AMERICA'S GOOD TERRORIST

AMERICA'S GOOD TERRORIST

John Brown and the Harpers Ferry Raid

CHARLES P. POLAND JR.

CASEMATE

Philadelphia & Oxford

Published in the United States of America and Great Britain in 2020 by
CASEMATE PUBLISHERS
1950 Lawrence Road, Havertown, PA 19083, USA
and
The Old Music Hall, 106–108 Cowley Road, Oxford OX4 1JE, UK

Copyright 2020 © Charles P. Poland Jr.

Hardback Edition: ISBN 978-1-61200-925-4
Digital Edition: ISBN 978-1-61200-926-1

A CIP record for this book is available from the British Library

Printed and bound in the United States of America by Sheridan

Typeset by Versatile PreMedia Service (P) Ltd

For a complete list of Casemate titles, please contact:

CASEMATE PUBLISHERS (US)
Telephone (610) 853-9131
Fax (610) 853-9146
Email: casemate@casematepublishers.com
www.casematepublishers.com

CASEMATE PUBLISHERS (UK)
Telephone (01865) 241249
Email: casemate-uk@casematepublishers.co.uk
www.casematepublishers.co.uk

To my daughters, Elisa and Lynette, whose love, achievements, and beauty have made their mother and father proud and blessed.

Contents

Acknowledgments

An author does not write a book in a vacuum. He is dependent on the support and help from numerous people, libraries, and archives. Not the least in importance is the moral support of family and colleagues. My wife, Betty, and our daughters have lived much of their lives with John Brown. For their understanding I am grateful. The help provided by my son-in-law, Paul, in solving computer issues has been a valued assistance. Colleagues the late Dr. Wallace Hutcheon has offered encouragement and Dr. Terry Alford, the authority on John Wilkes Booth, has graciously found materials for me relevant to my research. Researchers Bryce Suderow and Dr. Peggy Brown have been crucial in fulfilling my requests for difficult-to-obtain material. Aaron Parsons at the West Virginia Division of Culture and History provided gracious assistance in obtaining needed photographs. The author is grateful to South Lynn for not only his leadership in the restoration of the Kennedy House, but making it available and giving animated tours to my college fieldtrip classes on John Brown. Dennis Frye, the former chief historian at the Harpers Ferry National Park, has made available useful information. To Jennifer Hornby I owe a special debt of gratitude for her cheerful and expert editing. To the librarians and personnel in a host of public and private depositories, including those at colleges, universities, state libraries, the Library of Congress, national Archives, and National Battlefield Parks, I owe a debt of gratitude. This is especially true for the personnel at Casemate Publishers who made the publication a reality by working at home during the pandemic: Ruth Sheppard, publisher, editors Felicity Goldsack, Isobel Fulton, Alison Griffiths, and Daniel Yesilonis of marketing.

Introduction

John Brown is a common name, but the John Brown who masterminded the failed raid at Harpers Ferry in 1859 was anything but common. His thwarted efforts have left an imprint upon our history, and his story still swirls in controversy. Was he a madman who felt his violent solution to slavery was ordained by Providence or a heroic freedom fighter who tried to liberate the downtrodden slave? These bipolar characterizations of the violent abolitionist have captivated Americans. The prevailing view from the time of the raid to well into the 20th century—that his actions were the product of an unbalanced mind—has shifted to the idea that he committed courageous acts to undo a terrible injustice.

The debate still rages, but not as much about his ultimate goal as the method he used in attempting to right what he considered an intolerable wrong. Are citizens justified in bypassing the normal legal or governmental processes in a violent way when these fail, in the eyes of the dissenter, to correct a wrong that touched so many? Brown's use of violence was to strike terror into the hearts of slave-owners, terror that Brown hoped would intimidate them to free their slaves to ensure their families' safety.

Terrorism is a frightening element in our lives, especially since 9/11. Modern terrorism is varied and complex. The meaning of terrorism has changed over the last 200 years, making a simple definition difficult. It should not be confused with guerrilla warfare, insurgency, or criminal activity for one's self-aggrandizement. The FBI, US Department of Defense, US State Department, UK government, and individual authors give different definitions, but most identify the same common elements. David J. Whittaker, editor of *The Terrorism Reader,* addresses these issues and concludes that the fundamental aim of the terrorist's violence is to change "the system," motivated by the altruistic belief that "he is serving a 'good' cause designed to achieve a greater good for a wider constituency—whether real or imagined." Terrorists never acknowledge that they are terrorists and go to great lengths to obscure that identity. "All terrorist acts," according to Whittaker, "involve violence or the threat of violence." He defines terrorism as "the deliberate creation and exploitation of fear through violence or the threat of violence in the pursuit of political change."

Advancements in communication and weaponry technology have enabled modern terrorists to target indiscriminately and to inflict mayhem on civilians. Despite the differences between modern terrorist acts and Brown's own violent acts, when Brown's characteristics are compared to the definition of terrorism as set forth by scholars of terrorism, he fits the profile. Nevertheless, today Brown is a martyred hero who gave his life attempting to terminate the evil institution of human bondage. Brown's violent method of using terrorism to accomplish this is downplayed or ignored, despite his labeling by historians as America's first terrorist. The modern view of Brown has unintentionally made him a "good terrorist," despite the repugnance of terrorism that makes the thought of a benevolent or good terrorist an oxymoron. The title *America's Good Terrorist* reflects the shift in view of the violent abolitionist from villain to hero, and does not imply terrorism is benevolent.

CHAPTER I

The Making of a Terrorist

Nature's grandeur at Harpers Ferry laid an engaging stage for one of America's great dramas, John Brown's raid. The setting was a relatively small town walled in by water and cliffs, some 60 miles west of the nation's capital—by rail 70 miles west of Baltimore and 170 miles north of the Old Dominion's capital, Richmond. Captain Brown's "war of liberation" would bring excitement and anxiety of a magnitude previously unknown at Harpers Ferry. The raid had shocking repercussions that strained the political sinews binding the nation together, strained them almost to the point of rupture. But this raid was only the beginning. The residents of this town, located in an area of such unusual geographic beauty, had no way of knowing what impending trauma and change would invade their world.

The Golden Age of Harpers Ferry

The town's businesses clustered along the Potomac and Shenandoah shores on a neck of land shaped like a shark's head. The rivers' water powered the town's mills and factories. The Civil War and later floods would destroy and sweep away most of these businesses and the homes on the Shenandoah bank. Today the surrounding heights around Harpers Ferry, the confluence of two rivers, and remaining historic structures still provide magnificent scenery for gawking tourists, though most of the structures that were focal points during the abolitionist's raid have disappeared. Buildings hugging the cliffs or nearby along Shenandoah Street still stand, along with those on the lower part of High Street and North Potomac Street next to the armory site, which housed early businesses. Modern tourists may see dwellings such as the Harper House, which sits on rising terrain traversed by High Street. The most dramatic vista is still obtained by trudging up the stone steps to St. Peter's Catholic Church then continuing on the path past the remains of St. John's Episcopal Church to Jefferson's Rock. Behind it, on even higher ground, is a four-acre burial site, containing among the still and quiet remains those of the town's founder, Robert Harper. Further up on a plateau are several historic houses and buildings on Camp Hill, used in the 19th and 20th centuries by Storer College for African Americans.

Gone are the numerous structures that formed the town's heart. Only remnants remain of two of the three canals. The only building left on the outer rim of low land is the much-moved enginehouse, better known as John Brown's Fort. The bridges that replaced the two covered toll crossings have also been moved. Stone walls still frame the tip of land, but the one along the Potomac is all that remains of the masonry that surrounded the quarter-mile-long United States Musket Factory, the armory, that once consisted of 21 buildings. No trace can be found of the United States Canal, which entered from the west to power the armory's turbines. The modern visitor will only find railroad tracks, a train station, scattered loose railroad ties, and numerous unfriendly "No Trespassing" signs on 20-foot-high mounds of fill dirt running through what was the federal government's largest arms plant. These mounds obscure any view of the original armory grounds.

The nose of the shark's head, called the Point, was once home to a tollhouse, two rail depots, the Potomac Restaurant, Wagner House, and Gault House Saloon; all are gone. Just to the south, only vague and sunken outlines remain of the two arsenal buildings. Along the Shenandoah bank, wilderness hides the rail tracks to Winchester and covers land that was once three islands, Upper Hall, Lower Hall, and Virginius, that collectively form the outline of the shark's mouth. The Shenandoah Canal separates the islands from town, and the Shenandoah River borders them on the other side. A curving dam once funneled water to power machinery in most of the nine buildings of the rifle works on Lower Hall Island, as well as Virginius Island's tannery and iron, flour, saw, and cotton mills.

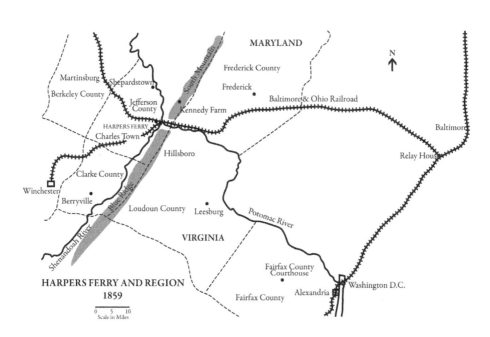

HARPERS FERRY AND REGION
1859

In warm weather tourists swarm the remains of the historic sites. Harpers Ferry of the 1850s was a thriving town nearing the end of its golden age. It was the site of numerous businesses; the most important was arms manufacturing. The US armory, the arsenal, the rifle factory, and other businesses employed a large number of the White wage earners among the town's 2,500 residents, half White and half Black. The majority of the White residents were from the North, considered foreigners by those of Southern heritage, and provided skilled workers for the town, as well as artisans for the government armory and for Hall's Rifle Works, which produced nearly 9,000 stands of arms in 1859. The region's economy did not foster large plantations and slaveholding. Although Harpers Ferry had 1,339 Black residents, only 88 were enslaved. The six Virginia and Maryland counties surrounding the town had a White population of 115,000, and 18,048 Black people who were enslaved, of whom fewer than 5,000 were men. Free Blacks in these counties numbered 9,800. In the Old Dominion at the time, a third of the residents were in bondage.

Railroads were integral to the town's prosperity, especially the Baltimore and Ohio or B&O, which made Harpers Ferry an important rail link between the East and the Ohio Valley. An additional railroad and canal supplemented the B&O: the Winchester and Potomac Railroad (which joined the B&O line at Harpers Ferry) and the Chesapeake and Ohio Canal, which followed the meandering northern banks of the Potomac River from Washington, D.C., to Cumberland, Maryland.

The federal armory had its genesis during the presidency of George Washington, who was impressed with the regional abundance of elements necessary for arms production: water power, iron ore, and hardwood timber. In 1796 the federal government purchased land from the heirs of Robert Harper, and that land became the site of the armory, then in the state of Virginia. Production started in 1798.

Economic growth and technological advancements in arms production caused growing pains for the area during its pre-Civil War golden age. Locals had lived in an isolated environment prior to the 1830s, and they clung to craft production and were slow to adopt technological advances because they feared these would bring lower wages. Federal authorities instituted measures to heighten control over arms production to eliminate lax work habits, such as employees' arriving at and leaving work whenever they wished. The people of Harpers Ferry resented the increased federal control, considering it an unwarranted intrusion upon the independence and the rights of the worker. Prior to John Brown's raid workers were similarly displeased with Superintendent Alfred M. Barbour's firing of more than 100 workers. Those who were retained took a 10-percent reduction in wages and had to abide by more rigid regulations.[1]

Harpers Ferry's unique setting has impressed travelers since the colonial era. A Philadelphia architect, Robert Harper, was so enamored with the region known as The Hole, or Peter's Hole, that in 1747 he purchased the land there from the first settler, ferry operator Peter Stephens. Harper's purchase and improvement of the

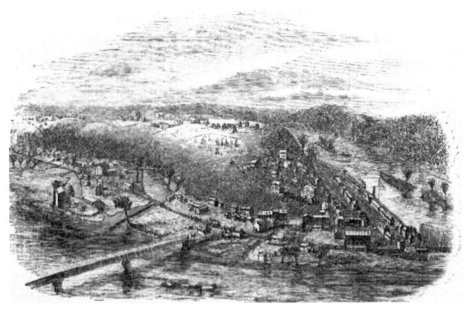

View of Harpers Ferry from south of the Shenandoah River in *Rambles in the Path of the Steam Horse*. (Library of Congress)

View of Harpers Ferry from the Maryland banks of the Potomac River. (West Virginia Archives, Boyd B. Stutler Collection)

ferry service resulted in a name change to Harper's Ferry.[2] Thomas Jefferson, in his *Notes on Virginia,* wrote about the area, apparently from a viewpoint on what has since been called Jefferson's Rock. He described the confluence of the Potomac and the Shenandoah Rivers and the mountains that bordered them as "one of the most stupendous scenes in nature."[3]

God's Avenger

Such was the setting John Brown selected for his attack upon slavery, an attack that the "Old Man"—as acquaintances and the press called him—believed would terminate that "evil institution." But it was not the grandeur of the scenery that attracted Brown. Instead it was the existence of the US arms facilities at Harpers Ferry, a town located in a border region that Brown wrongly assumed would supply numerous Black and White supporters who would liberate the slaves through guerilla warfare.[4] The original appeal of seizing federal property to obtain weapons for those he planned to liberate seemed to be less a motive at the time of the raid; by then, Brown had weapons for them. By 1859 he had more important motivations: retribution against a government that would protect slavery, and the publicity from such a bold act. Brown assumed this raid would launch his revolution. An additional attraction was the town's proximity to a mountain chain that Brown could retreat to and use as an avenue for deeper penetration into the slave kingdom.

Several threads ran through John Brown's life: business failure, debt, abolition, and religion. He enjoyed early business success, evolving from shepherd, tanner, farmer, and cattleman to real estate speculator and wool merchant, but fell upon difficult times. From 1831 to 1853 he was constantly in debt as a result of 15 business failures. Brown's dependence on credit, lack of judgment, and stubbornness doomed him in business deals. Debt frequently landed him in court, and by 1842 he was bankrupt.

Brown headed a large household and possessions were sparse. At one point, 12 Brown children slept in five beds. The family's austere life included plain clothing and food. Milk and water were their only drinks, although later in his life Brown sipped tea or coffee to avoid offending a well-meaning hostess. Tobacco and liquor were forbidden, and for some reason John would never eat butter. The one thing the Brown household had in abundance reflected John's priority in life: religion. They owned 11 Bibles and half a dozen New Testaments.

Brown's first wife, Dianthe Lusk Brown, delivered seven children in 12 years of marriage. In 1832 she died of heart failure three days after giving birth to a stillborn son. Brown lost nine of his 20 children—seven from his second marriage. While living in Ohio, Brown and his second wife, Mary Ann Day Brown, lost three children to dysentery within 11 days. Nine-year-old Sarah, two-year-old Peter, and one-year-old Austin were buried in the same grave as their four-year-old brother Charles, who had died two years earlier. Those years proved to be decades of frustration and despair.

Why did John Brown attack Harpers Ferry in an attempt to end what he considered America's greatest sin? One must look at the dominant anti-slavery influences in his life: his father, an abolitionist environment, Calvinism, slave revolts, Oliver Cromwell, guerrilla warfare, and a belief the government was guilty of malfeasance. John Brown's anti-slavery feelings formed in his early years. He was born in Torrington, Connecticut, on May 9, 1800, to Owen and Ruth Brown. His mother was the daughter of a Congregational minister, for whom John was named. In the 1850s, John Brown briefly sketched his childhood in an essay, "A Boy Named John." It was written in response to a request from one of his financial backers, Henry Stearns, and it focused on Brown's youthful errors, in hopes young Stearns would avoid them. The autobiography tells of the struggles and hard work in Connecticut and on the frontier in Ohio, of Brown's dislike of school, and of his proclivity to lie to avoid punishment. It also tells of traumatic events, including his mother's death, losses of a yellow marble and a bob-tailed squirrel, the death of his pet lamb, and the horror of seeing a young slave boy about his age beaten by a master with a shovel. At times during his youth, Brown wrote, he had a strong desire to die.

Brown had his lighter moments, often engaging in pranks. In his significant biography of Brown, Oswald Villard tells an unsubstantiated story of John's attempt to ignite gunpowder under his stepmother and then padding his pants to counter the sting of his father's thrashing. Hijinks aside, adult responsibilities were thrust upon John when he was barely an adolescent. When the War of 1812 started Owen sent his young son alone, barefoot and dressed in buckskins, to drive cattle over a hundred miles of wilderness from Ohio to outposts in Michigan. John was raised to revere strict Puritan values, and he was shocked by contact with the undisciplined, cussing, complaining soldiers. The shame of General William Hull's surrender of Detroit further disillusioned him. John's disdain for the military carried through into adulthood, when he refused to show up for mandatory militia drills, instead opting to pay fines. At 16 John was preparing to enter the ministry, but an eye infection and lack of funds doomed this ambition. He left school and returned to Ohio.[5]

Owen Brown had a profound influence upon his son. John's father, who was restless and moved frequently, was a stern disciplinarian who was liberal in his

Owen Brown, father of John Brown. (Library of Congress)

John Brown in 1850. (Library of Congress)

use of corporal punishment, a common practice of that era. A religiously devout man who was strongly opposed to slavery, Owen stuttered severely except when praying. Like his father, John would later move from place to place. Corporal punishment was passed down as well: John Brown whipped his sons, especially his older sons. When three-year-old Jason claimed a dream was real, John punished him for lying. John also kept a detailed account book of his son John Jr.'s sinful acts and the number of whip lashes each merited. John Jr. recalled that one Sunday morning his father said it was "time for settlement." He recounted, "[After] a long and tearful talk over my faults, he again showed me my account... I paid about one-third the debt from a nicely prepared blue-beech switch... Then to my utter astonishment father took off his shirt... [and] gave me the whip." The senior John Brown told the son to whip his bare back and to strike harder and harder as he took the remaining lashes for his son. Historians James Davidson and Mark Lytle contend that Owen's harsh treatment of John led to a deep feeling of "loyalty and submission countered by a strong desire for independence." John's similar treatment of his sons caused Watson Brown to tell his father, "The trouble is, Father, you want your boys to be brave as tigers, and still afraid of you."[6]

Yet John Brown was remembered fondly by his daughter Annie, a product of his second marriage. She recalled not just a rigorous disciplinarian but a caring, loving father. "He was very strict in his ideas of discipline," but he played with his children often, and "waited upon and cared for us at night." He never complained about getting up in the middle of a cold night and drawing a bucket of water to fetch his daughter a drink, "because he said that water that stood in the house was not good to drink." Before going to bed, he bounced Annie on his knee and carried her about, singing her to sleep and tucking her into bed. He continued the practice until she was nearly eight. She sat on his lap during business meetings, taking everything out of her papa's pockets to play with, and then carefully returning the items. He told Annie and her siblings stories and riddles and amused them "by making shadow pictures" of animals on the wall with his hands. Annie recalled, "He seldom ever came home from an absence of even a day without bringing the children something, such as oranges, nuts, raisins and fruits or popcorn, never candy, but books for those who were old enough to read. All children who were with him for a short time formed a strong attachment for him."[7]

The paramount influence of Owen Brown upon John was in religion and a hatred of slavery. Owen was a descendant of Peter Brown, who supposedly came over on the *Mayflower* in 1620, though records indicate Peter probably arrived a dozen years later. Owen felt people were, in the words of Jonathan Edwards, "sinners in the hands of an angry God." Owen was an orthodox Congregationalist and accepted Calvin's view of humans as wicked and feeble creatures whose duty was to resist Satan's temptations and live a life of Christian piety.

In his early years John considered becoming a minister, and he embraced his father's Calvinist view of a God of wrath and revenge, as well as the doctrine of predestination. As an adult John Brown diligently studied Jonathan Edwards's *On the Freedom of Will*, which fueled his evangelical fever. It also prepared him to debate a pious, overconfident minister, who, in their first argument, drowned out Brown's refuting of the doctrines of perfectionism and free will. Afterwards Brown said the preacher was not a gentleman. Word of this traveled back to the minister, who confronted Brown. Not only did Brown take ownership of the statement, but he pointed out that he had also said, "It would take as many men like you, to make a gentleman as it would take hens to make a cock turkey." Annoyed, the preacher engaged Brown in a second verbal sparring, and onlookers said Brown won the debate. Brown was devout, and religion so pervaded his daily life that he often turned business transactions into occasions for religious lectures and discussions.

No book received more of his time than the Bible, especially the Old Testament. Brown felt he had found his commission from God there, and he marked Old Testament passages about God's wrath in bringing about the slaughter of the wicked and the enemies of God's chosen people. Both Owen and John believed it was their Christian duty to fight wickedness, and in their eyes, the greatest wickedness in the US was slavery. Owen chose to fight slavery with the Underground Railroad, while John sought a violent solution. Years of studying Jehovah's violent destruction of the enemies of righteousness convinced John that God had chosen him to take action against slave-owners. His credo was one of his favorite marked passages: "… without the shedding of blood, there is no remission of sins." He also sanctified the use of violence while talking with Ralph Waldo Emerson at the transcendentalist's home in the late 1850s. Brown said he believed in the Bible and the Declaration of Independence and said, "Better that a whole generation of men, women and children should pass away by a violent death than a word of either should be violated."

One of Brown's favorite biblical characters was Gideon. Under divine orders Gideon delivered the Israelites from hordes of Midianites, who for years raided on camelback, plundering, burning, and conducting massacres. Gideon claimed God had assured him of victory if he reduced his forces from thousands to 300. He divided his small force into three companies and startled the enemy in a surprise night attack. His men blew their trumpets and revealed lamps they had hidden inside pitchers, shouting, "A sword for the Lord and for Gideon." Confused enemy troops attacked each other and fled, and Gideon won. This tale made an indelible impression on John Brown. Gideon's small force was victorious against the overwhelming numbers of an evil enemy; he used violence and an element of surprise to carry out God's will in a unique nighttime attack.[8]

Brown's study of violence in triumph over evil was not limited to his Holy Book. It extended to select aspects of history, and to leaders who felt their violent acts were part of a divine mission, especially Spartacus, Cinqué, Nat Turner, and Oliver Cromwell. Brown admired slaves who had led rebellions, but his idealization of them, as David S. Reynolds argues in his extensive biography, *John Brown: Abolitionist*, made Brown believe he would successfully spur a slave insurrection throughout the US slave states.

The life of Spartacus, who headed the most formidable of the many slave rebellions in Roman history, was also of great interest to Brown. Spartacus escaped from gladiator school to the mountains. Other men fleeing the cruel mistreatments of slavery joined him, and they formed an army that terrorized and laid waste to a large region, from the Alps to the southern tip of the peninsula, repeatedly defeating the powerful Roman legions. After two years the insurrection was crushed, Spartacus was slain, and 6,000 of his followers were crucified on the Appian Way to Rome as a warning to slaves.

John Brown admired Cinqué, who led a slave revolt upon a Spanish vessel, *Amistad*, while it was on the high seas. Nat Turner, who led a bloody insurrection in Virginia in 1831, was also especially revered. Brown would later emulate Turner's tactics by launching nighttime terrorist attacks at Pottawatomie Creek and Harpers Ferry. Inspired by Turner's use of crude weapons, Brown's men would use swords to hack their victims to death at Pottawatomie Creek, and Brown ordered 1,000 pikes to arm the slaves he expected to join him at Harpers Ferry.[9]

Brown's favorite historical figure was Oliver Cromwell, whom Brown patterned his life after so much that contemporaries called him the second Cromwell. Both had an agrarian background, were devoted Puritans, cared little about the state of their clothing, and believed they were commissioned by God to right wrongs through violence. Brown studied his second-favorite book—Joel Tyler Headley's *The Life of Oliver Cromwell*—a sympathetic biography of the man who led the republican forces in the English civil wars, overthrowing the monarchy and beheading King Charles I. Cromwell become a dictator in the name of ruling a republic and vigorously pursued his enemies: Catholics in Ireland, royalists in Scotland, and radical republicans such as the Levelers in England.

Brown read with keen interest of Cromwell's sense of divine mission and his speech to his people upon arriving in Ireland: "God has brought us here in safety... We are here to carry on the work against the barbarous and blood-thirsty Irish... to propagate the Gospel of Christ and restore the establishment of truth... and to restore this nation to its former happiness and tranquility." Cromwell invaded Ireland in 1649 with an army of 12,000 men to create a "godly" Protestant society. His army slaughtered civilians as well as soldiers and specifically carried out Cromwell's orders to kill priests, monks, and nuns. Catholic boys and girls were shipped to Barbados and sold as slaves. Catholic lands were confiscated. In the decade after Cromwell's arrival, about one-third of the Irish had been killed or died of starvation. Cromwell took a similar hard stand in dealing with the Levelers' mutiny: "You must cut these people in pieces or they will cut you in pieces." Inspired by his role models, Brown was convinced he was not only justified in carrying out the Pottawatomie Creek massacre and the raid on Harpers Ferry, but was following divine and historical precedent.

Brown pored over history books that dealt with guerrilla activities and insurrections. He was enamored with how the Portuguese guerrillas held their own against Napoleon's army in the Pyrenees; how the Maroons, slaves who rebelled against their Spanish masters, fled to the wilderness and formed communities that they defended with guerrilla tactics; and how Toussaint L'Ouverture liberated Haiti in a bloody struggle with Napoleon's forces. In his memorandum book, Brown copied select pages from Joachim H. Stocqueler's *The Life of Field-Marshal the Duke of Wellington,* published in 1852. He included details of Spanish guerrilla activity under the capable leadership of Mina, descriptions of broken mountainous terrain, and instructions for discipline and cooking. The notations included: "*See also* same Book Page 235 these words Deep and narrow defiles where 300 men would suffice to check an *army.*" Brown was convinced that with help, slaves could gain their freedom and form independent mountain communities.

The shivering fear and panic that swept over the South after Nat Turner's revolt in 1831 in southern Virginia convinced Brown of the value of using terror as a psychological weapon in destabilizing the institution of human bondage. Turner was a slave and self-appointed preacher who had visions and believed a solar eclipse was a divine signal to free the slaves. He gathered about 60 other men who were enslaved, many of whom were emboldened by stolen brandy, and led them on a killing spree. They took the lives of nearly 60 children, women, and men. The massacre began with his mild-mannered master and mistress. A hatchet and ax were used to hack them to death as they lay in their bed. Soon thereafter their baby was taken by its legs and its brains were smashed out upon a brick fireplace. The gruesome slaughter continued for several days. Fence rails, swords, razors, knives, and guns were also used to dispatch victims, whether they slept or fought back. Women fled their homes in terror, pleading for their lives, but were ruthlessly killed. Children were decapitated. The massacre's impact was seared upon the memory of Southern whites. Its impact was not lessened by the capture, execution, and deportation of the insurrectionists or by the fidelity of young Dr. Simon Blunt's slaves: after they were given a choice between fighting and leaving, they used hoes and pitchforks to drive away a surprised Turner and his mob.

Brown also learned from an uneducated ex-slave from Maryland, the indomitable Harriet Tubman, whom he called "the general of us all." The Appalachian chain that penetrated the heart of the slave states was, he said, "a veritable land of refuge." In 1858 he expressed to Wendell Phillips, a pioneer of abolitionism, that Tubman had used those mountains as the road to lead members "of her enslaved race from bondage to comparative freedom." When introducing her to Phillips, Brown said, "I bring you one of the best and bravest persons on this continent—*General* Tubman, as we call her." He explained she was "the most of any man, naturally, that I ever met with." Tubman was called Moses by those who sought freedom. Her dark skin bore the scars of beatings, but gone was the reputation she carried through early adolescence—when an overseer threw a weight at her, she suffered a severe head injury and was seen as a dim-witted person. According to her abolitionist friend, Sarah Bradford, who embellished Tubman's exploits, Harriet completed most of her 19 trips to free more than 300 slaves by taking different routes, including, after 1850, the scenic route to Canada by Niagara Falls. Her violation of fugitive slave laws led to collective rewards placed upon her head that supposedly amounted to $40,000; in reality it was $300. Tubman shepherded her flock through rain, snow, and swamps, carrying sleeping children in their arms and babies in baskets. Young ones were given opium to prevent betraying sounds. To stave off hunger Tubman traded her undergarments for food. She silently prayed for God's guidance and avoided seemingly certain capture.

Brown's admiration for Tubman was almost boundless. She was fearless and uncompromising and tolerated no whining, threatening to shoot anyone who wanted to return to their master. Brown believed she was a valuable ally in getting recruits from Canada and leading the slaves he would liberate from Harpers Ferry to freedom.[10]

In his 1857 autobiography—in which he refers to himself, curiously, in the third person—Brown wrote that early in his life he became "a most determined Abolitionist: [this belief] led him to declare, or *swear: Eternal war* with *Slavery*." Despite his claims, Brown's plans for attacking slavery emerged sporadically during a period of frequent financial and personal travails in the 1830s and 1840s. Although he claimed to have declared "eternal war with slavery" at age 12, not until 1834, at age 35, was there documented evidence of his wish. This desire to help people in bondage seemed to reach fruition in 1837, when a mob in Illinois attacked the office of anti-slavery editor Elijah P. Lovejoy, killing him. This repugnant act shocked Northerners, driving Abraham Lincoln toward moderation and anti-slavery activists such as William Lloyd Garrison to spurn violence in answer to slavery. Meanwhile, the murder fired Brown's anti-slavery passions to a new level. While listening to a eulogy for the slain Lovejoy, Brown and his father were deeply moved by the speaker's harangues against slavery and "Southern mob law." Legend claims that when the meeting was ending, John Brown rose from his seat, raised his right hand, and proclaimed to the world, "Here before God, in the presence of these witnesses, from this time, I consecrate my life to the destruction of slavery."

In the 1830s Brown's plans were relatively benign and nonviolent, in keeping with other abolitionists' attitudes. He wanted to adopt a "Negro" boy and start a school for black people in Pennsylvania or Canada, but a lack of money and time doomed this goal. In the late 1840s he published an article entitled "Sambo's Mistakes" in a little-known abolitionist newspaper, *The Ram's Horn*, published and edited by blacks in New York. In the article he urged black people to seek self-improvement and resistance. It was written from the viewpoint of a free black man who admits his minor foibles of wasting time and money, and of: "devouring silly novels & other miserable trash… as newspapers… instead of giving my attention to sacred & profane history which I might have become acquainted with the true character of God & of man." Especially significant was Sambo's admission, "I have always expected to secure the favor of the whites by tamely submitting to every species of indignity contempt & wrong, instead of nobly resisting their brutal aggressions from principle & taking my place as a man & assuming the responsibilities of a man a citizen, a husband, a father, a brother, a neighbor, a friend…" Sambo personified Brown's belief that black people had the capacity not only for self-improvement, but also for being equal to whites. At the time, for a white man, the concept was revolutionary.[11]

In 1890 John Brown Jr. wrote that around 1840 his father had his wife Mary and three teenage sons—John Jr., 19; Jason, 16; and Owen, 14 or 15—swear they would "do all in their power to abolish slavery":

> The place and the circumstances where he first informed us of that purpose are as perfectly in my memory as any other event in my life. Father, mother, Jason, Owen and I were, late in the evening, seated around the fire in the open fire-place of the kitchen, in the old Haymaker house where we then lived; and there he first informed us of his determination to make war on slavery—not such war as Mr. Garrison informs us "was equally the purpose of the non-resistant abolitionists," but war by force and arms.
>
> He said that he had long entertained such a purpose that he believed it his duty to devote his life, if need be, to this object, which he made us fully understand. After spending considerable time in setting forth in most impressive language the hopeless condition of the slave, he asked who of us were willing to make common cause with him in doing all in our power to "break the jaws of the wicked and pluck the spoil out of his teeth," naming each of us in succession, "Are you Mary, John, Jason and Owen?"
>
> Receiving an affirmative answer from each, he kneeled in prayer, and all did the same. This posture in prayer impressed me greatly as it was the first time I had ever known him to assume it. After prayer he asked us to raise our right hands, and he then administered to us an oath, the exact terms of which I cannot recall, but in substance it bound us to secrecy and devotion to the purpose of fighting slavery by force and arms to the extent of our ability.[12]

By the late 1840s Brown's views and proposals were becoming more militant. He had open discussions with blacks to try to recruit them. In 1847 at his first meeting with Frederick Douglass, in Springfield, Massachusetts, he discussed a scheme of guerrilla activity that was the closest that Brown had to a master plan. A former slave and leading black abolitionist, Douglass would become a close friend of Brown's. Douglass was opposed to violence. He tells of a conversation with Brown, who bitterly denounced slavery: "[Brown] felt slaveholders had forfeited their right to live, that slaves had the right to gain liberty in any way they could, did not believe that moral suasion would ever liberate the slave, or that political action would abolish the system." Brown laid out a US map on the table for his dinner guest, an intrigued but somewhat skeptical Douglass, and pointed out how the Appalachian mountain chain extended from Maine to Georgia. "[These mountains] are the basis of my plan," he told Douglass. "God has given the strength of the hills to freedom; they were placed here for the emancipation of the Negro race; they are full of natural forts, where one man for defense will be equal to a hundred for attack." He informed the self-educated and eloquent Douglass, "[The mountains] are full of good hiding places, where large numbers of brave men could be concealed and baffle and elude pursuit for a long time. I know these mountains well and could take a body of men into them and keep them there despite all the efforts of Virginia to dislodge them. The true object to be sought first of all is to destroy the money value of slave property, and this can only be done by rendering such property insecure." This in turn would compel slave-owners, out of paralyzing fear for their safety, to free their slaves.

Brown told Douglass he planned to take a select group of 25 men, divided into groups of five, to terrorize slave-owners. They would raid plantations, free slaves, and retreat to the safety of the mountains, whose inhabitants were non-slave-owners who had been squeezed off the fertile piedmont by slave-owners. Those enslaved people who did not wish to colonize in the mountains could escape the South by traveling north. Brown confided to Douglass that he did not want unnecessary combat, but if they were attacked, the situation was to be made as costly as possible for his assailants. His intent was not to bring about a general slave insurrection and slaughter of slave masters, but to begin on a small scale, posting his 25 handpicked men in "squads of five on a line of twenty-five miles. The most persuasive and judicious of these shall go down" from the mountains, said Brown, "to the fields from time to time, as opportunity offers, and induce slaves to join them, seeking and selecting the restless and daring."

When 100 carefully selected slaves were gathered, they would be well armed and entrenched in mountain forts, using draws and ravines to ambush the enemy. Brown had worked for Oberlin College surveying land given to the college, and he was familiar with the Virginia mountains. "If the slaves could be driven out of one county," he reasoned, "the whole system would be weakened in that State."

Douglass responded, "But they would employ bloodhounds to hunt you out of the mountains." Brown replied, "The chances are, we should whip them, and when you have whipped one squad they would be careful how they pursued." Still not convinced, Douglass said, "But you might be surrounded and cut off from your provisions or means of subsistence." The former slave, an orator, would later write that Brown "thought this could not be done... but even if the worst came he could but be killed, and he had no better use for his life then to lay it down in the cause of the slave." Douglass suggested converting the slaveholders rather than fighting. Brown became excited, or perhaps agitated, and said, "They would never be induced to give up their slaves until they felt a big stick about their heads." Brown said that his simple lifestyle was meant solely to save money to carry out his mission, and he had already delayed too long.

The night that Frederick Douglass spent with John Brown in Springfield gradually shifted Douglass's approach away from ending slavery by peaceful abolition. While speaking at an anti-slavery convention in Ohio, Douglass was interrupted by his good friend, the former slave Sojourner Truth, with the question, "Frederick, is God dead?" "No," he answered, "and because God is not dead slavery shall only end in blood." Sojourner, who believed in "the Garrison school of non-violence," was shocked, but she too would "become an advocate of the sword."[13]

Violence Is the Way to Freedom

In 1850 Brown traveled to Europe to sell wool. It was an unsuccessful financial venture, but he used the trip to research his plan. In Great Britain, France, Germany, and Austria he examined forts, studied military plans and ordnance, and observed soldiers. He came back even more convinced of the value of building forts in the eastern mountains. He planned to conceal forts in trees and thickets and connect them by secret passages for easy evacuation. If militiamen or bloodhounds pursued Brown's men, the pursuers would be unable to cut off significant areas or food supplies, and would meet their demise at hidden forts. Brown's guerrilla force would live off sustenance taken from the planters; they could subsist for several days on wild animals, roots, and fruit.

Brown's tactics were to be a modified and more militant version of the "running off slaves" of the Underground Railroad and an expanded version of what he would do in Missouri in 1858. The difference was that most of the runaways would take refuge in Southern mountains and swamps. In the late 1840s or early 1850s, after he first met with Douglass, Harpers Ferry became his primary target. His young daughter Annie said her father told her about Harpers Ferry nearly a decade before the attack. By the 1850s, however, Brown's militancy was calling him to action. Implementation still remained hazy, but his dedication to the violent assault on slavery was absolute. His inflexibility of purpose is illustrated by his words to a friend in 1858: "For twenty years I have never made any business arrangements which would prevent me at any time answering the call of the Lord... I have permitted nothing to be in way of my duty, neither wife, children, nor worldly goods. The hour is near at hand, and all who are willing to act should be ready." The forcible termination of slavery was now what he called his "greatest or principal object" of his life. In Brown's mind, "Slavery was a state of war to which slaves were unwilling parties and consequently they have," as he told Douglass, "a right to do anything necessary to obtain their peace and freedom." He said to another friend, James Redpath, "Any resistance, however bloody, is better than the system which makes every seventh woman a concubine."

His ultimate goal was constant, but his immediate objectives were more changeable. Brown talked of using terror to devalue slavery, and at times he planned to capture and govern a significant section of the United States. He claimed, "The land belongs to the bondman. He has enriched it, and been robbed of its fruits." During the years he spent in Kansas in the 1850s he first wanted to relieve Kansas by striking elsewhere, mainly Harpers Ferry. After going to Kansas he sought to create a situation where the pro-slavery and anti-slavery factions would fight it out. He continued to believe in this approach after the fighting between pro-slavery and anti-slavery settlers during the mid-1850s, referred to as "Bleeding Kansas." He wanted to provoke Southerners to follow through on their threats to secede so the "North would whip the South back into the Union without slavery."

Brown freely told prospective recruits of his plan, and he probably told Colonel Daniel Woodruff, a friend and veteran of the War of 1812, when they talked during the Kansas conflict in the mid-1850s. Brown is said to have vividly described the details of the evils in Kansas. He wished to relieve Kansas by striking Harpers Ferry. Such a strike would terrorize Virginia, detaching it from "the slave interests," capturing rifles to arm slaves, and destroying government facilities and stored arms that could not be carried off. Brown would later change his objectives: in the extensive orders he issued just before the celebrated raid, he would not mention the seizure of government weapons.

Brown's most intent listeners were family members. They were his sounding board. All the children knew Harpers Ferry was to be struck. Owen Brown later wrote he grew up "with the expectation of going with his father whenever he should attempt to carry out 'his plan'." While in North Elba, New York, from 1849 to ·1851, Brown talked openly to his family about attacking Harpers Ferry. Daughter Sarah recalled standing behind her father's chair, watching him sketch plans for forts to be built in the mountains near Harpers Ferry. She listened to him explain the placement of logs, the construction of roofs, and how trees could be felled and laid as obstacles for attackers. Another daughter, Annie Brown Adams, would later state, "I think I may say without any intention of boasting, that I knew more about his plans than anyone else, or at least anyone else who 'survived to tell the tale.' He always talked freely to me of his plans, from the time he first explained them to me, the winter before he went to Kansas, when I was eleven years old [in 1854]." After revealing his plans, she said, "He would say as if for a sort of apology to himself, perhaps, 'I know I *can Trust you*. You never tell anything you are told not to.'" She indeed kept his secret, but not without stress. Annie recalled that when Harpers Ferry entered into a school lesson, her "heart hammered" and she "shivered as with a cold."

Not all who heard Brown's plan for Harpers Ferry felt it was the best site to attack. It was too close to the nation's capital, and too easy to reach, on the rail lines. Destroying federal property would bring swift reprisal and certain defeat. Brown's son Salmon reveals that his dad did waver in his convictions and indicated his intent to launch his revolution elsewhere, including sites in the lower South. In the mid- to late 1850s the patriarch listed in his memorandum book these potential sites: Little Rock, Arkansas; Charleston, South Carolina; San Antonio, Texas; St. Louis, Missouri; Augusta, Georgia; and four Pennsylvania cities.[14]

Long a person of inflexible opinions and indomitable will, Brown had finally found specific direction and purpose. More than ever he believed that the sins of slavery must be "atoned in blood" and that he was the "instrument of God" to accomplish this. Brown would devote his life in the 1850s almost exclusively to fighting slavery.[15] His militant actions were in part triggered by the government's passing of laws that were, in his eyes, "abominably wicked and unjust": the Fugitive Slave Act of 1850 and the Kansas-Nebraska Act of 1854. Slaveholding interests dominated the Democratic Party and controlled the federal government, and Brown had no faith in the political process. He did not see a viable way to end slavery with the Republican Party or abolitionist organizations. Their tepid solutions shied away from violence—the only answer, to Brown—making them unappealing. "Talk was a national institution," Brown said, "but it did not help the slave." In Kansas Brown felt the anti-slave forces were weak in resolve and tactics. He felt justified in acting independently and made little effort to coordinate his military activities with other free-state forces. Brown was nearing the position of an anarchist, although he wanted to reform, not abolish, government. He believed a higher moral law dictated that he must act outside and against the law.

In 1851 Brown formed a militant organization of blacks in the Springfield, Massachusetts, area. Their purpose was to enable black men and women, by secret resolve, to violently resist attempts to enforce the Fugitive Slave Law. Brown assumed the mantle of a modern Gideon by attempting to raise a small army against pro-slavery forces. He named his organization after Mount Gilead, where Gideon was told by God to free his people from invaders. The United League of Gileadites was Brown's first attempt to organize slaves to defend themselves while seeking freedom. It was an attempt to prevent slave-catchers in the North from capturing and returning runaway slaves to their masters. Slave-catchers' actions were sanctioned under the Fugitive Slave Act of 1850, an act Brown felt that God meant as a warning to slave-owners and a signal to enslaved people to defend themselves. Brown instructed more than 40 black recruits, many escaping through Springfield by the Underground Railroad, to arm themselves so they could swiftly kill marshals sent to return them to bondage. After killing the marshals, they would flee to the homes of sympathetic whites, if necessary. If they were captured and taken to court—which, in most cases, would result in being sent back south—then other Gileadites were to smuggle gunpowder into the courtroom, create a diversion by lighting it, and free their comrade.[16]

In the mid-1850s Brown followed his sons to Kansas, a territory beset by tension over slavery and brutal acts committed by settlers on both sides. Brown's original intent was to temporarily and peacefully assist his two eldest sons' settlement on the frontier and return to his family in North Elba, New York, but plans changed. Brown later told a friend that fighting in the Kansas Territory never entered his mind until he heard the Missourians were planning to come into Kansas to vote. Stimulated by the warlike atmosphere, he sought revenge for numerous atrocities, particularly the attack made by pro-slavery settlers upon Lawrence, Kansas, that resulted in the killing of two Free State men.

Revenge took shape on a spring night in 1856, when Brown and seven men brutally murdered and mutilated five pro-slavery settlers in Pottawatomie, Kansas. Brown's so-called Army of the North, frenzied by the news of the caning of an abolitionist senator, Charles Sumner, went to three homes in the dead of night, dispatching or scaring away barking dogs and knocking on doors. They awakened the inhabitants, who found a tall, begrimed old man with a thin face in dirty clothes, a black cravat and straw hat ordering the adult males outside. The attackers were unmoved by the tearful pleas of the wives, including Mrs. Wilkinson's plea to spare her husband, because she was ill with measles. Brown asked, "You have neighbors?" She said yes, but she had no way of contacting them. "It matters not," Brown replied and forced her husband outside in stocking feet. Allen Wilkinson, William Sherman, John Doyle, and two Doyle sons were taken a short distance from their homes. Brown's men used their short two-edged swords, whetted to razor sharpness, to hack the men to death.

The next morning the Sunday sun revealed the gruesome sight of the mangled forms. Arms and fingers were dismembered, chests and faces were wounded, throats were cut. The elder Doyle's body had a hole in the forehead where Brown had fired into the dead body. Down at Pottawatomie Creek lay the mutilated remains of William Sherman, his left hand hanging by a piece of skin and his skull split open, with some brain tissue washed away. The victims did not own slaves, but it did not matter to Brown. In his eyes they were still the enemy, to be made an example of, "to strike terror in the hearts of the proslavery people." He said, "It was better that a score of bad men should die than that one man who came here to make Kansas a free state."

What Brown and his men did at Pottawatomie Creek shocked some of his sons and his men who had sat out the raid, as well as anti-slave settlers and Eastern abolitionists, who generally opposed violence. This raid caused Southerners to assume incorrectly that all Northerners were militant abolitionists. Even as Brown was leaving on the raid with four of his sons, John Brown Jr. had a bad feeling about what his father might do. He called out, "Father, be careful and commit no rash acts." (News of the massacre would later plunge him into temporary insanity.) But Brown had already said caution was the same as cowardice. It was his God-given duty to strike back at the "barbarians." When they had finished the killing, John's son Owen Brown, who participated in the raid, said, "There shall be no more work as that." According to his brother Salmon, while returning from the raid Owen "felt terribly conscience-stricken because he had killed one of the Doyles, and he cried and took on at an agonizing rate."

The disturbing news of what was done had reached Brown's men in camp ahead of the raiders. Upon return Brown was met by his trembling son Jason, whose hatred of bloodletting caused John not to confide in him about such matters. Jason demanded of his father, "Did you have a hand in the killings?" Brown responded, "I did not do it, but I approved of it." Jason replied, "Whoever did it… it was an uncalled-for wicked act." Annoyed, John fired back, "God is my judge, we were justified under the circumstances." But Brown wavered in his statements about the incident, stating once that he was probably responsible for the murders. On another occasion he said the five victims were ordained by God to die.

The Pottawatomie Creek killings did not intimidate pro-slavery settlers the way Brown had hoped. Instead the incident incited them to chant for war and revenge, and to escalate the violence, as with a fatal attack upon a Free Stater with a hatchet and knives. They threw their victim at his doorstep, where his wife saw her mangled, dying husband and became hysterical.[17] Authorities' and pro-slavery forces' attempts to arrest or capture "Old Brown" would fail. One was a young cavalryman, James Ewell Brown Stuart, who would later assist in the capture of Brown at Harpers Ferry.

The following months saw Brown fighting eagerly in Kansas's civil war, which he helped bring about. Guerrilla activity included nightly raids, illegal acts, and atrocities by both sides, including Brown's encouraging his men to steal cattle and horses from pro-slavery settlers. In battle he was a modern Gideon, defeating an opponent of greater numbers in the battle of Black Jack on June 2, 1856. On August 30, 1856, Brown and fewer than two dozen men held off and escaped from more than 200 pro-slavery attackers, who destroyed Brown's home and those of other "Free Staters" in Osawatomie. With tears flowing down his cheeks, an angry Brown watched as fire devastated Osawatomie. He vowed he would die fighting slavery and there would be no peace in the United States until slavery was ended. He said, "I will give them something else to do than extend slave territory, I will carry the war into Africa [the South]."

Even defeat in the battle of Osawatomie did not blunt the emergence of the legend of John Brown as an exceptional military strategist, "fearless antislavery warrior," and Terrifier of the South. He emerged from this strife with new confidence in the sanctity of his crusade against slavery. Emerson, Thoreau, and others lauded him for his courage. Despite Brown's religiosity, his dedication to fighting slavery in Kansas led to the curtailment of his religious rituals. Salmon later wrote, "I never saw father with a bible or testament in Kansas. He used to ask the blessing at meal times but I never heard him pray in Kansas."

Brown's life was not easy. Pro-slavery guerrillas murdered his son Frederick. Brown and his men were forced into hiding in the wilderness for long periods, enduring freezing weather, back-breaking labor, and food shortages, forcing them to eat whatever they could find, such as the toes of strange animals. Illness frequently laid up Brown and his men. These struggles took their toll on his health. He had been described as looking like an eagle, with a Romanesque nose, strong chin, stern mouth, and thick, wiry hair on a disproportionately small head. His most captivating feature was his keen blue-gray eyes, which Frederick Douglass described as "full of light and fire." But at this point in his life, his thin, sinewy frame made him seem much taller than his 5'10". He was stooped and emaciated, with a scrawny neck. At speaking engagements he wore ragged woolen clothes and cowhide boots full of holes. The "long, springing, race-horse" steps Douglass had observed were now a little slower. Privations had transformed Brown. He had maintained a capacity for hard work, but his "holy war" against the "forces of evil" aged him far beyond his 56 years. He was now Old Osawatomie Brown.[18]

The Search for Allies and Money

The abatement of violence and the establishment of a degree of order led Brown to leave Kansas in November 1856. He returned to the east, but not primarily to visit his wife and younger children in North Elba, New York. He saw little of them from the mid-1850s, instead communicating by letter. Brown had to be careful even when traveling in the North. He was still a wanted man being pursued by a US marshal. In a letter he wrote from Rochester, New York, in January 1858, Brown cautioned his wife and family, "Do not noise it about that I am in these parts."

Brown traveled extensively throughout the North, seeking support for his crusade—especially from eastern sympathizers known as the Secret Six. They were a mythic cabal of aristocratic northern abolitionists who would help Brown hide from the law and provide financial assistance, but not as much of the latter as Old Brown wanted. The Secret Six were men of outstanding social, educational, and financial standing. Four had degrees from Harvard, including Theodore Parker, who has been called one of the most impressive and learned Americans of his time. Parker knew 20 languages and had 16,000 volumes in his personal library. The Secret Six included two preachers, Thomas Wentworth Higginson, editor of the *Atlantic Monthly,* and Unitarian Theodore Parker; a world-renowned physician, Samuel Howe; two immensely wealthy gentlemen, eccentric Gerrit Smith and George Luther Stearns; and Franklin Sanborn, a young schoolteacher and secretary of the anti-slavery Massachusetts State Kansas Committee, who got married when his wife-to-be was on her deathbed. Upon meeting Brown in 1857 Sanborn was

The Secret Six, men who gave financial support to John Brown. (West Virginia Archives, Boyd B. Stutler Collection)

mesmerized by Brown's messianic zeal and introduced him to the other men. They would later call themselves the Secret Six.[19]

By 1858 Brown appeared ready to act. Though he was vague when sharing details of his plans, even with the Secret Six, Brown wrote an Ohio congressman that slaves would be liberated by bloodshed. He revealed to others that he planned to go to "Africa" or "China"—his code words for the South. Brown had earlier revealed his Harpers Ferry plan in detail to Hugh B. Forbes, whom he had hired for $100 a month to train his liberation army. Forbes was a mercurial alcoholic soldier of fortune who desperately needed money. He was struggling to make ends meet as a fencing instructor, a translator, and a New York *Daily Tribune* reporter. Like Brown, Forbes was uncompromising and had failed at business. He fancied himself a military genius, having fought with Garibaldi in the failed Italian Revolution of 1848 and authored a two-volume manual on military tactics, which he agreed to abridge for Brown's men. Forbes was captivated by Brown's idea of using guerrilla warfare to attack slavery. He was offered the job of Brown's drill master, but he envisioned becoming a general, perhaps a Garibaldi-like figure, in the fight against slavery. But that was the role Brown planned to play.

The relationship between the two soon deteriorated. Upon arriving in Kansas Forbes found few recruits and spent weeks drilling only one man, Owen Brown. John Brown and Forbes competed for control of an almost nonexistent army that lacked recruits, money, and weapons, and they argued heatedly over Brown's plan. From reading Garrison's *Liberator*, Brown incorrectly assumed that an attack on Harpers Ferry would send hundreds of slaves swarming to him, and he would arm them. Once Virginia was "liberated," Brown would continue God's work by moving southward through Tennessee, Alabama, and elsewhere, taking arms from local arsenals to arm the slaves he freed, and easily dispatching any inefficient local militia foolish enough to confront him. Forbes repeatedly argued that slaves would not swarm to Brown, insisting a better way would be to have small forces attacking several times a week along the upper slave borders of Maryland and Virginia, freeing small groups of blacks and running them to Canada. This would gradually shrink slavery and shove its frontiers further south. After a little over a month with Brown, frustrated and disillusioned by the lack of salary and fulfillment of his dreams, Forbes convinced Brown he had pressing business in the east and received permission to leave Brown and rejoin him in several months. He never returned.[20]

Mimicking the American Revolutionary Experience

In the winter of 1858 Brown had an extended stay at Frederick Douglass's comfortable home in Rochester, New York, where he spent a week in a bedroom, sprawled on a soft bed, with a board for a desk. He wrote and refined a "Provisional Constitution" that would create a new state in the Southern Appalachians for the freedmen he planned to liberate during his invasion. During meals Brown calmly explained the details of his invasion to Douglass. Douglass was shocked and horrified to hear of the destruction, violence, and terror resulting from a prolonged slave revolt. Brown was undaunted by his host's reaction and belief that Brown was overestimating the inclination of slaves to revolt.

That spring Brown convened a secret constitutional convention that met first in a schoolhouse and then in a Baptist church in Chatham, Canada, under the guise of forming a Masonic lodge for blacks. Brown saw the convention and his planned invasion as a response to a repressive institution that he considered a war on the enslaved. Here on May 8–10, 1858, a group of 46 people, 12 whites and 34 blacks, adopted Brown's Provisional Constitution for a government he planned to establish in the soon-to-be-conquered territories. Dr. Martin R. Delany chaired the meeting. He would become the highest-ranking African American in the Union army, as a major. Delany had been born in 1812 in Charles Town in Jefferson County, Virginia, only a couple of blocks away from where Brown would later be tried.[21]

The convention elected officials for the proposed new government, including Old Osawatomie Brown as its commander in chief. Patterned after the Declaration of Independence of 1776 and the US Constitution of 1787, the "Provisional Constitution and Ordinances for the People of the United States" took its justification from the 1776 document, and the mechanics of government, from the 1787 Constitution. The preamble of Brown's document contends that slavery was "a most barbarous, unprovoked, and unjustifiable act of war of one part of its citizens upon another portion," that it violated "those eternal and self-evident truths set forth in our Declaration of Independence." Since the government allowed the continued subjugation of blacks, the preamble said, it was necessary for a while to create a provisional government.

Like the existing central government, the provisional government would have three branches: legislative (one house of five to 10 representatives), executive (president and vice president), and judiciary (with a five-member Supreme Court), all selected by voters. Executives and legislators would serve three-year terms. The provisional president was not the commander in chief, a position Brown considered paramount since the implementation of the provisional government as well as slaves' freedom would come about through the violence of guerrilla warfare. As the commander in chief, Brown's position was that of a fourth branch of the government. All legislation of the proposed government had to have the approval of not only the president, but also the commander in chief. The convention filled the remaining positions of the provisional government by electing capable John Henry Kagi, who would later be second in command at Harpers Ferry, as secretary of war; eloquent Richard Realf as secretary of state; and George P. Gill, who had previously worked on a whaling ship in the Pacific, as secretary of the treasury.[22]

After the convention Brown was ready to launch his attack on Virginia, but circumstances forced him to delay. A shortage of funds, the revelations of his disgruntled drill master, Hugh Forbes, and pressure from most of the Secret Six forced Brown to go to Kansas as a diversionary tactic. Distrustful of Forbes, Brown had earlier sent his young secretary of state, Richard Realf, an Englishman, poet, and journalist, from Kansas to New York to find out what Forbes was up to. Realf never saw Forbes and became disenchanted with Brown's plans after reading *Limitations of Human Responsibility* by Dr. Wayland. Realf returned to England, supporting himself by giving lectures. John Cook, one of Brown's recruits, mistakenly believed Realf was collecting money for Brown. Realf later returned to the United States, to New Orleans and Austin, Texas, but had no contact with Brown.[23]

In the meantime, feeling betrayed by Brown and the Secret Six, Forbes—whom Osborne P. Anderson, a free African American who joined Brown, called "Judas" Forbes—had sent them abusive letters that warned of blackmail. He threatened to tell the world of Brown's plan if he was not paid. When the money failed to materialize, Forbes publicly exposed Brown's plan, denouncing his former employer and describing him to Senators William H. Seward and Henry Wilson as dangerous. Some of Brown's financial backers felt insecure because Forbes had blown their cover, and Brown's, so the Virginia plan was temporarily abandoned.

In late June 1858 Brown was back in Kansas, wearing a long gray beard and using the alias Shubel Morgan. In the summer and fall he suffered from the intermittent fever and chills of ague, or malaria, and needed to buy some time. In late December he launched a raid into Missouri. It was a limited assault on slavery. Brown and his men pillaged the homes of two Missouri planters, killing one of the planters, freeing 11 slaves, and carrying off wagons, horses, mules, and other property as reparations for those he was liberating. He then marched the 11 free blacks for 82 days and 1,100 miles through the dead of winter to safety in Canada. They arrived in mid-March 1859.

Brown was pleased with his efforts; in a way, the raid was a rehearsal for an attack on Harpers Ferry. On January 22, 1859, the New York *Daily Tribune* printed a letter from Brown describing his recent raid and claiming: "Eleven persons are forcibly restored to their 'natural and inalienable rights,' with but one man killed, and all 'Hell is stirred from beneath…' All Pro-Slavery, conservative Free-State, and doughface men, and Administration tools, are filled with holy horror." In *John Brown's War Against Slavery* Robert McGlone points out that the panic Brown created with the Missouri raid inspired him to do more than just run off slaves to the North. He abandoned the subterranean plan (to run off slaves through the mountains) for a more dramatic scheme to produce panic among slaveholders. He intended to implement the plan he had discussed with Forbes: swift nightly raids on plantations to build up a large force that would seize weapons from Harpers Ferry, moving southward and establishing bases in the Appalachians, and conducting raids on the lowlands. This would create terror, his primary weapon to destabilize slavery and ultimately embroil the nation in civil war. But Brown's failed efforts to entice black recruits would prove a factor in forcing him to reverse the order of his plan; first he would assault the federal armory at the confluence of Potomac and Shenandoah Rivers—with only a meager force.

Brown's raiding and guerrilla activities led to talk of rewards being placed on his head. The governor of Missouri proposed a $3,000 bounty, but he was unable to get his legislature's consent. The US president offered a $250 reward for the troublesome raider. Acting unperturbed, the game old man strode about in the North, pledging that he would die before being captured. Ridiculing the meager amount of his bounty, he jokingly and defiantly issued a $2.50 reward for the delivery of President James Buchanan to any Northern jail.[24]

CHAPTER 2

Launching the War of Liberation

After leaving Missouri in January 1859, Brown traveled throughout the Northeast again, seeking supporters and giving fiery speeches. By early June, he had urged the completion of a weaponry order he had placed two years earlier and arranged for his Ohio weapons and ammunition stores to be moved to Chambersburg, Pennsylvania. He made what turned out to be a last visit to his family in North Elba, New York. Then, in early July, under the alias of Isaac Smith, Brown headed for Harpers Ferry.

Brown targeted the Harpers Ferry area not only because of the federal armory and its weapons but because of information he recovered from black people who had lived nearby. He believed he could count on support from the high percentage of local free black people and anti-slavery whites—Quakers and Germans from Pennsylvania who were sympathetic to the Underground Railroad. The Railroad, or the Great Black Way, ran through Harpers Ferry, countering the slaveholders from tidewater Virginia, including members of prominent families such as the Washingtons, Lees, and Pages. To compensate for the loss of numerous runaways, in 1835 the Virginia legislature incorporated the Virginia Slave Insurance Company at Charles Town and unsuccessfully urged Pennsylvania to rescind its personal liberty law of 1826—which blocked the return of runaways—and instead enact legislation enabling the recapture of fugitive slaves. Few free blacks or slaves worked in the armory, arsenal, or rifle works at the time of Brown's raid. They labored nearby in the iron industry north of the Potomac River. The number of free blacks increased as the iron industry near Harpers Ferry sharply declined in the 1850s; by the end of the decade it was bankrupt. Many enslaved ironworkers were sold, and others purchased their freedom, staying in the area and working in the lumber industry and railroad. They formed black communities and churches, creating a seemingly favorable milieu for Brown to launch his war of liberation.

Brown had contact with men from Harpers Ferry, including Dr. Martin Delany, who had chaired the Chatham Convention. Another free black man, Joseph Richard Winters, born in Leesburg, Virginia, arranged a meeting between Frederick Douglass and Brown at the stone quarry in Chambersburg in 1859. Fugitives who used the Underground Railroad that ran northward through the sites of the iron furnaces swelled the black population of Chambersburg, making it an important conduit for the movement of men and weapons to the farm.[1]

Brown's Liberation Army

On July 3, 1859, Brown, his sons Owen and John Jr., and Jeremiah Anderson, a recruit from Kansas, got off the train at Sandy Hook, Maryland, across the Potomac and about a mile east of Harpers Ferry. They spent the night in this narrow hamlet. The next morning, on Independence Day, Brown and his companions set out on a quest to buy land for a dollar or two an acre. Soon they encountered a local resident. Brown introduced himself as Isaac Smith and his three companions as his sons, and he inquired about the price of land. He found the local price of $15 to $20 an acre too high, but a resident gave him a tip about a farm around five miles north of Harpers Ferry. Brown leased the farm from the widow of Dr. Booth Kennedy for $35 in rent, through March 1, 1860. The agreement gave him the use of two houses, pasture for a cow and a horse, and firewood. The main house sat upon a rise 300 yards north of the road, and 600 yards from it, across the road, was a cabin in a low swampy area, mostly hidden by shrubbery. By the second week of July Brown and his three companions occupied their new base.[2]

As summer turned to early fall, small numbers of anti-slavery men gravitated to the small rented farmhouse that served as the headquarters and staging area for Brown's war. Many of them were experienced veterans of Brown's guerrilla band in Kansas. Twenty-one men in all, 16 white and five black, would answer Brown's call and form the small army of the provisional government. They looked upon Old Osawatomie, whom they also called "Uncle" and "Captain," with respect that emanated not only from an admiration for their leader's certainty of purpose and hatred of the "peculiar institution," but also from his bravery and willingness to die for the cause. They openly embraced Brown's creed that slavery could only be abolished by violence.

Not all these men embraced his theology. John H. Kagi was an agnostic, and Aaron Dwight Stevens opposed slavery on moral rather than religious grounds. Jeremiah Anderson was described by his former high-school teacher as quiet and studious but morose and eccentric. It was assumed he would become a minister, but he rejected the idea and became a freethinker with spiritualist tendencies. The religious views of Canadian-born Stewart Taylor also differed from Brown's. Taylor's behavior was the most unique, causing Annie Brown Adams to describe him years later as generous and kind-hearted but a "crank," a fanatic, an eccentric dreamer who had opinions on all subjects that he called "Progressive ideas," that made him the "constant victim of jokes by the others, which he always took good naturedly." Annie Brown Adams found him to be a constant student, reading everything he could lay his hands upon, "interested in all the 'isms' of the day and in his religious views more of a spiritualist than anything else."

The men who gathered at the Kennedy house were not uneducated, uncouth ruffians, but a few had run afoul of the law.[3] Most had some education and were idealistic men in their twenties; the average age was 25. They were probably a little naive but were fired with youthful enthusiasm and righteous indignation. When the wife of the good-natured and fun-loving William Thompson pleaded with him not to go to Harpers Ferry for fear he would be murdered, his response was harsh: "O Mary, you do not think of any thing but self! What is my life in comparison to the thousands of poor slaves in bondage?"

Thirteen of the recruits had fought with Brown in Kansas. Brown's right-hand man, John H. Kagi, was gifted in speech and pen. The self-educated 22-year-old attorney had been forced to flee from the school-teaching job he started at 17 in Shenandoah County, Virginia, because of anti-slavery views. During his early life Kagi was a correspondent for the *National Era* of Washington, D.C., and *The Evening Post* and editor of the Topeka *Tribune*. He was imprisoned for several months for fighting in Kansas's civil war and later was severely injured by a pro-slave judge whom he had criticized for pro-slavery bias. The judge struck Kagi over the head with a cane and knocked him down on the courthouse steps. In self-defense, a dazed Kagi wounded his assailant by shooting him in the groin. Later the judge shot Kagi on sight. Kagi's life was miraculously spared when the bullet that struck above his heart was slowed by an inch-thick memorandum book. The bullet penetrated Kagi's coat and the book and stopped at a rib. Kagi is said to have removed the bullet with a penknife, causing the judge to say, according to a witness, "that if he had known Kagi possessed so much Pluck, he would have invited him to dinner."

Brown's most trusted assistant possessed such talents as organizational and executive skills, eloquence in writing and oratory, and total indifference to his personal appearance. A fellow raider, Osborne Anderson, describes Kagi as often going out "with a slouched hat, one leg of his pantaloons properly adjusted, and the other partly tucked into his high boot-top; unbrushed, unshaven, and in utter disregard of 'the latest style.'" When Kagi arrived at Harpers Ferry he planned to stay at the Kennedy house but was recognized. His reputation had spread to the the the region around Harpers Ferry, so most of his time from mid-July to mid-October was spent at Mary Ritner's boardinghouse on 225 East King Street in Chambersburg, Pennsylvania. There he coordinated the shipping of weapons, letters, and men to the Kennedy farm and received a number of visits by Brown. Henrie, as he was known, frequently attended to deliveries at the railroad depot, where he attracted attention. The town's newspaper *Valley Spirit* reported:

> Henrie was about the Depot at the arrival of every train, and was observed to scrutinize closely the passengers as they as they left the cars. He frequently met among the passengers, a person with whom he seemed to be acquainted. They appeared very shy with each other at first meeting but generally left the depot together.

The seat of Franklin County, Chambersburg was a key junction for bringing both men and weapons for the raid. The town's population of 4,000 included 500 free black people, in part because Pennsylvania was a haven for runaway slaves. Brown's men and weapons arrived by rail over the Cumberland Valley Railroad, and although the rail line went closer to the Kennedy farm, it was a poorly maintained track to Hagerstown in the slave state of Maryland. Brown deemed it prudent to use wagons to transport recruits and weapons, hidden in boxes, from Chambersburg to the Kennedy farm. These included 200 Sharps rifles that were meant to be loaned to Free State settlers in Kansas; these became embroiled in controversy between the National Kansas Committee and Massachusetts State Committee over ownership and the propriety of giving them to Brown. When considering whether to give Brown the money and weapons he had requested, the National Kansas Committee asked whether he intended to invade Missouri or any slave state. Candor would have imperiled his plans, so he adamantly refused to answer, saying, "I do not reveal my plans; no one knows them but myself... I do not wish to be interrogated; if you wish to give me anything, I want you to give it freely; I have no other purpose but to serve the cause of liberty." Ultimately George Stearns, as president of the Massachusetts State Kansas Committee and provider of funds for the purchase of weaponry, gained possession of the rifles and gave them to Brown. He had them shipped from Springdale, Iowa, to John Brown Jr.'s home in Ashtabula County, Ohio, along with 200 revolvers Stearns had bought. Brown's son had the weapons secreted about Ohio—in a store under coffins for sale and in a haymow—before they were shipped to the Kennedy farm.

Kagi stayed at the Chambersburg boardinghouse run by Mrs. Mary Ritner, the widow of Abram Ritner, who was the son of a former anti-slavery governor of Pennsylvania. At the boardinghouse, Kagi could see the garden from the open window of his rented room. Mrs. Ritner complained that a neighbor's "miserable" canine was once again trampling her garden, so her boarder took his pistol and proved his marksmanship. He shot the offending beast from 50 yards away and then threw the dog over the fence into its owner's yard. The dog's owner was a slave-trading neighbor who later claimed he would get revenge if he ever found out who was to blame.[4]

Another colorful member of Brown's force was a man in his mid-twenties, Aaron D. Stevens. The physically powerful 6'2" Stevens was born in Connecticut and ran away from home at 16. He fought in the Mexican War and years later almost killed an officer in a drunken brawl that nearly cost Aaron his life. In Trace, New Mexico, in May 1855 he was tried in a court-martial for mutiny, engaging in a drunken riot, and assaulting Major George A. H. Blake of his regiment. Stevens was convicted and sentenced to be shot. President Pierce commuted his sentence to three years' imprisonment, but Stevens escaped from Fort Leavenworth and used his years of military experience for the Free State cause in Kansas. He became the colonel of the Second Kansas militia, using the assumed name of Charles Whipple.[5]

John C. Cook was another fascinating character. He was an adventuresome soul and a womanizer whose expulsion from Yale for an unexplained indiscretion did not reflect favorably upon his prominent Indiana family. Cook served as a clerk in a New York law office and composed poetry with a facile pen. He met Brown in Kansas and later scouted Harpers Ferry, arriving there in June 1858, more than a year before the Old Man's arrival. He used several covers: schoolteacher, private writing tutor, traveling book and map agent, and canal-lock tender. His nervous, restless, and reckless disposition and proclivity for concocting outlandish stories—something he seems to have copied from his father—somehow made him engaging and likeable. He was well liked by those around Harpers Ferry, especially women. A slight young man, he was about 5'4" and 132 pounds, with long, silky blond hair, soft skin, and penetrating blue eyes, and he walked with his chest forward and his head leaning to the right side. Many women, regardless of marital status, found him irresistible.

Cook acquired knowledge of the armory and the region that made him an invaluable informant. At the Harpers Ferry raid, it was his plan to kidnap Colonel Lewis Washington. He favored not only seizing Harpers Ferry but also torching the town and railroad bridges and carrying off as many weapons as possible. Cook's judgment was not sound; he told Brown that political candidates in Maryland would join Brown's army and area slaves were also anxious to follow him. This misinformation contributed to Brown's miscalculating support for the raid.

As a marksman, however, John Cook lived up to his reputation. It was said his pistol shot could hit a 50-cent piece from a long distance. Salmon Brown recalls, "Cook was the best shot I ever saw. When the ducks and geese flew over us on the road he would always bring one down with his pistol." A Baltimore newspaper reported he could twirl a Sharps rifle "upon his finger, draw a bead at the five of clubs, and at a hundred yards knock out each spot." Other aspects of his reputation were less endearing to John Brown; he was an incessant talker and womanizer, getting involved with both married and unmarried women. He impregnated an attractive young teenager, Virginia (Jenny) Kennedy, the daughter of his landlady in the village of Bolivar, situated on high ground one mile west of Harpers Ferry. Virginia's lowly class and her own spicy reputation caused locals to act surprised that Cook was involved with her. Her reputation was not enhanced by the out-of-wedlock pregnancy, and tongues wagged in denunciation of such sinful behavior. On April 15, 1859, six months prior to the raid, the 18-year-old Virginia married Cook in a ceremony on the heights near Jefferson's Rock. The view was spectacular, of the two merging rivers running as one through an opening in the mountain range, a romantic and symbolic setting for their union. The next month Virginia gave birth to a son, John Jr. After the marriage the Cooks continued to live with the bride's mother in Bolivar, formerly known as Mudfort. The name was changed in 1825 to Bolivar after South American freedom fighter Simon Bolivar.

Cook was a dynamic little man. Salmon Brown found Cook "was just as much of an expert getting into the good graces of the girls at houses and hotels where we stopped nights and rainy days as he was shooting ducks." He added, "Cook was a little more than high strung, he was erratic." Cook's slight stammer, exacerbated by his rapidity of speech, did not lessen his charm. Salmon said "[Cook would] have a girl in a corner, telling them stories or repeating poetry to them in such a high-faluting manner that that they would laugh to kill themselves. He paralyzed the girls with his wit and audacity." He was deemed brave and engaging, but there was a catch: Salmon said, "I never thought he was over stocked with morality." Annie Brown found Cook to be "warm hearted, generous and brave... and whatever he did he did well." She thought he would not intentionally do harm. But Cook's lack of discretion and impulsive nature caused Annie's father to fear Cook's tongue: "[Brown] never knew what to expect of him."

Others at the Kennedy farm included Brown's sons Oliver, Owen, and Watson, and neighbors from North Elba, William and Dauphin Thompson, whose sister was married to Watson Brown. Watson left his young wife and a three-week-old baby boy when his older half-brother Salmon was unwilling to go to Harpers Ferry. Two young Quaker brothers from Ohio, Edwin and Barclay Coppoc, were small and delicate, with almost feminine behavior. Some of Brown's other men at the Kennedy house said, "They could not fight any better than girls." The Coppocs arrived at the Kennedy house along with Charles P. Tidd; Albert Hazlett; the Canadian-born wagon maker, shorthand expert, and spiritualist Stewart Taylor; the restless, likeable chain-smoking William H. Leeman, age 20; and Francis J. Meriam, the grandson of the president of the American Anti-slavery Society, who was somewhat of a misfit. He had lost the sight in one eye and exhibited erratic behavior, poor health, and quirky judgment. Taylor was the jokester at the Kennedy farm, and became the target of pranks. Tidd was easy to anger but retreated rapidly from his outbursts; he was musical, and a strong friendship grew up with Stevens as they enjoyed singing together.

The oldest member other than John Brown was Dangerfield Newby, a large, quiet man who was quick to anger. His age at the time has been estimated between 34 and 48, but he was probably about 39. He had been a slave in Culpeper County, Virginia, near the foothills of the Blue Ridge Mountains. Dangerfield had been freed by his white father, an aged Scotsman who freed his multiracial children in 1858 and moved with them to Ohio. Prior to going to Ohio Dangerfield apparently was hired out, working as a blacksmith on a canal that ran between Waterloo and Fredericksburg, Virginia. He married a slave woman, Harriet, who was a house servant living south of Manassas in Brentsville, Virginia, about 50 miles from Harpers Ferry. Dangerfield left Harriet and their six children behind; they were all owned by a doctor, Jesse Jennings. While in Ohio Newby attempted to raise the money to free his wife, but it is said Jennings reneged on his promise to sell her and one of the children for $1,000. While the amount was within the parameters of slave prices, it was a formidable amount for a laborer to obtain. At the time of his death Newby had only $741.55 in an Ohio bank account.[6]

It was against the Virginia slave code to teach enslaved people to read and write, but correspondence between the couple shows they were literate. Harriet's letters lack punctuation, but they eloquently reveal her plight, causing the modern reader's eyes to mist. She describes how she and her mistress had both recently had a baby. Her mistress became ill, and in Harriet's words, Mrs. Jennings "ben a grate suffering her breast raised and she had them lanced I had to stay with her day and night." Her mistress was unable to nurse her baby girl, so Harriet had to wet-nurse the infant in addition to caring for and nursing her own child. Her exhausting physical demands were made more burdensome: "[The servants are] very disagreeable they do all they can to set my mistress against me." In three letters to her husband in the spring and summer of 1859 Harriet said she missed him terribly and repeatedly expressed her angst, along with sharing news of their children. On April 11 she pleaded, "Dear Dangerfield com this fall with out fail money or no monney." A little over a week later she wrote, "Oh that bless hour when I shall see you once more." In what was probably her last letter to him, on August 16, 1859, Harriet wrote that she hoped his rheumatism was better and expressed her terror of being sold: "I want you to buy me as soon as possible for if you do not get me some body else will... Dear husband you [do not know] the trouble I see the last two years has been a terrible dream to me." Her master's need for money and the immediate likelihood of being sold made her fear the worst: "then all my bright hops for the future are blasted for there has ben one bright hope to cheer me in all my troubles, that is to be with you for if I thought I shoul never see you this earth would have no charms for me do all you can for me which I have no doubt you will."

Newby's failed attempts to purchase his wife and children's freedom and prevent them from being sold prompted him to join John Brown, whom he had met in Ohio, as a last hope for his family's liberation. His death would shatter Harriet's hopes and makes her fears a reality. She and her children were sold to a Louisiana slave dealer.

Four other African Americans joined Brown: Osborne P. Anderson, Lewis Leary, John Copeland Jr., and Shields "Emperor" Green. Anderson was a free man who worked as a printer before joining Brown in Canada in 1858. Most of the men of color who traveled to the Kennedy farm stopped over in Chambersburg with another black man, Henry Watson, a barber and trusted agent of the Underground Railroad. In addition to providing temporary shelter and meals prepared by his wife Eliza for black men, including Emperor Green, who were on their way to join Brown, Henry Watson helped by sending mail and supplies to the Kennedy farm. Emperor Green was a big-footed slave who escaped from South Carolina after his wife died, leaving his small son in slavery. Green was with Frederick Douglass when Brown asked him to join in the attack on Harpers Ferry. After Douglass rejected the invitation, Emperor Green accepted. He and Owen Brown, who was taking Green to the Kennedy house, were chased by law officials seeking escaped slaves and nearly captured, escaping only after Owen swam across a river with Green on his back.

A lack of education led the talkative Green to misuse large words, amusing others. Annie Brown described what Green called his farewell speech at the Kennedy farm to the two young Brown women who were being sent home before the raid. She called the talk "the greatest conglomeration of big words that were ever piled up." Someone asked Osborne Anderson whether he could understand what Emperor had said, and he responded, "No, God himself could not understand it."

Brown was not at the Kennedy house at the time but no doubt later found Emperor's speech amusing. Friend and supporter Richard J. Hinton said Brown was noted for terse, witty, and pointed expressions and "a quaint sense of humor which was no respecter of persons." The wife of a prominent Boston judge described Brown as having "a keen of sense of humor" about most things, including "blunders of the uneducated tongue." She described his laughter as "not making the slightest sound, not even a whisper or an intake of breath; but he shook all over and laughed violently. It was the most curious thing imaginable to see him, in utter silence, rock and quake with mirth."

Lewis Leary, a free black descendant of an Irishman named Jeremiah O'Leary who fought in the American Revolution under General Nathaniel Greene, left a wife and a six-month-old baby in Ohio to go to Harpers Ferry. John Copeland was a free black man born in North Carolina, who moved to Ohio with his parents and studied at Oberlin College. Leary and Copeland came together to join Brown. Copeland, who had earlier been hauled into court and accused of assaulting the marshal of Oberlin, was inspired to join Brown after reading letters from Kagi and John Brown Jr. to Leary. With money given them by two prominent attorneys of Oberlin, Copeland and Leary followed John Brown Jr.'s instructions to the Maryland hideaway. The judge in the trial of the raiders was impressed with Copeland's education, intelligence and dignity, claiming that if he had the power to pardon any of the conspirators, it would be Copeland, as he was by far the most worthy.

Mobilizing at the Kennedy Farm

These men gradually arrived at the time-battered farmhouse that nestled among rural hills. The house was compact, consisting of a small kitchen off the porch with a small stove, and a middle room used as both dining and living room, with stairs that led from living room to attic, where men drilled by day and slept on the floor at night. The basement kitchen was used for storage. The few kitchen utensils were made of tin. Furnishings were meager; boxes full of rifles and pistols served as chairs, and as a dressing table for Martha Brown, Oliver's wife. There were several outbuildings around the house and another structure across the road.

THE CABIN ACROSS THE ROAD
FROM THE FARMHOUSE

SCHOOL-HOUSE GUARDED BY
JOHN E. COOK

THE HOUSE AT KENNEDY FARM, MARYLAND
(West Virginia Archives, Boyd B. Stutler Collection)

Once he had settled at the Kennedy farm, John Brown sent Oliver back to North Elba for his mother and sister Annie. Oliver was preceded by his father's July 5 letter to his "Dear Wife," pleading for Mary and Annie to come for a short, safe visit without telling the neighbors. He urged Mary to bring only plain clothes, a few sheets and pillowcases, and whatever she could pack in a trunk and a clean bag, and not to worry about leaving the three young girls. Mary was against her husband's plan to attack Harpers Ferry and refused to go. Oliver's teenage wife, Martha, married at 15, went in her place with Annie. The morning they left Martha slipped coming down some stairs, was knocked unconscious, and severely sprained her ankle. Upon regaining consciousness she was told she could no longer travel. She went despite the pain. Martha and Annie were the only women at the Kennedy house and were compelled to explain the existence of unopened boxes to visitors; Annie wrote they claimed their mother "was coming soon and that she was very particular and had requested us not to unpack her furniture until she arrived."

Living in the small house the men frequently called the boardinghouse was confining and stressful for the inhabitants, who referred to themselves as prisoners and had to keep out of sight to avoid arousing suspicion among the locals. The attic had only a small window and must have been stifling in summer. Beds were primitive; men slept on the floor on bags the girls made out of coarse unbleached sheeting that was stuffed with hay. There were no sheets or pillows. After Emperor Green was spotted by a neighbor, Mrs. Huffmaster, Annie Brown recalled, "The colored men were never allowed to be seen in daylight outside of the dining room." Only thunderstorms at night allowed the men to let off steam outside; then they could enjoy running, shouting, and screaming. Nosy Mrs. Huffmaster heightened the men's concern about security and prompted them to provide a better defense. Owen and Watson Brown, the two Thompson brothers, and Jeremiah Anderson took their hay mattresses and spent the remaining nights in the log cabin across the road.

Unlike his rural neighbors, Brown did not work the land except to harvest some hay to feed his livestock. He didn't plant a garden—a universal practice of country folk—because of the labor required and the limited time he planned to be at the farm. All food had to be purchased. With the exception of Owen's purchase of a barrel of eggs, bought because it was cheaper than meat, food was obtained in small quantities to avoid suspicion. Most purchases came from Chambersburg, Harpers Ferry, or nearby hamlets. The daily routine started with breakfast, and when Old Brown was there he would read a chapter from the Bible and then stand to pray, always including a plea to the Almighty for the freedom of all slaves. After devotionals the men did a variety of activities, from preparing for the raid to just passing time. They studied Forbes's pamphlet, *Patriotic Volunteer*, and worked on their weapons and equipment. Cook obtained instructions from the Harpers Ferry arsenal for browning the rifle barrels. They made belts and pistol holders and assembled pikes by placing handles into spear heads. They also helped with housework. The men did most of the laundry, which Martha and Annie spread on the fence or ground, making sure to bring the clothes in as soon as they were dry. One day Mrs. Huffmaster, visiting, saw the clothes drying and remarked, "Your men folks has a right smart lot of shirts."

At the Kennedy house, Brown spent considerable time on a stool in the kitchen, where it was warmest, especially as the weather cooled. The rest of the house lacked heat. He also preferred the kitchen to the dining area, where the men often stayed, because he felt his presence inhibited their behavior. Recreational activities included playing cards, checkers, and other games, as well as singing, led by Stevens and his fine baritone voice. Old Brown encouraged and participated in discussions of various subjects, including a range of religious views. Some of the men even read Stevens's copy of Thomas Paine's *Age of Reason,* which led to lively discussions. For news they read Brown's subscription of the Baltimore *Sun,* collected from the Harpers Ferry post office, and magazines and other papers that Kagi sent from Chambersburg. For secrecy, important mail went to the Chambersburg post office and from there was taken by a trusted carrier to the raiders' headquarters in Maryland. Letters of minor importance came to Harpers Ferry addressed to "J. S. & Sons."

There were only two slave-owners, John C. Unseld and Terrance Byrne, near the Kennedy farm. Most of the residents around the Kennedy farm were Dunkards or Winebrenarians, pacifists who opposed slavery and would not let any minister preach until they knew his stand on slavery.[7] They had a church near the Kennedy house where Brown went almost daily, often preaching to the small congregation. During the day they had bush meetings held outside in a grove; at night they met in the church. Neighbors were impressed by Brown, his knowledge of livestock, and his willing assistance in helping them care for an ill cow, horse, or human. Brown fancied himself as having medical skills and occasionally performed a medical procedure on a sick neighbor.

Ironically, Brown had few animals at the Kennedy farm compared to the typical agrarian family: a dog, a mule, and a horse that turned out to be blind in one eye, which he purchased at Harpers Ferry; and from a neighbor, he bought a small farm wagon, a cow for milk, and three hogs to consume table scraps. A neighbor gave the mongrel pup, named Cuff, to Brown for removing a tumor from his mother's neck. Cuff made himself useful by barking with vigilance at neighbors who approached the house. Brown hired a brown mule, Old Dolly, from a local resident, James Magraw. The mule was to be returned to the owner in 30 days in the same condition as at the start of the transaction or Brown would have to pay the owner $160.[8]

Brown often left the farm to visit Kagi and seek money, making at least four trips from July 5 through October 16 to Chambersburg, Pennsylvania, 50 miles away. He usually traveled at night, as he needed less sleep than most, often rising at 3:00 in the morning. He rode on the back of Old Dolly, who also pulled his farm wagon. The vehicle was covered with the same coarse sheeting used to craft the crude mattresses. In late September and early October Owen Brown said he accompanied his father on several trips in the covered wagon to check whether the African American volunteers—whom he called "express packages"—had arrived. Transporting weapons could not have been an easy task for either a beast of burden or a horse with poor vision, but one of Brown's daughters recalled a Pennsylvanian bringing weapons to the Maryland farm in a large wagon.[9]

Henry Kyd Douglas, a future member of Stonewall Jackson's staff, who lived near Shepherdstown, 12 miles northwest of Harpers Ferry, gives a differing view. He recalled that as a young man he unknowingly befriended Brown. On a wet, muddy day Douglas encountered a kindly old gentlemen named Isaac Smith whose two-horse rickety wagon, overloaded with boxes, was stuck at the bottom of a hill. Douglas arranged for a horse and driver from his home near the Potomac River to pull the man's wagon out of the mud. The grateful old man told the youth the heavy load consisted of prospecting tools. Douglas was unaware of the sinister contents of the wagon or that his neighborly act aided Brown in his clandestine stockpiling.

It was vital that weapons hidden in the wagon remain undetected. The most unusual of these weapons were pikes. The handles were made of seasoned wood cut to Brown's specifications, six feet long, or pitchfork length. (Testimony of those examining them after the raid said the handles were five feet in length.) They were shipped simply tied together in a bundle, while the blades were tied together and boxed up. The pike was a most useful weapon, according to Brown, but it took months to acquire them. On the first day of 1857 Brown had traveled to Collinsville, Connecticut, 10 miles from his birthplace, to speak in the public hall about his Kansas experiences and to make an appeal for clothing for anti-slavery settlers. The next morning at the drugstore Brown showed those gathered there a double-edged blade, about eight inches long (a two-edged dirk), that he had taken from a Captain Pate in the Kansas fighting. Brown remarked that attaching these to poles about six feet long would make a "capital" weapon for settlers in Kansas to defend their homes. He then turned to Charles Blair, a local blacksmith whom Brown knew made edged weapons, and asked how much would it cost to make 500 to 1,000 of the weapon described. Taken off guard, Blair soon composed himself and named the price of $1.25 each for 500 and $1.00 for 1,000. A short time later Brown had Blair make a dozen samples. After making slight modifications Brown wrote out a brief contract stating the terms for the construction of 1,000 pikes at $1 apiece, with installment payments made within 30 days and 90 days for the completion of the manufacture of the pikes (near July 1, 1857).

After materials were purchased for 500 pikes and a few were made, Brown was unable to complete payment by the contract deadline. Blair stopped work and stored the handles and steel, and the few blades he had forged, in Blair's words, "were laid away." Blair later received a few letters from Brown telling of financial difficulties, the last in early March 1857. "Nothing more was heard from Mr. Brown at all, in any way or shape," Blair would testify, "until on the 3ᵈ day of June, 1859, the old man appeared at my door, unexpectedly of course, and said to me, 'I have been unable, sir, to fulfill my contract with you up to this time; I have met with various disappointments; now I am able to do so.'" Blair explained that he considered the contract void and was otherwise occupied, but he offered to turn over the raw materials he had stored. Brown said the materials were no use to him in that state. Blair, unaware of the real reason Brown wanted the pikes, and thinking they were to be sent to Kansas, agreed that upon full receipt of payment he would have a friend, Mr. Hart, complete the order. Blair left Brown's instructions with Hart, who completed most of the order for 1,000 pikes. As requested by Brown, Hart had them sent to J. Smith & Sons in the care of Oakes and Cauffman, Chambersburg, Pennsylvania.[10]

Brown was preparing for battle, but the two young women at the Kennedy house helped camouflage his preparations by lending the appearance of normalcy. Oliver Brown and the two young ladies had traveled from New Elba, journeying by boat from Troy down the Hudson River to New York, and from there, by rail to Harpers Ferry. Oliver's bride, 17-year-old Martha, was responsible for cooking and housekeeping at the Kennedy house. Martha was assisted by 16-year-old Annie Brown, her sister-in-law. But Annie's almost exclusive duty was what her father called being a "watch dog." He demanded "constant watchfulness." Annie was posted on the porch steps to meet callers and "parley long enough" that those inside could

Annie Brown (left), and Watson Brown with his wife Isabella. (Library of Congress)

remove suspicious-looking items that might reveal a gathering of men. If a visitor surprised them while eating, the men would seize dishes, food, and the tablecloth and climb to the attic above the dining room. If men were trapped in the kitchen, they would climb a ladder up to the attic. If visitors stayed for long periods at meal times, sometimes food would be carried up a ladder behind the house and passed through the small attic window to the men. Even when Annie was taking food from kitchen to dining room, washing dishes, or sweeping the floors, she was constantly looking out a window or from the porch for anyone approaching the house. Most of the time Annie sat on the porch or at the inside door, sewing, reading, or listening to the katydids and whippoorwills while keeping a constant lookout on the road. She later recalled that in the evening she enjoyed the fireflies and "looking at the lights and shadows on those fine old trees and the mountain ridge upon moonlight nights."

Shortly after the young women's arrival at the Kennedy farm, a diversion allayed the tedium of the daily routine. While her father was alone writing and she was sewing nearby, two wrens that had a nest under the porch came flying into the room through the open door. In Annie's words, they were "fluttering and twittering" in "great distress." She believed the birds were trying to get the humans' attention. They found, "A snake had crawled up the post and was just ready to devour the little ones in the nest." Said Annie, "[My father] killed the snake and the old birds sat on the railing and sang as if they would burst. It seemed as if they were trying to express their joy and gratitude for saving their little ones. After we returned to the room... [my father] thought it very strange the way the birds asked him for help, and asked if I thought it was an omen of his success. He seemed very much impressed by the idea."

Annie Brown's main challenge at the farmhouse came in the form of many unannounced visits by the diminutive Mrs. Huffmaster. The Huffmasters were a poor family who lived nearby and rented the garden behind the Kennedy house. Mrs. Huffmaster made visits to the garden, sometimes several times a day, with her four children, one of whom she carried in her arms. Annie called them "the little hen and chickens." The mother's garden visits were almost always followed by her entrance into the Kennedy house to chat. Annie remembers this was especially troublesome at mealtime, compelling the men "to gather up the victuals and tablecloth and quietly disappear upstairs." Annie called the woman's incessant visits "a worse plague than fleas." She said, "No one can ever imagine the pestering torment that little barefooted women and her four children were to us." One Saturday Annie and her father were at the Dunker Church and the remaining residents at the Kennedy house failed to be vigilant. Mrs. Huffmaster entered the house, surprising three of the men, one of whom was Shields Green, a black man. Another time she saw Charles Tidd standing on the porch. She assumed the white men were slave runners. Annie wrote, of Mrs. Huffmaster, "I used to give her everything she wanted or asked for to keep her on good terms, but we were in constant fear that she was a spy or would betray us. It was like standing on a powder magazine after a slow match had been lighted."

Months passed, and Annie wrote of mounting tensions and the men becoming overstressed by the long confinement and the mounting rumors of imminent raids by the law. To lighten their burden, the Brown girls would bring the men wild grapes, paw-paws, chestnuts, and bouquets of fall flowers from the fields and woods.

Meanwhile, Kagi spent most of his time in Chambersburg, Pennsylvania, sending weapons to Brown's base of operations. Of the 950 pikes, the spear heads and guards were in boxes, but the shafts made of ash wood were tied in bundles of 20 to 25 and passed off as pitchfork handles. Fifteen heavy boxes were filled with 198 Sharps rifles and 200 Maynard revolvers and labeled "mining equipment"; Kagi shipped them to "Isaac Smith and Sons." In September the weapons arrived at the Kennedy house. Most of the boxed rifles were stored in the one-room ground floor of the farmhouse, where crates leaned against walls or served as furniture. Some were stored upstairs, and others were across the road, in the log structure where pikes were stored in the attic. Several raiders slept in the log cabin to guard the weapons.

On Brown's trips to Chambersburg to fetch weapons, he was often accompanied by one of his sons or Jeremiah Anderson, who rode either in front, on one of the animals, or behind, looking out for danger. Their travels from Pennsylvania through Maryland aroused suspicion. A Maryland county sheriff anxiously inquired about "Isaac Smith and Sons, a mining firm that did not mine" and "cattle buyers who were not trading in stock." On August 20, 1859, three Iowa Quakers, led by David J. Gue, wanting to "protect Brown from the consequences of his own rashness" sent an anonymous letter to John B. Floyd, the unresponsive secretary of war, warning that John Brown would raid Harpers Ferry in a matter of weeks:

> Sir,—I have lately received information of a movement of so GREAT IMPORTANCE that I feel it is to be my duty to impart it to you without delay. I have discovered the existence of a secret association, having for its object THE LIBERATION OF SLAVES, AT THE SOUTH, BY A GENERAL INSURRECTION. The leader of the movement is OLD JOHN BROWN, late of Kansas. He has been in Canada, during the winter, drilling the negroes there, and they are only waiting his word to start for the South, to assist the Slaves. They have one of the leading men, a white man, in an armory in Maryland; where it is situated, I have not been able to learn. As soon as everything is ready, those of their number who are in the Northern States and Canada are to come, in small companies, to their rendezvous, which [is] in the mountains in Virginia. They will pass down through Pennsylvania and Maryland, and enter Virginia at Harper's Ferry. Brown left the North about three or four weeks ago, and will ARM THE NEGROES and strike the BLOW in a few weeks, and so that whatever is done must be done at once. They have a large quantity of arms at their rendezvous, and probably distributing them already. As I am not fully in their confidence, this is all the information I can give you. I dare not sign my name to this, but I trust that you will not disregard the warning on that account.

Believing John Brown to be a different man from the known abolitionist, President Buchanan issued a bounty for his arrest. The letter confused the less-than-astute Secretary Floyd, who knew the armory was not in Maryland but believed such an event could not occur. He ignored the warning.[11]

Brown went to great lengths to hide his purpose and his and his followers' identities. It was known that the quartz rock in the Harpers Ferry area contained meager amounts of gold. Years after the raid residents recalled Brown visiting places of business holding quartz fragments in his hand and claiming he had found gold. To hide their identity, the men modified their appearance, used aliases, used separate post offices for important and unimportant mail, and were ordered by their captain to be circumspect in speech and movement. All black recruits traveled to the farmhouse during the night from the home of a black barber, Henry Watson, in Chambersburg. The Old Man trimmed his beard to an inch or an inch and a half, thinking it a better disguise than "a clean face or long beard." A number of the men also grew facial hair. Before and during the raid Oliver, Edwin Coppoc, J. R. Anderson, and John Kagi had full beards, Cook had a moustache and Leeman had an imperial moustache. Additional steps of deception and vigilance included the use of aliases by key members, the ruse of their being in the cattle and mining businesses, having Annie serve as a civilian sentry, and carefully hiding their activities, even from Dunkard neighbors who also opposed slavery. Annie and her dad were friendly but secretive and successful in not allowing locals to enter their dwelling, with the exception of the overfriendly mother next door, who often entered the Kennedy House unexpectedly. Brown is said to have preached at a Chambersburg church that lacked a minister, but he quietly walked the streets going about his business, not initiating conversation.

To the two young daughters of Widow Ritner, when "Mr. Smith" stayed in town he seemed like a kindly old man. For fun on several occasions the Ritner girls rode a mile or two with Brown on his wagon as he left town with "mining equipment." His weapons were stored in warehouses once they arrived via the Cumberland Valley Railroad.

The men who were forming Brown's so-called army, however, were anything but discreet. Albert Hazlett and William Leeman were what Annie called "the hardest ones to keep caged of all 'my invisibles,'" with confinement "becoming almost unbearable at times." They would wander about in the woods or go to Cook's home in Bolivar Heights in the daytime. Many of the raiders were openly vocal about what they were up to. A number were writing home to family members or girlfriends of plans to attack Harpers Ferry. Two weeks before the raid Leeman wrote his mother:

> I am now in a Southern *Slave State* and before I leave it, it will be a *free state*, Mother... Yes, mother, I am waring [sic] with Slavery the greatest Curse that ever Infested America; In Explanation of my Absence from you for so long a time I would tell you that for three years I have been Engaged in a Secret Association of as gallant fellows as ever puled a trigger with the sole purpose of the *Extermination of Slavery*.

Brown lived in fear that John Cook's loose tongue would betray them all. While Cook was traveling as a book agent and selling maps in Loudoun County and the

Valley of Virginia, he openly told Quaker and Dunkard farmers there might be a "disturbance" or "active uneasiness" among the "darkies." Such talk no doubt increased Brown's concern, if not his anger.

In August Brown wrote from the Kennedy farm what is considered his most critical letter. Brown lamented the loose tongues of others to Kagi, who was extremely discreet and was addressed in the letter as "J. Henrie, Esq," one of several pseudonyms like "J. Henry" to hide his identity:

DEAR SIR – I got along Tuesday evening all right: with letters, etc. I do hope all corresponding except on business *of the Co. will be dropped for the present.* If every one must write some *girl*, or some other *extra* friend, telling or shoing [sic.] our location; and telling (*as some have done*) all about our matters; we might as well get the whole published *at once*, in the *New York Herald*. Any person is a *stupid fool* who expects his *friends* to keep *for him*; that which he cannot keep himself. All our friends have got *their special friends*; and they *again have theirs*; and it would not be right to lay the burden of keeping a secret on any one; at the end of a long string. I could tell you of some reasons I have for feeling rather keenly on this point. I do not say this on account of any tale-bearing that I accuse any — you of.

Three more hands came on from North Elba on Saturday last. Be sure to let me know of anything of interest.

"Yours in TRUTH"[12]

Dissent within the Ranks

The specifics of Brown's plan had severe flaws in what would prove to be an unrealistic scheme. According to his daughter Annie, he had changed his plan "for commencing while in Kansas and at one time thought of going down to the vicinity of New Orleans and working north from there." But ultimately he was overwhelmingly enamored with attacking Harpers Ferry. Revealing the specifics of his Harpers Ferry plan sparked heated arguments and anger among his men, and on a couple occasions, almost led to an open revolt. Brown's plan was rejected by others outside the farm. Brown asked Shields Green and Frederick Douglass, who was then living in Rochester, New York, and publishing the abolitionist newspaper the *North Star*, to meet him at a quarry outside Chambersburg. Pennsylvania. The site had been arranged by a free black man, Joseph Richard Winters. Born in Leesburg, Virginia, in 1816, Winters was known as "Indian Dick" because he was raised by a grandmother who was part Shawnee. After working at Harpers Ferry making sand molds, in 1830 Winters migrated to Chambersburg. Henry Watson, the Chambersburg barbershop owner, escorted Douglass and Shields Green to the quarry. Upon his arrival on Saturday, August 20, Douglass found "Isaac Smith" dressed in farm clothes and carrying a fishing pole in hopes of avoiding suspicion. Brown's trusted lieutenant, Kagi, accompanied the Old Man. Douglass had been aware for a long time that the old captain planned to strike Harpers Ferry, but Douglass was shocked when he found his old friend had replaced his plan of running off slaves in favor of capturing the town. When asked what he thought,

Douglass "opposed the measure with all the arguments" at his command, pointing out it would be "an attack upon the federal government, and would array the whole country against us." Brown's reply that his plan was just "what the country needed" further startled Douglass. Capturing Harpers Ferry would serve as notice to the slaves that their friends had come, Brown said. He said it would be impossible to defeat him once he was in possession of the town. Douglas rebutted respectfully, by saying that his friend's description made it sound as if he were about to enter "a perfect steel trap" with no escape. Unshaken by Douglass's argument, Brown claimed he would cut his way out, but he believed it would never come to that, because he would use the region's best citizens as hostages, which would allow him to negotiate an exit from Harpers Ferry. Douglass looked at his friend and asked how he "could rest upon a reed so weak and broken," and told him that Virginia "would blow him and his hostages sky-high, rather than that he hold Harpers Ferry an hour." The four men sat upon the rocks in the quarry as they—or, Brown and Douglass—debated the issue for most of a Saturday and part of the next day. Finally, in exasperation, Douglass turned to Green, saying Brown had changed plans and he was going home. In a last-ditch effort to convince the two formerly enslaved men to join him, Brown put his arm around Douglass, saying, "Come with me, Douglass; I will defend you with my life. I want you for a special purpose. When I strike, the bees will began to swarm, and I shall want you to help hive them." Unconvinced and starting to leave, Douglass asked what Emperor Green had decided. The response surprised him, that Green would go with the "Old Man." But Captain Brown had failed to enlist the aid of the friend whose help he so greatly desired. Despite Douglass's great sympathy for his friend's goal—if not his methods—Douglass had struggled mightily to be free and could not see throwing away his life on a futile adventure. He had suffered the hopelessness of bondage and the torment of the lash (although he had gotten the better of an owner who attempted to whip him in a two-hour fight). He had violated Maryland's slave code by learning to read and write and attempting to educate and encourage others to join him in an escape plot that was aborted by treachery. This escape attempt could have resulted in his being sold in the Deep South, or worse; instead Douglass was hired out as an apprentice at the Baltimore shipping yard. There he was attacked by four thugs who nearly took his life in an assault that included being struck from behind with a heavy handspike, repeated punches, and being kicked in the eye. Finally in 1838 Douglass boarded a train, escaping to the North. After enduring all this, to forfeit his life in a doomed effort—even for a noble cause—was not something Douglass felt he could do.[13]

Earlier, Hugh B. Forbes had argued heatedly with Brown over plans for an attack on slavery. In August 1859 at the Kennedy farmhouse, Brown's revelation of his Harpers Ferry plan was sharply opposed by a number of his men, including his three sons. Most had gathered at this rendezvous thinking they were going on an expanded hit-and-run raid similar to the previous year's foray into Missouri. The plan—to seize the town, armory, arsenal, and rifle works and hold them for an indefinite time until moving the war of liberation to the Deep South—angered and frightened them. Brown showed his men seven maps of eight slave states and slave statistics he had taken from the 1850 census in an attempt to convince them that by taking Harpers Ferry, a spontaneous revolution (under their leadership) would spread through the South.

Even Brown's sons Owen, Oliver, and Watson were unconvinced and denounced the plan as doomed to failure; they thought it would be suicidal for as meager a force as theirs to attempt to seize and hold a town in which they could easily be trapped and killed by militia or a Federal force. Charles Tidd became so angry he left and stayed for three days in Bolivar Heights at Cook's home. Salmon Brown, who refused to go to the Kennedy house, had prophetically told his brothers as they were leaving, "You know Father. You know he will *dally* till he is trapped!" According to Owen Brown, the men's opposition even weakened his father's resolve, causing him, on one of their wagon trips to Chambersburg, to remark, "I feel so depressed on account of the opposition of the men, that at times I am almost willing to temporarily abandon the undertaking."

Kagi left Chambersburg on Friday, October 14, to engage in the debate, supporting his captain and arguing they would leave Harpers Ferry before they faced armed resistance. Stevens, Anderson, Cook, and Leeman sided with their leader. Finally, young Oliver Brown, whose many visits to the Ferry had convinced him it was a suicide mission, stood next to his young wife and said, "We must not let our father die alone." There was no doubt his father was going to attack the Ferry, he argued, and if necessary the Old Man would launch his attack with six men. In an attempt to defuse the argument that the raid was doomed to fail, the old warrior told his men, "We have… only one life to live, and one to die; and if we lose our lives it will perhaps do more for the cause than our lives would be worth in any other way." Finally he threatened to resign as their commander, stating he would follow his second and third in command, Kagi, Stevens, or whomever the men selected to lead them. This the men unanimously opposed.

On August 18, 1859, Owen Brown wrote his father, who was apparently away on one of his trips:

> DEAR SIR – We have all agreed to sustain your decisions, until you have *proved* incompetent, and many of us will adhere to your decisions so long as you will. Your friend OWEN SMITH

Finally, Brown was able to bring everyone in line because of their respect for him and their dedication to fighting slavery although they still believed the plan was doomed. Edwin Coppoc, when captured, told a reporter that to counter their opposition to the raid, "(Brown) promised large reinforcements as soon as we made a demonstration."[14] Stewart Taylor, an excellent Canadian-born stenographer who had been distressed because he thought he was going to be left out of the Harpers Ferry venture, believed in dreams predicting his own death at the Ferry and talked about it calmly as an unalterable event. The touching letters between Watson Brown, who was approaching his mid-twenties, and his young wife illustrate the emotional turmoil of wanting to be home with loved ones while feeling a sense of duty to fight to rid an evil that would probably cost their lives. Watson left his wife shortly after she had given birth to a baby named in honor of Frederick Brown, who was slain in Kansas. "Oh Bell," wrote the young husband, "I want to see you and the little fellow very much but must wait. A slave whose wife was sold to go South was found hanging, dead" in an orchard. "There was another slave murdered near our place the other day, making in all five murdered and one [suicide since we began to live] here… I cannot come home as long as such things are done here… I sometimes think perhaps we shall not meet again." Bell wrote back, describing their baby's endearing behavior and giving encouragement. She concluded, "Now Watson keep up good courage and do not worry about me and come back as soon as possible. I think of you in my dreams."

Watson's compatriots at the Kennedy house also had doubts. One day while alone with Annie, Owen was looking at the old house and said, "If we succeed, some day there will be a United States flag over this house. If we do not, it will be considered a den of land pirates and thieves."[15] Owen and his compatriots' apprehension proved to be prophetic.

Final Preparations

Part of the preparation for the raid was evacuating the women. On September 29 Oliver took his sister Annie and young pregnant wife, Martha, to Troy, New York, and they continued on to New Elba, out of harm's way. Oliver hurried back to the Kennedy house. With the young women went any cheerfulness at the farmhouse. The men grew more somber as the impending raid neared. While at Harrisburg on their way north, Oliver, his wife, and his sister met Brown and Kagi returning from Philadelphia. It was the girls' last meeting with the Old Man.

Another woman who needed to get to safety was Virginia Kennedy Cook, John's wife, described by a friend as "an attractive young woman, large, regular featured, blonde in complexion, modest, quiet in manner." Her quiet demeanor was challenged when she was suddenly told she and her baby must leave their home just days prior to the raid, leaving behind most of her possessions and going to a place she had never been and to people she had never met. On the morning of October 6 Oliver Brown and Jeremiah Anderson pulled up in Brown's old covered wagon outside Virginia's mother's Mary Ann Kennedy's home in Bolivar, where the Cooks lived. Oliver and Jeremiah Anderson handed their comrade a note that, he recalled, read:

Mr. Cook – Dear Sir: you will please get everything ready to come with your wife to my house this morning. My wagon will wait for you. I shall take your wife to Chambersburg and will start early to-morrow morning. Be as expeditious as possible. Be very careful not to say or do anything which will awaken any suspicion. You can say your wife is going to make a visit to some friends of hers in the country. Be very careful that you do not let any of our plans leak out.

Yours, etc., J. Smith

Cook's later confession, despite inaccuracies, is relatively free from his proclivity for hyperbole, and maintains that he, his wife, and the two raiders sent to fetch them arrived that night at the Kennedy house in time for supper. Cook remained there while his wife and five-month-old child were taken by John Brown and his son Watson to Mrs. Ritner's in Chambersburg. It was October 7. Upon Captain Brown's return he told Cook his wife "liked her boarding place very well."[16]

Meanwhile, John Brown Jr. had been unsuccessfully scouting the North for recruits and financial support (financially depleted, his father had to borrow $40 from Barclay Coppoc to go to Philadelphia) but he obtained only moral support. Even blacks whom the elder Brown had helped liberate did not come forward, no doubt encouraged not to do so by Frederick Douglass's example. Harriet Tubman was also not on board, apparently because of illness. From the end of September to October 15 the last of the 21 men to join the Army of the Provisional Government arrived at the Maryland farmhouse: Osborne Anderson, Dangerfield Newby, Lewis Leary, and John Copeland. Kagi came down from Mary Ritner's Chambersburg boardinghouse, and Cook came from Bolivar Heights.

The last to arrive, on October 15, was the frail, one-eyed, emotionally erratic, and perhaps mentally deficient Francis Jackson Meriam. He had spent a week or more in Chambersburg, where he was busy penning letters and sending telegrams to Boston and other destinations. A number of his dispatches were expensive, costing as much as $6 each. Wanting to help free slaves and having heard Brown was in dire financial distress Meriam got $600 from an uncle, a prominent abolitionist, and met Brown in Philadelphia with the sorely needed money. After the meeting Meriam was sent to purchase items that included 40,000 Sharps rifle primers and percussion caps. Despite his fervor for terminating slavery, Meriam had some apprehension about his fate. Before he left Chambersburg he had Kagi take him to an attorney, Colonel A. K. McClure, to draw up a will. Dated October 9, 1859, it bequeathed his property to the abolition society of his native state of Massachusetts in the event of his demise.

The timetable for attack was fluid and depended on the arrival of men and money, which the arrival of Meriam helped remedy. Brown would have liked to have more men, especially black men, but by the end of September circumstances made immediate action imperative, in the minds of Brown and Kagi. In early October they wrote letters to John Jr. in Ohio instructing him not to send recruits to the Kennedy farm. Anyone arriving after October 10, in Kagi's words, "would be trying a very hazardous and foolish experiment… They must keep off the border until we open the way clear up to the [Mason–Dixon] line." Before recruits could come, he wrote, "We must first make a complete and undisputably open road to the free states." To do this, Kagi wrote, might take weeks or months and much labor. He also informed John Jr., "This is just the right time"—avoiding the incriminating words "attack Harpers Ferry." He listed many reasons why it was time to seize the Ferry. Among them were bountiful crops that were stored ready for use, a Christian revival, which made whites who just tolerated slavery examine their consciences, and slave discontentment being at a high level. He said, "The moon is just right." Kagi was especially agitated by the news of a despondent slave's hanging himself after his master sold his wife. Furthermore, Kagi contended, "We can't live longer without money—we couldn't much longer without being exposed." He could have added to his list of reasons the growing unrest of the men confined at the Kennedy house and Secret Six members' demands for action.[17]

Brown mimicked the American Revolutionary experience, forming his own army and patterning his Provisional Constitution after the original Constitution and the Declaration of Independence. In summer 1859, probably at the Kennedy house, he penned his own version of the Declaration of Independence, calling it "A Declaration of Liberty by the Representatives of the Slave Population of the United States of America." Jefferson's words in the original treatise make up most of the document, along with the argument for Brown's protest, which was based on John Locke's God-given natural rights—paraphrased by Jefferson as "life, liberty and the pursuit of happiness." Slavery replaced King George III as the oppressor and violator of inalienable rights. At the end of the declaration Brown added his own words: "Indeed; I tremble for my country, when I reflect that God is just; And that his Justice; will not sleep forever… Nature is mourning for its murdered, and Afflicted Children. Hung be the Heavens in Scarlet."[18]

Brown considered his small band to be at war as much as the minutemen and revolutionary soldiers in the Continental Army and state militia. Unlike the War for Independence, which was fought to get rid of an existing government, Brown's Provisional Constitution states, "[It] shall not be construed so as in any way to encourage the overthrow of any State Government of the United States: and look to no dissolution of the Union, but simply to Amendment and Repeal. And our flag shall be the same that our Fathers fought under in the Revolution."

Old Brown felt legitimacy and success demanded proper organization and rules. Salmon said, "Father had a peculiarity of insisting on *order*… He would insist on getting everything arranged just to suit him before he would consent to a move," a trait his son felt would likely "trap him" at Harpers Ferry. Over half the Provisional Constitution dealt with the organization of a military that could be made up of both males and females "of good character, sound minds and suitable age." Both soldier and civilian were required to "make a solemn oath… to abide by and support The

Provisional Constitution." Unlike modern terrorist screeds, this document states that both civilians and the military were forbidden to "carry concealed weapons… no needless waste of useful property," and only property of slave-owners should be confiscated; "nor shall any prisoner be treated with any kind of cruelty, disrespect, insult or needless severity," "[be] subject to corporal punishment," or be put to death without the "benefit of a fair and impartial trial." Furthermore, no harm should befall non-slaveholders who remained neutral. Harsher treatment would be given to those who betrayed the cause; anyone who was guilty of desertion would be executed. The same fate would befall "persons convicted of the forcible violation of any female prisoner." All in the organization were required to labor "for the general good." Brown's sense of morality strongly influenced the formation of not only the above provisions but also the article dealing with "irregularities." Profanity, indecent exposure, intoxication, quarreling, and "unlawful intercourse of the sexes" were prohibited as irregularities.[19]

Brown would later reemphasize and expand the provisions on military organization in the Provisional Constitution. He had spelled out nine agreements in the "Articles of Agreement for Shubel Morgan's Company" that were extrapolated from the Provisional Constitution, which the band of 14 men on his Missouri raid had to pledge to obey. For Harpers Ferry, Kagi and his leader spelled out regulations and orders that were more extensive.

Anticipating that large numbers of men, especially slaves, would join them after the attack on the Ferry as they penetrated the South, Kagi wrote out regulations for the organization of thousands of recruits under the heading "Headquarters, War Department Provisional Army, Harpers Ferry, Oct. 10, 1859. General Orders. No.1." The Provisional Army was to be divided into the following: company (72 men and officers), battalion (four companies), regiment (four battalions) and brigade (four regiments), for a total of about 4,600 men. Six days later Brown issued orders that spelled out assignments and the attack specifics.

It was Sunday, October 16, and Brown rose earlier than usual, calling the men to worship. He read a chapter from the "Good Book" that applied to the plight of the enslaved, followed with a prayer to God to help the army in "the liberation of the bondmen." Breakfast followed, and a sentinel stood outside the door to warn of approaching outsiders. Then came roll call, and at 10:00 a.m., assembly of a council chaired by Osborne P. Anderson; Brown felt it was symbolically and morally appropriate to put a black man in such a position. After the council adjourned, the Provisional Constitution was read, especially for four who had not previously heard it. Kagi, the adjutant-general and second in command to Brown, filled out commissions for newly appointed officers, who were required to take oaths of compliance. The legal basis of the commissions was the Provisional Constitution. In the minds of Brown and his men, these were issued by the top official of a legitimate government. Kagi wrote:

No. 5 *Commission*

Greeting:
Headquarters, War Department,
Near Harper's Ferry, Maryland,

Whereas *Oliver Brown* has been nominated a *captain* in the army established under the provisional constitution,

Now, therefore, in pursuance of the authority vested in us by said Constitution, we do hereby appoint and commission the said *Oliver Brown a captain.*

Given at the office of the Secretary of War, this day, October 15, 1859.

John Brown,
Commander in Chief.[20]

Most of the white men were made captains, and a few lieutenants—a disproportionate number of officers for such a meager force. This was in anticipation of large numbers expected to join them; Brown felt white leadership was vital in helping slaves obtain freedom. By now it was afternoon, and their commander in chief—himself a captain—issued 11 orders, based on Cook's scouting and recommendations. The orders spelled out who would stay behind to guard the weapons and later help deliver them to a schoolhouse for distribution to Maryland slaves, and to sympathetic whites from Pennsylvania and what would later become West Virginia. Orders spelled out which men would cut the telegraph wires; capture the watchmen; guard the wooden bridges over the two rivers; seize the armory, arsenals, and rifle works; and take hostages away from town. All men were ordered to stay at their assigned places in Harpers Ferry until the next morning. For the most part, until disrupted by opposing militiamen, Brown's men would closely follow their orders. The meticulous orders specified:

- Captain Owen Brown, F. J. Meriam and Barclay Coppoc would stay at the Kennedy house to stand guard until the next morning, when several men from the Ferry would join them with wagons to move arms and other items to an old schoolhouse about a mile from Harpers Ferry.
- Movement to Harpers Ferry should be as noiseless as possible, and arms hidden to avoid detection.
- The men would walk far apart and detain anyone they encountered until the rest of their comrades could leave the road undetected.
- Captains Charles P. Tidd and John E. Cook would walk ahead of the wagon transporting Brown. Upon their arrival at the Ferry, they were to tear down the telegraph lines along the railroad in Maryland, and they were to do the same on the Virginia side after capturing the town.
- Captains John H. Kagi and A. D. Stevens were to capture the Potomac bridge watchman and detain him until the enginehouse on government land was captured.
- Captain Watson Brown and Stewart Taylor would guard the Potomac bridge until the next morning. They were to be stationed on the bridge, a rod (16

and a half feet) apart. If anyone entered the bridge they were to let them get in between and then capture the intruder with pikes. Their Sharps rifles were to only be used as a last resort.

- Captains Oliver Brown and William Thompson would execute a similar order on the Shenandoah bridge and remain there until morning.
- Lieutenant Jeremiah Anderson and Adolphus (Dauphin) Thompson were stationed at the enginehouse with the captured watchmen. Once other buildings, including the rifle factory, were taken, they would be reinforced.
- Lieutenant Albert Hazlett and Private Edwin Coppoc were to occupy the armory opposite the enginehouse until the next morning.
- Adjutant-General John Kagi and John Copeland would hold the rifle factory through the night and stay until receiving further orders.
- Captain A. D. Stevens and men he would select from the raiding party would proceed into the countryside and capture select slave-owners, among them Colonel Lewis Washington, who would be forced to hand his historic weapons (pistols and a sword that supposedly belonged to Frederick the Great and General Lafayette) to Osborne P. Anderson, a black man. This was to be a symbolic gesture; "colored" men were viewed as possessions in the South, and Brown felt the South should be taught a lesson on this point.[21]

Despite his loose tongue, John Cook provided crucial information for planning. Months before the raid, while obtaining a wedding license, he asked the clerk for the official number of slaves in Jefferson County, and the clerk complied. Shortly before the attack, Cook said Captain Brown gave him $2 and "requested me to find out in some way, without creating suspicion, the number of male slaves on or near the roads leading from the Ferry, for a distance of eight to ten miles…" Cook traveled the road between Harpers Ferry and Charles Town, telling people he was gathering statistics "for a work to be published by John Henri, and to decide a wager between him and Mr. Smith." Earlier, traveling over the same road, Cook had obtained information from his visit to the home of a prominent local slave-owner; this information led to Brown's final pre-raid order. While in Harpers Ferry, Colonel Lewis Washington, the great grandnephew of the nation's first president, known by virtually all arsenal workers, was addressed by an engaging small man he had never seem but assumed was an "armorer," who asked, "I believe you have a great many interesting relics at your house; could I have permission to see them if I should walk out some day?" Taking advantage of the affirmative response, Cook arrived at the colonel's home in mid-September and curiously examined a sword, erroneously thought to be a gift of Frederick the Great, and a pistol from Lafayette, which were presented to General George Washington. Cook also saw newer weapons that included a double-barreled shotgun. Intrigued by the pistol given by Lafayette, Cook asked, "Does it shoot well?" Washington informed the intent guest he had only tried it out briefly a number of years earlier, and "It would never be shot again." According to Washington, Cook, a spinner of captivating yarns, informed the colonel, "he belonged to a Kansas hunting party and found it very profitable to hunt buffaloes for their hides." He revealed two revolvers in his coat, saying "he was in the habit of carrying them in his occupation, that he had been attacked with chills and fevers some time ago, and was wearing them to accustom his hips to their weight." Then he asked if Washington was fond of shooting, and Washington responded, "I formerly was." Cook then said. "You would possibly like to try these?" The two men went in front of the house "and under a tree stuck up a target, firing some twenty-four shots." Washington recalled his guest never introduced himself, but in "taking up his large revolver (the size used in the army) I found 'John E. Cook' engraved on the breech of it on a brass plate, and he said 'I engraved that myself; I borrowed the tools from a silversmith, a bungler, and thinking I could do it better myself, I did it.' I presume," asked Washington, "That is your name?" and was told it was. Before leaving, Cook invited his host to come see his special rifle, "a twenty-two shooter," but several weeks later when Washington "asked for him at the Ferry" he was told Cook had left. The colonel supposed "in all probability he had gone to Kansas, as he told me he intended to go" there "in a few days." The man whom Brown most feared would reveal their secrets had not only cased Washington's home without creating suspicion but, at least in this incident, temporarily covered his trail.

Cook was well educated, but his judgment left something to be desired. He incorrectly reinforced Brown's belief in spontaneous and widespread support of slaves for the raid and claimed that prominent political candidates of different parties in the 1858 Maryland election would also join his force.[22] This false information and his later confession would evoke Brown's scorn.

Noticeably missing from Old Osawatomie's detailed orders for the raid were instructions for taking federal firearms and transporting them to the mountains. This is surprising, because it was originally one of the paramount reasons for striking Harpers Ferry. The issue of seizing federal weapons is further muddled by conflicting eyewitness accounts. One man claimed Brown informed him at Harpers Ferry that: "It was not part of his purpose to seize the public arms. He had arms and ammunition enough… He only intended to make the first demonstration"—which would cause anti-slavery whites as well as slaves in Maryland and Virginia to flock to Brown. Another gentleman, while talking to the captured leader of the raiders in the Charles Town jail, claimed he was told by Brown that Brown intended to seize federal weapons. Brown made the same claim to armory officials who were held hostage on the morning of October 17; the gentleman said, "It was his [Brown's] determination to seize the arms and munitions of the government, to arm the blacks to defend themselves against their masters."[23]

Brown seems to have relegated taking federal weapons to a much lower priority as the raid neared. He wanted to arm slaves with weapons he considered superior to those in federal arsenals. In a discussion Brown had with his friend Augustus

Wattles at his frequently visited Kansas home, the free-state host said, "A forcible emancipation was worse than slavery." Brown ridiculed his friend by saying the plan was "to put arms in the hands of the slaves; give them a choice, stand behind them so as to protect them in a free choice; give them a free choice, and if they chose to go into slavery, let them stay: but if they chose to go out, sustain them in it." Wattles responded, "It was an impossibility to give them arms," referring to the expense and difficulty of supplying them. He was told by Brown "he had a plan for an arm for them better than a musket—a long pike."

Brown was now saying, "Give a slave a pike, and you make him a man. Deprive him of the means of resistance, and you keep him down." The pike, he told a Boston crowd, was a more formidable weapon for the inexperienced than the gun. "I would not give Sharpe's rifles to more than ten men in a hundred, and then only when they have learned to use them."

By fall 1859 Brown's reasons for attacking Harpers Ferry and seizing federal property were not only to show his contempt for a pro-slavery central government but also to commit a shockingly unthinkable act that would jump-start his revolution of forced emancipation.[24] The fear of slave revolt fueled by the searing memory of Nat Turner's killing of whites in Virginia and Toussaint L'Ouverture's Haitian massacre tormented the Southern mind and made terror Brown's paramount psychological weapon. Brown believed terrorizing slave-owners—through guerrilla raids that liberated and armed slaves—would undermine the resistance of the slave-owners, who, in their desperation to ensure their own survival, would free those they held in bondage.

One of Brown's final charges, which would not be followed by his men, who were eager to leave their restrictive base, was an admonition to kill only in self-defense. This was in no way a terrorizing request and stood in stark contrast to his mutilating retaliations at Pottawatomie Creek and the brutal mayhem of "Bleeding Kansas." Shortly before leaving their base, Brown said, "And now gentlemen, let me impress this one thing upon your mind. You all know how dear life is to you, and how dear your life is to your friends. And in remembering that, consider that the lives of others are as dear to them as yours are to you. Do not, therefore, take the life of any one if you can possibly avoid it; but if is necessary to take life in order to save your own, then make sure work of it."[25]

It was from the Kennedy house on a Sunday night in mid-October that Brown launched his war of liberation. During the night of October 16, 1859, Brown—after years of planning and dreaming of a raid upon Harpers Ferry—was on his way. He had repeatedly stated, "Twenty men in the Alleghenies could break Slavery to pieces in two years." He believed it was a divine mission with God on his side. Mesmerized by the success of other guerrillas in history who faced great odds, Brown was blinded by his own zeal. His confidence was buoyed and misled by his successes in Kansas and in liberating slaves from Missouri to Canada; neither militia nor federal forces were able to suppress him. Federal forces were thinly spread, making Brown believe they would continue to be a limited foe.

Brown was convinced Harpers Ferry was the fuse for his master plan. He believed that capturing this town would ignite a rapidly spreading slave uprising. Slavery in Virginia would soon collapse, followed by the same fate for that hated institution in the Lower South. Liberating guerrillas would raid plantations and federal arsenals to arm slaves to fight for their freedom throughout the South. Such a revolutionary force, Brown argued, could easily defeat militia or the "inefficient" soldiers of the US Army. Brown and his right-hand man Kagi believed the gradually increasing magnitude of their liberating raids would destabilize slavery by striking "terror into the hearts of the Slave States"; the whole institution of human bondage was "vulnerable" because of the South's "fear of slave rising."

Brown was counting on the psychological impact of terror to intimidate slave-owners. One of his friends and an early biographer, Richard J. Hinton, argued that Brown planned to hold Harpers Ferry long enough "to leave a startling impression on the country, and then by disappearance, to be followed by swift raids elsewhere, adding to the alarm that would exist. What John Brown seriously believed was, that slavery being vulnerable in all directions, could be frightened out of existence quite as much as fought out of existence."

As meticulous as Brown had been in planning, his orders were noticeably lacking a timetable, adequate supplies, or specifics for leaving the town. This would be his undoing. Brown's men were ordered to scatter over the lowest part of Harpers Ferry, along the rivers, which were walled in by precipices at the 1,200-foot or taller Maryland Heights and the nearly as daunting Loudoun Heights and Bolivar Heights behind the town. This would place his small force in jeopardy from any contending forces that might seize Bolivar Heights and the two bridges over the rivers. But to Brown this danger was apparently insignificant; the matter was in God's hands. He was starting what he considered to be a new American Revolution. Even if he and all his men were killed at Harpers Ferry, he believed their actions would not have been in vain. Few in history would have been able to die for so noble a cause; even a failed raid on Harpers Ferry would plunge the nation into an explosive confrontation, leading to a civil war, which would, Brown predicted, end slavery.[26]

CHAPTER 3

Igniting the Fuse: The Attack on Harpers Ferry

John Brown's guerilla attack, launched on a drizzling Sunday night, would advance through three phases over a 36-hour period. Despite early success, Brown's unrealistic expectations, defective planning, and inadequate leadership doomed the mission. It would not lead to the outcomes Brown expected, and would for a time leave him in a panic.

Phase One: Brown Takes Harpers Ferry

At 8:00 on the night of October 16, Brown was wearing a gray overcoat with a cape and had donned an old fur cap with a patent-leather visor bought while traveling from Kansas to Massachusetts. In *Voice From Harper's Ferry* Osborne Anderson, one of the raiders, recalls Brown saying, "Men, get your arms; we will proceed to the Ferry." It was a somber occasion. Brothers Edwin and Barclay Coppoc hugged and kissed each other, not knowing whether they would see each other again. Three of the men were less well suited for combat: Owen Brown, who had injured his right arm or shoulder throwing a stone in childhood, leaving him with only partial use of the arm; young and inexperienced Barclay Coppoc; and the well-meaning but unstable and sickly F. J. Meriam. These three remained at the Kennedy house to guard the weapons and would later assist in moving them to the nearby old schoolhouse a mile from Harpers Ferry, near the Chesapeake and Ohio (C&O) Canal, in a hollow where the road turns northward into the mountains. Brown and 18 men left the old dwelling in a manner that was called as solemn as a funeral procession. They wore gray shawls as topcoats to hide their weapons. Captains Charles Tidd and John Cook led the way. The rest followed their old leader, walking in pairs, each pair about 300 yards apart. That way, if they were to encounter anyone over the five miles or so of winding road, only the leading two raiders would be seen, giving the remaining men a chance to hide. Their leader rode on a one-horse wagon—pulled by a partially blind horse—that also carried pikes, crowbars, sledgehammers, and most of the 100 fagots the men had made by tying pine twigs with hickory sticks in bundles. They were for torching buildings and bridges.

The men arrived at the 300-yard-long covered bridge with its tin roof and clapboard siding, a bridge that carried rail, wagon, and foot traffic. They paused, were ordered to fasten their cartridge outside their clothing, and then launched their attack.

At first things seemed to go well for Brown's force; they seized the designated sites at Harpers Ferry, carrying out orders as smoothly as planned, without firing a shot. Tidd and Cook tore down telegraph wires on both sides of the Potomac. They were followed by raiders entering Harpers Ferry, which was unguarded except for unarmed civilian watchmen, one on the Potomac bridge, two at the armory, and one at the rifle works.[1]

The lack of protection of US facilities seems surprising in retrospect. Perhaps about 80 people in the country had some prior knowledge of Brown's impending attack, including some high-ranking government officials who had been warned that Brown was planning an attack on Harpers Ferry. But the mindset at the time was drastically different from today. The paramount risk to the armory and rifle works was unattended shop fires, and secondarily, wayward and mischievous locals intent on petty theft. The concept of armed invaders seizing what today would be a major defense plant was unthinkable, and civilian watchmen were rarely armed. Usually three were stationed at the armory and two at the rifle works, but on the night of the raid there was one less at each site. When the bell over the fire house and watchhouse rang out that the work day was over, it was then the duty of the fire-watchmen, as they were called, "to see that the fires in the forges and all necessary fire kept up in the workshops are put out, so there may be no danger from fire, and also to prevent any individuals who might come in during the night to pilfer." Arsenals lacked the fires of the shops, so it was deemed unnecessary to place watchmen there.[2]

Apparently neither the night watchmen nor anyone else imagined that people would do what Brown was doing. The flabbergasted watchmen were easily captured. The Potomac bridge watchman, William Williams, had walked from his home at Sandy Hook to work and was carrying a lantern from the other end of the bridge when he saw Brown and Cook, whom he knew, and was captured by Kagi and Stevens. At first he thought it was a prank. The captors and their prisoner headed toward the enginehouse on the armory grounds, where Jeremiah Anderson and Adolphus Thompson guarded him and the other captured watchmen in the armory.

Oliver Brown and Stewart Taylor remained just more than 15 yards apart on the bridge to capture intruders, using pikes to avoid attracting attention. Their rifles were to be used only as a last resort. Kagi and Stevens led the remainder of the self-proclaimed freedom fighters, with their prisoner, moving through the dark enclosure of the bridge and exiting off the left of the two split entrances into the unsuspecting and slumbering town. They turned sharply to their right and hurried past the shadowy outlines of clustered structures on the Point, passing on their left the toll house they had just departed, the B&O office, and the low-roofed Gault Saloon, and on their right the B&O depot, Wagner Hotel, and Potomac Restaurant.

Main entrance to the US Amory during the Civil War. Note the small and large gates have been removed and the bell in the tower is missing over the fire engine house now known as John Brown's fort. (Harpers Ferry National Park)

The hotel clerk, W. W. Throckmorton, was closing the doors when he noticed the one-horse covered wagon and men following it, but he assumed "some gypsies were going by" and continued closing down. After traveling 60 yards from the bridge, the raiders arrived at the eastern gates to the United States Musket Factory: the armory. Immediately to their left was a small gate for pedestrians, and in front of them the larger opening for wagons, with two swinging gates fastened by a large chain and padlock. The armory watchman, Daniel Whelan, was in the watchmen's small office, which was separated from the fire equipment on the other side by a solid brick wall.

Whelan heard the rumbling noise of Brown's small wagon and stepped outside to see what was happening. He carried a sword but left two dusty old muskets in a corner. Upon the roof tower hung a silent bell, used to summon workers and later dismiss them, that could be used to alert the whole town. After leaving the building—soon to be known as John Brown's Fort—through the smaller gate, he saw a wagon at the larger one, and two men attempting to open the padlock. Thinking it was the head watchman, he shouted, "Mr. Mason... hold on," and walked over to unlock the gate—only to find what seemed to him like more than several dozen armed men. He was ordered, "Open the gate." He refused. A raider leapt upon the limestone pier above his head while another grabbed his clothing through the iron bars, and about a half dozen men ran from the area of the wagon and thrust the ends of their rifle barrels into the chest of the startled watchman, demanding he surrender the key. Whelan defiantly refused to comply; a crowbar and large hammer were brought from the wagon, and one of the men, probably the muscular Stevens, twisted the crowbar in the chain. The chain broke and the raiders rushed into the armory grounds.

They immediately swarmed around the beleaguered and frightened guard. Whelan was in his late thirties and believed his life was ending prematurely. Cook, whom Whelan knew well, took the sword from him while—as Whelan testified before a committee of the Senate—he was told "to be very quiet and still and make no noise" or else they would put him "to eternity." Shaken by what was happening, Whelan willingly answered all their questions about the armory officers, causing Brown to say he "would have all those gentlemen [armory officials] in the morning."

The small wagon was moved past the enginehouse to the armory's office building. Next Brown ordered "all the men to dispatch out of the yard," his signal to seize the remaining designated sites, according to the armory watchman. That left only Jeremiah Anderson and Adolphus Thompson at each side of the large gate, with John Brown and his two prisoners. Brown told his captives, "I came from Kansas, and this is a slave state; I want to free all the negroes in this State; I have possession of the United States armory, and if the citizens interfere with me, I must only burn the town and have blood."[3]

Meanwhile, the watchman at the gate at the western end of the armory was oblivious to what was happening 300 yards away. Shortly after 1:00 Monday morning, after an eastbound train arrived, he was coming to see where Whelan was when Brown met him and marched him to the watchhouse. The men sent from the armory grounds, probably led by Stevens, assumed their pre-assigned positions by moving down Shenandoah Street.[4] Sixty yards away they stopped briefly at the two unguarded arsenal buildings housing the finished weapons made in the armory, leaving Albert Hazlett and Edwin Coppoc.

Soon after, Oliver Brown and William Thompson secured the bridge over the Shenandoah River. Half a mile from the armory, raiders captured the unarmed and unresisting guard, Samuel Williams—the elderly father of the watchman they had captured on the Potomac bridge—while he stood outside the buildings. They seized control of the rifle factory. Leaving John Kagi and John Copeland in control of what was formerly called Hall's Rifle Works, Stevens and the remaining men, with their new prisoner, walked back toward the armory. They picked up several stragglers in the streets before returning to the grounds of the massive musket factory.

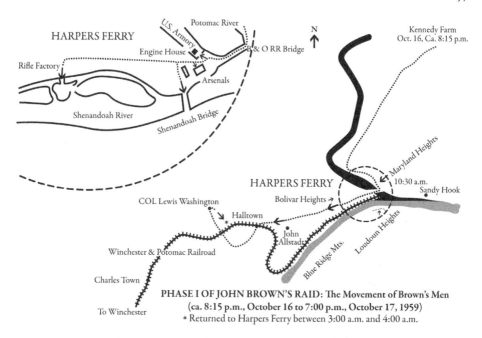

PHASE I OF JOHN BROWN'S RAID: The Movement of Brown's Men
(ca. 8:15 p.m., October 16 to 7:00 p.m., October 17, 1959)
* Returned to Harpers Ferry between 3:00 a.m. and 4:00 a.m.

After a brief discussion with their leader, Stevens chose Cook, Tidd, Green, Leary, and Osborne Anderson to implement Brown's 11th and final order. Their objectives were to initiate the primary purpose of the raid, to forcibly free and arm select slaves, and secondarily, to seize symbolic weapons while taking prominent hostages who could be exchanged to free more slaves. That is, the prisoners could be exchanged for slaves if they were not needed to ensure the raiders' safety and escape.

Their first target was five miles from Harpers Ferry: Beall-Air, the home of their potential prize hostage, Colonel Lewis Washington. He was a slave-owning small planter, possessor of historic weaponry, and a man of ancestry synonymous with obtaining America's "freedom from British tyranny." Arriving there about 1:30 a.m., Emperor Green and Lewis Leary were assigned to bring up Washington's carriage and wagon, along with any male slaves they found. Stevens, Cook, Tidd, and Anderson smashed in Washington's back door with a fence rail and walked to the front of the house to the first-floor bedroom where the colonel lay sleeping. The sound of the entry was muffled by walls and distance. Washington was the only white person in the house and on the farm; his overseer lived elsewhere, and his visiting daughter had left the previous morning. Washington was finally awakened by someone outside his bedroom door calling his name, as he said, "in an undertone." He assumed it be "some friend who had possibly arrived late, and being familiar with the house," had "been admitted in the rear by the servants." Washington later testified, "I opened the door in my night-shirt and slippers." He saw four armed men, three with rifles and one with a revolver in his right hand and a flaming torch in his left. He said (as Cook would confirm) they asked whether he was Colonel Washington, and he said yes and he was then told, "You are our prisoner." Looking at his captors, Washington was greatly surprised to see John Cook, the only one of the armed intruders he knew. The little man was again in the home where he had been a guest about four weeks earlier, but now he was part of what the colonel believed to be a gang of robbers. Washington noticed, "Each man had two revolvers sticking in his belt in front besides the rifle," and he commented to them, "You are a very bold looking set of fellows, but I should doubt your courage; you have too many arms to take one man."

Burning embers from the torch began falling upon the floor. Anxiously, Washington requested they come into his bedroom and asked them, "Light my candles, so as to prevent my house from being burnt." Getting dressed, the colonel said, "Possibly you will have the courtesy to tell me what this means; it is really a myth to me." Washington recounted, "[Stevens] spoke up and said, 'We have come here for the purpose of liberating all the slaves of the South, and we are able (or prepared) to do it,' or words to that effect." Once he had dressed, Washington "went into the dining room thinking... there was a better fire there," as the one in his bed chamber had gone out. Stevens immediately said, "You have some fire-arms, have you not?" The reply was yes but they were unloaded. "I want them," commanded Stevens, and Cook signaled they were in a closet. As all the weapons, old and new, were being taken, including two pistols presented to George Washington by Lafayette and a sword that, according to family tradition, Frederick the Great had given to George Washington and which the American general wore as a dress sword.

Following Brown's order to bring about a symbolic act, Stevens had Osborne Anderson step forward and take the sword. Brown later used these weapons to continue making symbolic gestures by wearing the sword during the raid and placing one of the revolvers in his belt. Both weapons had a history as the property of a liberator he was emulating in his own way—the man who freed colonial Americans from British tyranny.

Things at Beall-Air soon became more contentious, with an attempt to carry out Brown's directive to take any of the slave-holder's property that would help the crusade. Stevens said, "Have you a watch, sir?" "I have," replied Washington. "Where is it?" "It

Lewis Washington. (Library of Congress)

"Beall-Air," the home of Colonel Lewis Washington. (Library of Congress)

is on my person," replied Washington. "I want it, sir," ordered Stevens, who was not pleased when told, "You shall not have it."

Stevens admonished his captive to "Take care, sir." Washington was just as uncooperative in giving up his money. Stevens repeated the warning but was met with the reply, "You told me your purpose was philanthropic, but you did not mention... that it was robbery and rascality."

Yielding on the watch, Stevens changed the subject: "I presume you have heard of Osawatomie Brown?" "No, I have not," replied the colonel, according to his testimony. "You have paid little attention to Kansas matters," responded Stevens. Washington agreed, saying, "I had become so much disgusted with Kansas and related matters... whenever I saw a paper with Kansas at the head of it I turned it over." "Well," said Stevens—in a manner that Washington perceived as one of "great glorification"—"You will see him this morning." The conversation was then interrupted by an announcement that "The carriage was at the door."

Leaving his dwelling, Washington found that Emperor Green had driven Washington's carriage to the house, followed by Leary with the large four-horse wagon to carry away his slaves. To his surprise, Washington found the raiders only wanted the male slaves, taking the three who were there: two of the colonel's and one who was the husband of one of his servants. Washington said most of his servants were not present, "that being Sunday night." Later, upon hearing that there was trouble, one of Washington's slaves who had been away would get into the wagon at the Allstadts'.

Upon seeing that the two horses were incorrectly hooked to his carriage, Washington warned, "These horses will not drive in that way; they are high-spirited horses; they are on the wrong side." Tidd added, "This horse is reined too short." One of the carriage horses was shorter than the other, and Green had placed the small harness on the larger horse, so after going but a short distance they balked, refusing to move. Washington's house servant switched the horses and replaced Green, who was ordered from the driver's seat next to Tidd. Washington watched from the back seat of the carriage where he sat next to Cook. Things went well until they reached the large hill next to the Allstadts', where a hastily fastened harness came loose. On their way to the Allstadt house they stopped for a moment in front of a house a short distance from Halltown. They proceeded when Washington said no one was in the house but the recently widowed Mrs. Richard Henderson and her four or five daughters; he added, "It would be an infamous shame to wake them up at this hour of night."

Halfway between Washington's house and Harpers Ferry, two and half miles away, they reached the home of 50-year-old John Allstadt, a farmer and slave-owner. It was 3:00 a.m. on October 17. As Washington sat in the back seat of his carriage he could hear rails moving from the worm fence (a zigzagging rail fence) across the turnpike in front of the Allstadt house; the post-rail fence that bordered the house would have been more difficult to dislodge, with posts set in the ground. Most of the raiders walked to the back porch, to a door that led to the downstairs bedroom where Mr. and Mrs. Allstadt slept. The sleeping couple were awakened by banging on the locked door, causing John to go to the entrance to ask who was there. Allstadt recalled being told "to open the door directly or they would burn me up." He refused, and the door was immediately smashed open with a fence rail. Seeing a group of armed men with rifles, Allstadt struggled unsuccessfully to shut the door. Three men entered the bedroom and told John to dress himself. He asked their purpose and where they were taking him. Stevens replied that their intent was "to free the country of slavery" and they were taking him and Colonel Washington to Harpers Ferry, where "they had the armory in their possession."

From upstairs, the panic-stricken Allstadt daughters heard disturbing noises and voices, so they stuck their heads out a window and yelled, "Murder!" Outside, a raider pointed his rifle at the traumatized girls, ordering them to "go in and shut the window." In the meantime, Allstadt's 18-year-old son came downstairs, where he was grabbed by the collar and held until his father was dressed. The men were taken outside and ordered to get in the four-horse wagon with Washington's slaves, Sam, Mason, and Catesby, and seven from the Allstadt household, six adult males and one boy: Henry, Levi, Ben, Jerry, Phil, George, and Bill.

The group proceeded up the large hill to Bolivar, the carriage leading the way, followed by four armed raiders who walked in front of the large wagon. Near Bolivar, where a skirt of woods bordered the left of the road, the raiders, concerned about what they would encounter back at the Ferry, consulted one another a short distance away from the vehicles. Upon their return, one of the raiders said, "Boys, mind we may have a little fight," and the caravan proceeded toward the armory.[5] Their anxiety had merit.

While Stevens's raiding party was seizing Washington and the Allstadts, seizing their male slaves, and terrorizing the Allstadt women, many things were happening at Harpers Ferry. During the absence of the group led by Stevens the first gunshots were fired, inflicting the first casualties and alarming some residents—including one who would prove to be the town's Paul Revere figure. Around midnight a night watchman, Patrick Higgins, was carrying a lantern as he proceeded toward the rail entrance of the Potomac bridge to relieve William Williams. Both men worked for the Baltimore and Ohio Railroad, each serving 12-hour shifts. Instead of finding the bridge light and Williams, Higgins encountered darkness and two armed men. One man—Oliver Brown—grabbed him by the arm, ordering, "Come along."

After a short distance Higgins noticed pikes leaning against the bridge railing. Alarmed, the watchman struck Oliver in the right ear, knocking him against the railing. Higgins ran toward the Wagner Hotel and heard, "Halt!" Later he remarked, "Now I didn't know what 'Halt' meant then any more than a hog knows about a holiday." Oliver Brown's companion, Stewart Taylor, fired a rifle at the fleeing Higgins, knocking off his hat and creasing his skull. Breathless, Higgins ran into the Wagner Hotel with his scalp bleeding. In an excited manner he told W. W. Throckmorton, the young night clerk, "Lock your doors, there are robbers on the bridge—several men!" Throckmorton had heard the shot while going to awaken passengers for the soon-to-arrive train. The clerk thought "some rowdies from the canal locks" had fired at Higgins to scare him. Throckmorton awakened the passengers and tried unsuccessfully to borrow a revolver. He then walked to the B&O Railroad office to borrow a weapon from Hayward Shepherd, the free black baggage-master who always kept a revolver because of his tenuous position as a free black man in Virginia. (A New Englander traveling the C&O Canal observed that the young men of Harpers Ferry amused themselves "by gathering at the bridge evenings and waylay such darkeys as were caught out after 9 o'clock without a pass and as they called it 'wallop them.'"[6]) Finding Shepherd's pistol unloaded, the clerk left. On his way back to the hotel he noticed two armed men on the bridge, but things remained tranquil for the next hour and a half.

The eastbound train from Wheeling to Baltimore pulled into the Harpers Ferry station at 1:25 a.m. Monday. The conductor, Phelps, thought it strange that the night watchman was missing from his post on the bridge. The new passengers boarded, and he was preparing to move the train forward when Higgins, the missing watchman, appeared and told Phelps of his assault (which was confirmed by Throckmorton). Phelps told engineer William McKay to follow slowly. The conductor and two other men—a passenger and the train's baggage manager, Jacob Cromwell—walked cautiously ahead of the train to the bridge, with Cromwell carrying a lantern. Phelps thought he saw what he later testified were the "muzzles of four rifles resting on a railing and pointing at us." Immediately he shouted to the engineer, "Back!" As the train slowly backed up, a shot rang out.

The town baggage-master, Hayward Shepherd, looking for Higgins, whose whereabouts he was apparently unaware of, had entered the Winchester span of the bridge shortly before the three men; he had taken off his shoes to lessen any sounds of his approach. When confronted by the two raiders and ordered to "halt," a command he (like Higgins) did not understand, Shepherd was shot and ran toward Phelps, telling the conductor, "Captain, I am shot." The mortal bullet had entered the victim's back, traveling under the heart and emerging under his left nipple. The tall, likeable free black man staggered back to the B&O Railroad office with the assistance of his friend Higgins and Phelps. Higgins stayed with Shepherd to the end, bringing water as requested.[7] Shepherd died between noon and 1:00 Monday afternoon after suffering nearly 12 hours of agonizing pain; ironically, he was the first victim of Brown's war to liberate enslaved black people. It would have been of little comfort to Hayward Shepherd to know that was the aim of the raiders, the morning after he was shot.

Brown expressed his disapproval of the shooting, claiming his men on the bridge had bungled things. Shepherd's remains would be taken by train to his hometown of Winchester, Virginia, 32 miles away. Later he was interred there, in the black cemetery, amidst great ceremony, which included a procession led by a militia band, three Winchester militia companies, the mayor and other officials, and many white as well as black mourners; they all listened in reverence to the elderly black minister performing a graveside ceremony. None were more grief-stricken than his wife, Sarah Shepherd, and her six children who would never see Hayward again. The Winchester *Virginian* condemned Shepherd's killing, calling him a "worthy negro," and also condemned the raid, which was viewed as a threat to local whites. The *Virginian* obituary ended, "It is worthy of note the first victim of the pretended friends of the color race, was one of that class."

Shepherd was a free black man who had been given permission by the county court to remain in Jefferson County. He used to come home, to 438 North Kent Street, after several nights at work. He attended to everything in the rail office when his friend, agent and mayor of the town, Fontaine Beckham, was absent. The bond between the two was strong, but their relationship was stormy. The townspeople were often amused to see Shepherd walking from the railroad office with a pack on his back on his way to Winchester, swearing he would never work another day under Beckham, provoked by contradictory or unreasonable orders from the stationmaster. But Shepherd always returned after Beckham sent a messenger with concessions that resolved the conflict.[8]

Hayward Shepherd, baggageman and free African American was the first fatality of the raid. (West Virginia Archives, Boyd B. Stutler Collection)

Back on the train, passengers heard a shot and Shepherd's agonized cry and ran frantically about. Women and children were screaming. Approximately 10 minutes later Oliver Brown and Stewart Taylor left the bridge and starting walking toward the armory gate, possibly to ask what to do about the train. Brown had given no instructions; either he had forgotten or he was unaware of the train's schedule. The two men were met by a tall raider from the armory, probably the six-foot-two, light-skinned, multiracial Dangerfield Newby, who was born in 1815 in nearby Fauquier County, Virginia. Before returning to Brown's headquarters with young Brown and Taylor, he became concerned about the passengers who came out of the hotel and depot located between the hotel and B&O office near the Shenandoah River, and he gave them a warning; one witness believed he said, "The first man that fires at me I will shoot." Throckmorton, who had borrowed a revolver from a passenger, fired at the raiders and proceeded toward the armory, along with Phelps. Two raiders behind the armory gates fired back. Fortunately for the participants, darkness prevented accurate marksmanship. After emptying his revolver and borrowing another one—because carrying pistols for one's safety seemed to be the norm—the clerk returned to the hotel and hurried passengers inside. Throckmorton saw three men (Brown, Taylor, and Dangerfield Newby) return to the bridge and calmly walk within five or so feet of a local doctor who stood at the corner of the depot before he ducked inside, so Throckmorton attempted to protect those in the hotel by putting out the lights. Ten minutes later, around 2:00, one of the men came out of the bridge and told the conductor, who had returned to the railroad office, "You can come over the bridge with your train," in retrospect raising the question of whether the intent was only to stop foot traffic. Phelps was alarmed for the safety of himself and the passengers, and he replied, "I would rather not, after these proceedings." He asked, "What do you want?" The answer was, "We want liberty and are intent to have it." Phelps said, "What do you mean?" The reply was, "You will find out in a day or two." Throckmorton, Phelps, and his passengers waited anxiously until daylight and noticed men who "appeared to be in blankets" in the armory and passing back and forth between the bridge. They also saw the arrival of wagons carrying Washington, the Allstadts, and their slaves.[9]

In a building across from the hotel and 50 steps opposite the railroad bridge, a slumbering 35-year-old physician, John D. Starry, was awakened by a gunshot and Hayward Shepherd's cry of distress. Jumping from his bed to look out the window, Starry saw people scurrying about and two men he deemed to be "low fellows" leaving the bridge. He dressed hurriedly and rushed into the street to witness the exchange of gunfire and "three low fellows" returning to the bridge. The physician walked into the B&O office. There he found Hayward Shepherd "lying on a plank upon two chairs." Upon examining the stricken man, he realized Shepherd had carried his last load of baggage.

Unable to retard the suffering man's pain and impending death, the doctor left to observe what was happening outside. At this point Starry was puzzled about what was happening. The town physician has been depicted as "slow-witted" for spending much of the night watching the raiders and remaining uncertain about their intent, but that is perhaps too harsh an appraisal. Other residents and passengers were also confused about the purpose of the shootings and movements of the armed strangers. The unarmed doctor wandered about talking to raiders and watching them until dawn, attempting to figure out what was going on. Amazingly, he did not become a hostage. Old Brown was later puzzled as well; capturing him would have prevented the doctor's Paul Revere-type sounding of the alarm and might have delayed the militia for hours or half a day. After the insurgent leader's capture, Starry claimed, "[I asked Brown] if he was at the armory gates when I was there, but he said he was not, and did not know why I had not been taken a prisoner."

Starry said he walked toward the armory to "inquire why they allowed persons to go in and out the gate, when they knew they were shooting down those whom they met in the street." Nearing the entrance, he called for the watchmen, but a stranger told him, "Halt." He asked for watchmen Medler and Murphy but was informed by the guard that he did not know them; the guard added, "There are a few of us here." Without saying another word and with curiosity unsated, Starry left. He walked up Shenandoah Street then down to the Winchester Railroad and back to the B&O office. Meanwhile, the raiders on the bridge were wondering when the train was going to cross. Starry later testified that while he stood on the platform at about 3:00 a.m. a member of the "party from the bridge hailed me to know if that train was coming over—the train which they had stopped. I told him I thought it very doubtful; I did not think it would come over until after daylight; we did not understand their movements, and should like to know what they were doing." Starry was told virtually what was said to Phelps an hour or so earlier: "Never mind, you will know in a day or two." The doctor asked "if he expected to stay there a day or two," but receiving no answer, Starry walked around the station and watched the armed men, "sometime very close, and sometimes further off," until dawn.

At about the time when Dr. Starry and the raiders were speaking, Phelps was approached by an elderly man, who said, "The party who have arrested me allowed me to come out on condition that I tell you that you might cross the bridge with your train." The conductor told Mr. Koise, a citizen of the town, even more emphatically what he had said earlier: "I will not cross the bridge until daylight that I might see whether it was safe." It is curious that Brown and his men repeatedly attempted to get the train to leave, knowing it would negate the benefits of having cut the telegraph lines; if the train left, word of what they were doing would spread. Probably they wanted to eliminate the nuisance and risk of passengers who were not directly under their control between the Potomac bridge and Brown's scattered meager force; these passengers were a variable they had not counted on. The old captain may have concluded he and his men would be gone from the Ferry before any danger from releasing the train could befall them.

At about 4:00 Starry heard a wagon traveling down a street, and from a different vantage point Phelps saw a carriage and wagon enter the armory yard, with about 12 people jumping from the larger conveyance. Approximately an hour later, around 5:05, both Phelps and Starry witnessed, in the physician's words, "a four-horse team driving over the Baltimore and Ohio Railroad bridge… In the wagon there were three men standing up in the front part, with spears in their hands… and two were walking alongside armed with rifles." Unbeknownst to Starry and Phelps, it was Colonel Washington's wagon, with one of the colonel's slaves driving, armed with his master's shotgun, and three of the Allstadt slaves standing with pikes. At least two, if not all three, armed raiders, Cook, Tidd, and Leary, walked alongside the wagon. They were going to move weapons Brown had collected from the Kennedy farm to the schoolhouse, as well as take a neighbor of Brown's hostage and free his slaves.

All the new arrivals who had been brought to the armory by the carriage and wagon were chilled from the damp and cold that had accompanied the darkness and were anxious to warm themselves at the watchhouse stove. Washington, the most prized prisoner, had assumed he was taken by robbers until he arrived at the armory gate. The sight of armed men in control of the government facility made things seem more ominous. When the carriage that carried Washington stopped in front of the enginehouse, Brown greeted him with some consideration, saying, "You will find a fire in here, sir... it is rather cool this morning." Washington and the Allstadts were taken to the watchhouse, and all their servants—as they referred to their slaves—went to the unheated enginehouse but repeatedly came, according to Washington, into the heated room to warm themselves, "each negro having a pike in his hand." After a while Brown approached the colonel, who testified about their conversation: "[Brown said,] 'I presume you are Mr. Washington.' He then remarked to me, 'It is too dark to see to write at this time but when it shall have cleared off a little and become lighter, if you have not pen and ink, I will furnish them to you, and I shall require you to write to some of your friends to send a stout, able-bodied negro; to release you, but only on the condition of getting your friends to send in a negro man as a ransom.'" Washington said that the wiry old raider added, "I shall be very attentive to you, sir, for I may get the worst of it in my first encounter, and if so, your life is worth as much as mine. I shall be very particular to pay attention to you. My particular reason for taking you first was that, as the aide to the governor of Virginia, I knew you would endeavor to perform your duty, and perhaps would have been a troublesome customer to me; and, apart from that, I wanted you particularly for the moral effect it would give our cause, having one of your name as a prisoner."

After watching most of the night, as dawn neared John Starry knew something had to be done. In his view, "Strangers seemed to have possession of the public works." He got on his horse to notify Archibald Kitzmiller, the acting superintendent. First he went to "rouse up" the men at the mill and cooper shop on Virginius Island; then, hurriedly riding past three raiders who were walking from the armory to the arsenal, Starry rode up High Street to the acting superintendent's home, and then went back down to the rifleworks. There he saw armed men walking about, and he headed "back uphill, and tried to get the citizens together... to get rid of these... very troublesome" fellows. After sending messengers to Charles Town and Shepherdstown to get militia help and to the B&O Railroad to prevent eastbound trains from going to Harpers Ferry, he wrote that he arranged for "the Lutheran church bell to be rung to get citizens together to see what sort of arms they had; I found one or two squirrel rifles and a few shot guns... I could not find guns fit for use, and learning from the operatives and foremen at the armory that all the guns they knew of were... [the thousands boxed up] in the arsenal and in possession of the raiders..." The physician continued his frenzied activity by racing six miles to Charles Town to make sure help was coming.

While he was away citizens armed themselves with guns found in one of the armory workshops, guns that had been moved a few weeks earlier to keep them out of high water. However, the citizens lacked ammunition. With the limited supply of lead in the town's stores soon exhausted, women assisted in slowly melting pewter plates and spoons into balls with bullet molds, which two armory workers, John McClelland and William Copeland, had stealthily obtained; they had moved into the enclosure of the armory, entered the stockhouse at the back, and taken two bullet molds and all of the percussion caps. This allowed citizens to fire—sporadically and ineffectively—at Brown's men in the morning. Some took their own weapons and confronted their unwelcome visitors. Around 7:00 that morning townsman Alexander Kelly armed himself with a shotgun and neared the corner of Shenandoah and High Streets, about 100 yards from the armory. Before he could shoot, gunfire from raiders put a hole in his hat, and he scurried away. Moments later at the same intersection a more deadly fate befell an Irish grocer, Thomas Boerly. Despite being described by a contemporary as having "Herculian strength," after shooting at the arsenal raiders, he was struck in the groin. Some contend it was a bullet from a rifle-musket fired by Dangerfield Newby, while others say the shot came from the armory. He died a short time later with a local physician, Dr. Clagglett, at his side.[10]

Shortly after 6:00—before Boerly's death—Brown again showed some concern for his prisoners by ordering food. He sent a young black man with a note addressed to the "hotel keeper or clerk of the Wagner house" that said:

Oct. 17
You will furnish forty-five men with a good breakfast.
CAPTAIN SMITH

Throckmorton read the note and, surprisingly, went to the captain. Brown received him politely, showed him the prisoners, asked the clerk whether he knew them, and reaffirmed that he wanted breakfast for "forty-five men as soon as possible." Throckmorton was explaining he would do the best he could, when the train conductor, Phelps—who was anxious to get his train moving and had come to the armory—interrupted their conversation. Upon seeing "a black boy" deliver a note to the Wagner House, Phelps had gone to investigate what it meant. First he asked Edwin Coppoc, who told him, "We don't want to injure you or detain your train," and said Phelps could have left earlier.[11] "All we want is to free the negroes," said Coppoc. Phelps was sent to the armory gate, where he asked the guard the same question and was told, "There is Captain Smith—he can tell you what you want to know." After Brown responded to Phelps's question about whether he was Captain Smith, the conductor asked if he could move the train, as, said Phelps, he had "women and children who were frightened nearly to death." Apparently annoyed by the failure of the train to leave during the night, Brown imperiously replied, "No, Sir." Phelps than asked why Brown had stopped the train. Brown, in turn, said, "Are you the conductor of that train?" Phelps responded in the affirmative, and Brown said, "Why, I sent word to you at 3 o'clock that you could pass."

Phelps explained to Brown his fear of moving the train after Shepherd was shot; the conductor said he believed the passengers and train might be harmed. The captain's mood seem to soften, and he apologized, saying he was "very sorry"; according to Phelps's account, "it was not [Brown's] intention that any blood should be spilled... it was bad management on the part of the men in charge of the bridge." Phelps than asked what security he would be granted that the "train would pass safely" and asked the captain to walk ahead of the train, over the bridge, along with him. Phelps said that Brown "called a large stout man [Stevens] to accompany him." Ever aware of the need to keep the upper hand, Brown bristled when one of the passengers, a Mr. McByre, asked to accompany Phelps. The old captain, according to Phelps, "ordered him to get into the train, or he would take them all prisoners in five minutes." He did not see Throckmorton going to some of the passengers before they boarded the train: "Throckmorton was begging them to make an alarm and have a military company here as soon as possible."

As clouds hid the rising sun Brown and Stevens took rifles and accompanied Phelps across the bridge, passing one of the captain's sons along with Taylor and Newby, who were guarding the entrance. Once across, Brown told the conductor, "You doubtless wonder that a man of my age should be here with a band of armed men, but if you knew my past history you would not wonder at it as much." Brown had frequently expressed this sentiment before, during, and after the raid, elaborating upon it to his hostages, as Terrance Byrne later testified. Byrne, a local resident who lived near the Kennedy farm and became one of Brown's hostages, said Brown stated that he went to Kansas "a peaceful man" who was "hunted down like a wolf by the pro-slavery men," men who took the life of one of his sons. "Now I am here," said Brown.

Continuing his conversation with the conductor, Brown explained his purpose, talked of getting sizable reinforcements, and ordered that no additional trains were to travel through Harpers Ferry. By this time, around 6:30, the train had left the bridge. Phelps claimed he "bid [Brown] good morning, jumped on my train, and left him."

If Phelps made a promise to do no harm to Captain Smith when he pleaded with the captain to let the train leave, as eyewitness Throckmorton is quoted in the New York *Herald*, his word was not kept. Testifying at Brown's trial, the conductor would make no mention of such a pledge. At 7:05 a.m. October 17, from outside Frederick, Maryland, he telegraphed William Smith, the right-hand man to B&O president John W. Garrett. Phelps wrote that the train had been stopped at Harpers Ferry by armed abolitionists who controlled the federal armory, cut the telegraph wires, and fired at Phelps and the baggage master, severely wounding a "colored" porter. Phelps said, "They say they have come to free the slaves, and intend to do it at all hazards... The leader of these men requested me to say to you that this is the last train that shall pass the bridge, either east or west. If it is attempted it will be at the peril of the lives of those having them in charge… It has been suggested that you had better notify the Secretary of War at once."

Disbelieving and unconcerned about what he read, William Smith waited two hours, until 9:00, to send a rebuke: "Your dispatch is evidently exaggerated and written under excitement. Why should our train be stopped by abolitionists and how do you know they are such and that they number a hundred or more? What is their object? Let me know at once before we proceed to extremities."

Phelps—in all likelihood annoyed—wired back at 11:00 a.m., from Ellicott's Mill, Maryland:

> My dispatch was not exaggerated, neither was it written under excitement, as you suppose. I have not made it half as bad as it is. The Captain told me that his object was to liberate all the slaves and that he expected a reinforcement of 1,500 men to assist him. Hayward the negro porter was shot through the body and I suppose by this time is dead. The captain also said that he did not want to shed any more blood.

The conductor concluded by saying he would tell Smith everything upon his arrival. But John W. Garrett, the president of the railroad, had already taken action. He had read Phelps's original message and at 10:30 a.m. had telegraphed US President James Buchanan, Governor Henry Wise of Virginia, and Major-General George H. Stewart, who commanded the First Light Division of Maryland volunteers in Baltimore. Garrett's message said that an insurrection was occurring at Harpers Ferry by free blacks and whites.

Buchanan and the secretary of war, John B. Floyd, would respond by sending US Marines to quell the rebellion. Virginia's excitable governor, Henry Wise, worked to defend his state by rounding up the Richmond Grays as the militiamen of Baltimore prepared to move. A press dispatch informed the Baltimore newspaper press "of a formidable negro insurrection at Harper's Ferry… led by about 250 whites with a gang of negroes fighting for their freedom."[12]

Back in Harpers Ferry, after escorting the train across the bridge, Brown had returned to the armory and some of his men had continued to walk about the Point, when the food for his prisoners arrived. The hotel clerk and one of the hotel servants, anxious to help, carried food in a basket to the armory. Throughout the morning prisoners were allowed to roam about the lower armory as long as they stayed away from the gates. Some, like Colonel Washington and the Allstadts, doubted the good intentions of their captor in feeding them. Washington recalls, "[After] Brown invited me to breakfast… I went to several of the prisoners and suggested the impropriety of touching it, for said I 'you do not know what may be in it; the coffee may be drugged for the purpose of saving a guard over you.' I advised them not to take it."

Lack of sleep, strain, and preoccupation prevented the old captain from eating. The clerk offered to bring a special breakfast but lamented he only had water for Brown to drink, but Brown, in a departure from his usual habits, told him "he must

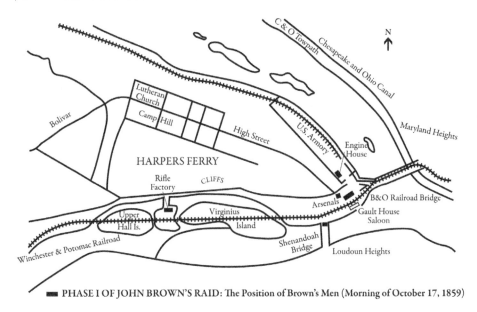

■ PHASE I OF JOHN BROWN'S RAID: The Position of Brown's Men (Morning of October 17, 1859)

have coffee as he felt fatigued." During their conversations the clerk asked about pay for breakfast. Brown told him that "he should want dinner at three o'clock for perhaps 200 men, and he would pay for the whole then." With half of Meriam's $600 in gold coins in his pocket, he was capable of paying the bill.[13]

After breakfast Washington asked Throckmorton to take Washington's horses from the armory and put them in the hotel stable, paying special attention to the colonel's mount. The clerk recalled ordering the slave who accompanied him to return to the hotel, but the slave defiantly replied, in Throckmorton's words, that "he would when he was ready and… he was as much boss as I was… This amused Old Brown, who laughed at me, and I told him there was no n***** blood in me."

Before the clerk left, Brown let him know he was the leader of a serious mission. "I have come here to free slaves of your surrounding country, I take possession of this government property and arms to assist me in doing so. I can have five thousand men here in less than twenty-four hours at my call." Brown and his men would repeatedly state their purpose, especially their leader, who spoke in what Colonel Washington called "general terms," such as: "This thing [slavery] must be put a stop to." The old captain was, however, usually specific. He repeated his objective so frequently to new arrivals it was practically his mantra early in the raid. Brown said Throckmorton would be given permission "to pass backwards and forwards" if he kept quiet, and if not, Brown warned that he "would take possession of the hotel."

Around breakfast time at the armory, the raiders who were sent with Washington's heavy farm wagon travelled into Maryland. They would encounter Terrance Byrne, a slaveholder in his forties who lived less than a mile and half south from the place Brown rented. Byrne left his place between 5:00 and 6:00 in the morning for a six-mile ride along the narrow, winding mountain road. A little after daylight, about a mile and a quarter in the direction of Harpers Ferry he passed a four-horse-drawn wagon going in the opposite direction driven "by a colored man." As Byrne "passed the tail end of the wagon" he heard, "Mr. Byrnes, Stop." The rider later testified, "I reined up my horse and looked back and recognized John E. Cook... who approached me on the right side of my horse." In an apologetic manner Cook said, "I am sorry to inform you that you are my prisoner."[14] Byrne smiled and said, "You are certainly joking." While Cook was saying, "I am not," and jerking the rifle with a barrel protruding out his coat in an attempt to be taken seriously, C. P. Tidd stepped toward the mounted rider, pointing his rifle at Byrne and saying, "No parley here, or I will put a ball in you; you must go with us to your place; we want your negroes." According to Byrne he was told: "They had possession of the armory, bridge, and telegraph and before night would have the canal; that Colonel Washington was a prisoner at Harpers Ferry and that his fowling piece was carried by one of the negroes" with them. To enlist Byrne's cooperation they offered him a deal. If he "would give up his slaves voluntarily their captain would enter into an article of agreement... to protect" him and his property. Rejecting their proposal, Byrne told them: "I looked to the State government, or, if that failed, to the federal government to protect me in my person and property." He was told, "They will have them anyhow."

Byrne and his captors reached the Byrne home, where at least three family members were going about their morning. Byrne later recalled that when he was back at home, he whispered to his brother James, sitting on the porch: "civil war" or "servile war." Once inside, Cook, Tidd, and Leeman annoyed Byrne by sitting without an invitation. The three had been up all night walking over 20 miles, and they were in no mood to stand on the niceties of etiquette and ceremony. Fatigue and hunger were taking their toll, especially on Leeman, who sat "by the side of the fireplace... and put his head against the mantel and drew his cloth cap" down. Cook asked Leeman if he was sleepy and hungry, and the chain-smoking raider, a year out of his teens, replied yes. Cook seemed more energetic and gave the brothers, according to Terrance Byrne, "a higher law speech," stating, "All men were created equal." Terrance Byrne's mind raced with anxious thoughts, paying little attention to Cook's oration and ignoring the time indicated by the clock on the mantel; he was traumatized and wondering about his fate.

In desperation Byrne asked his sister to call to their visiting cousin, who was upstairs, to come down—Byrne later described her as a lady of "considerable nerve." Seeing the intruders, the intrepid woman blurted out: "Cowhide those scoundrels out of the house; why do you suffer them to talk to you?" She ignored the raiders' menacing rifles and revolvers. Soon Cook told Terrance's brother, "Mr. Byrne, we want your slaves." James replied, "Captain Cook, you must do as I do when I want them—hunt for them." Terrance recalls in his account that it was "too early in the morning... My brother's servant and my own two men had left home the Saturday evening preceding and had not returned yet, Monday morning....They did not want the negro women and children at that time." Not having time to wait around for the slaves to return, Tidd and the black people brought with them travelled with the wagon to retrieve weapons from the Kennedy house and outbuilding while Cook and Leeman remained to guard the two brothers.

Tidd and the African Americans—including one of Washington's slaves, who drove the four-horse team—arrived at the house around 11:00 a.m. While they fed and sheltered the team from the rain, Owen Brown, who had assumed cooking duties after the young girls departed, prepared a meal, after which they rapidly loaded the wagon with gunpowder and boxes of Sharps rifles and revolvers before setting out to the schoolhouse and stopping at the Byrne house. Terrance Byrne noticed on Tidd's return that the wagon was filled with boxes. The raiders took off with Terrance and the mysterious boxes to the schoolhouse, a mile from Harpers Ferry. Surprisingly, the raiders left behind James Byrne, who pleaded ill.

They arrived at the one-room schoolhouse late in the morning to find the teacher, Lind F. Currie, instructing nearly 30 boys and girls, aged eight to 16.[15] They were struck with fear when Cook burst in with expensive weapons—a $25 Sharps carbine and two revolvers worth at least $15 each—and a large knife at his side, demanding possession of the building as a depot for arms and placing boxes in one corner of the room. Currie, a farmer-teacher in his early thirties, would later testify that Cook told him "he thought I had better keep on the school and we should not be interrupted." Currie said that was impossible: "The children were then very much alarmed, and I could not do anything with them. They were not in a condition to engage in their usual duties, and it would be impossible to keep them there." They all left in a frightened state, hurrying to their homes, including their instructor. As the teacher left the school, Byrne tried to reassure him, saying he would be fine because he was not a slave-owner; apparently Byrne was unaware Currie was a farmer and slave-owner. Before returning to his home, Currie got permission to walk a friend's frightened young child home, after which he returned to the schoolhouse, finding only Cook and one of Washington's slaves, who carried a pike. Cook retained the teacher until late afternoon, engaging him in long and varied conversations about how they were going to free the slaves, attitudes of North and South, and when questioned, how many men Brown had; Cook responded vaguely, saying maybe 5,000 to 10,000. Finally as the afternoon waned, Currie promised not to reveal what had happened at the schoolhouse and was allowed to leave. Taking the road to the Potomac River, avoiding the gunfire he could hear in the embattled town, Currie crossed to Virginia to join his mother and slaves at his home three and half miles from Charles Town.

Leeman left to escort Terrance Byrne to the armory. Byrne recalled that the morning was damp, which caused Leeman to carry his Sharps rifle under his blanket with only a portion of the barrel showing. After only 100 to 150 yards they met "one of Brown's party, whom I [Byrne] had known by the name of [William] Thompson." The jovial raider came up smiling. "He was armed and I think had a blanket over his shoulders. He extended his hand and said, 'How are you, Byrne?' I said, 'Good morning Mr. Thompson, I am well; how are you?' I was then disposed to put on a cheerful face, and I asked him what was the news at Harper's Ferry. He said the people were more frightened than hurt." It then started to rain, and at Leeman's suggestion they sat under a tree along the road waiting for the shower to stop. The normally silent Leeman huddled with Byrne under Byrne's umbrella and remarked, "Our captain is no longer [Isaac Smith but is] John Brown of Kansas notoriety." This made Byrne's strained cheerfulness more difficult to sustain as his mind, he said, "was busy with the future. I was fearful of civil war. I was under the impression that unless they were in great numbers they would not be foolish enough to make an attack on the borders of two slaveholding States."

Byrne was not alone in this assumption. The residents and hostages at Harpers Ferry, including Colonel Washington, thought Brown had a large force. Brown encouraged this impression by talking about the impending arrival of reinforcements and not revealing his numbers. According to Washington, Brown answered evasively at the armory when someone asked how many men he had. He replied, "I cannot exactly say. I have four companies," which he said were scattered over different sites. Listeners misinterpreted this to mean he had at least several hundred men.

After the rain stopped later that morning, Thompson walked with Leeman and Byrne to the bridge, where they passed guards who included "a white man wearing a mitt." Byrne did not remember the man's name but said, "As soon as he saw me he took it off and shook hands with me." Once on the Virginia side of the bridge, Thompson stopped as Leeman took his prisoner to the armory. Byrne saw Brown moving about in front of the enginehouse; Brown did not speak to his newest hostage. Inside the watchhouse, Byrne still pretended to be cheerful by remarking, "Good morning, gentleman; I hope I am in good company."[16]

The hostages, seized one or two at a time, had swelled in number to nearly 40 with the arrival of armory workers and officials. They joined the five townsfolk taken prisoner before the arrival of Washington and the Allstadts. Among the first prisoners were Albert Grist and his son, who were seized while returning home across the Shenandoah bridge after a meeting on Sunday night. Upon seeing the rifles of Oliver Brown and William Thompson, the father asked whether the town was under martial law. As the two surprised residents neared the end of the bridge they were asked by a man carrying a spear, "Were many slaveholders about Harpers Ferry?" The elder Grist replied there were not. Soon John Brown came up and remarked, "You have got some prisoners," and the Grists were taken to the armory. Exhausted, they lay down while Brown explained that his object was to free the slaves. The father replied there were not many there, and the old captain replied, "The good book says we are all free and equal," and told his captives they would remain unharmed as long as they were peaceful. Around 3:00 that morning Brown sent the elderly Grist to tell the train conductor it could leave. Instead Grist left the message with someone he knew, Fontaine Beckham, the B&O Railroad agent and mayor of the town, probably telling him to relay the message. When Grist returned to the armory Brown told him he could go home, but Grist refused, fearing he would be shot by raiders who were unaware he had been freed.

Brown was courteous and concerned for the welfare of his hostages, repeatedly reassuring them they would not be harmed. On Monday morning he let them move about within the armory and, in some cases, they were allowed to reassure family members of their welfare. Despite Brown's acts of kindness and consideration, a cloud of uncertainty fueled their fears. Washington heard the muscular Stevens make some less-than-reassuring comments to a young hostage during the night. According to Washington, the raider asked the young man "what his view in reference to slavery was, and the young man said, 'Of course, being born south, my views are with the south on the subject.'" Stevens then asked "if he was a slaveholder. He said he was not. 'Well,' said Stevens, 'you would be the first fellow I would hang, for you defend a cause not to protect your own interest in doing so,' and he used an oath at the time." As gunfire increased that day, so did the hostages' anxiety.

Among the early-morning arrivals at the armory was the rotund, inventive master machinist, Armistead Ball, who entered the gate about 5:00 a.m., having been awakened by Benjamin Hobbs, an armory employee, with some startling news—in Ball's words, "that persons were at the armory carrying off government property." Soon after Ball came elderly bell ringer James Darrell to summon employees to work, master armorer Benjamin Mills, and acting superintendent Archibald Kitzmiller, who had been alerted to problems by Dr. Starry. Between 8:00 and 9:00 came the unsuspecting paymaster's clerk J. E. P. Daingerfield, who upon seeing the night watchman Daniel Whelan, ordered him to unlock the smaller gate. When Whelan moved to comply with the command, Brown stepped forward to take and keep two keys from the watchmen, saying he was the man who could open the gate. Daingerfield was escorted to the watchhouse.

The earlier arrest of machinist Ball had been more abrupt, but he was soon treated with a degree of kindness. Upon his arrival Stevens seized him without explanation and took him to Brown, who repeated his mission to free slaves. Ball remembers: "[Brown] told me his object was to free the slaves, and not the making of war on the people; that my person and private property would be safe; that his war was against the acquired system of slavery; that he had the power to do it and would carry it out." Then, Ball said, Brown gave "permission to return to my family, to assure them of my safety and get my breakfast." The two armed men who escorted him respectfully "stopped at the door, breakfast not being ready." Ball returned to the armory and later "was allowed to return home again under escort." Brown told Ball and the other armory officials, Kitzmiller, Mills, and Daingerfield, that "it was his determination to seize the arms and munitions of the government, to arm the blacks to defend themselves against their master." The old captain, Ball recalls, then made a somewhat redundant proposition to the officials "to deliver into his possession the munitions of war belonging to the Government," while adding "that they were already in his possession, as we were."[17] This objective soon dwindled in priority as skirmishing began, when local militia came to subdue him, as Frederick Douglass had warned. Brown's practice of allowing hostages to move about with some freedom ended as the morning waned and pressure on him increased.

Phase Two: Militiamen Trap Brown

Brown and his small band of insurgents had seized and maintained authority over much of the town, relatively unchallenged, from Sunday night through Monday morning. As noon approached, however, time was running out for Brown and his men. Kagi, who was still in the rifle factory, realized their plight and anxiously pleaded with Brown by messenger; twice that morning he had Jeremiah Anderson deliver his request that they adhere to the original plan and retreat to the mountains before it was too late—but to no avail.

While Tidd was moving weapons from the Kennedy farm to the school, he went to the bridge, where some of the boys begged him to convince Brown to leave immediately. Like Kagi, Tidd was unable to move the old man. Brown felt having hostages guaranteed him not only the opportunity to escape whenever he needed and wanted but also to control the resistance against him until reinforcements (comprised primarily of those in bondage) arrived. He instructed Mr. Grist, whom he released early Monday morning, "to tell the people outside to cease firing or he would burn the town; but if they did not molest him, he wouldn't molest them." Brown frequently reminded hostages that their safety "depended on the good conduct of our citizens" and "if the citizens were willing to risk their lives and those of the prisoners to capture him, they must abide by it" and endure the dangers.

The immediate threat to Brown during the day of October 17 took the form of local militia and townsmen. They were motivated by Dr. Starry's Paul Revere-like warnings. Starry had not only alerted the town, he had sent messengers to nearby Charles Town and Shepherdstown while he searched in vain for weapons. In desperation, Starry rode the six miles to Charles Town to hasten that town's assistance. There he found the town buzzing with excitement and confusion.

Frantically, people from the countryside fled to Charles Town to join the townsfolk in stopping the bold intruders, whoever they were, at Harpers Ferry.

The Virginia *Free Press* graphically reported that amidst ringing of bells and "the long roll of drums and strident notes of fifes," two companies assembled outside the Charles Town courthouse: the Jefferson Guards and a hastily formed unit of boys and men armed with varying types of weapons—most inferior—ranging from muskets, squirrel-guns, and pistols to pitchforks. From the courthouse they marched to the Winchester and Harpers Ferry railroad depot, met the northbound train, and forced the passengers off the train. By 10:00 a.m. nearly 100 men from Charles Town were on their way to take on a force they knew little, if anything, about. Its size, purpose, and leader were unknown. Why was Harpers Ferry the target of the attack? Two of the men from Charles Town who went to fight the insurrectionists, Leonard Sadler and Samuel C. Young, were nearly 70 years of age. According to the local press, a Presbyterian minister, visiting his brother-in-law in Charles Town, "with musket and cartridge box in hand" also joined the fight.

Citizens left in Charles Town soon became afraid that the news of the attack on Harpers Ferry was a ruse created by robbers, who planned to rob and plunder the unprotected and defenseless town and farms. By early afternoon, at a meeting at the Charles Town courthouse, the men and boys who were left in town agreed to get their guns and guard their village. Their fears of an attack by "desperadoes" were not lessened, according to one eyewitness, until midnight. At that time a dispatch from Harpers Ferry informed the Charles Town "stay-at-homes" that a "band of abolitionists" led by "Osawatomie Brown of Kansas" had attacked Harpers Ferry. The Charles Town home guard disbanded and retired for the night.[18] After hurrying Captain Rowan of the Jefferson Guards off at Charles Town, Starry remembered, he returned to Harpers Ferry, where he discovered the citizens had found some guns in workshops. "I assisted from that time until the night, in various ways, organizing the citizens to the best place of attack, and sometimes acting professionally [as a physician]."

Still, the raiders were not seriously menaced until the arrival of the Charles Town militia. The militiamen traveled about half the distance by rail. Disembarking at Halltown, they were marching the remaining distance when Colonel Robert W. Baylor of the Third Regiment Cavalry, the senior officer, and Colonel John T. Gibson of the Jefferson Guards were incorrectly informed by a citizen that "not only the Winchester, but Baltimore and Ohio Railroad tracks had been taken up." At Halltown, Baylor and Gibson were also told, as rumors exaggerated the situation, that the "insurgents" were "in large numbers," maybe "300 to 500 strong," that they had taken "75 to 100" local citizens as prisoners, and slaves had been "carried off." The colonels, thinking they faced a sizable foe that considerably outnumbered their own militiamen and volunteers, sent orders to the nearby towns of Winchester and Shepherdstown for reinforcements. For instance, Colonel Baylor sent Captain Barley, a conductor on the Winchester line, back to that town by rail to deliver a message to Colonel L. T. Moore of the Thirty-First Virginia Militia: "You are ordered to muster all the volunteer force under your command, fully armed and equipped, and report to me, forthwith, at Harpers Ferry."[19]

In the meantime, the march of the Charles Town men from Halltown to Bolivar, the high ground just west of Harpers Ferry and Brown's men, was not a pleasant one. According to newspaper accounts, a "cold easterly wind" blew "a dashing, drenching rain" in the faces of the militiamen, most of whom had failed to bring their raincoats during the excitement. After arriving around 11:30 a.m. at Camp Hill, the high ground on the outskirts of Harpers Ferry, Colonel Baylor reported they found the citizens "in very great excitement." The militiamen rested for half an hour as their officers, headed by Colonels Baylor and Gibson, contemplated the plan of attack. They decided to cut off the raiders' avenues of escape by seizing control of the Potomac and Shenandoah bridges and select buildings in front of the armory entrance. This would buy time until help arrived to assist in subduing an opponent believed to be greater in number and armed with superior weapons: "Sharps rifles and revolvers."

To entrap Brown it was crucial to gain control of the bridges. The Jefferson Guards, under Captain J. C. Rowan, were sent to take possession of the Potomac bridge. They marched rapidly from Camp Hill to the Potomac northwest of Harpers Ferry, to a point at which, according to the New York *Herald*, "the water was deep enough to allow the company to cross the river in flat boats." In pouring rain, two squads crossed the river two miles above Harpers Ferry at the Old Furnace west of the Dam no. 3 (Armory Dam), built using timber cribs filled with stone that zigzagged across the Potomac to use large rocks in the river for support to facilitate flowing water to the armory and later the C&O Canal. They rejoined on the Maryland shore, where, continued the *Herald*, they "proceeded in a running march" down the Chesapeake and Ohio Canal towpath toward the bridge. The men anxiously approached the bridge. "For a half a mile or more they felt exposed as a target for the enemy from the armory yard, and from the mountain above." But all escaped "unscathed," according to the *Herald*, as they marched "midway into the bridge."

It was now around noon on that rainy Monday and things were abruptly changing for the raiders. They could no longer move about on the Point unfettered and were, according to an observer, "easy targets." They were unconcerned about their safety because Cook had reassured them the townsfolk lacked weapons. Concerned about the militiamen on the bridge—his escape route to Maryland—and armed men from Charles Town streaming down High Street behind him, Brown went to Colonel Washington. Washington later testified that Brown, without saying why, said, "'I want you to walk with me;' and we went from one room [watchhouse] to the other [enginehouse]." Brown repeated the process until he had secured his trump card, 10 of the more prestigious hostages: Washington, Allstadt, Terrance Byrne, Joseph Brua,

Reason Cross, Israel Russell, and armory officials Archibald Kitzmiller, Benjamin Mills, Armistead Ball, and J. E. P. Daingerfield, along with one of Washington's slaves and three of Allstadt's slaves. Brown had them secured behind sturdy brick walls and two heavy wooden doors with inaccessible high windows above them. Confident securing these prisoners would give him the upper hand, Brown told Byrne that citizens and militia would not attack as long as he had them with him as hostages. It would be difficult to free them from Brown's makeshift fortress, leaving him with what he believed was unanswerable bargaining power.

The Jefferson Guards waited at the bridge as Captain Rowan, cut off from communication with the commanding colonel, sent three messengers seeking further orders. When no messengers returned, the Mexican War veteran captain ordered his men to charge from the bridge into the street in front of the armory yard. This drove back three raiders, Oliver Brown, William Thompson, and Dangerfield Newby, a mixed-race former slave. Two of the three men retreated into the armory. Newby lay dead in the street, his throat cut from ear to ear, with arteries ripped away. Some claim a local sniper named Bogert, one of the armorers, fired a musket from an upstairs window of Mrs. Stephenson's house at the corner of High and Shenandoah Streets, near the armory, and a six-inch spike hit Newby.

Jefferson Guards attack and force Brown's men from the Baltimore and Railroad bridge. (*Frank Leslie's Weekly,* West Virginia Archives, Boyd B. Stutler Collection)

Dangerfield Newby. (Library of Congress)

Rowan's men took positions around the armory wall, trapping Brown's men not in the arsenal of the rifle works but inside the armory. They had successfully taken Brown's escape route to Maryland and severed his connections with supplies and his few raiders north of the Potomac. They had sustained just one casualty: Samuel C. Young of Charles Town, nearly 70 years of age, received a "severe wound in the left breast" and arm as the bullet hit his torso and "shattered his left arm immediately below the shoulder."[20]

While the Charles Town Guards were gaining control of the Potomac bridge, two companies of local citizens, many of whom were armorers, hastily formed on Camp Hill under Captains Lawson Botts and John Avis. Armed with only three rounds of ammunition, they moved to seize the Shenandoah bridge and the houses directly in front of the two arsenal buildings and complete the entrapment of Brown's raiders. Botts's command of 40 men descended to the base of the hill under Jefferson's Rock to avoid being fired upon by the raiders, then took possession of the Shenandoah bridge. After leaving a strong guard at the bridge, the rest of Botts's men moved along the banks of the river toward the Point and the Gault House Saloon, at the rear of the arsenal. After scaling a high wall—some claimed incorrectly it was 30 feet high—the volunteers entered the Gault House Saloon through a basement window and occupied it. This position gave them command of both the entrance to the armory and the bridge over the Shenandoah. The saloon proprietor, George W. Chambers, had been firing at the raiders but had ammunition for only one more shot. At this time, Avis and a handful of men took possession of the houses, commanding the arsenal yard.

The Virginia *Free Press* reported that the command, under Charles Town jailer Captain John Avis, took "possession of the houses directly in front of the arsenal," as instructed. Brown was cut off from his men at the rifle works and in Maryland, leaving his only possible escape route through the western end of the armory; this was not viable because he lacked boats to cross the Potomac. The plight of Brown and his men was becoming increasingly desperate. Brown agreed with his hostages to release them near a canal lock once he and his men were allowed to cross into Maryland. It was Lock 34, the second lock west of the bridge and near the road that led northward. This would give him access to his schoolhouse-arsenal and an escape route through hilly terrain to the Kennedy farm and Elk Mountain.

From Monday through Tuesday morning Brown negotiated periodically with the prisoners, armed citizens, and later, militia. On Monday morning, hours before organized resistance began, Brown had agreed with the armed men surrounding him to exchange Washington and Allstadt for the freedom of two slaves. In the confusion of escalating events, however, this plan was never carried out. That morning, stressed and anxious captives, fearful of their fate, attempted to negotiate a cease-fire through repeated trips by hostages Joseph A. Brua and Israel Russell. Brown let them leave the enginehouse to seek a compromise, which resulted in Brua's pleading with the townspeople to cease their sporadic firing, which endangered the lives of Washington and the other hostages. At one point that morning, according to Washington, Brua got a "promise the people would not fire while negotiations were pending." That agreement was unenforceable. There was no central control over citizens who were enraged by Brown's seizure of family members, friends, and neighbors; the mortal wounding of Hayward Shepherd; the Monday morning killing of Thomas Boerly; and, later, the afternoon deaths of George W. Turner and Fontaine Beckham, a popular old mayor who was unarmed. Citizen fury accelerated to its highest point after what were seen as wanton murders, making compromise more and more unthinkable.

Morning negotiations failed. During the afternoon with the arrival of militia the situation became more threatening for both captives and captors. When firing commenced, the frightened hostages fell to the enginehouse floor. Armistead Ball accurately assessed their feelings: "We were in danger, and almost any proposition that was made was accepted to secure our safety." Despite Brown's saying, in Ball's words, "he was too old a soldier to yield the advantage he possessed in holding hostages" early Monday afternoon he wavered momentarily from his constant insistence on being allowed to cross unfettered to one of the C&O Canal locks, where he would release the prisoners. Concerned about his worsening plight just after the Jefferson Guards took possession of the Potomac bridge, he was open to other suggestions. He asked hostage Reason Cross to draft a proposal, which greatly heartened his captives. Washington recalled that "Brown should retain the possession of the Armory, that he should release us, and that the firing should stop." Realizing this would make him vulnerable because it would relinquish his main bargaining power, Brown vetoed the plan. Instead he gave an opportunity to his adversaries, asking Kitzmiller—aided by a few others—to draft another proposal. He sent hostage Reason Cross, escorted by raider William Thompson, from the enginehouse to negotiate, under a white flag to cease fire. They were fired upon and Thompson was seized as prisoner. His hands were tied and he was dragged to the Wagner House.

As soon as they were fired at, Stevens wanted to fire back from the enginehouse. Brown—surprised and angered by what he considered foul play—fumed that, according to press accounts, "he had within his power to destroy the place in half an hour, but would not do so unless resisted." Acting armory superintendent Kitzmiller told Brown the situation was worsening, and, finding Brown open to suggestions, Kitzmiller attempted to negotiate with Brown who said he would fight those who supported slavery, if needed, to free the slaves. Kitzmiller was surprised, then angry, and finally disgusted with Brown, who expected Kitzmiller to get the militiamen to leave the Potomac bridge and allow Brown's men to reach the Maryland shore. He told the acting superintendent to get the company of riflemen on the bridge to leave. To do this, Kitzmiller, escorted by Watson Brown and the burly Stevens, walked toward the bridge and waved his handkerchief to prevent being fired upon. He told Watson and Stevens to stay behind.

As Watson and Stevens passed the B&O depot, they were fired upon from the Gault House Saloon (prior to the arrival of Botts' Charles Town militiamen). Stevens was struck; he cursed and fired back while shouting he had been deceived. Both raiders would be seriously wounded by the weapons of Thomas Percival and saloon proprietor George W. Chambers. Watson was shot—some contend in the bowel—and received an agonizing and fatal wound, but he somehow struggled back into the enginehouse, where he vomited blood. Lewis Washington later testified that despite Watson's being "wounded in the breast, the ball passed around to the side, but he took his weapon again and fired frequently before his suffering compelled him to retire."

Kitzmiller went home and Stevens did not return. Struck by two shots—some say three, and others, four—Stevens lay bleeding in the street. Witnesses in the enginehouse first thought he was dead but became deeply moved upon hearing him moan and seeing him writhing in agony as he was pelted by a heavy rain. They pleaded for someone to come to the raider's assistance. Brown was deeply annoyed that the enemy would fire on his men while they carried a white flag, and he refused to send anyone, saying they would be shot. Unable to withstand what he was seeing, hostage Joseph A. Brua disregarded his safety and, with great courage and compassion, ran from the enginehouse. He carried Stevens to the Wagner House, where he received medical attention. Surprisingly, Brua kept his word to Brown, returning to the enginehouse as a hostage. On a later occasion he would not return.[21]

Around 1:00 less compassion was shown when the youngest raider, William Leeman, tried to escape by running through an opening in the stone wall to the Potomac River. He surrendered but was shot on a rock in the middle of the river. About an hour later there was more violence involving Colonel Washington's close friend, George W. Turner, who was a West Point graduate, a veteran of the Seminole War, and a prominent farmer and slave-owner who lived five miles south of Charles Town. Turner rode into town with his shotgun and was shot in the neck and instantly killed. As with other incidents during the raid, there are conflicting details. One account maintains he was killed on High Street 50 yards from the intersection with Shenandoah Street when firing at the raiders. Another version contends he was killed on High Street while talking to a traveler who left a train that had stopped prior to entering the town because of the raid. Nevertheless, Turner's death accelerated locals' thirst for revenge.[22]

Confusion continued as the militias and townsmen attempted to coordinate their attacks on Brown, ignoring Hall's Rifle Works during the early assaults—an oversight that Dr. Starry and John Irvin, a young man of the town, tried to remedy. Starry helped round up men while John Irvin went to Colonel Baylor to say he had discovered insurgents in possession of the rifle works and with a small force he could capture them. Baylor ordered 12 to 15 men to go with Irvin to attack. They planned to attack from the bluff opposite the rifle works and shoot the insurgents through the windows. Minutes after taking position on the bluff they saw five men running toward the Shenandoah River. Kagi had waited anxiously most of the day for Brown's approval of his pleas to leave, approval that was never given; eventually he ordered the men to leave the building they occupied in an attempt to escape. As they reached the road behind the building they discovered they were surrounded by shouting men who started shooting. The beleaguered raiders ran toward the river, thinking it was their only avenue of escape. They were unaware they were running toward a dozen or so men with Medlar, who was in charge of the local men across the river, who also would try to kill them.

According to an eyewitness, the Reverend Charles White, a Presbyterian minister who served churches in Harpers Ferry and Berryville, "When the villains ran they crossed the Winchester Railroad and made for the river... We ran immediately toward... them—the Bolivar men pressing on them from the mountain—we on one side." John Copeland, one of the men attempting to escape, said, "We remained there [at the rifle works] until Monday about 2 oc. p.m. ... On entering the river we turned and fired one round at those who had by this time opened fire upon us from all sides." As the raiders tried to escape by wading across the Shenandoah, the surface of which was punctured with numerous outcroppings, they were fired upon by the group of men from Harpers Ferry who had earlier crossed the bridge over the Shenandoah to the eastern banks of the river. Caught in crossfire, some of the small band of raiders abandoned their weapons as they struggled to continue to wade across. John Kagi and Lewis Leary led the way, 10 to 12 feet ahead of Copeland and the two local slaves. By Copeland's account, their hopes diminished when the two leading men were about two thirds across the river and Kagi was "shot through the head and sank beneath the river." Realizing the "chance of escape had left us" Copeland recalled that Leary stood up on a large flat rock and turned looking toward the rifle works when he was struck in the back. Copeland said:

> I had succeeded in getting above some stones that were just above me in the river & floated down behind them & remained so until they thought we were all killed when some of them coming out to where Leary was discovered me & I was pulled up out of the water with the intention of being shot. But some of those that were present not being such cowards as to want to kill a man when discovered & a prisoner prevented it.

The attempt to escape had ended in disaster. John Kagi, the most capable of Brown's men, had responded to a friend's warning the year before that they would all lose their lives if they attacked Harpers Ferry: "Yes I know [Richard] Hinton, *but the result will be worth the sacrifice.*" Kagi died, partially fulfilling this prophecy. A wounded Lewis Leary would linger in pain for 10 hours before dying among the wooden barrels, hoops, and staves in a cooper's shop in town, while his surviving comrade John Copeland was hauled off to the Charles Town jail to await trial. The two slaves met a similar dismal fate. One of Colonel Washington's slaves, a coachman named Jim, was chased into the water with the raiders and drowned attempting to cross Herr's Dam, which funneled water to power equipment on the islands that formed eastern Harpers Ferry. A slave owned by Allstadt sought sanctuary with the attacking citizens.

From the pockets of the limp body of Kagi, notes were recovered, written "on ivory tablets"; they included the listing of one recent week's daily activity and communication with Meriam and "J. B, Jr.," and the arrival of Leary and Copeland.[23]

An eyewitness watching from a hill wrote that for nearly one hour that Monday afternoon he saw a running, random firing kept up by the troops against the rioters. Frightened women and children in town ran shrieking in every direction "until they realized the soldiers were their protection." Then "they took courage, and did good service in the way of preparing refreshments and attending the wounded." During the day citizens gathered in small clusters, peering from behind fences or corners of houses on high ground, as rain fell sporadically. Bystanders anxiously watched the action below as other men in small groups discussed what was happening, often swearing, and interrupting their conversation only to spit tobacco juice from their

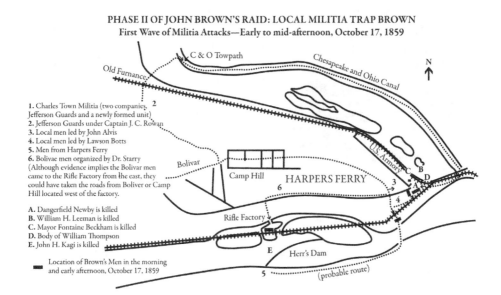

PHASE II OF JOHN BROWN'S RAID: LOCAL MILITIA TRAP BROWN
First Wave of Militia Attacks—Early to mid-afternoon, October 17, 1859

1. Charles Town Militia (two companies, Jefferson Guards and a newly formed unit)
2. Jefferson Guards under Captain J. C. Rowan
3. Local men led by John Alvis
4. Local men led by Lawson Botts
5. Men from Harpers Ferry
6. Bolivae men organized by Dr. Starry (Although evidence implies the Bolivar men came to the Rifle Factory from the east, they could have taken the roads from Boliver or Camp Hill located west of the factory.

A. Dangerfield Newby is killed
B. William H. Leeman is killed
C. Mayor Fontaine Beckham is killed
D. Body of William Thompson
E. John H. Kagi is killed

Location of Brown's Men in the morning and early afternoon, October 17, 1859

Lewis S. Leary. (Library of Congress)

John H. Kagi. (Library of Congress)

mouths. None was more curious than the town's mayor, Fontaine Beckham, railroad agent of the B&O for the 25 years of its operation and county magistrate for even more years. His nervous disposition was exacerbated by what was happening to his town, and by the death of Hayward Shepherd; Shepherd was an employee, and despite their squabbles, was a man for whom Beckham had great affection.

Shortly prior to 3:00, disregarding warnings of the danger, Beckham stood on a B&O Railroad trestle and repeatedly peered around the water tower 30 yards from the enginehouse. "If he keeps on peeking, I'm going to shoot," said Edwin Coppoc, sitting in the enginehouse doorway. Beckham took another peek, and the raider, whose Quaker mother would have disapproved of such a violent act, fired but missed. "Don't fire, man, for God's sake! They will shoot in here and kill us all!" screamed some of the prisoners. Others laughed. Disregarding their pleas, Coppoc fired again at the unarmed mayor, whose hands were in his pockets. Beckham fell dead, and his killer moved to the watchhouse to fire another shot, leaving only Brown's son Oliver in sight. Oliver sat in the partly opened enginehouse doorway; he saw someone peering over the stone wall of the railroad trestle and sighting his gun. Young Brown jerked his rifle up to shoot, but before he could discharge his weapon the other man fired, leaving Oliver with a mortal wound in the chest. Oliver fell backward saying, "It's all up with me." He vomited blood and was in agonizing pain during the brief period before death claiming him.

Edwin Coppoc gives a different version of Oliver's death in a condolence letter to Mrs. Brown: "Oliver lived but a very few moments after he was shot. He spoke no words, but yielded calmly to his fate."

Gault House Saloon owner George W. Chambers had warned the mayor not to go on the railroad trestle to the water tower. He recalled seeing his stricken friend "lying on his head and his neck twisted." "[I] ran up and laid him straight on the railroad track, and then came off." Some claim Beckham's body remained at the death scene for several hours before being removed in a wheelbarrow by a local woman, leaving some of the deceased's gray hair on the railroad tracks where he had fallen. In all likelihood the body was removed by the mayor's son-in-law Mr. Hough, who brought the body to Beckham's house, 15 paces from where he was killed. The tower at the death scene was now scarred by the 30 or so shots fired from the enginehouse that afternoon. When the hostages told him he had killed the elderly, well-respected mayor, Coppoc deeply regretted what he had done. The popular six-foot-tall Beckham, now dead at the age of 64, had befriended not only Shepherd but another man of color, Isaac Gilbert. Beckham obtained freedom for Gilbert's wife and three children by purchasing them and liberating them in his will. Beckham's death would provoke unrestrained retaliation.[24]

Shortly after Beckham died, in midafternoon, a second wave of militia units arrived, reinforcements from Martinsburg and Shepherdstown, (West) Virginia. Immediately upon learning of the alarming disturbance at Harpers Ferry, residents of Martinsburg hurried to their designated meeting place at the guardhouse. There they elected a veteran of the Mexican War, Captain Ephraim G. Alburtis, to take command. Around 2:00 about 30 men in two railroad cars left their hometown for Harpers Ferry. The volunteers from Martinsburg, who were mainly B&O employees, arrived near Harpers Ferry by rail at 3:00 p.m. They left the train east of Furnace Station, about a mile from the town where the Potomac River bends sharply northward. Alburtis and his men climbed up a ravine to Bolivar, about a mile west of Harpers Ferry, and were joined by two militia companies (the Shepherdstown Guards and Hamtramck Guards) and a small body of dismounted cavalry. Colonel Baylor ordered the Martinsburg men to go near the southern bank of the Potomac and approach the armory from above as he led the two Shepherdstown companies down High Street to the arsenal. Upon entering the armory from the upper, or western, end—probably through the gate at that end—Alburtis divided his force into three groups to sweep down through the armory. The captain led one group of about 25 men down the center of the armory, a similar number took the area behind the shops, and the third group proceeded down through the shops. As Alburtis and his men approached the lower end of the armory, they were fired on by Brown's men, who were in the enginehouse and on the corner between the enginehouse and the pay office. The Martinsburg men returned fire with weapons that included those described as squirrel rifles and fowling pieces, forcing all the raiders into the enginehouse. From this position the raiders kept up a continual fire through a four- or five-inch opening in the door. Alburtis's men briskly returned fire during the heated skirmish, dashing forward, cheering. They smashed in a window in one of the two rooms of the enginehouse, which were separated by a solid wall, and freed at least 30 hostages. On the other side of the wall Brown's dwindling force barricaded itself and 11 prisoners. They were trapped despite their superior weapons, although their Sharps rifles brought them a temporary reprieve by forcing the ill-equipped Martinsburg men, who had only pistols and shotguns, to pull back.

The men of Martinsburg had not only cut off the only remaining possible escape route but nearly captured the enginehouse and the raiders—a feat, Alburtis argued, that could have been accomplished if he had been supported as expected by other militia companies. Instead, after eight warriors were injured and in need of medical care, Alburtis halted the assault. His men had fought well. The actions of young George Wollet were noteworthy: he was in the forefront until he was shot in the wrist. Other wounded soldiers included a Martinsburg attorney in his early twenties, George Murphy, who was shot in the leg below the knee after he was one of the first to rush to the enginehouse window and smash it with the butt of his musket. After he was wounded, Murphy limped along with a captured Sharps rifle slung over his back, cheering his associates and urging them to continue the attack. More fortunate than Murphy was his fellow townsman, a Mr. Watson, a 75-year-old who was unhurt when the stock in his gun shattered as he raised it to fire at the raiders.[25]

Trapped, Brown barricaded himself, his few men, and the prisoners inside the enginehouse; the insurrectionists fastened the two large double doors with ropes but allowed enough play so men could fire out through the opening. The three

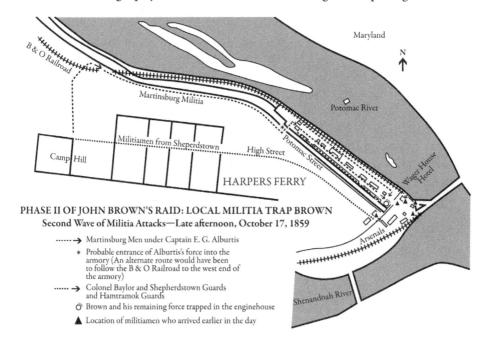

PHASE II OF JOHN BROWN'S RAID: LOCAL MILITIA TRAP BROWN
Second Wave of Militia Attacks—Late afternoon, October 17, 1859

······→ Martinsburg Men under Captain E. G. Alburtis

* Probable entrance of Alburtis's force into the armory (An alternate route would have been to follow the B & O Railroad to the west end of the armory)

······→ Colonel Baylor and Shepherdstown Guards and Hamtramok Guards

Ó Brown and his remaining force trapped in the enginehouse

▲ Location of militiamen who arrived earlier in the day

A contemporary sketch showing the attack on the engine house by Baltimore and Ohio railroad employees led by Captain E. G. Alburtis. (*Frank Leslie's Illustrated Newspaper*, Library of Congress)

Allstadt slaves Brown had kidnapped had discarded their pikes, and some crawled under the firefighting equipment to take a nap. Brown handed masonry tools to an enslaved man named Phil Lucker, who belonged to Mrs. Allstadt, saying, "You're a pretty stout-looking fellow; can't you knock a hole through there for me?" Using the masonry tools Phil Lucker complied for a while, making as many as four loopholes in the brick wall through which to shoot. But gunshots dampened his will to continue; Armistead Ball would later testify that it was "getting too hot for Phil." Brown picked up the tools and completed the work.

Brown's fate was sealed, though he was temporarily secure in the enginehouse. His force at the rifle works was eliminated, and his two men at the arsenal, Osborne Anderson and Albert Hazlett, would escape in a stolen boat to Maryland. The details of their escape, which probably started late Monday afternoon, are unclear as the fictional and unreliable account by Anderson leaves the truth obscured. His version of the story was meant to refute accusations of desertion by contending they did not leave until after Brown's capture on Tuesday morning. According to Anderson's not-altogether-reliable *A Voice from Harper's Ferry,* he and Hazlett took off after the fall of the rifle works, believing Brown captured. Anderson contends the two men were hoping to join their team at Kennedy farm, so they left the arsenal from the back. They climbed a wall, walked south on the railroad tracks that led to Winchester and paralleled the Shenandoah, and captured an armed man, who informed them of the fate of those at the rifle works. With compassion, they released the man who pleaded for his life, taking his gun, which he supposedly said they could have. The two fugitives then climbed up 100 feet or so among the rocks on the high ground above the town. They hid in the rocks, and as daylight faded, supposedly they fired back at those shooting at them—which was highly improbable. The story goes that under the cover of night they descended from the rocks and walked behind Harpers Ferry to Bolivar Heights, then along the B&O tracks and to the site of an old sawmill known as Keep Triest, where the Potomac bent sharply northward. Not far from the Old Furnace Station, they are said to have untied a boat and rowed to the Maryland shore. To reduce the chance of detection they shunned crossing the canal at the locks across from town. There were scattered houses, blacksmith and boat repair shops, and a post office, making it risky to reach the road to the Kennedy farm.

Instead, contends Anderson, the two men walked along the canal path northward more than five miles, passing Lock 37, or Mountain Lock, and crossing under an arch beneath the canal that drained a small creek into the Potomac northwest of the Kennedy house. Anderson and his comrades may have been aware of this area from their nightly rambles to escape the confines of the boardinghouse. Following the creek to the nearby road from Antietam, they traveled to the Kennedy farm to obtain food. Finding the house empty, ransacked and void of food, because Owen Brown and his party, who were escaping, had taken the food with them to the mountain a mile away, they walked in the rain on a rocky and muddy road back toward the Potomac. They reached the schoolhouse around 2:00 a.m. Fatigued, hungry, and fearing they would oversleep in the schoolhouse and be captured, they wearily climbed and spent the night nearby on Elk Mountain. According to Anderson's fictional account, they awoke after sunrise to gunfire from across the river and moved toward the river. From there they saw troops firing at "colored men… stationed by Tidd at the school house," wounding one. His companion approached Anderson and Hazlett, but they were unable to persuade him to join them. After seeing militiamen occupy the schoolhouse, Anderson and Hazlett started an arduous journey toward Pennsylvania.[26]

At about the time when Anderson and Hazlett probably left the arsenal, John Cook attempted to help his beleaguered comrades in the armory. While guarding the weapons at the schoolhouse he heard a disturbing increase of gunfire around the armory shortly after Charles Tidd started back to the Kennedy farm for a second load of weapons. Anxious to find out what the shots meant, the hyperactive Cook had to wait until around 4:00, when Tidd returned. Taking one of Allstadt's "negroes," Cook left for Harpers Ferry, encountering several people; most were acquaintances from his earlier job on the canal. All gave an increasingly gloomy picture of what was happening across the river. Near the schoolhouse he was told, in his words, by "a negro woman" that there was "hard fighting." Cook went a short distance to Lock 34, near the school and nearly a mile from the bridge, where the lock keeper's wife, Mrs. George Hardy, and her friend Mrs. Elizabeth Reed said a number of the raiders had been killed. Cook promised to free Mrs. Reed's husband from the enginehouse and walked toward the Potomac bridge, despite Mrs. Hardy's plea that he avoid the Ferry because it would cost him his life. He came across two friends who told him Brown and his men were trapped. Cook sent the black man—who had become more frightened upon hearing each account of events—back to the schoolhouse, and climbed up part of the base of Maryland Heights. He positioned himself in a tree overlooking the Potomac. With a spyglass he saw his leader was in trouble at the armory, being fired upon by a group of men on High Street. Cook fired at them from the tree. Despite being an excellent marksman, his diversionary gesture was futile. He soon fell 15 feet as a returned shot cut the limb that provided his support.

Bruised and cut, Cook continued his journey toward the bridge. Seeing the faces of potential enemies peering at him from the store 50 yards away, he took shelter behind a crane on the canal. Pointing his cocked rifle at them, he beckoned them to come to him. Only one man complied, but he reassured the raider there were no armed men in the store. Feeling safe, Cook proceeded to the lockhouse, where William McGregg answered his many questions and revealed that seven raiders had been killed, including two who had tried to cross the rivers. McGregg pleaded with Cook to leave before his enemies came, and Cook started back to the schoolhouse. He stopped at the home of an Irish family for coffee and food. It was there he received the unsettling report John Brown had been killed at 4:00 that afternoon.

When Cook reached the schoolhouse—which would later be described by a reporter as being in a "gloomy hollow"—Cook's suspicions were aroused. The shutters and door were closed and no one answered his calls. After a fruitless search of the woods behind the school, he entered the darkened building with a cocked pistol and lit match to find that the shapes in the middle of the room that had assumed were crouching men were only boxes. Cook left for the Kennedy dwelling, and after a while he encountered a group of men about 50 yards away who ordered him to halt. Cook demanded they do the same. Familiar voices responded, revealing it was Charles P. Tidd, Owen Brown, Barclay Coppoc, F. J. Meriam, and "a negro who belonged to Washington" (the only one riding a horse)—they were all heading back to the schoolhouse from the Kennedy farm.

Tidd stayed at the schoolhouse while the others went back to the Kennedy farm, arriving between 2.00 and 3.00 that afternoon. Gunfire could be heard in the distance, urging them toward Harpers Ferry so they could help fight. Owen remembers feeling somehow they would never return to the Kennedy house: "I told some of the neighbors where they could help themselves to provisions and things, if they wanted them, and I tied [the dog] to the crude staircase" so he could not follow. Later Owen learned that the dog barked and growled furiously to ward off interlopers. "Arming ourselves with rifles and revolvers," Owen writes, "we started toward the Ferry in the rain." On the way they met and challenged a man who turned out to be Tidd; he brought unwelcome news that many of their men had been killed and the others were trapped with no chance of escaping from the hundreds of militiamen who controlled the bridges and town. "The fact is, boys," he concluded, "we are used up; the best thing we can do is to get away from here as soon as possible."

Opposed to deserting their friends, Owen Brown proposed going to the schoolhouse, gathering the slaves left there, and going up to Maryland Heights and "without long range guns divert or frighten away the enemy, and let our people escape." Tidd still thought things were hopeless but agreed to go to the schoolhouse and get the local slaves he had stationed in the woods behind the schoolhouse. Upon colliding with Cook, Owen Brown, Coppoc, and Meriam received more chilling details: "Our men are all killed but seven." To Owen Brown, Cook said, "Your father was killed at four o'clock this afternoon." Owen and Cook argued in the rain and darkness while Owen refused to accept Cook's assessment that "it would be sheer madness to attempt a rescue."

Tidd said he had he left the other black men at the schoolhouse, but Cook pointed out they had run away, along with the man he had sent back from the canal. Owen finally persuaded Cook they should go to schoolhouse. Once there Owen had difficulties getting the strong-willed, stout former lumberman, Tidd, to follow. Revolver drawn, Tidd reluctantly followed Owen, with only the illumination of a candle to guide them into the structure where enemies could be lurking. They found only the weapons they had taken there that day and, in a corner, nearly a barrel's worth of sweet biscuits Owen had made to feed the slaves who John Brown assumed would join him. Owen hurriedly stuffed as many biscuits as he could into a bag, along with about 20 pounds of sugar in another bag that bore his father's initials. He then joined the rest of the men outside. There they lingered for perhaps an hour, calling out to the black men. In Owen's words: "The only answer that came to us out in the rain was the firing at Harper's Ferry a mile away." Finally realizing his rescue plan from the heights would be folly—it would at most take few lives of the enemy and "would surely cost" their own lives—Owen and the men headed back to Kennedy house.

Some of Brown's Men Flee

After a hasty supper at the boardinghouse, which would not be safe for long, Owen threw the bags of biscuits and sugar onto the horse. Quickly the men seized what they could carry, planning to sort out and bury the excess on the mountain. While ascending the mountain and contemplating their escape, Owen "ordered the negro to turn his horse loose." "Why?" came the response, along with prolonged resistance arguing that the "horse is worth more'n a hundred an' fifty dollars." With difficulty Owen convinced the man "that his life was worth more than a horse," and the horse was released. They halted in the laurel at the base of the mountain behind their secondary base at the cabin across the road from the boardinghouse (a mile away), thinking they were safe for the night and in a position to help any other unlikely escaping comrades who might come to the Kennedy house. There they made their beds in the cold and rain by spreading an India-rubber blanket on the ground, a woolen blanket on top of it, another for a cover, and an India-rubber blanket on top. "Thus," claimed Owen, "two men clubbing together had furniture for a good bed in the wettest weather."

Thirty-four-year-old Owen, the oldest of the group by at least a decade except for 30-year-old Cook, had been a woodman and Underground Railroad "engineer." In his account, "[I] told the boys if they stuck by me I felt pretty sure I could I could get them safely through to the North, and to Canada, if necessary." The camp was "dark as only a laurel thicket can be on a starless, rainy night," and gunfire could still be heard at intervals. "I told the boys my plan," recalls Owen. Their best direction, in his view, was to first follow the mountain ranges northeasterly into Pennsylvania then move northwest "toward our friends or Canada… traveling only at night upon the edges of the clearing; sleeping and hiding by day in the thickets on the uninhabited mountain-tops; shunning all traveled roads at all times, except as we are obliged to cross them in the night." No fires were to be built, according to Owen, and his plan included "buying or stealing no provisions" and "not speaking aloud till we should, at least, get beyond Chambersburg, Pennsylvania." Hearing the plans for such an arduous journey and fearing being a fugitive, Washington's slave started complaining of rheumatism, stating he was afraid he could not go with them.

The men went to their beds, spaced about 15 feet apart for the sake of safety. Owen warned the black man that going back would cost him his life while also attempting to reassure him by saying he was "reasonably sure I could get him to freedom if he kept with us." Owen's suspicions increased when the black man began groaning and complaining of rheumatism, saying he could not lie comfortably and wanted to sit up. Owen arose and sat down on the bed next to the complaining man to keep an eye on him, but after two nights without sleep, the raider dozed off. Around 3:00 Tuesday morning Owen awakened to find the man had run off. Fearing he would reveal their location and plans, Owen roused the others, who agreed they must immediately leave and make changes in their route northward. They hurried to the top of Elk Mountain and then rushed to the other side. Tuesday night they crossed into Pleasant Valley to the ridge beyond, South Mountain, starting what would prove to be their journey to the Quaker State and beyond. Their trip rivaled that of Anderson and Hazlett in difficulty.[27]

Arrival of More Militia

At dusk and during the night, while two groups—Owen Brown, Cook, Tidd, Coppoc, and Meriam in one, and Anderson and Hazlett in the other—wandered around north of the Potomac, each unaware of the other group's movement, a third wave of militia units arrived. Three uniformed companies—the first of the militia to show up in uniform—arrived from Frederick, Maryland, under Colonel Shriver, a Frederick attorney. They were soon followed by Colonel L. T. Moore's Thirty-first Regiment from Winchester (including the Continental Morgan Guards, Mount Vernon Rifles, and Marion Guards), who traveled by rail to Halltown. From there they marched through Bolivar Heights to Harpers Ferry, entering the armory ground around 5:00 p.m. They took position in the yard and on the B&O trestle, 75 to 100 yards from Brown's men. Hours later five companies of Baltimore volunteers followed, and finally, before midnight about 90 US Marines arrived. During the night the governor of Virginia, Henry Wise, accompanied by Company F of the First Virginia Regiment, was coming as rapidly as he could.

By midafternoon Monday, men who were eager to fight had gathered at Camden Station from all parts of Baltimore. A special 11-car train left the station at 4:15 p.m. amid great cheers from an immense crowd. The first car carried liquor and provisions, and six cars carried the military, which included the Independent Greys, Law Greys, Baltimore City Guard, Wells Riflemen, and McComas Riflemen and numbered 201 muskets. The remainder of the cars conveyed passengers and citizens not in uniform, including one car of rough-looking men of various dress and weapons. One man was armed, according to the Baltimore *Exchange,* "with a long duck gun, carrying over his shoulder an immense pouch filled with buck shot; another had on a cocked hat and military roundabout, with two horse pistols in a belt on each side." Railroad personnel "attempted to prevent" some of these 50 to 60 "characters" from boarding, "but they were bent on a fight, and pleaded hard for a chance to take part in the fray, and soon filled up one car." The next morning they would crowd near the armory gate to shoot Brown and his men, causing the New York *Daily Tribune* headline "Roughs Eager for the Fray."[28]

Some 150 miles south, in the Old Dominion capital, the night started with men of the company assembling fully equipped for an inspection and last drill before the October 19 celebration of the 1781 American victory at Yorktown. Within 10 minutes of assembling, they received orders from the governor, who accompanied them on an all-night sleepless journey northward. They were hurried in cars of the Richmond and Fredericksburg Railroad Company that carried them from Richmond to the landing on Aquia Creek to take a boat to Washington. Roll was called aboard the vessel, revealing 67 present. Fourteen others had sneaked home in the darkness on the way to the depot but would accompany a regiment the following day; the next-day regiment would proceed no farther than Washington because the raid would have been terminated.[29]

Fear and paranoia spread far beyond Harpers Ferry and the immediate surrounding communities. Parke Poindexter of Company F, accompanying Wise to Harpers Ferry, found "all the volunteers and regular soldiers at [the nation's capital]... on duty patrolling the city, as well as the police-force of some one hundred men, expecting an attack upon the city of Washington." Fear swept north of the Mason–Dixon Line. The New York *Herald* recorded the fear of black people in Pennsylvania: "Arms recently furnish to a colored voluntary company in Philadelphia have been taken away in consequences of the Harper's Ferry Affair."

The news of the raid that Poindexter heard in Washington was not reassuring, as 800 to 1,000 men were rumored to be tearing up the railroad tracks, which would necessitate marching eight to 10 miles on foot to reach the Ferry, where a much larger force would confront them. After being joined in Washington by a company of volunteers from Alexandria, they marched through rain and mud in the darkness from the boat landing to the nearby B&O Railroad depot, where they received refreshments and then started for the Relay House, south of Baltimore, where they would turn west to Harpers Ferry. Ammunition was distributed among the men on board the train that would take them as rapidly as possible to the troubled town. Poindexter looked at people lined along the tracks in, he observed, "a great state of excitement. Men, women, and children cheered vociferously, waving their handkerchiefs, as the train bore on our splendid company at almost lightning speed. After traveling two hours we began to near the infected country, and the men prepared for an attack. About three hours the train suddenly stopped"; this was because of false information that the track had been torn up. They proceeded with passengers whose emotions were heightened, for rumors were flying. When they reached three miles of their destination they met a train going the opposite direction and were informed the troublemakers had been captured.

Brown Attempts to Negotiate His Freedom

Long before Wise and the volunteers left Richmond, the night before Brown's capture, the Old Man had tried in vain to negotiate his way to freedom. Colonel Robert Baylor reported that immediately after the Martinsburg men ceased their attack, Brown again attempted to use his hostages to negotiate an escape. He sent prisoner Isaac Russell to the colonel with, in Colonel Baylor's words, "a verbal communication, stating if I would permit him to cross the bridge with his prisoners to some point beyond he would set them at liberty." Baylor responded, "I say to you, if you will set at liberty our citizens, we will leave the government to deal with you concerning the property as it may think most advisable." In Baylor's account, Brown still believed his possession of hostages would get him out, and he countered.

CAPT. JOHN BROWN answers:
In consideration of all my men, whether living or dead, or wounded, being soon safely in, and delivered up to me at this point, with all their arms and ammunition, we will then take our prisoners and cross the Potomac bridge, a little beyond which we will set them at liberty; after which we can negotiate about the government property as may be best. Also we require the delivery of our horse and harness at the hotel.

JOHN BROWN

In writing, Baylor adamantly insisted his original terms would be the only ones accepted.

Alexander R. Boteler, the congressman from the Harpers Ferry district who claimed to be present during these negotiations, later gave a more colorful and embellished version. Boteler wrote that before the arrival of the Frederick militia four or more of the key militia commanders—Baylor, Gibson, Alburtis, Botts—and several local citizens, including the congressman, held a conference on whether to immediately assault the enginehouse or wait until morning. Those who had been freed by the Martinsburg men protested that to attack the enginehouse at night would imperil the lives of the remaining hostages, which had been the salient factor in not using an artillery piece brought with one of the arriving militia units. Before making a final decision a popular but eccentric local farmer, Samuel Strider, who lacked succinctness, was sent to demand Brown's immediate surrender. Boteler writes, "Tying a white handkerchief to the ferrule of a faded umbrella," Strider went "marching up to the door of the enginehouse," calling out "in stentorian tones, 'Who commands this fortification?'" "Captain Brown of Kansas," was the reply. "Well, Captain Brown of Kansas," continued the farmer in his high-pitched voice, "I am sent here, sir, by the authorities in command, for to summon you to surrender; and sir, I do it in the names of the Commonwealth of old Virginia—God bless her!"

Brown said, "What terms do you offer?" After saying he had heard nothing about them, Strider asked what Brown wanted, and Brown insisted he be allowed to cross to Maryland to a point on the C&O, where he would release the prisoners. Strider demanded Brown put it in writing—which at first he refused to do, claiming it was too dark to write—but the farmer got his wish after responding, "Pshaw! That's nonsense… and if you don't write your terms down, in black and white, I won't take 'em back to those who sent me." Brown finally complied and wrote the note Baylor quoted above.

The proposed terms were taken to those in charge, read by each, and handed to another. When the note was handed to Lawson Botts, who would later become Brown's first attorney during his trial, in Boteler's account, he threw it "contemptuously upon the floor, and placing his foot on it saying: 'Gentlemen, this is adding insult to injury. I think we ought to storm those fellows without further delay.'" Regardless of the accuracy of details given by Boteler, the argument for caution set forth by former hostages, and the fact that Brown was trapped and unable to escape in the darkness of that rainy night convinced Baylor, Gibson, and others to postpone an assault until morning.[30]

The arrival around dusk of the Sixteenth Regiment of Frederick, Maryland, led to another round of talks with Brown.[31] He continued to cling to the belief his hostages were his ticket to freedom, once again insisting he be allowed to cross to the canal and free his prisoners there. Rumors of trouble at the Harpers Ferry alarmed Frederick residents that Monday morning, prompting Colonel Edward Shriver to hurry by rail to the site of the disturbance. Finding what he believed to be a servile insurrection of several hundred, he returned to his hometown. Finding that town authorities had offered help, and President Buchanan had accepted, 170 men hurried on a special train provided by the B&O Railroad. Shriver recorded that shortly after embarking, they arrived at Monocacy Junction, three miles south of Frederick, where they received "apparently well authenticated reports... that the forces of the insurgents had been largely increased... to six hundred armed slaves, and they had strongly fortified the [Potomac] Bridge." Shriver immediately ordered the cannon belonging to Frederick "to be forwarded by the earliest train." Disembarking at Sandy Hook, Shriver later wrote, he had been told the insurrectionists no longer controlled the bridge but was still apprehensive about who might be on the crossing. He had his men charge into the dark and foreboding enclosed structure with fixed bayonets. Arriving uncontested on the Virginia shore, Shriver offered the services of his command to Colonel Baylor, who immediately, according to Shriver, "placed detachments of each company on guard" around the trapped insurgents, which the Maryland colonel learned was all that remained of a meager force of fewer than two dozen men. Commanders and the men of the Frederick companies "warmly asked they might be led to the assault of the building occupied by the Insurgents without delay." Baylor nixed the request, again pointing out the danger to hostages who included a well-known cabinetmaker from their town, George B. Shope.

From 11:00 p.m. to midnight, according to Shriver, Captain Thomas Sinn, who was "with his detachment of his company on guard in front of the building occupied by the Insurgents was hailed and invited to it for the purpose of conference in regard to the terms on which the Insurgents proposed to surrender." When Sinn arrived outside the enginehouse, he found the raiders' leader, who introduced himself as John Brown. Brown repeated his terms and complained that his men had been shot down like dogs while carrying truce flags. Captain Sinn replied that by taking up arms and doing what they had done, they must expect to be shot like dogs. Brown replied he was well aware of the perils of what he was doing and would not "shrink" from responsibility, but considering he had control of the town and could have burned and massacred its inhabitants, that should entitle him to something. Furthermore, he added that neither he nor his men had killed unarmed men. When it was pointed out that they had killed the unarmed mayor of the town, he expressed regret, and the conversation ended. Sinn immediately went to tell Shriver of the raider's demand. This prompted the colonel, accompanied by Sinn and an adjutant, to hold "a parly [sic] with Captain Brown and the gentlemen whom he held prisoners. He repeated to me," Shriver later wrote in his report, "the same terms adding only if escorted to the Canal lock [Lock 33]... with all his men and their arms, he asked no farther favor than he & his men should not be shot down instantly by a body of men posted for the purpose, but on being allowed a brief period for preparing for fight, he was willing to take his chances for death or escape." [31]

The attacks on his men under flags of truce had angered the rebel leader. Brown repeatedly denounced and distrusted militiamen and other armed citizens as they violated the protocol of this traditional combat procedure. He also considered them inferior as warriors and was therefore willing to take his chances in combat with them if he was able to get his remaining men armed and near the wooded mountain on the Maryland shore. But once again Brown's proposal was rebuffed; Shriver later reported he informed the abolitionist "he was completely surrounded by an overwhelming force and every avenue of escape effectively guarded—that his life was assuredly forfeited and urged him to permit his prisoners retire." The old raider, unshaken by the ultimatum as he and his wife had long anticipated that he would likely be killed, reminded the colonel of the purpose of taking hostages by informing him "they were gentlemen and he should be sorry to hurt a hair of their heads, but he secured them as hostages for his own safety and the safety of his men and should use them accordingly." Shriver was convinced Brown would not surrender or release the prisoners unless on his unacceptable terms, and so the stalemate continued. Shriver retired from the enginehouse and attended a conference "with all the Field Officers present" where "it was resolved and announced by Colonel Baylor the commanding officer that at daylight the position of the Insurgents should be assaulted and taken with the Bayonet, in order to secure as far as possible the safety to the prisoners." This seemed, according to Shriver, to appease the Frederick men's ardor for an immediate attack. Detachments of Frederick men and Virginia men, relieved every two hours, continued to guard the beleaguered raiders in the enginehouse.

Meanwhile, Captain Sinn walked to the Wagner House, becoming disgusted by the drunken citizens hollering, screaming, and indiscriminately firing their weapons. There Sinn found additional repugnant conduct; a few young toughs were taunting the gravely wounded Stevens by pointing their revolvers at him. Stevens did not flinch. Sinn drove the men from the room, saying, "If this man could stand on his feet with a pistol in his hand, you would all jump out the window." But the wounded raider's harassment did not end, and after hours of intense suffering his disillusionment deepened as he realized Brown's raid was futile. After Stevens was shot, he had lain on the street, cussing and moaning under heavy rain, and had said to Kitzmiller, "I have been cruelly deceived," to which Archibald responded,

"I wish I had stayed home." The next morning when a reporter from the Baltimore *Exchange* was taken by Colonel Baylor to Stevens, the reporter found about 20 angry men crowded around the bed in the Wagner House, shouting threats ranging from hanging to being shot. The correspondent wrote that the suffering raider said,

> There are twenty-two of us, and we are all under John Brown. We came here to free the negroes. Brown made us believe that we only had to strike the blow, and thousands of negroes would join us. I have found that he has deceived us, and if I had known what I know now, I would not have been here. We were not to receive any money for this work, and we had no design to rob the paymaster's department. I feel very bad and it hurts too much to talk.

The reporter left to talk to Brown, leaving many of those crowded around Stevens still clamoring for his death.[32]

After visiting Stevens on Monday night, Sinn remembered the plight of the suffering wounded young raiders with Brown. With compassion, Sinn returned to the enginehouse with a surgeon in his command, Dr. William Taylor Jr. The doctor attempted to "staunch the wounds" of Watson Brown and promised to return in the morning. This turned out to be possible only after the raiders were captured.[33]

Robert E. Lee and Marines Arrive

The stalemate continued through the night, becoming the problem of Colonel Robert E. Lee, who arrived and assumed command late Monday night. The arrival time varies according to participants, whose attention swirled around the dramatic events; times given vary from 10:00 p.m. Monday to 2:00 a.m. Tuesday. It seems likely he arrived shortly before midnight.[34]

Before the Marines and the future Confederate icon arrived, the number of militiamen in the river town had swelled as they traveled by special trains. From Winchester, Virginia, came another militia company from Winchester headed by R. B. Washington, and later 17 railroad cars carried five companies from Baltimore. Volunteers totaled 201 men under the command of Major-General George H. Stewart, and laborers showed up to repair rail and telegraph lines.[35]

Earlier in Washington President James Buchanan, Secretary of War John B. Floyd, and Secretary of the Navy Isaac Toucey, and in Richmond Governor Henry Wise, had been scurrying about to muster men to suppress the insurgents. James Ewell Brown—"Jeb"—Stuart later wrote to his mother that the dispatches received by the president were "whispered very cautiously... through the War Department" to keep them secret, fearing an insurrection in the nation's capital. Lieutenant Israel Green, the ranking officer on duty at the Washington Naval Yard, was sent to Harpers Ferry. Green was to report to the senior officer, and if there should be no such officer he was to take charge and protect the government property. At the same time three companies of artillery at Fort Monroe, two days away in southeast Virginia, were ordered to the same destination.

Earlier that day Secretary of War Floyd had sent James Ewell Brown Stuart to summon Robert E. Lee to Washington. Lee was an army colonel on leave from duty in Texas, who was at his Arlington family estate, a short distance from the capital, on the southern banks of the Potomac River. Stuart, a Virginian like Floyd and Lee, was also in Washington on leave from military duty in Kansas, seeking a patent for the inventions he planned to manufacture and sell to the army. Upon learning of Harpers Ferry's troubles, Lieutenant Stuart immediately volunteered his services to Floyd, who sent him on his second visit in two days to the lieutenant's friend and former superintendent at West Point and father of his classmate Custis. For Lee, these were welcome interruptions from the tedium of his work as an executor, as he attempted to untangle legal matters dealing with the estate of his late father-in-law, George Washington Parke Custis.

When the president and secretary of war placed Lee in command of the Marines to quell the uprising, Stuart volunteered as his aide. Lee immediately telegraphed Green, who received the instruction at Frederick Junction to proceed to Sandy Hook—the small hamlet on the northern bank of the Potomac about a mile north of the Ferry—and await his arrival. Stuart recalls he barely had time to borrow a uniform coat and a saber before joining Lee. They hastily boarded a car pulled by a locomotive that had left Camden station in Baltimore at 7:30 p.m., which Stuart claimed "sped… very rapidly in pursuit" of the train Jeb thought was 20 minutes ahead of them carrying Green and the Marines on their six-hour journey from the nation's capital to the insurrection site.

Lee arrived near midnight under a light rain and spent the next hour or more talking with militia leaders and prominent civilians and reconnoitering the situation. After conferring with Baylor and Shriver he discovered there was a meager group of trapped troublemakers—far less than the 3,000 rumored in Washington's halls of power. The nearly a dozen hostages included Lewis Washington, a descendant of the first president and a cousin of Lee's wife, Mary Custis. This made the plight of hostages personal; Lee reported it "was a subject of painful consideration," and "to prevent if possible, jeopardizing their lives" he approved and planned to implement the militia commanders' resolution to "storm the Insurgents position at daylight by a charge of the bayonet." This was a decision Lee regretted in hindsight: "I should have ordered the attack at once."

After assessing, Lee had the Marines disembark from the rail cars, leaving behind the two howitzers, and march across the bridge and into the armory through what Israel Green called a back gate. Orders were sent by the new commander canceling a previous one for the movement of three artillery companies from Fort Monroe to the insurrection site. Between 1:00 and 2:00 Tuesday morning Lee ordered the volunteers to march out of the armory and gave "control inside to the marines, with instructions to see that none of the insurgents escaped during the night." The Frederick militia were to maintain security of the Potomac bridge. The Baltimore men were to stay on the Maryland side to thwart any attempt to send reinforcements to the beleaguered raiders.

While planning to implement a dawn attack upon the enginehouse, Lee—according to Colonel Shriver—"announced that he deemed it due to the volunteer military present that it should have the privilege of conducting operations" and "requested that each company… assign two men who shall compose the storming party." First he wanted to give Smith (the believed name of the insurrectionist leader) the opportunity to surrender, which would give the hostages their best chance of escaping unscathed. At around 2:00 a.m. Tuesday Lee instructed Stuart that shortly after dawn he should walk to the enginehouse under a white flag and read the following demands:

> Headquarters Harpers Ferry
> October 18, 1859
> Colonel Lee, United States army, commanding the troops sent by the President of The United States to suppress the insurrection at this place, demands the surrender of the persons in the armory building. If they will peaceably surrender themselves and restore the pillaged property, they shall be kept in safety to await orders of the President. Colonel Lee represents to them, in all frankness, that it is impossible for them to escape; that the Armory is surrounded on all sides by troops; and that if he is compelled to take them by force he cannot answer for their safety.
> R. E. Lee
> Colonel Commanding United States Troops

Lee further instructed that upon the rejection of surrendering, which Lee anticipated, Stuart would wave his hat to signal an attack on the enginehouse.[36]

Darkness temporarily stayed the capture of Brown, but it brought little solace or slumber to him, his men, or the hostages. The dark confines of the enginehouse blunted their vision but not their senses of cold, hunger, and thirst; it did not lessen their angst over what dawn would bring or the pain of the wounded and dying. To rest, they had to sit on the fire engines or the hard brick floor where the body of studious Canadian-born Stewart Taylor lay, dead from a bullet that had struck his forehead. Nearby Brown's two wounded sons lay dying. According to Coppoc, Taylor's death was not instantaneous, as he lingered "about three hours after receiving his wound" suffering intense pain and begging the men "to kill him."

The eerie and uncomfortable situation inside the enginehouse, and random firing by drunks outside, did not shake the resolve of Old Brown, who, to his prisoners' surprise, had shown concern for their welfare. Nevertheless the circumstances had to be at least unnerving, and to some, like the teenage John Thomas Allstadt, frightening. Confusing Oliver with Watson, Allstadt later said, "In the quiet of the night young Oliver Brown died," after begging "again and again to be shot, in the agony of his wound, but his father replied to him, 'Oh you will get over it,' and, 'If you must die, die like a man.'" After a while Oliver "lay quietly in a corner" prompting his father to call "to him, after a time. No answer. 'I guess he is dead,' said Brown." This callous paternal response is rejected by Terrance Byrne's testimony.

Byrne also watched Watson writhing in agony and begging his father to kill him so he could be released from his excoriating torment. Later Byrne recalls the father saying something like, "No, my son, have patience; I think you will get well; if you die, you die in a glorious cause for liberty, or freedom." Earlier Brown had asked Captain Simms to obtain a physician for Watson, and later, upon being taken from the enginehouse, his first concern was a suffering Watson, as the father pleaded for his "noble-hearted" son to be treated kindly.[37]

Only four of the trapped raiders and their commander remained unharmed: Edwin Coppoc, Jeremiah Anderson, Dauphin Thompson, and Shields Green. The liberated slaves in what had become Brown's fort, as well as those in other locations, were now anything but supportive. They had long since discarded the pikes given them upon their arrival. In the stillness of the night Brown occasionally asked, "Men, are you awake?" At other times he held intermittent conversations as he had during the day with his captives Washington, the elder Allstadt, and Daingerfield about his determination to liberate all slaves. Daingerfield "found him as brave as a man could be, and sensible upon all subjects except slavery." Daingerfield would later author an inaccurate and self-aggrandizing article in *Christian Century Magazine* that contradicted his testimony at Brown's trial a quarter century earlier. Daingerfield in the article claimed that he told Brown he and his men were committing treason against Virginia and the United States. Supposedly this alarmed Thompson and Anderson, stripping away their youthful naivety and altruism, and they asked their leader, "'Are we committing treason against our country being here?' Brown answered, 'Certainly.' Both declared, 'If that is so, we don't want to fight any more. We thought we came to liberate the slaves and did not know that that was committing treason.'"

Phase Three: Defeat and Capture

By midafternoon that rainy Monday local militiamen and citizens had trapped Brown. By midnight about 600 men surrounded him. All of them were militiamen and armed locals except the Marines. Together they made escaping virtually impossible for the 59-year-old leader of the raiders. He remained barricaded in the enginehouse with 11 hostages, only four uninjured raiders, and one of Washington's and three of Allstadt's slaves. With an amazing calmness and despite numerous earlier failures in bargaining for his freedom, the weary old man still clung to the view that having hostages would lead to his escape. It was his only hope.

Although Brown's position had deteriorated during Monday and become precarious after the plucky charge of the men from Martinsburg, the militiamen—despite their vastly superior numbers—made no serious attempt to capture him. Why not? This was the question that later greatly annoyed Governor Wise of Virginia, as it appeared that the Old Dominion could not defend herself against a meager band of fewer than two dozen "lawless ruffians." On the surface, Colonel Robert

W. Baylor's justification of his handling of the Virginia militia, especially of the actions after dark on Monday, seems plausible. Fear of harming the hostages in the enginehouse, his troops' exhaustion level, and inclement weather prompted Baylor to post guards around the armory; Baylor hoped to prevent Brown's escape while postponing "another attack until morning," a position later endorsed by Robert E. Lee. What Baylor's report ignores are the rowdy and barbaric acts on Monday afternoon by some of the militiamen and citizens, which critics maintain indicates that the militia and volunteers' forces were out of control.

The shock and fear first evoked by the seizure of Harpers Ferry by an unknown band soon changed, by Monday afternoon, to wrath and revenge. Blinding rage, unleashed and fueled by Brown's raid, soared to uncontrollable heights as news spread of the deaths of several prominent local citizens at the hands of what their fellow townspeople called "wanton, malicious unprovoked felons." As friends and families anxiously awaited to hear the fate of the hostages, wild reprisals were made against the raiders. Men roamed the streets, frequented the town's bars (Wagner House and Gault House Saloon), shouted wildly, and fired their weapons indiscriminately during the day and into the night; reason, restraint, and propriety were dulled while their base passions of hate and revenge were inflamed by booze and mob psychology.

The body of the large mixed-race raider, Dangerfield Newby, who joined Brown to free his wife and six children from bondage, lay in the street outside the armory, some say within 20 steps of the enginehouse. Newby's corpse became an inviting target for the unrestrained rage of drunken militiamen and citizens, from the afternoon of October 17 to the afternoon of the following day. Witnesses wrote: "Infuriated people beat the body with sticks, put them in the wounds, shouted curses on" the corpse and "otherwise degraded themselves" by dragging the body into the gutter and slicing off ears as souvenirs. A dog sniffed the "coagulated blood which surrounded the head, and finally hogs tugged at the body." One ran its snout into the hideous, gaping wound, large enough to "admit the fore part of an ordinary foot," and "drug out a very long or elastic, stringy substance... one end being in the hog's mouth and the other in the man's body." With Newby's fatality died his loving wife Harriet's last hope for freedom.[38]

Others also became victims of the militiamen's and townsmen's anger. On Monday afternoon Brown had finally realized the hopelessness of his plight and tried unsuccessfully, under two separate flags of truce, to bargain for his freedom. On both occasions, militiamen and armed citizens ignored the white flags. Under the first flag, in the afternoon, they seized raider William Thompson and put him in the Wagner House. Later that afternoon, in retaliation for a raider's bullet killing the Mayor Fontaine Beckham, citizens took Thompson to the Potomac bridge. There they shot him a dozen times and threw his bullet-riddled body to the shallow water below, where, according to witnesses, it "could be seen for a day or two... with his ghostly face still exhibiting his fearful death agony."[39] He was an additional target for unrestrained rage.

Drawing showing William Thompson thrown into the Potomac River and William Leeman, who had reached a rock in the river being shot at from above. (West Virginia Archives, Boyd B. Stutler Collection)

The second flag of truce had seen raider Aaron Stevens struck by several shots and seriously wounded, and Watson Brown mortally wounded. Watson, despite the severity of his wound, continued to fire from the enginehouse until his deteriorating condition made it impossible. The following morning he was barely able to walk. Earlier the same afternoon the youngest of the raiders, 20-year-old William H. Leeman, impulsive by nature and at times difficult to control, had tried unsuccessfully to escape. Throwing away his rifle and cutting off his accoutrements with a Bowie knife to lessen impediment in the water, Leeman fled through the opening in the eastern end of the armory stone wall into the Potomac River. Coming under heavy fire, "he stopped on a tiny islet." There, according to a widely spread story, the unarmed youth threw up his hands and pled, "Don't shoot," but despite his surrender, he was slain. One account maintains that Harpers Ferry resident G. A. Schoppert "waded out," put a pistol against Leeman's face "and fired, blowing half his head off." The militiamen then cut off "the boy's coattails" and accoutrements, "sat the mangled form against the rocks and then... spent with others, the afternoon in target practice on the dead body." That afternoon, Leeman's body was riddled with shots fired from undisciplined militiamen and other individuals, especially those who had captured Sharps rifles in the fray and were eager to try them out. When tiring of "this *sport*" wrote a reporter for the Frederick *Herald*, "a man waded out" to where Leeman lay "and *set him up, in grotesque attitudes,* and finally pushed him off, and he floated

William Thompson. (Library of Congress)   William H. Leeman. (Library of Congress)

down the stream." The Baltimore *Sun* found the mutilation of the body was "of very questionable taste and propriety." Finally lodging near the middle of river, Leeman's black hair, according to the *Sun* could be seen "floating upon the surface of the water and waving with every ripple." Upon the body was found:

HEAD-QUARTERS WAR DEPARTMENT
  Harper's Ferry, Md.
Whereas, W. H. Leeman has been nominated a captain in the army established under the *Provisional Constitution*; now therefore, in pursuance of the authority vested in me by the said constitution, we do hereby appoint and commission the said Wm. H. Leeman captain.
  Given at the office of the Secretary of War, this day, 15th of October, 1859.
    JOHN BROWN
    Commander in Chief

In 1900 Schoppert made an affidavit supported by Colonel Gibson maintaining the killing of Leeman was justified because he was armed with a pistol and knife and refused to surrender. Letters were found on his corpse from his sister and mother that revealed poverty in his father's household; the Richmond *Whig* said it was "the condition of the lowest negro." The *Whig* ridiculed what it called "Abolition Charity"—Leeman forsaking his impoverished family and his aged invalid mother's lament to him "that if she had had money to buy medicine she could get well, but that she *could not raise a dollar to save her life.*"[40]

  Amid such madness there were contrasting acts of courage and decency. One was a woman's unsuccessful attempt to prevent the revenge killing of William Thompson.

Miss Christine Fouke entered the parlor of the Wagner Hotel to find Thompson seated in an armchair with his hands tied behind, and guarded by some citizens. She listened as they questioned him about his motives and those of the other raiders. His answers were the same, reflecting a naivety and previous youthful enthusiasm about how Brown had fostered an expectation of ease for accomplishing their mission. This heightened Thompson's and others' disillusionment when their lives were in peril as the raid was failing. Christine Fouke later wrote, "He (Thompson) had been taught to believe the negroes were cruelly treated and would gladly avail themselves of the first opportunity to obtain their freedom, and all they had to do was to come to Harper's Ferry, take possession of the armory and arsenal, which would be an easy matter, and then the colored people would come in mass backed by non-slaveholders of the Valley of Virginia." Thompson was told by someone, "I imagine you regret that you did not succeed in running off the darkies." He replied "that he regretted having engaged in the attempt, and if it were to do over again he would decline." Hearing that Thompson was recently married, Miss Fouke later wrote that she walked up to the prisoner saying, "Mr. Thompson, you had much better have stayed at home and taken care of your wife, and pursued some honest calling, instead of coming here to murder our citizens and steal our property; that their first act was to kill a free colored man, because he would not join them in their wicked scheme."

Shortly after learning of the killing of Beckham, Harry Hunter, his grand-nephew and militiaman from Charles Town, and Charles Chambers, a saloon keeper, hurried to the Wagner Hotel seeking retribution. They burst into the room, their guns pointed at their captured victim, who sat in a chair, still guarded by several citizens. Miss Christine Fouke immediately threw herself in front of Thompson and the weapons of the avengers. She was protecting not only the raider from what she considered an illegal act, but also the welfare of her sick sister in the next room; Fouke believed that for her sister, the shock of such a "great outrage" of killing "the man in the house however much he deserved to die" might "prove fatal." About a month later Fouke became concerned about the Saint Louis *Republican* claiming she had saved Thompson's life. She wondered what her neighbors would think, and others of the South, about a resident of the town who aided one of the outlaws. On November 27 she wrote the Saint Louis *Republican* to set the record straight. After listing the reasons for her actions, she concluded with, "I simply shielded the terribly frightened man, without concern for him, until Col. Moore, I think, came in and assured us, on his honor that he would not be shot in the house. That was all I desired."

Despite Christine Fouke's efforts, Thompson was dragged outside by the throat and executed. Before Hunter and Chambers repeatedly shot their victim at the bridge, Thompson told them, in one last act of defiance, according to Hunter's testimony, "Though you may take my life, 80,000,000,000 [others say it was 80,000,000] will rise up to avenge me, carry out my purpose of giving liberty to the slaves." Hunter later justified the killing by testifying that "villainous Abolitionists" had shot down his "loved uncle and best friend" and "I felt it my duty, and have no regrets." After throwing Thompson's corpse, mangled by a dozen or more musket balls, in the Potomac River, Hunter and Chambers went back to Wagner House to take the life of Stevens. Finding him suffering and probably dying, they spared him and headed out after other raiders with plans to shoot them all.

Other acts of courage countered the vengeful wrath of armed citizens and militiamen. Hostage Joseph Brua ran from the watch room in the enginehouse to aid a critically wounded raider who lay bleeding in the street, and the good Samaritan returned to continue being a hostage as promised. (Later, when Brown sent him to work toward a cease-fire, the shooting became too intense for him to return.) Another act of kindness was by Dr. Starry, who used his horse to shield and save a frightened John A. Copeland. Copeland, a free black raider who had been captured trying to cross the Shenandoah River, was saved by Starry from a potential lynch mob, some of whom were knotting their handkerchiefs amidst shouts of "Hang him, hang him!"

Intervention by a local Presbyterian predicant, Charles White, saved the life of one of Allstadt's slaves. As John Kagi and a few other raiders fled the rifle factory to the Shenandoah, a slave—who was, some say, armed with a pike—ran toward the townsmen and the preacher, who were beckoning the slave to come forward. The slave surrendered to this group of townsmen and informed them that he had been forced to guard the rifle works or forfeit his life. Then, an observer recounted, a "reckless fellow... leveled his musket" virtually point-blank at the black man's head, stating that he had orders from the captain of the Charles Town Company to kill the slave. The parson placed himself in front of the slave and ordered the "reckless" man not to fire, while others seized his weapon.[41]

With such frenzied events, it is inevitable that accounts of the raid would differ; but no accounts differ more than those dealing with the militia actions. One eyewitness, in contrast to a local newspaper's editorial praise of local units, wrote a scathing indictment of the militia's role on Monday, October 17. Except for the Hamtramck Guards' coolness, preparedness, and propriety, according to the commentator, the units were drunken, loudmouthed cowards. Furthermore, while the Hamtramck Guards waited for orders from Colonel Baylor (which never came), the only commands were given by those whom an eyewitness called "drunken fellows, whooping and bellowing like a pack of maddened bulls... too drunk many of them to hold their guns." During the excitement of Monday afternoon, this witness recounted, "the Martinsburg party, drunken and maddened, made an attack upon a building" and released prisoners who could have freed themselves—"had they not been too cowardly." While some of the Martinsburg men "were getting away from this building" (the enginehouse), "some of their own" men "opened fire... upon them and this accounts for" all their casualties. "Late in the evening Colonel Baylor called for twenty volunteers to storm the enginehouse, but could not get a single man from all the brave and bold from Martinsburg, Harper's Ferry, and Charlestown." That afternoon the Charlestown Guards were "scattered in every direction." "Their captain could not get them in their ranks, and did not the whole evening." As for the Harpers Ferry men: "They have not got a man who will stand his ground."

Colonel Robert Baylor, who took from Colonel John Gibson command of the Virginia militia soon after the arrival of men from Shepherdstown and Martinsburg between 3:00 and 4:00 Monday, was not exempt from controversy and criticism. Aggressive leadership, critics asserted, would have subdued Brown without outside help. Soon after the raid, controversies arose over the interpretation of Virginia's militia law and Baylor's right to assume command. State, local, and personal pride led to a brief but contentious and deteriorating relationship between Colonel Baylor and Governor Wise, culminating in the governor's removal of Baylor from militia duty on October 31, 1859. Wise said that Baylor had never legally been in command of all the local militia; upon releasing him from service, the governor accused Colonel Baylor of having acted "without orders and improperly interfering with command." An auditing board rejected Baylor's demand for $193.98 for 20 days of service. Instead they ruled he was entitled to payment for only four days of service, as he had disbanded the only company under his command and gone home. Confusion over who was in command certainly did not benefit militia activities on the critical day, October 17. Colonel Gibson did not recognize Baylor's command until midafternoon. Nevertheless, the truth regarding the leadership and actions of local militia units lies somewhere among the praise from the local press, Colonel Gibson's reports, and the picture of a motley, bloodthirsty, uncontrollable, drunken mob. Despite elements of the latter and numerous shortcomings, some quite serious and repugnant, the militia units and citizens had all but captured Brown.[42]

The erratic behavior of the militiamen—many with inadequate weaponry and lacking bayonets—may explain why Lee changed his mind about having them charge the enginehouse on Tuesday morning. His becoming aware of their lack of discipline probably made him turn to the more trustworthy professionals to rescue civilian hostages and subdue their captors through the use of the blade, not the bullet. Over the years it has been repeated on the printed page that Shriver and Gibson turned down Lee's offer that select men of their units make the attack, saying the risk was too great for men with families. Shriver's report remained unpublished and hidden among long-forgotten boxes marked "Miscellaneous Papers" in the Maryland archives until near the end of 20th century, and it refutes the traditional explanation. At daylight Tuesday morning, October 18, select militiamen, says Shriver, formed a storming party that waited for some time "to discharge the duty of making the assault" until "it was announced to me & by me to the companies that Col. Lee had determined to storm the position with the Marines alone."[43]

At 6:30 a.m. Tuesday Lee ordered Israel Green to pick 12 men for the storming party. They were to use only their bayonets and cautioned not to attack the black men Brown had seized unless they fought. They were to direct their assault only at the insurgents. While assembling the storming party, the Frederick and Baltimore militias were positioned adjacent to the enginehouse; Lee had recently ordered the Baltimore men from the shore across the Potomac bridge. The excitement was too much for one militiaman from Baltimore who, according to a Baltimore paper, had a "fit" (seizure) and had to be carried away.

As the drama and suspense of the impending attack increased, the streets around the armory were cleared, and 20 or more roughs from Baltimore, bearing a musket or rifle, huddled at the armory gate, anxious to fire on the insurgents. They were first warned not to endanger the civilian hostages by firing, and then were ordered away from the scene. After selecting 12 of his best men, Green picked a dozen more as a reserve, stationing them alongside the enginehouse with "a number of men provided with sledge hammers to batter in the doors." Lieutenant Green walked to the stone abutment between the two large wooden doors that were the entrances to the enginehouse. He stood there ready to order the assault if Brown failed to capitulate. Stuart, with Samuel Strider of Harpers Ferry, bore a flag of truce and gave Lee's written demands to the old man, pointing his carbine at Brown through the ponderous wooden doors with heavy wrought-iron nails cracked open about four inches.

The man they called Smith stood inches away, with his body pressed against the four-inch opening, and Stuart immediately recognized him as the troublemaker he had dealt with in Kansas, John "Old Osawatomie" Brown. The raider leader countered Lee's demand with his own, the same he had repeated many times the day before. Stuart said the only conditions Lee would accept were those in the written note. Brown remained, as Washington witnessed throughout all negotiations, "very solicitous to have some capitulation by which he could gain his terms, and very obstinate in reference to his terms." The stalemated parley, Stuart recalls, "was a long one" with the raider captain presenting "in every possible shape with admirable tact, but all amounting to the only condition he would surrender upon to be allowed to escape with his party. Armistead Ball, Stuart stated, "appealed to Brown on the grounds of humanity to the prisoners" and his own men "not to persist in spilling blood." Brown replied he was aware of what he was doing and the consequences; "that he was already proclaimed an outlaw" with $3,500 on his head. Stuart continues, "Many of the prisoners begged me with tears to ask Col Lee to come & see him [Brown]." It is claimed that Lewis Washington was not one of them, blurting out, "Never mind us, fire!"

Lee stood calmly on a slight elevation outside the armory, 40 feet from the enginehouse. He was dressed in civilian clothing, unarmed, without the facial hair for which he was later known, bearing just a dark mustache. Recognizing the voice

Brown trapped in the fire engine house waiting for the US Marines to attack. (*Frank Leslie's Weekly*, Library of Congress)

of a family member and descendant of the American Revolutionary leader and first president, Lee is said to have responded, "The old revolutionary blood does tell!" Washington's last statement and Lee's response may be more fiction than fact.

Waving his large plumed hat, similar to that which he would wear as a Confederate cavalry leader, Stuart made the prearranged signal. A crowd he estimated at 2,000 spectators observed intently; their eyes were drawn to the bright uniforms of the Marines, with their blue trousers, dark blue frockcoat, white belt, and French fatigue cap. Two Marines—some claim three—started pounding with heavy sledgehammers on the now closed doors as those inside "fired rapidly at the point where the blows were given upon the door." The strenuous blows had no effect except to make a loud noise, as the doors were fastened from the inside with rope, allowing some give and absorbing the impact of the blows. An additional impediment was two old fire engines braced against the door with fastened brakes, which Brown had hurriedly moved to block any unwanted entrance. Soon realizing the futility of their action, Green ordered the hammering to desist. "Just then my eye," Green later testified, "caught sight of a [heavy] ladder, lying a few feet [25 yards] from the enginehouse." He ordered the reserve of 12 men "to catch it up and use it as a battering-ram." Immediately dropping their muskets and seizing the ladder, from 25 yards away they started running toward the enginehouse. Despite the "tremendous assault" the first attempt failed to penetrate the door. The second try with a 40-foot ladder broke through, creating what Green described as "a ragged hole low down in the right-hand door," which was "splintered and cracked some distance upward. I instantly stepped from my position in front of the stone abutment, and entered the opening" safely, as "Brown had moments before emptied his carbine," firing at the opening. Green continued, "Getting to my feet, I ran to the right of the engine which stood behind the door, passed quickly to the rear of the house, and came up between the two engines... The first person I saw was Colonel Washington, who was standing near the horse cart, at the front of the enginehouse. On one knee, a few feet to my left, knelt a man with a carbine in his hand, just pulling the lever to reload. 'Hello, Green,'" were Washington's words as, according to Green, "he reached his hand to me. I grasped it with my left hand, having my saber uplifted in my right, and he said, pointing to the kneeling figure, 'This is Osawatomie.'" As he said this, Brown turned his head to see whom Washington was speaking to.

> The whole scene passed so rapidly that it hardly made a distinct impression upon my mind. I can only recall the fleeing picture of [a hatless] old man kneeling with a carbine in his hand, with a long gray beard falling away from his face, looking quickly and keenly toward the danger that he was aware had come upon him... Quicker than I thought I brought my saber down with all my strength upon his head. He was moving as the blow fell, and I suppose I did not strike him where I intended, for he received a deep saber cut in the back of his neck. He fell senseless on his side, then rolled over on his back. I think he had just fired as I reached Washington, for the marine who followed me [Private Luke Quinn] received a bullet wound in the abdomen...

Quinn died from his wound within a short time. The fatal shot that struck him might have been fired by any number of the insurgents, "but I think it was from Brown." Green recalled, "Instinctively as Brown fell I gave him a saber thrust in the left breast. The sword I carried was a light uniform weapon, and either not having a point or striking something hard in Brown's accouterments" not only did not penetrate, but bent double and remained so, thus not inflicting a fatal wound.

"By this time," Green said, "three or four of my men were inside," as was their paymaster, Major W. W. Russell. In an impulsive act Russell also leaped through the opening, carrying only a rattan switch. "They came rushing in like tigers, as a storming assault in not a play-day sport" as one of their comrades was dying and another, Private Matthew Ruppert, was suffering from a ghastly facial wound. He was shot in the mouth but would survive.[44] Despite Jeremiah Anderson's and Dauphin Thompson's cries of surrender, both were fatally impaled by bayonets as the Marines found, according to Green, "one man [Thompson] skulking under the engine, and pinned another fellow [Anderson] up against the rear wall." With the other insurgents taken prisoner, Green testified he "ordered his men to spill no more blood, and the contest ended. The whole fight had not lasted over three minutes."

With the fight over, Green had a chance to observe the enginehouse, which was so thick with smoke from black gunpowder it was difficult to see across the room. He found in the rear behind the "left-hand engine" the huddled hostages—all but

Sketch showing Marines using a ladder to batter a hole in one of the engine house doors. (*Frank Leslie's Weekly*, Library of Congress)

the intrepid Washington, who remained in the front. Those in the rear "were the sorriest lot of people" Green said he ever saw. "Begrimed and soiled" by their long imprisonment, "without food for over 36 hours, in constant dread of being shot… huddled up in the corner where lay the body of Brown's son and one or two others of the insurgents who had been killed." Washington's filthy condition made him refuse to leave the enginehouse until he had a pair of gloves to hide his dirty hands. When he did leave, wrote a Baltimore reporter, "The mountains reverberated with the shouts of the multitude"; people crowded the streets and railroad platform and hung out all the windows in the vicinity. The main interest of one eyewitness, Henry Kyd Douglas, in watching those leaving the fort was not the appearance of Brown (whom he had months earlier helped with his stalled wagon full of disguised weapons) but that of Lewis Washington. Douglas admired the colonel's "coolness and nonchalance." "[When] walking quietly away from the fort with some excited friends, he took from his pocket a pair of dark-green kid gloves and began pulling them on" as he walked toward the Wagner House. When a friend asked if he would like to "take something" to eat or drink as he walked toward the Wagner House, a smiling Washington said, "Thank you, I will. It seems a month since I've had one."[45]

The details of the capture of Old Osawatomie are conflicted and incomplete. This confusing event lasted only a couple of minutes in a dark smoke-filled room amid heightened emotions, shots being fired, and the swirling movement of Marines rushing in. It was difficult for witnesses to explain precisely what had happened. Over the years faded memories muddled the view even more. Green's and J.E.P. Daingerfield's articles on the capture of Brown, written a quarter century after the event (1885), and Lewis Washington's interview by a reporter shortly after the raid, were major influences molding the traditional version of what happened. In Washington's version of Brown's behavior, he states, "all the insurgents wished to surrender but Brown... [who] exhibited during his capture coolness and courage seldom equaled." Oswald G. Villard's copious influential biography of John Brown, first published in 1910, perpetuated the idea that during the firing "he never faltered." For a century and half the insurrectionist leader has been depicted as courageous, defiant, refusing to surrender, fighting to the end until he was captured after being knocked senseless from blows by Green's light sword. Washington's claim of Brown's defiance, coolness, and bravery has credibility in describing his behavior during the raid up to the time the Marines rushed in; and then it runs contrary to other witnesses' testimony of a defenseless Brown with his head down and arms up in a feeble attempt to protect himself from Green's attack. Green admitted he "saw little of the situation until the fight was over." His memory of Brown "with a long grey beard" was inaccurate, as Brown had severely trimmed his whiskers. Neither Green nor Lee mentioned the Marines firing after they witnessed two comrades becoming casualties—one was hit fatally, and the other was wounded, losing part of his lower lip. The men were wounded while manning the ladder to batter through the door, and not after entering the enginehouse as Green and tradition contend. Concerned for their welfare, the Marines fired their weapons to clear the way for their entrance, disregarding orders to use only bayonets (and causing the prisoners, at Colonel Washington's suggestion, to raise their hands to distinguish themselves from the raiders).

Seven of the eight hostages who testified at Brown's trial agreed their captor treated them well but gave contradictory testimony over who fired and surrendered. The senior Allstadt stated, "Think that Capt. Brown shot the marine who was killed; saw him fire." Lewis Washington and Daingerfield contradicted not only each other but themselves. Terrance Byrne testified that prior to the Marines' entrance, their beating sledgehammers on the door caused Brown and his men to fire and then close the door and ram a fire-engine against it. Then a brief interlude occurred during which a frightened raider, possibly Dauphin Thompson, turned to Brown, saying, "Captain, I believe I will surrender." Brown responded, "Sir, you can do as you please." The man, who had been on his knees, got up, turned to Byrne and said, "Hallo, 'surrender' for me." Byrne supposedly "hallooed at top" of his lungs, along with John E. P. Daingerfield, but they could not make themselves heard outside. Edwin Coppoc, it is said, now urged Thompson to get down, "or have your head shot off."

Jeremiah Anderson, becoming more apprehensive about his fate, joined Thompson in wanting to surrender as both men laid down their weapons, recalled Daingerfield, but during the attack they picked them back up to renew the fight; and both lost their lives to Marine bayonets. Daingerfield also testified he saw Edwin Coppoc try to fire twice, but each time the cap exploded. Brown himself seems to have surrendered before the entrance of the Marines. He adamantly insisted the afternoon after his capture and on subsequent occasions that he spared the lives of his attackers by stopping the shooting and surrendering, not for his benefit but for others'—but the repeated loud yells of surrender went unheard outside.

In stark contrast to Daingerfield's claims, the day after the end of the raid Lewis Washington stressed that Brown resisted to the end and gave "no cry of surrender." Only one of his men shouted, "I surrender," as the door was being smashed in. Washington said Brown shouted out, "There's one surrenders—give him quarter," immediately firing his gun at the door as the Marines and raiders exchanged fire. When cross-examined at Brown's trial, Washington repudiated the above, saying he was kept with other hostages at the back of the enginehouse for safety, so he could not say for sure whether the Marines fired after breaking into the room or who said what. "The noise was great, and several shouted from inside that someone had surrendered the prisoners." Confusing matters more was the testimony of John Allstadt, who claimed he saw Brown fire or point his gun at the door. Armistead Ball stated several times under oath that he never saw Brown "fire from the engine house."

The sequence of the leathernecks entering through the broken door is also not clear. Tradition has Lieutenant Green first, followed by Major Russell, and then Privates Luke Quinn and Matthew Rupert. It is inferred the first two men were not fired upon because the raiders were surrendering, and except for Green's flimsy blade, they had no weapons. The ominous appearance of the two Marine privates with fixed bayonets on their guns is said to have heightened the threat to Brown's men, who fired, mortally wounding Quinn and maiming Rupert.

Years after the raid Daingerfield drastically changed and embellished his version of the end of the raid and depicted himself as a key figure, and Israel Green as leaping through the air, superhero style, to strike the raiders' leader. Green would refute this as fanciful.

Termination of the raid, according to a New York *Daily Tribune* reporter, was not brought about by Israel Green, but by Major W. W. Russell. Although Lieutenant Green was in command of the Marines until Lee's arrival, the secretary of the navy had requested Major Russell accompany them, but because Russell was the paymaster he could not exercise command. Nevertheless, as the Marines attacked, Russell risked his life as a number of shots had been fired by both sides; he rushed in unarmed and was the first man to squeeze through the shattered door. Perhaps using his imagination more than relying on fact, the reporter states that Russell heard someone give a cry of surrender and ordered the Marines to cease firing. Seeing another volley was about to be fired, he grabbed a Sharps rifle from one of Brown's men, pointed it at his own men, and said he would "shoot the man who fired another gun." Later, in the paymaster's office where Russell had Brown and

Stevens placed, the bloodied raider leader looked up, recognized the major, and said, "You entered first. I could have killed you, but I spared you." Appreciatively, Russell bowed and said, "I thank you." Russell let a reporter from The Baltimore *Exchange* into the room. The prone raider leader answered questions but seemed stunned and lacking in any understanding of the reaction of the angry crowd, complaining that "the crowd who were clamorous for his blood were treating him unkindly and unfairly, after the kindness and leniency he had shown the citizens and the town."[46]

Seeing the few remaining insurrectionists captured and the hostages freed, witnesses felt relief mingled with trauma at the grotesque aftermath. Eleven stiff and torn raider corpses were strewn about the town in several buildings, on the street, and in the two rivers. Four local men lay lifeless, and eight wounded received care in more dignified surroundings. Brown and the other wounded were carried out of the enginehouse and placed on the grass on the armory ground, including Jeremiah Anderson, who was dragged out while vomiting gore. Stuart took the raider leader's bowie knife as a memento. A mob pressed forward to get a look at Brown, whose hair was matted with blood, Anderson, and the fatally wounded Marine, whose screams of agony penetrated the air. Nearby Watson Brown was dying a lingering death that would take his life 24 hours after his capture. After seeing this tall, handsome man just a week past his 24th birthday, a Richmond militiaman wrote, "I could not help feel sorry for him. He suffered such excruciating pain from his wounds that before he died he seem to have grown to be an old man." In front of the enginehouse Old Osawatomie, according to Green, regained consciousness, and it was discovered his injuries, cuts on his head and side, were not fatal as had been assumed.

Once the contest was over militiamen and civilians rushed forward onto the armory grounds as authorities shouted "Order!" in an attempt to restrain them. It was becoming more difficult to control the throng of armed onlookers, who greeted the captives with unnerving shouts of "Shoot them! Shoot them!" and a repeated chorus of "Hang them!" as they pushed forward to get a glimpse of the dead and wounded, especially Brown. In response, Major Russell moved the raiders inside where they could be more easily protected by sentinels standing guard over them.

Dr. William Tyler Jr., who attended the dying Marine, and two other physicians accompanying the Frederick militia rendered what service they could, including wrapping a bandage on Brown's head. Also providing medical aid was Dr. David M'Laughlin who found, according to the Baltimore *Sun,* on the "notorious 'Ossawottamie Brown' the sum of $305 in gold, which was handed over… to major Russell of the marine corps." A militiaman from Richmond, Parke Poindexter, unaware of all that was done and the limits of what the physicians could do, thought medical care was given selectively. He wrote, "Those wounded the surgeons supposed to be mortally so were permitted to remain without sympathy or medical relief; the rest were taken" to a place "where their wounds were dressed." The Baltimore

(Left to right top) Dauphin Thompson, Jeremiah Anderson, Oliver Brown, (left to right bottom) Stewart Taylor, Virginia Governor Henry Wise. (Library of Congress)

Sun reported that the arsenal grounds were where the wounded Marine Quinn was taken: "the apparent place of his death."

When the freed hostages started leaving the place of their confinement, Shields "Emperor" Green discarded his weapons, the carbine and bowie knife in its sheath that each raider carried. He tried to avoid arrest by pretending to be one of the slaves captured by the raiders, but the ruse failed when Washington informed the Marines Green was in the raiding party.

Those in bondage scurried back to their homes by Tuesday night. They arrived several days before their masters; Washington spent two days with his friend Governor Wise, and Allstadt's harrowing and frigid experience left him with hoarseness and a cold. Allstadt was unable for several days to visit his critically ill and most valuable slave, Phil, a 20-year-old who had followed Brown's commands to make holes in the enginehouse wall to fire through. Phil was jailed in Charles Town, where he was suffering even greater ill effects than his master. Allstadt visited Phil and found him too ill to move, dying from pneumonia. All the other Allstadt slaves returned, as did Washington's, with two exceptions: Jim, whom Washington had hired from Dr.

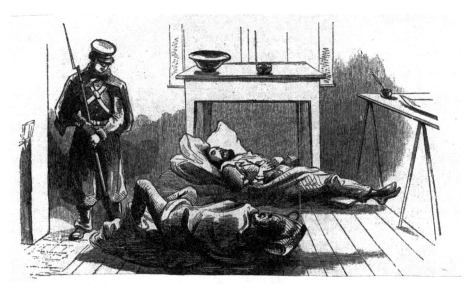

Sketch by David Strother of John Brown and Aaron Stevens in the paymaster's office. (*Frank Leslie's Weekly*, Library of Congress)

Fuller, had drowned in the canal while escaping from Hall's Rifle Works; and the colonel's servant had escaped from Owen Brown early Tuesday morning. According to Washington his slave fled to the Potomac River and was "put across by a white woman in a boat." Thursday after the raid Washington returned home and took his "negro boy" who escaped from Owen Brown to Maryland to catch his horses, said to be "running up the mountain." Once on the Maryland side of the Potomac the slave, said Washington, "showed me where he had hidden" a double-barreled shotgun he had been given to carry prior to his escape.

The thousands Brown thought would flock to him proved a wishful dream. Even the few in bondage whom he thought he was liberating did not support what he was doing; the uncertainty of their fate dimmed any ardor for their participation. Years later Annie Brown Adams wrote, "My father expected the slaves to recognize and accept him, as a Moses, sent to deliver them from bondage. This they did not do, and I do not think [they] even at this day, have any, or at least, very little appreciation of the sacrifice made by John Brown and his men on their account."

Southerners argued Brown failed to get enslaved people to flee to him because he did not understand the bond between slaves and their owners. Examples illustrated in the press included a group of black people in Georgetown the day Brown was captured who offered their services to the mayor to help suppress the insurrection; Bawley, a slave in Culpepper, who was supposedly given permission by his owner to go to Charles Town to get a shot at an abolitionist; the Virginia state legislators who contemplated raising a regiment of free blacks to repel future abolitionist incursions;

and the wish of Governor Wise to guard Brown and others at Charles Town with a majority of slaves, with one white man for every 10 black. The Richmond *Enquirer* reported a number of slaves in Staunton, Virginia, wanted to contribute money for the cost of volunteer guards in the raid's aftermath.

The picture of slaves repudiating Brown's attempt to free them understates what happened, while the opposite view of raider Osborne Anderson in *A Voice From Harper's Ferry*—stressing the extensive involvement by black people—seems to overstate the case. The possibility of freedom naturally appealed to those in bondage. One of Washington's slaves, who was away when the raiders struck Beall-Air, voluntarily joined them at Allstadt's. Tidd stated that the Allstadt and Washington slaves who accompanied him to the Kennedy farm were ecstatic about being free until learning of the raid's failure. Two men informed him they had planned to run away the next summer. The failure of the raid brought about the chilling possibility of being captured and severally punished or sold to work in the cotton fields of the Deep South. This prospect drained enthusiasm for continued black resistance. Some were unsure you could trust a white man leading a revolt and felt more comfortable pursuing freedom on foot, using the Underground Railroad, than through combat.

The raid ended before Brown could attract more supporters, free or enslaved. Free black people in Chambersburg claimed they would have come to Brown's aid if it had lasted longer. Washington and others claimed their slaves' behavior after the raid was subdued but returned to normalcy. This claim was also echoed in Southern newspapers. But a significant change occurred among slaves in the area of the raid, according to local resident Jennie Chambers, who said they were less reliable and secretly congregated without their owners' awareness. Reverend Charles White wrote in early November 1859, "Several masters have been beaten or attacked by their servants." Torching of slave-owners' property increased. Slaves were eager to know as much as possible about the raid yet were fearful of their owners' knowledge of their interest. They secretly spread information among themselves.[47]

Early Tuesday morning, soon after Brown's capture, Washington found his carriage in front of the enginehouse "a good deal shot to pieces," as the recipient of numerous stray shots. His horses were more fortunate, safe in the stable, although without feed and water for almost as long a duration as the 40 hours their owner claimed he was without sustenance. The colonel testified he also retrieved the sword Frederick the Great allegedly gave to General George Washington, which Brown "carried in his hand all day Monday, and when the attacking party came on he laid it on a fire engine, and after the rescue I [Washington] got it."[48]

Confiscation of Brown's Property

While Washington retrieved his cherished relic, and soon after Lee had secured the captive raiders inside on Tuesday morning, Lee sent the Baltimore Greys on the other side of the Potomac to search for Cook, the only raider they were aware at the time had escaped. The Greys were also told to seize weapons deposited in the schoolhouse. The black man who had run off from Owen Brown and Cook's slumbering party near the Kennedy house had done what they feared, but he apparently only informed authorities that Cook was in the mountains. The movement to the old schoolhouse had finally occurred after much confusion and the insistence of a frustrated John C. Unseld, a retired mechanic in his mid-fifties who rented out his farmland; he and Byrne were the only slaveholders in the neighborhood. Unseld and Brown had visited each other but never entered the other's house. Unseld learned of the raid Monday morning and later that day was told by his son's teacher that Cook and several others had seized the schoolhouse. Tuesday morning Unseld went to Harpers Ferry, urging militia officers and political leaders to have militiamen sent to the schoolhouse, telling them Cook and others were still there. He was first rebuffed by officers from Charles Town, Colonel Baylor of the Virginia militia and Captain Simms of Frederick, Maryland. They gave the excuses that their company was dismissed, they could not do it then, and they lacked authority. Frustrated, Unseld had attorney and Democratic politician Charles Faulkner relay his request to Colonel Lee. The colonel replied that a company had been sent an hour earlier. Inquiring what company was sent and told it was the Baltimore Greys, a now-upset Unseld told Faulkner this was incorrect; Unseld had a short time before overtaken their captain on the way up Camp Hill and requested troops be sent to the schoolhouse, to be told he would do so after he had breakfast.

Seeing Congressmen Boteler, Unseld asked him to get Lee "to send a company over to the school-house" and to tell him "Nobody will go there." Again a message came back, this time stating the Greys had gone several hours earlier. After having Lee pointed out to him, Unseld, by now annoyed, walked up to the colonel. Lee told him, "My dear friend, they have gone two hours ago." Unseld convinced Lee this was not the case, and accompanied Lee to a lieutenant, and then the captain of the Baltimore Greys; both claimed their orders to go to the schoolhouse had been countermanded. Less than pleased, Lee immediately sent the company with Unseld as their guide to the site of the school, a mile away.

At the building the men removed a door latch in the form of a chain running through a staple with a stick holding it together. Unseld and two militiamen pushed strenuously, but the door kept springing shut. After three or four shoves it was open enough to enter, and to their surprise, they found no one there. Instead there were about 15 boxes, about four feet long and a foot square. The men eagerly pried them open to discover new 1852 model Sharps rifles, revolvers, and lying about, a number of picks. The 40 to 50 men there, Baltimore militiamen and curious locals, didn't hesitate to help themselves to rifles and pistols—and justified these acts out of need and as the spoils of war. It was decided to take the remaining weapons back to Harpers Ferry, but they lacked means until they spotted Washington's wagon behind bushes in a ravine south of the schoolhouse. Near the wagon they found three horses, one tied to the wagon, the others loose. They caught one of the loose animals and hitched it along with the tied-up horse to the wagon. The remaining weapons were loaded onto this wagon and onto a one-horse conveyance belonging to a local named Beck. When no one wanted to drive the team, Unseld volunteered, having one of the militiamen ride his horse back to town, where the weapons were turned over to the acting superintendent of the armory, Archibald Kitzmiller.

After learning about the weapons at the Kennedy farm, between 11:00 a.m. and noon, Lee sent Jeb Stuart and Israel Green, and a few Marines who went on foot, along with Washington's gladly loaned wagon. They were accompanied by Unseld and his young son, who apparently had been with his dad since early morning.

The deserted dwelling was entered first, and the men found it had been ransacked earlier by nearby neighbors and folks from Sharpsburg. Alexander Boteler later collected 50 to 100 letters carried off by Brown's neighbors. Greeting Green and the company were the barks and growls of a pup a Baltimore reporter describes in exaggerated prose as a "huge savage looking mastiff, tied with a rope to the railing" of steps to the second floor. In the kitchen they found two barrels of flour, a large quantity of sausages and cured hams, several pounds of butter and lard, abandoned tin utensils, and a cookstove where embers still smoldered and water remained hot in its boiler. Ascending to the attic, they found six mattresses stuffed with corn husks. But it was the floor under the attic where they found incriminating items. Unseld testified that no weapons were found in the house, which was devoid of furniture except for a table and stove, but what caught the eye of this investigating group was a number of carpet-bags, trunks, and papers, many in a large box. In these containers and strewn about were found small, elaborate maps of seven Southern states. The maps bore ink crosses, some circled, marking extensive targets for slave liberation. They also found an accurately traced map from Chambersburg to the Kennedy house, Forbes' Manual, the "Provisional Constitution," "General Order No. 1," Brown's "Vindication of the Invasion," the roll of Brown's men, along with what many Southerners would consider the most incriminating of all: more than 100 letters, some from secret Northern backers. To the emotionally agitated mind of the suspicious Southerner, all this would be looked upon as conclusive proof of a vast Northern conspiracy sponsoring attacks throughout the South. Even Unseld's young son expressed his immediate disapproval when he found a map of the Kansas Territory in the Kennedy House. He tore the map to shreds.

Green and Unseld were the first to enter the log cabin across the road, leaving a Marine to guard the entrance. They were greeted by boxed firearms and two- to three-foot-high piles of neatly folded quilts—called counterpanes at the time. They opened boxes of men's clothing and boots, knives, forks, spoons, picks, and short- and long-handled shovels that, along with a few found at the house, were intended to be used to dig earthworks. The most imposing numbers of weapons were found in

TARGETED SOUTHERN STATES AFTER VIRGINIA

Brown's original maps were destroyed. The large map is based on newspaper descriptions of the selected counties in four Southern states with a high percentage of slaves. Targeted counties were indicated by cross marks and in a few select areas circled crosses. South Carolina had two places marked with a cross with two circles. Georgia had more than twice the number of targeted counties as any of the other three states, South Carolina, Alabama and Mississippi. The smaller map shows Brown's plan to use the Appalachian Mountains as his invasion route of the lower South.

the cabin's loft. Most of the pikes were piled in a corner next to a window that had been nailed shut. On the floor nearby were two straw ticks with a pike blade under each, where raiders slept, guarding their arsenal. Green ordered Unseld to break the window open. The two men started heaving the pikes out the open window until Unseld became exhausted and refused to continue. Green then had two Marines sent up to finish the task. The pikes and other items far exceeded the capacity of the one wagon to carry them. Curious neighbors eagerly took all the clothing, shovels, and many other items, including pikes. Attempting to get rid of the pikes, Green told the onlookers, "You can have five apiece," and soon upped the amount to 10, and finally to 50. In all, more than 400 were given away before the remaining 483 were taken to the Ferry and delivered to Kitzmiller at the armory. Of those, 175 had broken handles from being thrown from a second-story window.

Nearly 50 different types of items of interest were found in the Kennedy house and cabin, including 625 envelopes; a major-general's sword; 40 shovels; spades; pickaxes; clothes, blankets, and odds and ends to outfit a large number of men; the original 954 pikes delivered to Brown; 102 Sharps rifles bearing the stamp "Massachusetts Manufacturing Company, Chicopee, Mass."; many of the 200 Massachusetts Arms Company revolvers paid for by abolitionist and Brown backer George L. Stearns; and a large quantity of ammunition, including 10 kegs of gunpowder, 13,000 ball cartridges for Sharps rifles (slightly damaged by water), and 23,000 percussion caps for pistols. What was not carried off by individuals would be turned over to the acting superintendent and stored in one of the arsenal buildings.

Poorly armed militiamen and others at Harpers Ferry eagerly awaited the return of the party sent to the Kennedy farm; those waiting wanted to get free weapons like the ones of the Maryland militiamen sent to the schoolhouse. The inadequacy of militia weaponry is cited in the report of Colonel Moore, who stated that of his 135-man Winchester regiment, fewer than 30 had weapons "that would fire with any effect." Moore warned, "If the State expects her volunteers to protect her, she must arm them better." Need, plus the allure of the most advanced firearms, negated restraint and triggered greed. As Stuart and Green's men arrived around 6:00 p.m. militiamen waiting on the Maryland side of the Potomac bridge leaped upon the wagon, helping themselves to weapons and anything else that caught their eye. This practice continued into the town, where men grabbed and contently left with weapons, including some from the arsenal. Unsuccessfully trying to bring about order, Wise made a militia company responsible for distribution. Its members handed out weapons to friends, failing to establish any degree of restraint, let alone order. Half the 200 Sharps carbines and 200 revolvers had been carried away, leaving 104 Sharps rifles and 102 pistols stored in the arsenal. Carrying around captured items had its dangers: George Dillard, a stranger from Staunton in town on business, was mistaken for a raider and was seized, threatened, and detained for walking around with a pike and several blank books in his pockets. The items had been given to him by Governor Wise.[49]

The vocal governor of Virginia had arrived with 200 Richmond militiamen in the afternoon before the return of Stuart and Green. He seemed disappointed his arrival was after the raid had ended, but felt compelled to give numerous speeches during the day and evening in addition to spending much of the afternoon—along with others—interviewing Brown. In a conversation the governor had with the troublemaker he claimed to have told Brown "he need not answer questions unless he chose." The insurrectionist leader replied that "he had nothing to conceal—he had no favor to ask." Brown added something unpleasant to the nervous governor: "he had arms enough for two thousand men, and could get enough for five thousand if they were wanted."

Stuart later wrote he would meet and talk with Wise at Harpers Ferry and again "on the Cars [train] between Harper's Ferry and Charlestown—while they were taking the prisoners to the latter place." Stuart found Wise to be "a queer genius." Upon returning to Richmond, Wise made a speech in which he praised Colonel Lee as "fit for any command on earth." Stuart felt this compliment was correct and allowed that Lee "deserves a gold medal from Virginia." But Stuart was annoyed by the passage in Wise's message to the Virginia legislature in which the governor said, "I telegraphed to Col. Lee to grant no terms [to Brown]—Col. Lee granted no terms…" Stuart wrote, "You see the Old Fox [Wise] makes out by implication that Col. Lee was acting in obedience to his [orders]... [What a] gross and outrageous injustice of Col. Lee who if he ever received such a dispatch received it after the whole affair was over."

In the letter written to his mother the last day of January 1860, Stuart expresses his great concern about his own reputation and displays a healthy ego. He complains about false newspaper accounts of his role at Harpers Ferry. Stuart states that Green complained to him that his sword was so dull (being a common dress sword) he could not hurt Brown with it, "but my Sabre" was heavier and "like a razor." He continues, "If I had commanded the Stormers my sabre would have saved Va. the expense of B's trial." Stuart was pleased that Lee, in his report on Harpers Ferry, expressed thanks to "Russell (Israel Green) and myself, he mentioned by name first which in view of my being junior in rank to both is a significant compliment to me."[50]

There were other untruths that emerged from Brown's infamous raid. Over the years questionable to untrue stories frequently circulated in the press—claims by Brown defenders of abuse of the captured raiders. They include a farmer spitting "his tobacco expectoration into the throat of dying Anderson," reporter John Hanna attempting to stomp on Old Brown as he lay on the ground, and Brown lying on the floor of an armory building with undressed wounds for 18 hours. One of the more accurate accounts was recorded by one of the onlookers at the surrender scene. A southerner from South Carolina, C. W. Tayleure was a Baltimore newspaper reporter who strongly disapproved of what Old Brown and his men had done, but was greatly impressed with their "serenity, calm courage, and devotion to duty." He was especially drawn to Brown's dying son. Watson's calmness amidst intense pain, the grime covering his face, and his penetrating stare fascinated the reporter and evoked his sympathy. He brought Watson a cup of water and "improvised a couch for him out of a bench, with a pair of overalls for a pillow." Tayleure recounts his talk with Watson: "'What brought you're here?' He replies very patiently, 'Duty, sir.'" After a pause the reporter asked, "Is it then your idea of duty to shoot men down upon their own hearth-stones for defending their rights?" Exhausted, Watson replied, "I am dying; I cannot discuss the question; I did my duty as I saw it." This conversation occurred in the compartment of the enginehouse (watch house) adjoining that in which the defense had been made, and was listened to by young Edwin Coppoc with perfect equanimity, and by Shields Green with uncontrollable terror as a guard stood nearby. Despite his calmness, Coppoc was deeply moved by the plight of his suffering comrade Watson Brown. Watson had been shot at 10:00 Monday morning, and despite being in great pain at around 3:00 that afternoon, he fought bravely during the charge against them. After that Coppoc wrote Watson "kept getting worse" until around 3:00 Wednesday morning, "when he died." He suffered greatly. During those last hours Watson "complained of the hardness of the bench on which he was lying" and Coppoc "begged hard for a bed, or even a blanket, but could obtain none for him. I pulled off my coat and put it under him and placed his head in my lap, in which position he died without a groan or struggle." [51]

Watson's father and the muscular Stevens—who was taken from the Wagner House as ordered by Major Russell to a nearby building containing the armory offices—lay next to each other according to writer Oswald D. Villard. As described by the biographer, they had "clotted and tangled hair, their faces, hands and clothing powder-stained and blood smeared" as they lay on makeshift beds covered with old bedding. An onlooker attracted by the unfolding drama, who had hurried that morning by train from his home in nearby Martinsburg, was one of their early visitors. David N. Strother, a popular illustrator for *Harper's Weekly* who signed his work "Porte Crayon", first witnessed the town as crowded with military of varying arms, uniforms, and levels of organization—from the quiet efficiency of the Marines to "half armed, half drunk and noisy militiamen" who amused themselves by shouting at the raider corpses in the Potomac. Walking past the arsenal to the armory, Strother saw the unnerving "bloody corpse" of Dangerfield Newby, "whose glassy staring eyes and fallen jaw was hideous to behold." He wrote, a "dog was smelling the mass of coagulated blood surrounding his head as a couple of hogs were rooting at the body." Moving on to the armory grounds, he saw three more "ghastly stiff" bodies in and outside the enginehouse, and beside the wall, "Jerry Anderson wallowing in death spasms and half clothed in vestments grimed with dirt and blood." A Marine protected "the dying wretch from disturbance, while a crowd, greedy of horrors" pressed forward "to get a look at him." Suddenly in "the midst of this tragic scene" Strother "heard a voice, speaking in tones of petulant rebuke to the rude men. It was a mountain beau with a girl on each arm, who seemed disgusted and astonished at the want of manners among the vulgar" and said "'Gentlemen, just give room here. Can't you stand back and let the ladies see the corpses?'"

A friend beckoned the Martinsburg man to enter as he passed a window of the building containing the offices, including that of the superintendent and paymaster. Upon entering, Strother saw a priest kneeling beside Luke Quinn, whose pain induced "cries and screams made one's flesh creep." When the priest attempted to visit Brown, Congressmen Boteler claims he witnessed Brown angrily shout, "Get out to here—I don't want you about me—get out." The clergymen then bowed and left.

Near the dying Marine, in the adjoining office, Strother found Brown and Stevens. Both were guarded by a sentinel. Strother described coming upon "a stout comely man" lying with his hands "folded helplessly across his breast," motionless. His breathing was barely perceptible, and he occasionally moved his eyes from side to side. Strother wrote that the second man was an older man lying "with his head on a leather traveling sack" and his body covered with an old quilt, with his feet "near a fire which had been hastily kindled in the fireplace." The elderly man's "strongly marked face, iron grey hair and white beard dirty and matted with blood" had "fresh puddles oozing from wounds in his head," collecting "on the floor and traveling bag." Strother did not know these men or their history when he was informed they were John Brown, "the leader of the robber band," and his lieutenant, Aaron Stevens. He started quietly sketching them when movement and noise in armory yard caused Strother's acquaintance to exclaim, "They are putting up a scaffold," as he ran to the window. Hearing this comment, according to Strother, Stevens lay motionless as usual, "but the unnatural restlessness of the eyes betrayed his emotions." Strothers said Brown "began turning side to side, his eyes rolled wildly and his groans drowning the cries of the wounded [Marine], denoting the most ungovernable fear."

The guard, seeing the situation differently, tried to ease Brown's pain. The captain agreed to being comforted by being turned and given several sips of water. The old man became calmer, claimed Strother, when informed that what his friend had heard was only nosy men rummaging through Brown's wagon, discovered behind a building. But soon anxiety returned as alarming threats were uttered by men passing the window. Strother discontinued his sketching and soon left with several authorities who came to check on Brown, treating him civilly and reassuring him as he "begged that he might not be given up to the mob to be lynched."

Brown's post-capture panic is also the assessment of Winchester militiaman Lewis T. Moore. After serving as a colonel in the Confederate army he wrote to a friend, "John Brown at the time of his capture and for an hour after his capture, was more stricken and paralyzed with fear than an human being I ever saw before or since this occasion… During our late civil war I saw men in all situations, but in the entire time of that trying period I saw no man afflicted with fear so seriously as was Brown on the morning of his capture at Harper's Ferry."

Weakened by two nights without sleep, with little or no nourishment, the stress of combat, the death of one son and fatal wounding of another, and pain from bleeding wounds, Brown's capacity to cope with the trauma was lessened. He believed there was a life-threatening, unruly mob. To die immediately by their hands would abort any opportunity to explain his divine mission and would diminish it, for it might be depicted as the actions of a demented outlaw. He realized for the first time that his years of planning and his God-directed freedom crusade for the enslaved had failed, along with his plan for the hostages to secure his escape. He felt demoralizing terror and was forced to face the reality of the predictions of his sons and his friend Frederick Douglass.

Strother writes that upon meeting Lee, Green and Stuart remarked that Strother "had no prior knowledge about Brown." Strother's interest was piqued, and he returned with Stuart to continue his sketch of the man Stuart had said "is the celebrated John Brown of Kansas notoriety, a man so infamous for his robberies and murders that if people knew his antecedents he would not be permitted to live five minutes." Stuart had little sympathy for Brown, whom he damned and claimed was faking serious injury. Stuart "spoke roughly" to Brown, according to Strother, ordering him to pull down his blanket for the artist to get a better view of his head. But the dirt and blood got in the way of Brown's face, causing Stuart to suggest someone should be sent to clean him up.

Stevens's anger toward Brown expressed in the Wagner House was now replaced with compassion; upon seeing his bloodied leader treated the way Brown was being treated, Strother recorded Stevens's saying, "Yes, it is a shame that a man like that should be maltreated and neglected. Not a surgeon has been near him and no one has paid him the least attention. If there is any manhood in you, and you are not a sett [sic] of old women you should have him cared for." Annoyed, Stuart responded, "You are a son of a bitch, you had better keep silent. Your treatment is to be that of midnight thieves and murderers, not of men taken to honorable warfare." Stuart taunted the prisoners, asking why they hadn't brought their own surgeon. Stevens grew silent. Stuart's belief that Brown was faking serious injury was shared by Congressman Boteler, who also visited Brown that day and sketched him, claiming he found the Old Man standing up and examining the wound in his side.[52]

Interrogation of Brown

Tuesday afternoon more visitors assembled around Brown, forming an impromptu interrogating group averaging about a dozen men, military officers, politicians, reporters, and a few curious onlookers. They included Robert E. Lee, Jeb Stuart, Virginia Governor Henry A. Wise, Senator James Mason of Virginia, Congressmen Clement L. Vallandigham of Ohio and Charles James Faulkner of Virginia (who lived not far away), and prominent locals Colonel Lewis Washington, Andrew Hunter, and David Strother. Reporters furiously scribbled in shorthand. A lengthy three-hour interview took place, much of which would be published in the New York *Herald*. When the *Herald* reporter arrived shortly after 2:00 p.m., he found Brown answering the questions of Senator Mason, who had recently arrived from his home in Winchester, 30 miles away. Shortly after questioning began, Lee offered to clear the room if the two injured prisoners found it annoying or painful. Brown rejected the offer, saying he was "glad to make himself and motives clearly understood." If he had been fearful earlier, as Strother thought, he was not now. The *Herald* reporter writes he was courteous and affable, conversing "freely, fluently and cheerfully, without the slightest manifestation of fear or uneasiness, evidently weighting well his words, and possessing a good command of language." He made a favorable impression on those who heard him. Brown assumed sole responsibility for the raid and its failure. He refused to implicate others while arguing the correctness of his divinely sanctioned duty to free slaves. The interview provided an opportunity to gain respect from many who heard him calmly and lucidly respond to their questions. Listeners were impressed by the depth of his unwavering commitment; he had sacrificed his life for a cause, though it was one the witnesses found repugnant. After the interview Wise would say Brown was "the gamest man I ever saw." Strother, no admirer of Brown—later referring to him as that "greasy old thief"—nevertheless found him more impressive during the interview than the vain Virginia governor. The artist wrote that the old man "answered all questions considerably and directly without attempting argument or prevarication" and candidly stated his objective. Strother said, "That he purposely misstated some things... we have clearly ascertained, but that general tenor of his confession was truthful I am inclined to believe."

The lengthy dialogue was wide ranging and often unrelated as questioners blurted out queries that suddenly came to mind as well as those of longer duration. The questioners considered it an interrogation, but to the old captain it was a press conference, an opportunity to get his message across. He was reluctant to reveal the details of his plans but expansive in explaining his justification, purpose, and the goal of his actions. The topics he covered included the raid, the correctness and morality of what he was doing, Kansas and other places he had traveled to, his supporters, the Kennedy farm, the "Provisional Constitution"—which Brown urged be carefully read—and a compliment from a physician, a Dr. Biggs, on the expertise of Brown's lancing a boil on a woman's neck.

Those who surrounded Brown needed to know whether his actions at Harpers Ferry were part of a Northern conspiracy to encourage those in bondage to violently gain their liberation. The New York *Herald* reporter's coverage was detailed. To Senator Mason's query—"Can you tell us, at least, who furnished the money for your expedition?"—Brown said, "I furnished most of it myself. I cannot implicate others." "If you would tell us who sent you here—who provided the means—that would be useful information of some value," said Mason. "I will answer freely and faithfully about what concerned myself—I will answer anything I can with honor, but not about others," replied Brown. When the Ohio congressman, Clement L. Vallandigham, repeated Mason's question, "Mr. Brown, who sent you here?" Brown answered, "No man sent me here; it was my own prompting and that of my Maker, or that of the devil, whichever you please to ascribe it to. I acknowledge no man in human form." When asked who his advisers were, Brown said, "I cannot answer that," but added, unreassuringly to his listeners, "I have numerous sympathizers in the entire North." To the question "Where did you get arms to take possession of the Armory?" he responded, "I bought them." He was asked, "In what state?" and replied, "That I would not state."

In answering Mason, Brown added that his tardiness in leaving was the reason for his capture, and he was late because of his concern for the hostages. He argued that his restraint and compassion were in marked contrast to the behavior of the militiamen. He said, "It is my own folly that I have been taken. I could easily have saved myself from it had I exercised my own better judgment, rather than yield to my feeling." When asked if he meant he could have saved himself by immediately escaping, he responded in the negative. "I had the means to make myself secure without escape, but I allowed myself to be surrounded by a force by being too tardy." "Tardy in getting away?" asked Mason. Said Brown:

I should have gone away; but I had thirty-odd prisoners, whose wives and daughters were in tears over their safety, and I felt for them. Besides, I wanted to allay the fears of those who believed we came here to burn and kill. For this reason I allowed the train to cross the bridge, and gave them full liberty to pass on. I did it only to spare the feelings of those passengers and their families, and to allay the apprehensions that you had got here in your vicinity a band of men who had no regard for life and property, nor any feelings of humanity.

This prompted charges he and his men had shot down innocent citizens. Mason said, "But you killed people passing along the streets quietly." "Well, sir, if there was anything of that kind done, it was without my knowledge," countered the captive raider leader. "Your own citizens, who were my prisoners, will tell you that every possible means were taken to prevent it. I did not allow my men to fire, nor even return a fire, when there was danger of killing those we regarded as innocent person, if I could help it. They will tell you that we allowed ourselves to be fired at repeatedly and did not return it." More than one bystander could be heard stating, "That is not so" and pointing out, "You killed an unarmed man [Beckham] at the corner of the house over there [at the water tank] and another besides." "See here my friend," responded Brown, "it is useless to dispute or contradict the reports of your own neighbors who were my prisoners."

Brown also countered others who condemned him. When a uniformed militiaman asked the number of men used in the raid and was told it was 18, he asked, "What in the world did you suppose you could do here in Virginia with that number of men?" "Young man," said Brown, "I don't wish to discuss that question." "You could not do anything," responded the militiaman. "Well, perhaps your ideas and mine on military subjects would differ materially," said Brown. When asked what his wages were as commander in chief, he said, "None." Stuart responded, "The wages of sin is death." The old abolitionist countered, "I would not have made such a remark to you, if you had been a prisoner and wounded in my hands." Someone called Brown a "robber," to which he responded "You [slaveholders] are the robbers. If you have your opinions about me, I have my opinions about you." The governor of Virginia then said, "Mr. Brown, the silver of your hair is reddened by the blood of crime, and it is meet that you should eschew these hard allusions and think upon eternity." "Governor," Brown answered, "from appearance [I am] not more than fifteen or twenty years [ahead of you] in the journey to that eternity of which you kindly warn me; and whether my tenure here shall be fifteen months, or fifteen days, or fifteen hours, I am equally prepared to go. There is an eternity behind and an eternity before, and the little speck in the center, however long, is but comparatively a minute." Brown concluded his countering argument: "The difference between your tenure and mine is trifling and I want to therefore tell you to be prepared; I am prepared. You all [slaveholders] have a heavy responsibility, and it behooves you to prepare more than it does me."

Brown was repeatedly asked what he was trying to do and why. Vallandigham asked, "Did you expect a general rising of the slaves in case of your success?"

"No, sir; nor did I wish it. I expected to gather them up from time to time and set them free," said Brown. To Mason's question "How do you justify your acts?" Brown said, "I think, my friend, you are guilty of a great wrong against God and humanity—I say it without wishing to be offensive—and it would be perfectly right in any one to interfere with you so far as to free those you willfully and wickedly hold in bondage. I do not say this insultingly." When Mason responded, "I understand that," Brown added, "I think I did right, and that others will do right to interfere with you at any time and all times. I hold that the Golden Rule, 'Do unto others as you would that others should do unto you,' applies to all who would help others to gain their liberty." Stuart said, "But you do not believe in the Bible." "Certainly I do," responded Brown. When asked, "Do you consider this a religious movement?" Brown said, "It is in my opinion, the greatest service a man can render to God." He was asked, "Do you consider yourself an instrument in the hands of Providence?" "I do," was the reply. "Upon what principle do you justify your acts?" a bystander asked. Brown said, "Upon the golden rule. I pity the poor in bondage that have none to help them; that is why I am here; not to gratify any personal animosity, revenge or vindictive spirit. It is my sympathy with the oppressed and the wronged, they are as good as you and as precious in the sight of God." "Certainly," responded the bystander, "but why take the slaves against their will?" Brown claimed he "never did." The bystander persisted: "You did in one instance, at least." In a strong, clear voice Stevens agreed with the questioner, correcting his captain: "You are right. In one case the negro wanted to go back." Stevens was asked where he was from and how far away he lived from Jefferson County. Before he could respond, Brown stopped him by saying, "Be cautious, Stephens, about any answer that would commit any friend. I would not answer that." The *Herald* reporter observed that the seriously wounded Stevens "turned partially over with a groan of pain, and was silent."

While being questioned about the places he had been, Brown shifted the subject of his response, wanting the bystanders and *Herald* readers to appreciate his motives:

> I want you to understand, gentlemen—you may report that I want you to understand that I respect the rights of the poorest and weakest of colored people, oppressed by the system of slavery, just as much as I do those of the most wealthy and powerful. That is the idea that has moved me, and that alone. We expect no reward, except the satisfaction of endeavoring to do for those in distress and greatly oppressed, as we would be done by. The cry of distress of the oppressed is my reason, and the only thing that prompted me to come here.

This prompted a bystander to ask, "Why did you do it secretly?" Brown said, "Because I thought it necessary to success; no other reason."

Near the end of the interview the New York *Herald* reporter asked Brown, "I do not wish to annoy you; but if you have anything further you would like to say I will report it." To this and the remaining queries he warned of the impending termination of human bondage. With resolve Brown gave his justifications, framing them in a way that tried to show self-sacrifice, civility, concern, moderation, and reasonableness, and cast himself as a victim. "I have nothing to say, only that I claim to be here in carrying out a measure I believe perfectly justifiable, and not part of any incendiary or ruffians, but to aid those suffering great wrong." Brown warned Southerners, "You had better—all the people of the South—prepare themselves of that question that must come up for settlement sooner than you are prepared for it. The sooner you are prepared the better. You may dispose of me very easily; I am nearly disposed of now; but this question is still to be settled—this negro question I mean—the end of that is not yet."

Brown portrayed himself and his men as victims of rash acts, both before and after the Marines attacked. He bitterly decried the shooting of his men under the white flag; he viewed this as a flagrant violation of fairness and the rules of combat. Describing their capture, he insisted that, "The Marines fired first and they were obliged to return the compliment"; he intentionally put his and his men's actions in the best possible light. Confusion from the suddenness of events and his own head injury or unconsciousness from Green's blows may also have been factors in his explanation. He was mistaken about received bayonet wounds, saying, "These wounds were inflicted upon me—both saber cuts on my head and bayonet stabs in the different parts of my body—some minutes after I had ceased fighting and had consented to a surrender, for the benefit of others, not for my own… There had been loud and long calls of 'surrender' from us—as loud as men could yell—but in the confusion and excitement I suppose we were not heard. I do not think the major [Russell], or any one, meant to butcher us after we had surrendered."

To newspaper correspondents and others around him, he gave as an example of his restraint the sparing of the life of Major W. W. Russell, whom a reporter incorrectly identified in his column as Lieutenant Stuart. Referring to a major who stood nearby during the interrogation, Brown said, "I could have killed him just as easy as a mosquito when he came in, but I supposed he came in only to receive our surrender."[53] He also told of his benevolent treatment of the hostages. "We assured the prisoners that we did not wish them any harm, and that they should be set at liberty… We took them in the first place as hostages and to keep them from doing any harm and to guarantee our safety." When asked why he did not surrender before the attack, Brown said he did not believe it was necessary. "I exercised my best judgment, not believing the people would wantonly sacrifice their own fellow-citizens, when we offered to let them go on condition of being allowed to change our position about a quarter of a mile. The prisoners agreed by a vote among themselves to pass across the bridge with us. We wanted them as a sort of guarantee of our safety; that we should not be fired into." Brown's final example was his attempt to avoid killing; he said, "We did kill some men in defending ourselves, but I saw no one fire except directly in self-defense. Our orders were strict not to harm any one not in arms against us."

Brown also attempted to depict his liberation of slaves and confiscation of slave-owners' property in as conservative a light as possible. After he explained about his military restraint, someone asked him, "Brown, suppose you had every n***** in the United States, what would you do with them?" He immediately responded, "Set them free." He was asked, "Your intention was to carry them off and free them?" "Not at all," quipped the raider captain. Expressing the fear and anxiety of many Southerners, a bystander said, "To set them free would sacrifice the life of every man in this community." Brown disagreed, saying, "I do not think so." The bystander countered. "I know it. I think you are fanatical." To this Brown said, "And I think you are fanatical. 'Whom the gods would destroy they first made mad.' And you are mad." Someone asked, "Was it your only object to free the negroes?" "Absolutely our only object," said Brown. "But you demanded and took Colonel Washington's silver and watch?" Brown said, "Yes, we intended freely to appropriate the property of slaveholders to carry out our object. It was for that and only that, and with no design to enrich ourselves with any plunder whatever."

The interview ended with those who had heard the raider leader more impressed with his courage, calm, and eloquent responses than the content of his explanations. The implications of his efforts and motives horrified Southerners, and words could not explain them away. Even Governor Wise, who was greatly impressed by Brown's qualities, would ultimately insist on his death as retribution. To others the interview was the genesis of the emerging legend of John Brown, which placed the cloak of martyrdom on the violent abolitionist. That cloak would have been denied him if the blade of the Marine officer had taken his life.[54]

While the interview with Brown was taking place Tuesday afternoon, militiamen returned to their homes in places such as Frederick, Maryland. Around 7:00 p.m. thousands crowded the streets near Baltimore's Camden Station to welcome back their warriors who had left them the previous afternoon. In the interim many had hung around the station, curious for news and indiscriminately interrogating passengers from the west. A band played as they cheered to welcome back their conquering heroes only to find the men exhausted. They left their cars looking haggard, wearing filthy uniforms, desiring only to return to the comfort of their beds.

Back at the scene of the raid that same night, unease still prevailed in the aftermath of trauma, providing another memorable night for Joseph G. Rosengarten, a director of the Pennsylvania Railroad. Rosengarten had happened to arrive in town on Monday afternoon and witnessed the shooting of Captain Turner. Later that day Rosengarten was arrested as a suspect, and he spent Monday night in Charles Town jail until Governor Wise had him released on Tuesday. He returned to Harpers Ferry Tuesday night in time to find the town "made hideous by the drunken noise and turmoil of the crowd." Wise's impoundment of all the horses made the sober militiamen disgruntled, as they were now forced to trudge home on foot. Intoxicated militiamen remained—a couple of them shouted wildly they were John Brown's men, as others fought and squabbled with each other, stopping only long enough "to pursue and hunt down some fugitive negroes." Finally the governor of Virginia ascended to the porch of Wagner House. In disapproval, Rosengarten listened to Wise "haranguing an impatient crowd he addressed as 'Sons of Virginia!'" After speaking for one or two hours the governor went inside, where he and his staff huddled at a table illuminated by flickering candles. They pored over the letters and other documents which elicited the governor's commentary; he claimed to find irrefutable evidence of Brown as the instrument of a Northern conspiracy. The emotionally charged men saw a conspiracy, not only in letters from the "Secret Six," maps taken from a trunk at the Kennedy house of targets throughout the South, and captured documents drafted by the leader, but also in benign newspaper clippings, letters, and notes. Some of these were taken from citizens who had ransacked Brown's headquarters.[55]

Disposal of Dead Raiders

Before dark, late that evening, a wagon traveled over the area of combat. Men gathered into it the nine dead black and white insurgents, including the dripping remains from the converging rivers. Men pitched the bodies into the wagon, intentionally violating traditional segregation as the bodies were carried off for burial. Local resident James Mansfield was given $5 to dispose of the contemptible remains of Oliver Brown, William and Dauphin Thompson, Dangerfield Newby, Stewart Taylor, John Henri Kagi, Jeremiah Anderson, William Leeman, and Lewis Sheridan Leary. All were deemed unworthy of a proper burial in the town cemetery above Jefferson's Rock. James Mansfield and his brother-in-law James Giddy took the bodies for disposal across the Shenandoah bridge, turning right and rolling along the eastern river bank for a half mile across from the rifle factory, near the midriver rock where Kagi was killed. The bodies' treatment was devoid of any ceremonial reading of scriptures, prayer, or somber words. This was starkly different than the military honors given the Marine who had emigrated from Ireland, Private Luke Quinn; he was interred at St. Peter's Catholic Cemetery in Harpers Ferry. Quinn's formal funeral was conducted by another Irish immigrant, Father Michael A. Costello, believed to be the clergyman Brown had harshly banished from his presence shortly after his capture.

On the Shenandoah shore men dug two graves and lowered into them two wooden pine store boxes six feet long, four feet wide and three feet deep, with four bodies stuffed in one, and three in the other, along with what Mansfield would recount in a later notarized statement: "a couple" bodies were "without [a] coffin of any kind." There the bodies remained until 1899, in unmarked and soon-forgotten graves at the edge of the rippling waters of the Shenandoah, a Native American word said to mean "beautiful daughter of the stars." Near the end of the 19th century, during one of their many excursions to search for the graves, Dr. Thomas Featherstonhaugh and

L. A. Brandenbury of Washington, D.C. happened to stumble across James Foreman, who lived nearby on the mountain. Foreman had witnessed the burial and took them to the long-sought-after site; at the edge of the water were two sunken spots several feet apart. Featherstonhaugh wanted proof. Not expecting to find anything, on September 16, 1895, he had Foreman and his son use shovels to unearth one of the graves. After digging three feet they found the rotting top of a wooden box six feet long, four feet wide, and three feet deep, made out of inch-thick lumber. Most of the box was below the water line and constantly kept wet, keeping that part in better condition than its top. They removed the sunken and decaying top and stared at the backbone of a raider stuck to it, and at what Featherstonhaugh called "great masses of woolen tissue" from the blankets they wore as shawls "surrounding each one of the dead men." Reaching down into the ooze inside the crude casket, Featherstonhaugh removed a shattered skull he assumed was Newby's, having heard Newby was struck near the head by a railroad spike. Satisfied, they took a photograph

Photograph taken on September 16, 1895 of the opening of one of the graves of Brown's men on the bank of the Shenandoah River. On the left Dr. Thomas Featherstonhough, center James Foreman, son of Lewis Foreman on the right. (West Virginia Archives, Boyd B. Stutler Collection)

and closed the grave, leaving the others undisturbed and placing as markers two large flat stones taken from edge of the river.

Some doubted Featherstonhaugh and Brandenbury's discovery, so the physician wrote a statement verifying his claim and had it notarized in Jefferson County (now West Virginia) on April 21, 1899. The same year on July 29, early on that Sunday morning, Featherstonehaugh, with the help of others, had the remains he had found dug up. They included large bones, a few buttons, a belt buckle, fragments of ponchos, and the shaggy bear coat worn by Oliver Brown. What was left of the nine men was placed in a trunk and sent to John Brown's farm in North Elba. There the remains were laid to rest in a single coffin near their leader, his son Watson, Aaron Stevens, and Albert Hazlett, in a manner that was in stark contrast to their original interment. The Rev. Joshua Young, who had conducted the service for John Brown 41 years earlier, and his bishop led the funeral. The ceremony ended with the piercing and somber noise of the US infantrymen of the 26th Regiment firing a salute over their graves.

The body of Watson Brown was not buried with his comrades' in the mass riverside graves. His lingering death occurred after their interment. Somehow curious medical students attracted to the site of the raid got hold of his body and that of Jeremiah Anderson, who was killed in the enginehouse. According to one account when they left the train prior to reaching the town they found a body lying on the riverbank with papers that made them mistakenly presume it was Owen Brown. Some claim the remains were placed in a box; others say the body was crammed into a barrel and taken back to Winchester Medical College by medical students who were pleased with their fortune in obtaining a cadaver.

This was the beginning of a macabre journey for Watson's corpse. At the medical college the body was flayed, a preservative was applied, and blood vessels were injected with a red fluid to facilitate its use as a specimen, particularly for the study of the circulatory system.

The corpse still served this purpose when the Union took control of Winchester and used the medical college as a Civil War hospital in spring 1862. Dr. Jarvis J. Johnson, a major and the regimental surgeon of the 27th Indiana Volunteer Infantry, found and took charge of what he called a "large symmetrical and anatomical human body or frame" in the college museum. With General Nathaniel Banks's permission, Johnson removed it to Winchester's "Academy Hospital." This prompted visits by prominent citizens, including a professor of Winchester Medical College, informing the doctor that the cadaver was one of John Brown's sons. Johnson said the "professor strongly appealed to [Johnson]" to return the body in the name of medical science, for the benefit of future students, once the medical college (which had recently burned) was rebuilt; the body was also meant as a display of warning of the consequences of Brown's so-called evil assault on slavery in the Old Dominion. Johnson responded he

Watson Brown. (Library of Congress)

had "too high esteem" for Brown and his sons' "heroic" effort at Harpers Ferry "to leave the body upon the soil of Virginia hence I should send it to the free soil of my own State."[56] In summer 1862, by express, Dr. Johnson sent Watson's body back to his home in Martinsville, Indiana. He kept the remains in his office for a time until the body was borrowed by the local lodge, Knights of Pythias, who wanted the cadaver for their initiation ceremony. Storage in a shed led to some ravaging of the body by insects.

Watson's mother, Mary Ann Brown, was unaware of these events. She moved to California thinking her son had been given a decent burial but on January 27, 1863, received what was meant to be a consoling letter from Union soldier Horatio N. Rust stating that during Banks's occupation of Winchester in 1862 Watson's body had been taken from the medical college by members of the 10th Maine Regiment and was buried. This proved to be untrue. Rust went on to say, "You would certainly be pleased to know... friends in New York were very glad to know th[e] remain wer[e] laid to rest by other than th[e] Hands of the Nativ[e] Savages whom God seems to be punishing most severely by this war. How terribly Harpers Ferry and vicinity suffered and how justly I can h[e]artily say Amen." Years after the war Dr. Johnson read in the newspaper that construction of a monument was being considered for John Brown, but his wife knew nothing of the remains of their sons. He wrote the Chicago *Tribune* announcing he had one of the bodies. Upon learning this on her way back to visit John Brown Jr., Mary Ann Brown asked her son to go to Martinsville in hopes of finding the body. It was not a task John Jr. was looking forward to. On the evening of Sunday, September 10, 1882, he wrote his wife an emotional letter describing what he found after arriving at Dr. Johnson's house, where the remains had been carried from the nearby office. With Dr. Johnson, a number of other physicians, and prominent citizens, John Jr. gazed at what he expected to be the remains of either Oliver or Watson. There on end leaning against the wall was a long, narrow box covered with a cotton cloth instead of wood. As the white covering was pulled away, John Jr. observed:

My first impressions will remain with me forever. It seemed to me to have, notwithstanding its ghastly appearance, a pleading expression as if to say 'Come and take me.' I could hardly resist the impulse to clasp it in my arms… As soon as I could choke down my feelings I began a careful survey. The muscles of the mouth had been stretched unnaturally, probably to expose the teeth as much as possible. Two or three of the front teeth are broken as if they had received a blow forcing them inward toward the roof of the mouth. Several joints of the fingers and toes are missing. It is said they were cut off and carried away as relics by Confederates when it was in their hands at Winchester. The body has suffered a good deal of waste form the ravages of insects. The height corresponds well to that of either Watson or Oliver. The hole corresponding to the wound as reported at the time which Watson received can plainly be seen.

With the help of surgeons John Jr. had the remains positively identified as that of his brother Watson. The bereaved brother took the body to his home at Put-in-Bay, Ohio, an island in Lake Erie. On October 13, 1882, he buried it next to his father's body in North Elba in "the shadow of a great rock," 23 years after Watson's last breath.[57]

Incarceration of Captured Raiders

On Wednesday, October 19, 1859, the morning Watson died and the day after the end of the raid and the burial of raiders on the Shenandoah bank, John Brown, Aaron Stevens, Edwin Coppoc, and Emperor ("Shields") Green were delivered to the sheriff of Jefferson County and the US marshal of the Western District of Virginia and taken by train to jail in Charles Town to await trial. Governor Wise, Senator Mason, and other prominent men accompanied the transfer of prisoners, and an agitated crowd of several hundred followed them to the train. To ensure the safety of the prisoners, they were escorted by the reliable US Marines under Lieutenant Green; the only remaining militia company was passed over. Stevens and Brown were incapacitated by their wounds and were carried to the train in a wagon. Coppoc and Green walked between the files of Marines as the disgruntled mob pressed around them shouting, "Lynch them! Lynch them!" Wise responded loudly, "Oh, it would be cowardly to do so now!" The crowd slackened their pursuit as the prisoners were safely placed on the train. Although Brown had recovered enough from his wounds to support himself, no handcuffs were placed upon him.

The excitement at the Ferry was not yet over. In the first half of the 19th century slave insurrections left a lingering paranoia among Southern whites. Unlike the other slave revolts, Brown's raid was led by whites, renewing and intensifying white Southerners' fears of numerous slave uprisings triggered by the North. The night after the Harpers Ferry raid, Wednesday, at around 9:00, a James Moore from Pleasant Valley, Maryland, brought hair-raising news of people being massacred by a body of men. He said that at about sunset the men descended from the mountains, killing the Garnett family and "from the cries of murder and screams of the women and children, Moore believed the residents of the valley" were being massacred. Excitement subsequently increased "in the village of Harpers Ferry," Lee reported, "by the arrival of families [from nearby] Sandy Hook, fleeing for their safety." Lee thought the occurrence of the horrors improbable, but he would take no chances that "some atrocity might have been committed." He and Green, Stuart, and about several dozen Marines went the four and half miles to the scene of the alleged massacre, only to find it was a false alarm. "The inhabitants of Pleasant Valley were quiet and unharmed, and Mr. Garnett and his family safe and asleep." Moore had mistaken the cries of whippoorwills for the sounds of his neighbors being massacred. Returning to Harpers Ferry, Lee's job was done. Later that night Lee, with Stuart, Green, and the Marines, took a train back to Washington. He had identified and suppressed the insurgents.[58]

CHAPTER 4

Anguish and Travail

The raid sparked grief, stress, and trauma, especially for the participants and their families and friends. Tearful mourners grieved the deaths of locals Thomas Boerly, George Turner, Fontaine Beckham, and Hayward Shepherd. The raiders' families and friends mourned as well. Their loved ones' angst was compounded by worry over the fate of those who were captured, and by the condemnation by northern neighbors, who looked upon them with suspicion. As relatives of violent criminals, their reputations were tainted.

Angst and Grief

Isolated in the North Elba mountains, Brown's wife and family were spared censure from neighbors, but word of the raid's outcome was delayed. It took several days for the news to trickle back to their humble dwelling in the Adirondack highlands. On the afternoon of Friday, October 21, 1859, a copy of the New York *Times* dated October 18 brought the disturbing news that made it impossible to cling to hope that the rumors they had heard the day before were untrue. In the meantime, in Chambersburg with her baby, Virginia Cook succumbed to feelings of despair. A contemporary described her as "frenzied with grief." In addition to her distress about her husband, she was stranded and penniless, unable to purchase passage to an uncle's home in Brooklyn, New York, or to pay for her temporary quarters in the room behind the parlor in Mrs. Ritner's boardinghouse. She first thought of returning to her home in Harpers Ferry. Franklin Keagy—a relative of raider John Kagi and resident of Chambersburg who boarded at Mrs. Ritner's—dissuaded Virginia. In Harpers Ferry, he said, she would likely be harassed and possibly even arrested. Moved by her plight, Keagy obtained money from a benefactor and placed the funds in Virginia's hands, telling her she could now go to her uncle in New York. As he started to leave the room, "She awoke," Franklin Keagy writes, "as it were from a dream, and breaking out in a flood of tears, with clenched hands raised above her head, she exclaimed: 'Oh, sir, how can I thank you for your kindness to me. God bless you.'" The next day Virginia left for her uncle's home. Concerned about her welfare, her uncle arrived at Chambersburg while Virginia was heading north. She had been at Mrs. Ritner's for two weeks.

Brown's female relatives would also suffer. Belle and Martha Brown's husbands, Watson and Oliver, were already dead. The fate of the Brown widows would only worsen. Belle had lost not only her husband but also her two brothers (the Thompsons), her father-in-law, and her brother-in-law. As for Martha, she was still devastated from the loss of her husband when, five months after Oliver's death, she gave birth to a girl in March 1860. Martha named the baby Olive in honor of her father. Annie recalled Martha telling the family, "If it lived she should try to live to care for it, but if it dies I shall die too as I shall have nothing to live for." A few months later the child died. Annie held the dead infant for the weakened mother to kiss goodbye, and when Annie took the baby away, she noticed two teardrops from the grieving mother were left on the small face. Later Martha was awakened and asked to take some medicine. Knowing death was near, she said, "No not now, wait until Oliver comes, he will be here soon, and Watson too." Martha saw Belle, Watson's widow, standing nearby and asked if she had "any message to send Watson… I shall see him soon." Martha departed from this world soon after that, at the age of 17.

Belle would also suffer the anguish of losing a child. Her little son Freddie had been born shortly before Watson left for the Kennedy farm. The boy missed his father, and when he saw other fathers playing and hugging their children, Freddie sadly remarked, "I have not dot any papa, bad men tilled my papa." He died from membranous croup at the age of four. As he was dying, Annie Brown Adams said he pointed his small hand upward, saying, "See, see," as if he saw his papa coming.[1]

The Travail of the Fugitives

Virginia Cook's husband and six other escaping raiders wandered in two separate groups of two and five, each unaware of the others' slow, fatiguing meanderings northward in the mountains of Maryland and Pennsylvania. In the first part of their odyssey both groups struggled to reach Chambersburg. Osborne Anderson and Albert Hazlett reached the town first, after traveling for almost a week.

Crossing the Mason–Dixon Line from the slave state of Maryland into the free state of Pennsylvania did not substantially lessen the danger for either group of fugitives. They were all wanted criminals. Residents of Franklin County, Pennsylvania, were embarrassed and appalled that Brown had used Chambersburg, their county seat, as a vital juncture from which to launch his insurrection.

Chambersburg housed 500 black people, most of whom lived crowded into dilapidated houses and shanties and worked as laborers and domestic workers. A number of black people had emigrated from Harpers Ferry and the surrounding

Raiders who escaped: (left to right top) Osborne Anderson, Barclay Coppoc, (left to right bottom) Charles P. Tidd, Owen Brown, Francis J. Meriam. (Library of Congress)

region, including the notable Dr. Martin Delany and the Reverend Thomas W. Henry, whose name was given in one of the letters found in Brown's carpetbag as a person to be trusted. Thomas Henry served as a minister in the African Methodist Episcopal Church in Chambersburg; its members supported Brown. Prominent church members included William Goodridge, Delany, and longtime resident Henry Watson, whose barbershop was the center of the area's Underground Railroad.

The white population of Chambersburg and the county was divided on the treatment of fugitive slaves. Some made a living by catching and returning escaped slaves; others, along with free black people, helped them escape. Brown's raid accelerated these tensions, and his supporters in Chambersburg and elsewhere were watched and viewed with suspicion as abettors in the dastardly raid, turning them into unwelcoming hosts whenever fugitive raiders knocked at the door.

Entering Chambersburg one night around 2:00, Anderson hid his rifle before going to the home of an acquaintance. There he was reluctantly befriended by William Goodridge, a wealthy black businessman and Underground Railroad agent. Goodridge provided a hasty meal for the famished Anderson while lamenting the likelihood that Anderson's presence would lead to his arrest by a US marshal.

Anderson contends he fled out the back door as a marshal knocked at the front. Making his way eastward, Anderson boarded a train at York, heading toward Canada by way of Philadelphia. To avoid detection he changed his clothes three times and hid on the train during the day.[2]

Anderson, like Hazlett, came from the Quaker State. Neither man was welcomed home. Anderson was bitterly disappointed by his parents' rejection when he arrived at their home in West Chester, a short distance west of Philadelphia. His parents spurned their son, whose actions they must have disapproved of—for perhaps no other reason than his putting them in jeopardy. According to Annie Brown, he later told her "with tears in his eyes… that his own father turned him from the door, threatening to have him arrested if he ever came again; that most of the colored people he met turned the cold shoulder to him as if he was an outcast."[3]

For Brown's followers, the rigors of the journey north led to exhaustion and frayed tempers, sparking disruptive arguments that made it difficult for them to stay together. Hunger and fatigue were their greatest antagonists, slowing the steps of the weakest and most debilitated first. Hazlett, and also Meriam, lacked physical stamina for trudging up and down mountains, across valleys, and through streams in the cold, rain, and snow. The tall slender Hazlett was unaccustomed to physical strain, and he hobbled along with blistered feet until, in Anderson's words, he "at last gave out, completely broken down." He was unable to walk the 10 miles to Chambersburg. Hazlett begged Anderson to go on without him, stating it was Anderson's best chance of escape and claiming that he himself would be fine. Hazlett said the next day he would throw away his rifle, go to Chambersburg, and catch a stagecoach.

On the way Hazlett was given a ride by Hiram E. Wertz, a resident of Quincy who was on his way to pick up his mail in Chambersburg. Hazlett was dressed in an ordinary fashion, but his white rolled-up blanket with ends tied together and hung over his shoulder marked him as an outsider. The two men conversed on varying topics, but when Wertz brought up Harpers Ferry, his passenger remained silent. When they reached New Franklin, four miles southeast of Chambersburg, Hazlett asked to be let out. As he stepped down from the buggy, a revolver dropped from his pocket. It was a rare weapon in those parts. The young man hurriedly scooped up the weapon, thanking Wertz, and took the road to the right. Hazlett boldly strolled into town, going to Mrs. Ritner's boardinghouse.

When Wertz arrived in the town he found men talking of capturing Cook for a $1,000 reward, and Wertz thought he had given Cook a ride. After seeing the young red-haired Hazlett in town, Wertz told the constable. Three men searched Mrs. Ritner's house to no avail. In the garden they found a box with a blanket sporting the initials W. H and the pistol Wertz claimed to have seen. Constable M. W. Hauser and Sheriff Charles T. Campbell continued the pursuit, taking the afternoon train north; one would get off at Shippensburg and the other would ride to Carlisle. The next day when one of the pursuers was returning toward

Shippensburg, he saw and arrested the fugitive, whom he assumed was Cook, one mile south of Carlisle and about 35 miles from Chambersburg. The prisoner claimed to be William Harrison. Rumors circulated that he was Albert Hazlett, but the true identity of the man they detained in the Carlisle jail was unknown until after he was returned to Virginia.[4]

Little detail is known about Anderson and Hazlett's travels from Harpers Ferry to Chambersburg beyond that they followed the South Mountain range northward, taking a similar route to the fugitives who followed them. Owen Brown shepherded his group the best he could. They crossed valleys and roads in darkness, viewing passing strangers with apprehension, on their way to reach the next formidable stretch of forest. To avoid capture they spurned roads until they reached western Pennsylvania, traveling almost exclusively at night in the lower part of the mountains. By day they slept and hid in the thickets of uninhabited mountain tops, at times becoming confused about their location or the time of day or night, since they lacked what Owen Brown called "time pieces." They endured extensive hardship from hunger and trudged over rugged terrain, at times leaning on their guns as canes in rain and snow. They were pursued by local citizens on horses who took the main roads and were accompanied by barking hounds. The fugitives' endurance was taxed by fatigue, causing John Cook and Charles Tidd to demand risky acts to lessen their plight. Arguments resulted. In the first week or so they argued in strained whispers; Owen Brown pleaded that they must avoid rash acts. He bribed his companions with money and rations to keep them from traveling on roads, firing weapons, and igniting fires for warmth and cooking until they were in western Pennsylvania. Fatigue led to frequent short rests, during which the raiders would fall asleep for a few minutes, a practice Owen patterned in part after his father, who was adept at sleeping while riding a horse in Kansas. Only infrequently did they sleep at night so a man suffering from overexertion or illness could rest.

About 20 miles north of Harpers Ferry, Owen, Cook, Tidd, Coppoc, and Meriam faced their first menacing challenge while crossing the Baltimore turnpike through the mountain gap east of Boonsboro, Maryland. Coming in sight of the pike, they saw about a hundred fires. A large party of men was accompanied by large and small dogs, and the hounds bayed so loudly, Owen claimed, "I never heard so much barking before in my life." The fugitives assumed the men and dogs were looking for them. Crossing below the gap, at a creek, they headed undetected toward the mountain, unseen except by some hounds running by who chased a red fox. The dogs stopped for only a moment to glance at the worried fugitives.

While traveling toward the heights Owen looked back but could not see Meriam. Going back to the creek bank, Owen found the tired, weak Meriam could not climb the steep bank. Owen called strong Charles Tidd to help, and with impatience, Tidd helped Owen pull up the exhausted man, bruising him against a protruding root.

Daylight found the group leaving tracks in the bare soil of a newly plowed field where they heard the clatter of 40 to 50 horsemen. They dropped and hugged the ground until the riders passed, and then they finally made their way up the mountain. Near the summit of South Mountain they came to a round gray stone tower, 34 feet high. On top of it they saw a white rag flying on a pole. Thinking it was some sort of unfinished monument or lookout tower, Owen was the only one willing to exert the energy to climb the circular stairs to the top. From there he gazed westward, overlooking the impressive sight of a valley and Boonsboro, four miles away. Boonsboro's citizens had completed the structure in 1827, after two years of labor, as the first monument to George Washington.[5]

From the monument the men struggled northward. Owen wanted to bypass Chambersburg, but the men had long since consumed all the food they had and were tired of subsisting on uncooked field corn and an occasional apple or raw potato. Unlike Anderson and Hazlett, who lit fires of dry leaves and twigs to cook field-foraged corn, Owen and his group did not light fires. Without fire, they could not enhance their meager fare or dry and warm themselves after wading barefoot through chilly waters. Cook, the only married fugitive, was anxious to see his wife and baby boy and insisted on going to Chambersburg. He was battered and bruised from his fall near Harpers Ferry and suffered additional injuries from a fall on the rocky heights of South Mountain, which left him limping; but it was the search for food that led to his downfall.

South Mountain ran east of Chambersburg, forcing the men to leave the mountain. When Tidd smelled the enticing aroma of fresh-cooked pies near a farmhouse, none of Owen's arguments could dissuade him from going. Yielding despite his worries, Owen agreed on the condition that Cook go instead, believing the smooth talker was less likely to arouse suspicion. Cook returned after two or three hours with the best food they had seen since fleeing: several loaves of bread, a bag of salt, boiled beef, and a pie. Not only had he and his golden tongue procured the provisions, but he was given a meal during what he called a splendid visit with the farmhouse residents. He convinced them that he and his hunting party "were too far from home to get back for dinner."

Before sunset the same day their most violent disagreement occurred. Enraged, Tidd ordered Cook to stop repeatedly firing the old pistol taken from Colonel Washington's house that had belonged to George Washington. Cook argued that he fired the gun to make it appear as if they were hunters, as he had told the farm family. The two men taunted and threatened each other with weapons, and when Owen and the others separated them with great difficulty, Cook and Tidd angrily vowed to settle the matter later.

Continuing their movement, the group was forced to cross a wide stream. Cook wore boots with loose soles, which Owen had repaired with the needle, thread, and pocketknife he carried, along with a pair of scissors. The boots were too tight to remove, and Cook could not cross barefoot with the others. Owen attempted to carry Cook across, but the sharp rocks on the bottom cut into his feet, compelling him to drop his passenger into the water.

After splashing through the stream, they crossed two valleys and a mountain and then came to the woods of another mountain before daylight. Thinking it was safe, they continued in what they believed to be the direction of Chambersburg. Cook's anger at Tidd seemed to increase; he and Owen frequently walked ahead of the others while he alternated between fuming about how Tidd had wronged him and expressing eagerness to see his family in Chambersburg. (He was unaware they had left.) Owen had long been concerned about the two men; he had checked Cook's impetuousness when Cook wanted to seize mounts out from under their riders, and when Cook and Tidd had wanted to shoot black squirrels chattering in the trees. Owen said that Cook's "imprudence would be so great that he would never see his wife and child again." This proved to be prophetic.

Soon others demanded food, and young Coppoc volunteered to obtain it, but Cook was deemed the better choice. Owen again warned of the danger as he gave Cook money and a red silk handkerchief to hold his purchases. Leaving his rifle and taking only a revolver, Cook set out on his mission on the morning of Tuesday, October 25, 1859. Owen recalls, "Cook hadn't been gone long when two ravens flew over our heads, croaking dismally. You may think it is queer, but it struck every one of us as a bad omen."[6]

Cook never returned. When he came off the mountain at midday, he arrived near the village of Mont Alto, 14 miles from Chambersburg. He entered a clearing where a group of men were working in a ravine under the supervision of Claggett Fitzhugh, a man of Southern birth and sympathy and the manager of Mont Alto Iron Works. Fitzhugh was talking with Daniel Logan, a muscular mountain man with limited education who was savvy in catching fugitive slaves and wayward lawbreakers. A Chambersburg abolitionist attorney who would befriend Cook recorded, "Aware of the reward for Cook, Logan saw a small man entering the clearing with his revolver carelessly resting on his left shoulder and his pistol arm swinging loosely by his side." He quietly said to Fitzhugh, "That is Captain Cook; we must arrest him; the reward is a thousand dollars."

Cook boldly struck up a conversation with the two seemingly friendly men, again claiming to be part of a deer-hunting party from Chambersburg seeking to purchase bread and bacon. Logan told the half-starved thin man, who sported a sparse mustache and beard on his fair-skinned face, that he owned a store and Cook should follow him. As Logan and Fitzhugh walked on each side of the fugitive, they grabbed him by the arms, causing Cook to immediately jam his hands in his pockets. Surprised, Cook struggled in a futile attempt to escape from the larger, stronger men, who disarmed him and placed him in an open buggy. He was unbound, but they warned him that if he attempted to escape he would be shot. "Why did you arrest me?" Cook is said to have asked as they were traveling to Chambersburg. "Because you are Captain Cook," Logan bluntly replied. According to his lawyer, A. K. McClure, Cook said to the men, "They will hang me in Virginia, won't they?" "Yes, they will hang you," responded Logan in an unsympathetic tone. "Do you want me hanged?" "No," said Logan. Cook said, "Then you only want the reward?" The answer was yes.

Cook now thought he saw an opportunity to make a deal for his release. He said he was John E. Cook and the bulge in his pocket he had earlier claimed was a picture of his wife was actually his pocket book. Upon taking it, his captors found boldly inscribed on the inside, "John E. Cook, Harper's Ferry," a receipt for $2, a note for $11 to be paid over six months, an incriminating order from Brown appointing Cook captain, ammunition for a Sharps rifle, drawings of roads around Harpers Ferry, and a piece of parchment six inches long and one and a half inches wide with a string tied to it. Upon the parchment it was written:

> One of a pair of pistols presented by Gen. Lafayette to General Washington, and worn by Gen. W. during the Revolution—descended to Judge Washington, and by him bequeathed to George C. Washington, and by him to Lewis W. Washington, 1854.

Cook told his captors the firearm was left in his carpetbag back on the mountain, a half mile from his capture.

Cook claimed he could get the reward amount and much more from his brother-in-law Ashbel P. Willard, governor of Indiana, and his sister's husband, a wealthy merchant in New York. Logan did not believe him, but when Cook asked whether anyone in town would serve as his attorney, Logan agreed to contact Colonel A. K. McClure to serve as the prisoner's attorney; McClure could contact Governor Willard for the ransom.

Around sunset the arrival of the three men in Chambersburg created excitement and attracted the attention of the town's residents, including James W. Cree. The captors placed their prisoner in room number 9, at the head of the second flight of stairs in the Franklin Hotel, located in the center of Chambersburg. Cook was guarded by Fitzhugh as Logan looked for McClure. In the meantime a curious James Cree was admitted to the room to see the prisoner, who sat on the bed. What Cree saw aroused his sympathy: "A more pitiable looking object I have never seen. He was ragged, tattered, and dirty, and the shoes he had on were hardly the upper. At once my heart went out to the poor forlorne, wretched creature." He refused to answer to the name of Cook, but was greatly indebted to Cree for getting him a lavish supper, enough for four men, and devoured it all while telling how he had been deceived by Fitzhugh and Logan.

The little raider's fortunes were not improving. Unable to find McClure and work out a deal, Logan contacted Daniel Reisher, the justice of the peace, for a hearing to place Cook in securely in jail. A crowd followed as Cook was taken to the small office of Reisher, now crowded with the town's attorneys. The small office was illuminated by two narrow windows. Curious onlookers packed the hallway and gathered outside as McClure approached the office, having returned to town after looking at some property. Seeing him, Logan left the office, asking, "My God, Colonel McClure, where have you been. I have been looking for you more than an hour. That's Captain Cook and I had agreed to bring him to you." There was nothing the colonel could do to prevent Cook from going to jail. His identity was known, by his own admission to Logan and Fitzhugh, and by the testimony of a gentleman from Hagerstown, who claimed earlier he had been introduced to the prisoner as Mr. Cook. There was also the incriminating evidence found upon him: the damning commission issued by John Brown, hand-drawn road maps of the Harpers Ferry area, and the slip of paper identifying the pistol stolen from Lewis Washington. Three hundred excited and curious townspeople followed Cook through the streets to the jail. Only at street corners where lamps were burning were they rewarded with a glimpse of the celebrity outlaw.

McClure's first opportunity to talk with his client was in a jail cell. The lawyer observed was a man with "long silken blonde hair that curled carelessly about his neck; his deep blue eyes were gentle in expression as a woman's, and his slightly bronzed complexion did not conceal the soft, effeminate skin that would have well befitted the gentler sex. He was small in stature… nervous, and impatient. He spoke in quick, impulsive sentences, but with little directness save in repeating that he must escape from prison." McClure pointed out that the next night would be better for an escape because it would be less embarrassing for the sheriff and less dangerous for all. He assured his client that a requisition from Richmond for his extradition could not reach Chambersburg the next day or night. The jailer seemed to have sympathy for Cook, as he took the colonel to see the builder of the jail to see where their prisoner could be placed to increase his chance of escape.[7]

Returning home, the colonel discovered his sympathetic wife and her friend planned to immediately visit Cook with bundles of women's clothing and have him leave dressed as a woman, with one of the two ladies remaining in jail. McClure informed them this was unnecessary because the following night Cook would be free. But Cook's luck deteriorated further; he never had the opportunity to escape. Several days earlier, thinking they had captured Cook when Hazlett was seized, a requisition for John Cook was sent from Richmond. It arrived on the train Wednesday morning, October 26. The bearer went directly to the region's highest judge who happened to be in town, and not the sheriff, and obtained the legal approval that his papers were in order. He was able to spirit away Cook before McClure was aware of his departure.

Owen Brown and his companions waited, unaware, all day into Tuesday night (October 25) for Cook's return. Thinking he might be lost, they started calling out his name at 2:00 a.m. They finally gave up their last glimmer of hope that he would return and supposed that he might have gone to one of their hiding places in Chambersburg. They were unaware he had revealed that he had companions and that the townsmen would soon scour the area for them and for Cook's carpetbag.

Boldly, the four remaining fugitives took to the road, with Owen warning them to stay alert and be ready to hurry out of sight and, if needed, to fight. When a man riding a fine horse rode toward them, Coppoc walked up to a house to ask directions. His companions, whose nerves were frayed, thought seriously about killing him. Owen said, "We had been chased and lived like wild beasts so long we felt blood-thirsty." Fortunately for the rider, he went by, acting as if he hadn't seen them. Upon Coppoc's return he and Tidd walked through the village of Old Forge, leaving Owen behind to help a feeble Meriam to safety. The men agreed to meet at one of the two hiding places at Chambersburg. Both groups of two set out, with Tidd and Coppoc never getting more than 40 yards ahead of Owen and Meriam. They stopped at the corner of the street in Chambersburg that led to Mrs. Ritner's. Despite Owen's insistence they should not go there, Tidd and Coppoc continued on. Meriam collapsed in exhaustion in the middle of the street and lay motionless, using his luggage as a pillow.

Once at Mrs. Ritner's, Tidd knocked on the door, to no response. He entered the garden and got a bean pole tapping on a second-story window. Mrs. Ritner put her arm out the window, frantically waving him away, and Tidd blurted out, "Mrs. Ritner, don't you know me. I am Tidd." "Leave, leave!" came a frightened whisper. "But we are hungry," pleaded Tidd. "I couldn't help you if you were starving," she whispered back. "Leave; the house is guarded by armed men!" Frightened, Tidd and Coppoc returned to the two men they had abandoned.

The men hurried to find a hiding place, with the three more able-bodied men telling Meriam to come along. After some distance, Owen looked back for Meriam, who was nowhere in sight. Owen returned to the original street corner, where Meriam still lay in the street, apparently asleep. Owen jerked him up, telling him that "his life depended on him walking a half mile or at most a mile farther to a hiding place." Daylight was approaching.

The men traveled only a short distance from Chambersburg and hid, lying motionless in a briar patch in a field. They were surrounded by the town's streets and the railroad tracks with trains passing, including a train carrying Cook back to Virginia.

From their hiding place the men waited. They saw a man with a gun appear near the woods, and at first they thought he was Cook, but he proved to be a local man gone squirrel hunting. Around noon a cold rain with snow and sleet whipped about by wind set in, with no more cover than a patch of thorns. Six to eight oxen came to investigate the fugitives. The beasts stared intently at the strange creatures who lay still and speechless amid the thorns. The men were fearful the herd would attract unwanted attention, but the animals wandered off.

It became evident the group could not successfully continue their escape with the debilitated Meriam. He could no longer walk any significant distance, and at night he was useless for warmth, as he threw off no body heat when the men slept together for warmth. He would not have made it that far had it not been for Owen Brown's beneficence. Early in their trip Owen, despite having an immobile arm from a childhood injury, had to carry Meriam's weapons and gear, along with his own and at times a bag of field corn—all while urging the weak raider to persevere. Owen's endurance and capacity for labor are impressive, considering he had been what Annie called "a cripple" since boyhood, his right arm and hand "withered and almost useless." She found him somewhat odd but honest, always ready to help others with his good arm and hand, and, in her words, the "most unselfish person I ever knew."

Others were not as compassionate toward Meriam, who slowed them with his many physical liabilities, which included a glass eye. That afternoon in the briar patch outside Chambersburg, Owen repaired Meriam's torn coat and cut off his beard with scissors to alter his appearance, hoping it would enhance the man's chances of escape by catching a train at a nearby station. While discussing Meriam's leaving, as they shivered from the cold wind, ice, and snow, Coppoc insisted he leave with Meriam. An argument ensued, first in whispers and then—when the winds increased to a higher velocity—in full voice until Owen was nearly hoarse. Owen said to Coppoc that his leaving with Meriam would increase suspicion and the likelihood of their being caught: "I need you with us and you need yourself with us, for defense, and especially to keep warm nights. We have lost too many already; we shall freeze if we lose you now. When it is safe you will be the next to go." Turning over on his elbow, Owen could see tears of frustration and disappointment streaming down the cheeks of the young man, who came from a nonviolent Quaker family.

Toward nighttime the men became alarmed when a boy entered the field on horseback. He was searching for something, circling around the briar patch only 16 feet from the prone raiders. When the boy spotted the oxen, his face brightened, and he started hollering for them to accompany him back to the barn. The fugitives were relieved.

Owen believed their best chance, once they'd taken care of Meriam, was to go to Meadville, in Crawford County, in northwestern Pennsylvania, where he had friends. If this proved unsafe they could cross the state line to Owen's brother John's home in Ashtabula County, Ohio; if it was also unsafe there, it was an easy and short distance to Canada. They thought it best to leave all Meriam's weapons in the briar patch, except for a pistol and what ammunition he could conceal. The others knew they would have to continue on foot, so they left three Sharps rifles, three full cartridge belts, and everything else in the way of arms except their Navy revolvers and what Owen called "one heavy gun each." The left-behind ammunition and weapons, including one with "C. P. Tidd" inscribed on the mounting, would be found by some boys on Thursday morning, October 28.

Through pelting snow, in darkness, the fugitives moved toward the road opposite the railroad tracks. There they said good-bye and Godspeed to Meriam, who had his own money and would take only $5 from Owen. Tidd and Coppoc remained at the corner of the field as Owen took the hand of the feeble Meriam and led him for a while to make sure was able to make his way toward the railroad station. There he boarded a train, going first to Philadelphia, then to Boston, and on to Canada.

The three remaining raiders started the second and longest phase of their odyssey. They continued moving northward, looking for anti-slavery Quaker farmers who might offer food, shelter, and temporary employment until pursuit of the fugitives waned. They also became bolder in the ways they traveled and obtained food, often shifting their time and place of travel from night to day and using roads through what were considered densely populated agrarian areas instead of wilderness. They shifted from secretly spending nights in barns, killing chickens, and milking cows to openly getting what they needed from members of the Society of Friends. Walking on main roads in central Pennsylvania, the three men attempted to deflect suspicion away their shabby, gun-toting appearance by being friendly and freely conversing with the folks they encountered. Owen introduced himself as Edward Clark; Tidd, as Charles Plummer; and Coppoc, as George Barclay—three woodchoppers looking for work. When offered work, they found the salary inadequate or some other difficulty that prevented their acceptance. When Harpers Ferry became the subject of conversation, they pretended to know little of the event.

Leaving the outskirts of Chambersburg, the three fugitives walked through country in the darkness, wading through the hip-deep swiftly moving waters of a creek 30 yards wide. Once across, Owen's bare feet were so numb he could not feel them on the snow. After trekking a mile they reached a fork in a road and were unsure which road to take, so they retraced their steps. They spent three hours of warm slumber in a barn near the creek, where they were again greeted by a barking dog. As they rested they heard the sounds of roosting chickens, but groping around in the darkness, they came up empty handed. That night they moved on, leaving tracks in the snow in a heavily populated area. They were again forced to hide in a briar patch before dawn, spreading their blankets in the middle of the path and cutting some briars to cover themselves before going to sleep. At midday the sun appeared, melting the snow and awakening them. A cow and sheep passed by, and then came a boy and a dog who picked up their scent, jerking the boy at the other end of a rope in an attempt to reach the hiding men in an open field. Fortunately for the men, the lad insisted on going forward while cursing the canine for wanting to hang himself. "He probably"—in Owen's words—"came much nearer hanging us" than the men realized at the time. When darkness approached, two fat pigs wandered by the hungry men in the briar patch. For two hours Owen imprudently ran about trying to catch and smother one of them; if he'd been successful, the piercing sounds of a squealing pig in distress would have resonated throughout the area. Instead Owen went to a nearby field and brought back what had become their staple: dry corn.

After dark they took a road leading toward Tuscarora Mountain, which brought them to a traditional Pennsylvania barn. Owen felt around the sides of the barn, looking for chickens, while the other two stood guard. Catching and quietly wringing the necks of a Jersey Blue hen and rooster, Owen placed them in his cloth bag, and the three walked to the mountains for a safe place to cook and eat their dinner. On the way Tidd and Coppoc got ahead of Owen, who would later write he felt especially vulnerable walking alone through a village, when wind blew off his hat. He chased it while passing four men who were talking about the "powerful exhortation of Brother"—apparently they were leaving a prayer meeting and paid little attention to a man running for his hat. Catching up with Tidd and Coppoc, Owen "remonstrated with them upon the danger of separating so in such a place."

On the mountain they dressed the hen and rooster. As soon as Tidd removed the feathers from the hen's leg, he cut it off and barely warmed it on the fire. The men could not wait for the hen to be cooked, and they devoured it raw, crushing the bones and swallowing everything. Tidd cooked the remaining bones and ate them. After burning the feathers and placing the dressed rooster back in the bag, they continued walking, passing more men before coming to an orchard, where they added apples to the dead rooster's bag. The second or third night after eating the hen, they cooked and ate the rooster on the side of an Appalachian ridge. They feasted in a hollow with a spring surrounded by beech and hemlock, above pitch pine trees that frequently that grew in soil with a high salt content, making Owen proclaim, "We had salt!"

Several nights later they stole four or five hens from a barn, going again to the mountains to find an abandoned log shanty used in the spring by people who peeled bark from hemlock trees to use it for tanning hides. Using stones piled up in a corner of the dirt floor as a fireplace, they cooked and devoured the chickens and apples. Tidd, who had gorged himself on chicken, bones, and apples, complained of upset stomach, but the other two slept contentedly. Rain struck the bark roof of the first building they had spent the whole night in since leaving the Kennedy house. Waking around noon, they found Tidd still complaining. Owen and Coppoc wandered around on the mountain, seeing but unable to get a shot at a flock of geese. They returned to the hut to find Tidd groaning and unable to travel that night. Leaving Coppoc to care for Tidd, Owen walked three miles and returned with his bag full with apples from an orchard. They spent their second night in the hut but without sleep as Brown and Coppoc watched and gave what comfort they could for their moaning ill comrade. They let him rest in the hut during the rainy next day, and they resumed traveling that night.

They stole their food by freely helping themselves to chickens, a guinea hen, apples, and occasional milk from farmers' cows. Even a red fox that circled and barked at them before running off was viewed as a delicious potential meal. One time when a cow would not stand still to be milked, Owen boldly climbed into a granary near the farmhouse, filled his pockets with ears of corn, and used it to entice the cow to let him milk her dry. They ate better living off stolen farm products, but their travel was again interrupted when Owen developed a debilitating headache. He would write that the men felt it "strange that none of us seemed to have any ailments, on dry hard corn, – except a little dizziness from being so weak; but as soon as we got the luxuries of chickens and guinea-fowl, apples and salt this sort of trouble commenced."

Forty-odd miles northwest of Chambersburg, they had little idea where they were, other than Pennsylvania, so they decided to risk walking the roads in the daylight. They tidied themselves, with Owen cutting Tidd's and Coppoc's hair. Their first encounter was a man on horseback, who was suspicious of the gaunt men carrying weapons, but they disarmed him with conversation, and he allowed Coppoc to ride his horse as he walked. When asked how far they were from Bellefonte, where Owen had heard there were Quakers, who might offer work, they were told it was a considerable distance but they were about 10 miles from the Juniata River. Soon the man departed, going up a farm lane. Proceeding a short distance on the road the three wayward men boldly ventured into an apple orchard in daylight, filling their bag with forbidden fruit before resuming their journey to the river. There they purchased, from the women who ferried them across the river, doughnuts and bread and butter that they found irresistible. They walked a short distance along the towpath of the Juniata Canal, which ran the distance of 127 miles from Hollidaysburg to where the Juniata and Susquehanna rivers merged. Walking long after dark hid their shabby condition, and when a canal boat approached they asked for a ride and were told it was going to Huntingdon Falls, about seven miles away. Resting on hay stored for the horses was their only leisure travel as they were carried four miles an hour on the canal boat. The jovial captain conversed with his passengers and ate most of their apples. Leaving the captain before daylight at Huntingdon Falls, they walked six to seven miles on the road to Bellefonte and spent the day resting in an old structure that housed two horses and sat away from the road. They did not know the day of the month or the number of days of their torturous wandering.

After walking another mile, nearly 60 miles northwest of Chambersburg they saw an appealing warm blaze in a fireplace through the window of a home next to the road and knocked on the door. Owen said an "honest, simple minded farmer" answered and gave them permission to stay the night. His stout, good natured wife sat them at her supper table, where they devoured innumerable flapjacks and everything else she placed in front of them. Near the end of the meal the farmer casually mentioned Harpers Ferry, and they asked him the news, saying they had heard about it but they did not know the particulars. This surprised the farmer, who stated the county had not been this excited in 20 years. He let them read the

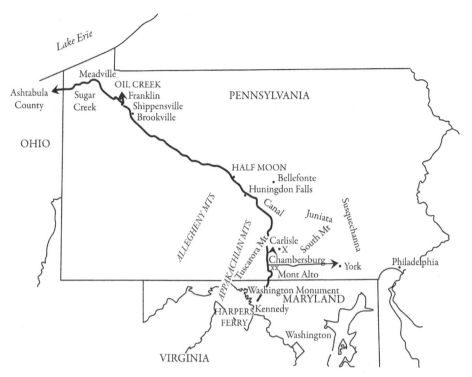

Route walked by fugitives from the raid. Seven fugitives fled north in two separate groups following similar routes to Chambersburg. Albert Hazlett and Jeremiah Anderson separated shortly before reaching Chambersburg. Hazlett was captured near Carlisle as Anderson escaped by turning eastward and taking a train at York. John Cook in the five-man group was seized near Mont Alto. The rest escaped. Francis Meriam got to safety by taking the train at Chambersburg, and Barclay Coppoc got out of harm's way by taking the stage at Half Moon. Owen Brown and Charles Tidd walked to northwestern Pennsylvania. Tidd stayed at Oil Creek as Owen walked to Ohio.

weekly newspaper that had arrived that afternoon. Tidd was first to grab the paper and started reading aloud. Emotions welled as Coppoc and Owen listened intently. Tidd read the details of Cook's arrest when their host interrupted, informing them that one of John Brown's sons had escaped, along with others who were still at large. Their host told the men that Old Brown had not been killed but had been wounded, and, "It was not certain yet whether he would live to be hanged, for he had been tried and found guilty." Tidd now reading silently became deeply moved by the news that his good friend Stevens—whom he had spent hours singing with in the Kennedy house—was shot while carrying a flag of truce. Again the farmer gave them additional information, saying the "very latest news was a man named Coppoc had been tried, too, and found guilty." Shaken by the news of his brother Edwin, Barclay Coppoc stared pensively at the fire, struggling to keep his composure.

Owen was anxious to learn about his brothers but dared not ask. He hoped that since no mention of them had been made, it was a good sign. After a few moments of silence Tidd handed the paper to Owen, who read it aloud for Coppoc's benefit. Seeing his name in large letters in the middle of the page, Owen read that first and felt strange reading aloud in front of strangers a detailed description of himself and the offer of an "extravagant reward." He dared not stop reading for fear of creating suspicion. Years later he recalled reading the article that gave all the details of the raid, including how "Thompson, was butchered when a prisoner, and how my brother Watson was shot while carrying a flag of truce, and though mortally wounded, fought till the gun fell from his hands." Hearing Owen's quivering voice, the farmer's wife, who had already read the article, now "paused in her domestic work until the reading was over." Upon discovering it was November 4, 1859, Owen realized it was his 34th birthday: his most memorable one. He was surprised to learn they had been traveling for just 17 days; the long, difficult days of travel had made it feel more like six weeks to him. The travelers sat by the fire and talked of the dead and wounded as long as they dared before going to bed.

The next morning the men paid their hosts for their kindness and asked for directions to Bellefonte and for the names of Quaker families along the way. The farmer told them of Benjamin Wakefield, who lived not north but 20 miles northwest. Walking now in a northwestern direction, they reached the Wakefield farm on a Saturday about sundown. They decided it would appear less threatening if only one of them appeared, so Tidd went first to the house and found Wakefield and his son loading wheat. Tidd told the elderly gentleman he was said to be a kindly and neighborly man; Tidd had two more friends, and he hoped the gentleman would let all of them spend the night. "Thee and thy friends may come," responded the Quaker. When they appeared with their guns he held up his hands, saying they could not bring weapons into his house. After arguing, a compromise was reached. The guns could be brought in if they were unloaded. Then the Quaker startled the three fugitives, calmly saying he knew who they were; they were from Harpers Ferry.

They asked how he knew, and he replied, "[They] were so gaunt." He said he knew they were hunted like wild beasts and were strongly opposed to slavery. A discussion of slavery and the activities in Kansas followed. Their host talked them into staying most of the Sabbath, stocked them with provisions, showed them the way on his pocket map to his cousin's 40 miles away, near Half-Moon. As they left he advised them to travel at night. They followed his counsel, journeying by night and staying as far away as possible from the highway.

Several nights later they had consumed their provisions and were forced to steal corn and apples and to raid a henhouse. Upon venturing back upon the highway, their guns created such suspicion that they headed back to the mountains. Approaching the village of Half-Moon late one night, they had the good fortune of meeting a man who told them the way to the house they sought. Owen said, "We walked boldly through the village to the farm-house and aroused the inmates." The motley-looking threesome told the man as he leaned out a second-story window, "Mr. Wakefield sent us." The Quaker seemed, as Owen put it, "disposed to let us in; but at this stage of the interview another window, apparently in the same second-story room, opened and three night-capped heads [of wife and two daughters] were thrust out. No, we couldn't come in... they cried in chorus. They knew who we were; we were traitors; our lives were forfeit." The fugitives pleaded; Owen said, "We had merely risked our lives for the freedom of millions of helpless slaves" and offered to "pay twice any sum they would ask." They were unmoved, saying "that they were not in favor of slavery, themselves, but they were also not in favor of putting it down by force." Owen said, "[the man] was on our side, but when he said anything in our favor it seemed to go worse with us than ever. His arguments excited more fury in the night-caps than ours."

Finally the older woman pulled her head back inside. Owen recounted, "Two younger voices said 'Well father, if you want to take in murderers, you may, but don't ask us to wait on them!'" The young women slammed the window shut. Things looked bleak, with, as Owen put it, "three female tongues ready to betray us, and the man of the house not daring to take us in." Suddenly the door opened and the Quaker showed them to their beds.

The next morning at breakfast the mother and two daughters refused to eat with the undesirables. The Quaker gentleman turned down money to pay for their room and board, so his three guests showed their gratitude by accompanying him to the field and shucking corn. The ladies seemed to be more accepting at the noon meal and finally accepted some silver coins from the men, who wished to express their appreciation for the ladies' culinary efforts. Tidd and Coppoc went back to the field to shuck more corn while Owen went to Half-Moon. He was preparing to send Coppoc home by getting rid of most of their guns, cartridge boxes, the old Washington pistol, and other items they wanted to save. They planned to send them along with Coppoc by stage and rail to his home in Salem, in Columbia County, Ohio.

Owen purchased three carpetbags and visited several shoe stores to find a box large enough to hold items to be shipped to Ohio, including the pistol, which Cook took and later returned to Washington through Owen. After his errands were complete, Owen returned to the home of the pacifist Quakers. The following morning, Coppoc gathered his carpet-bag and the box of munitions and joyfully departed by stage for his home in Ohio.

Tidd and Brown left on foot for Owen's old friend in Townsville, in northwestern Pennsylvania—along the direct route to Owen's brother John's home in Ashtabula County, Ohio. Each carried a carpetbag and a Navy revolver; Owen's was the one he had in Kansas. Both men vowed they would not be taken alive as they crossed over the Allegheny Mountains.

Fearing recognition because Owen's description was now common knowledge, they shied away from railways and telegraphs while traveling in daylight through towns and stopping at farmhouses. They still used aliases and pretended to be woodcutters. Owen estimated they averaged 25 miles a day even though most of the time it rained or snowed. They traveled over what is now Route 322 through Brookville, Clarion, Shippensville, and Franklin; the region was the center of the coal industry and the nascent oil industry. From Franklin they traveled up Sugar Creek to Randolph, staying a day or so with old Mr. Gilbert, who had helped Owen's father start his first tannery in Richmond, Pennsylvania, years earlier.

One afternoon they walked to Townsville and into the store of Owen's old friend George B. Delamater. He was out, but his partner, Orange Noble, who had never seen them, whispered in Owen's ear that they were safe. His friend, whom he had not seen since childhood, arrived and took both fugitives to his home, where they worked, still using their aliases. After a week Tidd was sent down Oil Creek, where he stayed for months, becoming interested in the oil business. He later told Thomas Wentworth Higginson that his escape convinced him "that twenty-five men in the mountains of Virginia could paralyze the whole business of the South and no body could take them." The topography, he argued, was ideal for guerrilla warfare because its crags and laurel bushes discouraged pursuit; those hunting him had restricted their travel to the roads. He reaffirmed what his leader had claimed.

Owen stayed in Townsville for several weeks until men came looking for him. He fled to Oil Creek, and then on to Elk Creek, and finally to Ashtabula County, Ohio, where his brothers John and Jason resided. Owen had walked for more than a month, covering more than 350 grueling miles. He crossed and traveled on the Tuscarora and the ranges of the Appalachian and Allegheny mountains, all arcing diagonally northeast through the Quaker State. The man Annie called a cripple had survived one of the most exhausting and unique escapes, winning contests against both nature and man. But his flight was not over. Being in Ohio did not end his running. For months Owen, John, and Jason dared not stay very long in one place.[8]

Life After Escape

All the escaped fugitives except Tidd joined the Brown family at a memorial service on July 4, 1860, at the North Elba grave site of the family patriarch and leader. Other supporters in attendance included Thaddeus Hyatt, James Redpath, and Richard J. Hinton. Only five of those who had been at the Kennedy house were there: Owen and Annie Brown, Barclay Coppoc, Francis Meriam, and Osborne Anderson. Except for Tidd, the rest were dead. It was the first and last family reunion after John Brown's death. During the ceremony Richard Hinton read letters and papers from Wendell Phillips, Frederick Douglass, and Henry David Thoreau and introduced the escaped raiders "for whom the pirate-state of Virginia offered a reward of $1500." Moved by the occasion, Anderson then came forward upon the platform, proclaiming, with great emotion, a larger meaning for the failed raid and the grave he stood near. Garrison's *Liberator* summarized and edited the remarks, making them more eloquent than the original speech:

> This was the first occasion in his life when he felt that he could stand on a Fourth-of July platform. That day to him had hitherto been a lie and a juggle. Thank God, it was no longer so! By the light of that grave's sacrifice, he knew the Declaration of Independence held more than 'glittering generalities.' He had gone to Virginia not as a mulatto, but as a man. Thanks God for this struggle! Costly as had been the sacrifice, it would yet amply be repaid.

Days prior to the ceremony Annie and Belle, Watson's widow, spotted a man in their yard who appeared to be weeping and praying at the grave of John Brown. Finally recognizing the man as Anderson, Annie went out to talk with him, the only black Harpers Ferry comrade of her father's to survive. After he asked about her family and said it was a pleasure seeing her, he concluded with, "God bless you dear girl" and started to leave. Annie insisted he enter the house and meet Watson's wife and son Freddie. The former raider shared his plight since the raid—he was rejected, hunted, and broke—and the Browns welcomed him into their home. He stayed there until after the memorial. Upon leaving their modest home, he apologized to Annie for staying so long, but said he dreaded going, in her account, "back into the world where he would be so friendless and alone."

It was difficult for survivors and family members of Brown's liberation force, but it was especially so for Anderson, whom Annie found "modest and unassuming in conversation." He moved back and forth from Canada, considered going to Africa, and served, according to his father, the last several years of the Civil War as a recruiter of black soldiers for the Union forces. Sometime after the war he moved to Washington D.C. and lived with a caring friend until consumption took his life on December 10, 1872. Poverty plagued him after the raid, forcing him to ask others for money. He received some from Richard Hinton and received $209.34 from the John Brown Fund—the same amount this fund gave to Owen Brown, John Brown Jr., and the widows of Leary and Cook. It was not enough to sustain Osborne Anderson.

A printer by trade, in 1861 Anderson was able to publish *A Voice From Harper's Ferry*, in hopes its sale of 15 cents a copy would provide him with economic stability. Except for his service in the military, his financial woes continued to the end. According to one source, it delayed the burial of his body by at least six months. He was eventually buried in Columbia Harmony Cemetery. His unmarked grave was later moved, with others, from Washington D.C. to Maryland.[9]

Shortly after Barclay Coppoc's escape, a Virginia agent with a requisition from Governor Wise went to Iowa to bring him back to Virginia to stand trial. The governor of Iowa, Samuel Kirkwood, refused, calling the warrant informal. The Virginia agent then sought the aid of a US marshal, but with no avail; Coppoc had been warned by a friend and fled on horseback.

Coppoc's life was nearing its end. He returned to Kansas to help some slaves escape from Missouri, and his second attempt to do the same nearly cost him his life. In July

1861 Coppoc became a first lieutenant in the 3rd Kansas Infantry, but only several months later, on the night of September 2, he had the misfortune of being on a train that fell 40 feet from a trestle that had been burned by Confederates into the Platte River. The next day he died from injuries and was interred in Leavenworth, Kansas.

Of the five fugitives who eluded the law, only Owen lived a long life. It came to an end on January 9, 1899, at his mountain home in California. He was six feet tall, analytical, firm in his sense of morality and what is correct—including opposing smoking—but he was even tempered and giving. This sandy-haired raider also was the only one of the escaped raiders who did not join the Union army, perhaps because of his physical disability. His arm was also the reason he gave for never marrying. Unlike his father, he was agnostic and optimistic. His savvy and cautious leadership had been crucial in the escape of all the members of his group besides Cook.

Tidd, whose full name was Charles Plummer Tidd, dropped the surname to avoid detection. He enlisted as Charles Plummer and became a sergeant in the 21st Massachusetts Volunteers. He died of enteritis, an inflammation of the intestines accompanied by diarrhea, on February 8, 1862, on the transport vessel *Northern*. His comrades landed on Roanoke Island, attacking and defeating former Virginia Governor Henry A. Wise's Confederate forces, inflicting casualties that took the life of one of the Confederate general's sons.

The enfeebled Francis Jackson Meriam would live only three years longer than Tidd. Meriam journeyed from Canada to his New York home the day John Brown was hung. After returning to Canada for safety, he later returned, joining the Union army. While serving as a captain in the 3rd South Carolina Colored Infantry he was wounded in the leg. He died suddenly in his bed on November 28, 1865, just after the end of the war.

The residents of Ashtabula, Ohio welcomed with open arms fatigued Owen and Barclay Coppoc and any others of Brown's men seeking protection from the agents of the vengeful governor of Virginia and federal government. Brown and many of his men had relationships developed with the people prior to the raid. The search for those thought to have helped Brown led many in Ashtabula County to be fearful of being arrested. This prompted them to form a secret society called Blackstrings, because of their insignia of a small black string sewed into the neck button hole in their shirts. A thousand or more men are reported to have taken an oath "to fight Virginia or the United States to prevent the arrest of anyone as a witness or as a conspirator" —a defiant gesture similar to that of the Sons of Liberty during the pre-Revolutionary War protests in Massachusetts against what they considered unwarranted acts by the British crown and parliament.[10]

CHAPTER 5

An Agitated Nation

The 36-hour raid left 17 men dead, including 10—nearly half—of Brown's liberation force. It was more than just a dismal failure. The impact of Brown's raid was traumatic and far reaching, and its emotional storm swept across the country and even reached Europe's shores. Brown's actions exacerbated the sectional bitterness and paranoia of the 1850s and earlier, and further diminished the American capacity for reasonableness and tolerance. The South was horrified; moderate Northerners were shocked; and anti-slavery activists spouted praise for Old Brown as a hero and martyr. Even the Republican press was shocked and at first denounced Brown, but as praise for him spread, these papers gradually drew a distinction between their repudiation of Brown's raid and their high regard for the courageous and noble old man who led it. So unnerved were authorities in Philadelphia that by October 22, four days after the raid, the adjutant-general had taken away all the arms that had recently been given to a black volunteer company in the city.

John Brown was the central topic in Congress the winter after the Harpers Ferry raid. Animosity ran rampant, and quarrels were so acrimonious that politicians feared for their safety. As a precaution, Senator Zachariah Chandler of Michigan put himself on a fitness regimen and took up target practice. Many Republicans carried pistols and escorted colleagues who did not. Allegedly Benjamin Wade of Ohio brought pistols into the Senate chambers and boldly set them on his desk as a warning to his enemies. As terror swept through the South the Southern press frequently repeated the assertion that once the raid started, only one slave had voluntarily joined Brown, and others in bondage had failed to flock to him. With righteous indignation Southerners decried the attempt by Northerners to ignite a servile insurrection against Southern whites. Among the disturbing evidence were captured weapons on the Kennedy farm and the nearby school, which were intended to arm approximately 1,500, maps of Southern states that marked sites believed to be targets for attacks, and letters from Secret Six members Samuel G. Howe, Gerrit Smith, and supporter Frank Sanborn.[1]

Uncertainty over the state of the nation was spreading. Select letters found at the Kennedy house were printed in the New York *Herald,* along with indicting headlines like the one on October 29, 1859: "The Exposure of N*****-Worshipping Insurrectionist." Its editorials branded all the Secret Six but gravely ill Theodore Parker, who had gone to Italy in an unsuccessful attempt to restore his health, along with others, as traitors to the Union and nation. Horace Greeley's rebuttal of the *Herald* in his New York *Tribune* failed to allay fears. Abolitionist William Lloyd Garrison, who abhorred violence, denounced Brown's actions as "misguided, wild, and apparently insane." Many of Brown's supporters were unnerved by their being implicated as accomplices. Cook denounced Frederick Douglass as a coward whose failure to bring the needed large number of reinforcements to the Ferry doomed the raid. This denouncement caused Douglass to flee to Canada and then to England, where he was less likely to be kidnapped and brought back for prosecution. The Secret Six feared that men would come to their homes to take them away for prosecution, and the members' behavior was inconsistent and at times erratic. Only T. W. Higginson stood his ground, refusing to leave the country and chiding others who did. Instead he helped raise a Worcester vigilance committee to guard him from being seized to testify against Brown or be tried with him. He did state that he would testify at the Mason committee, but he was never called. Higginson would command a black regiment during the Civil War and would become a staunch advocate of the immediate implementation of Brown's attack upon the South. Secret Six compatriots George Stearns, Frank Sanborn, and Samuel Howe fled to Canada out of fear of prosecution for treason—twice in Howe's case. Some stayed only a few days, while others lingered. The behavior of Gerrit Smith was the most bizarre of all. He seemed to go insane, spending most of November and December in a mental institution in New York. After his release his mental state was considered too fragile for him to testify before the Mason committee.

In August 1859 Gerrit Smith wrote, "For insurrection then we may look any year, month, any day. A terrible remedy for a terrible wrong! But come it must unless anticipated by repentance and the putting away of the terrible wrong."

After the raid members of the Secret Six—except T. W. Higginson—muted and hid their endorsement. Some destroyed papers and denied their culpability, claiming they only vaguely knew of Brown's plans. This would be the tenor of Howe and Stearns's testimony before the Mason Committee.[2]

Southern Fears and Repression

Southern editorials condemned the treasonable outrage at Harpers Ferry by what the Baltimore *Sun* called "a handful of fanatics... fiends in human form" who were supported by the sentiment and anti-slave rhetoric of the black Republican "oppressive party of the north." Southerners perceived the news of the seizure of items from the Kennedy farm as conclusive evidence of an extensive Northern conspiracy to destroy slavery by the violent means of triggering slave revolts. This belief further inflamed the raw emotions and longstanding Southern fears of slave insurrection and renewed the all-too-vivid memory of Nat Turner's 1831 revolt in Southampton County, Virginia; nearly 60 whites, mainly women and children, had been killed by slaves. The gory details were recalled in several columns of the New York *Herald* the day after the raid on the Ferry ended. Southern extremists saw Brown's raid as ample justification for secession. Even moderates in the South took little reassurance from the many Northern editorials repudiating Brown's raid or from numerous meetings in the North reaffirming the sanctity of the Union and proclaiming the insanity of Old Brown and his raid. Slaveholders were shaken with fear in places such as Augusta County, Virginia—terror that Brown had hoped would make slave-owners free their slaves. Instead, some took the precaution of selling slaves in the lower South.[3]

The white Southern fear that Northerners would provoke slave revolts muted the numerous voices of Northern moderates. It was all too galling to the South that Brown's martyrdom was growing. Northern intellectuals and abolitionists called Brown a "saint" and compared him to Christ. Northern and Southern Democrats charged that the "invasion of Harpers Ferry" was a Republican plot and demanded a congressional investigation. Fearing political damage in future elections, Republicans, including Abraham Lincoln, promptly refuted the charge and denounced Brown's raid. Later a special US Senate committee, composed of three pro-slave Democrats (James M. Mason of Virginia, Jefferson Davis of Mississippi, and G. N. Fitch of Indiana) and two Republicans from the North (Jacob Collamer of Vermont and James R. Doolittle of Wisconsin), investigated the raid for seven months (December 16, 1859 to June 14, 1860). They interviewed 32 witnesses and issued warrants for four more—John Brown Jr., John Redpath, Frank B. Sanborn, and Thaddeus Hyatt—who ignored their summonses. Hyatt and Sanborn were arrested. Hyatt spent three uncomfortable months in a District of Columbia jail refusing to testify, and Redpath was released from custody by the Supreme Court of Massachusetts on habeas corpus before the marshal could take him south. Brown Jr. and those with him armed themselves and successfully avoided arrest. Two of the Secret Six would testify. After returning from exile, Dr. Howe and George Stearns testified before the Mason Committee, answering extensive questions about Kansas, the weapons Brown received, and their support of Brown.

Howe, who earlier issued a disclaimer in the press about any prior knowledge about Harpers Ferry, was asked at the Mason committee, "Had you ever, at any time, from [Brown] any intimation of an organized attempt or effort, on his part to be made, to produce an insurrection among the slaves in the slave States of the South?" "Never," Howe responded.

Stearns followed suit when asked, "Did you ever [before the raid] have any intimation that that was contemplated to be done, intended to be done like what occurred at Harper's Ferry?" His reply was, "No, sir; I never supposed that he contemplated anything like what occurred at Harper's Ferry."

The committee, chaired by James M. Mason of Virginia, issued a majority report summarizing the raid; it concluded Brown's raid was "simply the act of lawless ruffians under the sanction of no public or political authority" by which Brown intended "to commence a servile insurrection on the borders of Virginia" that would spread throughout the South. The report stated that federal legislation would be futile in preventing future insurrections, with the possible exception of ensuring armories and arsenals had military protections, such as naval yards and forts. The majority report concluded from the testimony that, "It does not appear" Brown "intrusted even his immediate followers with his plans, fully, even after they were ripe for execution," but privately Mason thought otherwise. He was unable, after testimony, to tie supporters such as Dr. Samuel Howe and George Stearns directly to Harpers Ferry. The report concluded that through their money and influence they must have had responsibility for facilitating Brown's acquisition of weapons, with which Brown would attempt "to excite servile insurrection." To guard against such acts in the future, the report said, free states must enact appropriate legislation that would help "guarantee" the "security of peace between the States of the Union."

The conclusions of the majority report were strongly refuted in the brief minority report of the two Republican senators denying any connection of Northern abolitionists or Republicans to the "treasonable conspiracy of John Brown and his associates" and accusing the committee of exceeding its investigatory authority. Amazingly, Collamer and Doolittle went beyond accepting the veracity of the testimony of Howe and Stearns, concluding the committee's investigation reveals "that the people of the free states have had no complicity with this atrocity." Twenty thousand copies of both reports were printed but were given little notice by the press or public. The abolitionist paper *Liberator* briefly mentioned the report, stating that "the Mason committee mountain had labored and brought forth a mouse."[4]

The committee's tepid conclusions failed to change or calm minds, especially those in the South. Before the US Senate committee's finding was published, an investigation of the "Harpers Ferry Invasion" by a joint committee of the Virginia legislature concluded that a widespread Northern conspiracy was present that posed a dangerous threat not only to the Old Dominion but to the entire South.[5] People throughout the South concurred. With most Southerners convinced that they faced the twin menaces of internal slave revolts and "invasion from without," militia units were drilled and expanded to be combat-ready as a watchful eye was kept on all strangers, traveling salesmen, itinerants, and especially Northern preachers, since they might be abolitionist agents. Convinced that Brown supporters were planted insidiously throughout the South, the Southern press asked in frustration and fear, "Where will this infernal plot end? The ramifications are spread all over the South. The very lives of her citizens are at stake," as "many a lurking foe is concealed under the garb of a clergyman"—or a Yankee teacher, traveling lecturer, itinerant vendor, or bookseller. In Virginia the Shepherdstown *Register* warned, "'The irrepressible conflict' spoken of by Northern fanatics has already begun," while a New York *Herald* headline said, "Virginia Arming for Civil War." The Baltimore *Sun* reported by early December 1859 that disunion proposals had rapidly increased in number in the South Carolina legislature. The dissolution of the Union was seen as inevitable, and some pending resolutions argued that "the best interests of the South require it" to secede "as soon as possible." Another resolution called for the "election of Southern delegates to a Southern congress to form a Southern Confederacy"; and still another proposed all the Southern states pay a portion of the expenses incurred by Virginia "in the Brown invasion and then demand indemnity from the non-slaveholding States." The editor of the conservative Savannah *Republican* warned, "If we cannot conquer abolition at the ballot box we are ready to meet it either in the courts or in the field."

Brown alone did not create sectional discord or cause the Civil War. Varied economic interests in different regions spawned sectional rivalry over land, slavery, internal improvements, tariffs, and the Bank of the United States. These differences threatened to rupture the Union before Brown took action. New England's disaffection with the War of 1812 was expressed as talk of secession, whereas secession was the pointed reply of South Carolina to President Jackson's threat to force compliance after its nullification of tariffs in 1828 and 1832. Vocal Southern fire-eaters bellowed for secession during the crisis over slavery in the Mexican Cession after the Mexican War. In the antebellum era, Southerners believed their unique way of life—of slavery, cotton, and plantations—faced increased peril, which accelerated their intolerance. The kindling for igniting sectional conflict was abundant long prior to 1859. Most conflicts were temporarily snuffed out by compromises.

Brown accelerated not only the threat to the South but also Southern intolerance to any criticism of slavery in the antebellum era. The growth of cotton and the expanding demand for slaves had supplanted Jeffersonian liberalism with a conservatism that demanded conformity in the defense of the institution. The increasing attacks on slavery had gradually shifted Southern attitudes about slavery from a temporary thing to a permanent institution. The shift was complete in 1831 as the result of the assault upon the institution by Nat Turner, William Lloyd Garrison's *The Liberator,* and the debate in the Virginia legislature over abolishing slavery in the state. These attacks resulted in the South's taking the offensive and demanding all Southern intellectual life justify slavery. Slavery's defenders claimed it civilized black people, was justified by the Bible and the US Constitution, provided cheap labor necessary for cotton production, and maintained white supremacy. After 1830 the issue of slavery splintered religious denominations, with Baptists, Methodists, and Presbyterians splitting into Southern and Northern branches. The debate led to the rejection of all reforms—except temperance—that might spur an attack on slavery, and it forced Southern critics of slavery to head north. These critics included the activist Grimké sisters, who left their slave-owning father's home in Charleston, South Carolina, for Philadelphia.

The sectional conflicts preceding Harpers Ferry created a fragile political environment that intensified Southerners' reaction to Brown's raid, making it even more emotional and extreme. After the Harpers Ferry attack the South demanded at least expulsion or punishment of outsiders, and censorship and repression of words or deeds by anyone—Yankee or Southerner, white or black—who had any potential, regardless of how remote, of stirring up the slaves. In Texas a 60-year-old minister who believed slavery was sanctioned by the Bible received 70 lashes on his back because, from the pulpit, he criticized the treatment of slaves. In the month of Brown's execution, December 1859, 39 residents who opposed slavery were kicked out of Berea, Kentucky. At about the same time, an Englishman was jailed in Alexandria, Virginia, on "suspicion of being Richard Realf, Brown's Secretary of State" in a proposed provisional government. Several months later a man was lynched in South Carolina because he was believed to be an associate of Brown's. The *East Floridian,* with a headline "Served Him Right," reported a slave master's executing a map-selling traveling agent who was caught late one night "preaching abolition to the negroes." The slave-owner had his slaves hang the offender from the joist of a building and then immediately dig a hole and bury him. In Lynchburg, Virginia, anyone found on the streets after 10:00 p.m. was arrested as a possible Brown supporter. In Savannah at the time of Brown's execution, a shoemaker born in Massachusetts was tarred and feathered for expressing abolitionist sentiments.[6]

You could be expelled from the South for the slightest failure to adhere to what was deemed necessary for the defense of slavery. A music teacher—who was married to a Southern woman and had lived in Georgia and Alabama for nine years—repeatedly spoke out in favor of slavery. The musician refused to play the flute in a ceremony expelling a Northern book peddler from town because he felt it was unjustified, and the musician received a written warning to leave the state immediately or be tarred and feathered. He left for the North before daylight.

Even the law overlooked violence in the name of intolerance of any written attack upon the peculiar institution. A mob in Newport, Kentucky, tossed a printing press and printing materials, valued at the time at about $3,000, into the Ohio River. When the proprietor sought redress against the rioters in court, he found the judge siding with the state attorney general: that the free press "constituted a nuisance which the citizens had the right to abate."

John Fletcher, who lived in Norfolk, Virginia, found it was dangerous to criticize slavery. He was jailed for issuing "seditious language" after temporarily delaying his arrest by threatening to kill a constable with a knife. A similar fate was experienced by a man near Great Falls, Maryland, who expressed "a feeling of sympathy with the late rebellion at Harpers Ferry." He was put in the county jail.

Northern laborers in the South were often insulted and were the objects of violence. A Georgia village expelled a Northern mechanic because he was found with a clean shirt rolled in a New York paper containing a sermon by the abolitionist Henry Ward Beecher. An Alabama merchant of 20 years in Benton, in Lowndes County, was given 30 days to leave the state because he sent his children to a New York school where black people attended along with whites. A young Irish stonecutter named Power, in Columbia, South Carolina, found authorities unforgiving after saying "[Slavery] caused a white laborer at the South to be looked upon as an inferior, and degraded, man." Seized by a vigilance committee and turned over to the mayor, Power was jailed for three days for issuing "treasonable words." As thousands watched, he was dragged through muddy streets three miles out of town. There he was given 39 lashes, covered to his waist in tar and feathers, and put shirtless on "the negro car" on the train to Charleston. At every station the engineer whistled for a mob to gather to jeer at the man. After spending a week in a Charleston jail amid threats of mob retaliation, the traumatized man was sent north.

Even more trauma was met by a Northern man in Pulaski County, Virginia, who was believed to be an agent of an abolition aid society or the Underground Railroad. The influential citizens bestowed vigilante justice upon the accused. He was hung by the neck until nearly dead then taken down. When he recuperated enough to be hung again, his torturer did so, repeating the process five times in all, in memory of John Brown and his four chief companions. Finally he was sent off with warning from captors "that if ever caught in Virginia again, he would have to take the sixth and fatal leap."

Brown's raid had a strong economic and psychological impact on the South. Censorship in a number of Southern states included the burning of anti-slavery books in public ceremonies. Blacklists named Northern companies that were "suspected of abolitionist tendencies" and were to be boycotted. Southerners talked of economic separation until abettors of Brown in the North showed a returning consciousness of their duty to the South by acts showing they supported the Union and were prepared to defend the constitution from fanatical invasion. In Richmond women wanted to boycott Northern goods, while the city's merchants met at noon on November 28 seeking the best manner of getting up a direct trade with Europe. Yankee drummers in the south fell upon hard times, finding business dull and sales few.[7] A Richmond newspaper went so far as to advocate legislation "that will keep out of our borders every article of Northern manufacture or importation." With acts that were similar to protests by the colonists before the American Revolution, antebellum Southerners formed boycotts and obtained non-intercourse agreements. In the weeks prior to Brown's death, numerous Virginia county meetings were held, and resolutions passed, often endorsing the idea of non-intercourse with the North, as well as establishing vigilance committees to seek out and question all suspicious characters. In the Georgia Senate the introduction of a bill to allow licensed Northern salesmen into the state met with such an outcry from voters that it was dropped.

A countywide meeting in Orange County, Virginia, on November 28, 1859, endorsed non-intercourse with Northern businesses, established vigilance committees for every part of the county, called for a Southern convention to be held in April 1860, and warned the Union would be dissolved if a "Black Republican President" was elected. In a mass meeting in Lynchburg, a Parson Brownlow, protesting "the Harpers Ferry raid," said that he "would rather be with the South in Pandemonium than with the abolitionists." The preacher added that he intended to instruct his family "not to bury him in a Yankee coffin," but if an emergency compelled them to do so, "they must leave both ends open, so that when the devil or abolitionists came at one end he could crawl out at the other."[8]

The New York *Herald* reported in late November that "Vigilance Committees" were "being organized in every county, town and village of the commonwealth" of Virginia. During this time Virginia law required all postmasters and deputy postmasters to search for and burn on the spot any abolitionists' materials mailed in the state. In early January 1860 a meeting of concerned citizens in Savannah, Georgia, established a vigilance committee of 25 men "to detect and expose such persons as may be suspected of entertaining or uttering sentiments hostile to slavery." A number of resolutions were passed. One stated the citizens were "looking forward to a time when all the ties which now connect us with the Northern States of this confederacy may be severed." Additional resolutions demanded avoiding Northern purchases, establishing in-state normal schools to train teachers for free schools that would only use textbooks authored by Southerners and "printed on Southern paper by Southern presses." The Southern Rights Association agreed with establishing commercial independence and otherwise proposed less-radical solutions for Southern defense. The group met in Richmond in late November 1859 and proposed "to use all lawful and constitutional means to arrest the further aggressions of the non-slaveholding States on the vital interests and constitutional rights of the South."

Restrictive bills were introduced in Maryland's House of Delegates that would prohibit manumission by deed or will, prohibit immigration of free black people from outside the state and grant free blacks older than 18 the unlikely choice of becoming a slave upon their request before the court—such self-identified slaves were to choose an owner. Another bill would empower police commissioners to have sheriffs arrest vagrant free blacks over the age of 14 and sell them to the highest bidder "as a slave, to serve until the first day of the ensuing January." It was the attitude of the Maryland legislature that free black people had no other rights beyond freedom.

The Arkansas legislature passed an act "giving the free colored population of the state the alternative of migrating before January 1st, 1860, or becoming slaves." While some preferred servitude, according to the Cincinnati *Gazette,* most of Arkansas's free blacks went north; "upward bound boats" were "crowded with them."[9] Near Harpers

Ferry the Shepherdstown *Register* gave notice on November 12 that "A meeting of citizens of Shepherdstown and vicinity, will be held at the Town Hall, on Saturday, the 26th, for the purpose of adopting such measures as may be deemed best, for the removal of the free Negro from among us."

Even Northern newspapers were unwelcome in areas of Virginia. Postmasters such as "R. H. Glass of Lynchburg, informed the New York *Tribune* they would no longer distribute the paper." Disdain for the North was also expressed by several hundred Southern medical students who left Philadelphia en masse after Brown's raid and were welcomed in Richmond by a large cheering crowd. On December 20, 1859, hundreds of the students met and "resolved to secede" from those in Philadelphia. Jefferson College lost about 200 students, and the University of Pennsylvania, 100. Richmond Medical College admitted 150 without cost (except for graduation fees) because the students had paid fees in Philadelphia already. The *Richmond Inquirer* stated this would aid "in the independence of the South." As all things Northern were repudiated, the Southern press defended its position by arguing that no slave voluntarily joined Brown during his raid, slaves were well treated and did not want to be free, and more "wives of Northern men... run away from their husbands than slaves from their Southern masters."

Ironically, Brown's raid to free the slaves had the immediate impact of greater repression of all black people, free or enslaved, in the South. Southern slave patrols were expanded to monitor slave behavior, and ferret out and suppress any hint of trouble. A loose and defiant tongue could be potentially fatal for a slave. While Brown waited in jail for his impending execution, Jerry, an enslaved man in nearby Clarke County, Virginia, responded to a white stranger's inquiries by boasting that he and other slaves approved of the Harpers Ferry raid and would help break Brown out of jail if "they could stop the [slave] patrol so they could get about." Furthermore, Jerry added, buildings were burned once the patrols commenced. He said, "We will keep on burning until they are stopped." Jerry was later tried and sentenced to execution for "plotting and conspiring to incite slaves to rebel and make insurrection.[10]

Free blacks were viewed with suspicion. They were considered unwelcome trouble-makers and, in some Southern states, had to leave or be forced back into slavery. In Berryville, Virginia, where Jerry was tried, a newspaper editor called for the removal of free blacks from Clarke and Frederick counties because, he said, "This fungus population" was "becoming more and more obnoxious in the section of the state every day" since Brown's raid. Even black people from a foreign country were dealt with harshly; a black British sailor in Georgia was illegally sold into slavery for allegedly "enticing a slave to run away." In Maryland a slaveholders' convention proposed bills to the legislature that imposed fines on free blacks coming into the state.[11]

Civilians such as Amanda Virginia Edmonds were caught up in the whirlwind of events in the aftermath of Brown's raid, and some felt an increasing fear and disdain for black people. Edmonds lived at her ancestral home of Belle Grove, nestled at the base and shadow of the Blue Ridge Mountains in upper Fauquier County, Virginia, two miles south of the small village of Paris and about three miles from Ashby Gap. Known as Tee to family and friends, this stern-looking but spirited young woman was in 1859 just entering her twenties. Her fair hair, piercing blue eyes, high cheekbones, hair combed severely behind slightly protruding ears, and small mouth presented a somber and moderately attractive face. Not immediately apparent was the fiery spirit that inhabited her slender frame.

Tee Edmonds had been raised in an upper-middle-class family that owned a modest number of slaves, including house servants, who shared much of the wearisome day-to-day toil of providing a home for Tee and her nine brothers and sisters. Provided with a better-than-average education, Tee spent her youth in a manner typical of that time and place. Restricted by antebellum standards of proper ladylike behavior, Tee was schooled in voice, was reserved in the presence of visiting males, and was devoted to family and friends; their visits and her own travels to their homes were the highlights of her week. Like her beloved "Pa," Captain Lewis Edmonds, she liked people. But her father's fondness for and trust in his neighbors put the family in a financial bind. His impulsive, generous nature caused him, unwisely, to sign notes for friends, which they failed to pay. He faced financial ruin and was forced to mortgage Belle Grove and eventually (in the 1850s) to sell his slaves. Shortly after his death in 1857, Tee, with tearful eyes, witnessed the sale of personal property, including her father's horse and saddle, in an attempt to settle her father's debts and save the farm.

A year and a half later, Tee, like others in the South, was shocked and angered by Brown's raid. "While we move," she recorded in her diary, "in the bright, beautiful world, unsuspicious of the enemies prowling around, just waiting for our lives, O! What a blow!" "The 16th of October [at the start of Brown's raid] will be an eventful day in the period of our lives. To free the slaves of the South, that our dear old State should be made a free State! O! The idea is overbearing that they should attempt anything like that!" For weeks after the raid, she wrote, the excitement was "very, very great" around her community "and over the [Blue] Ridge."

John Brown had shattered the thin veneer of tranquility between whites and blacks in the South. None in bondage responded as Brown had envisioned, but after the raid, there were more frequent torchings of slaveholders' property by disgruntled slaves. In contrast to Tee's writing of earlier affection for slaves and sadness felt when family slaves were sold, she began to talk of seeking revenge against local rebellious slaves. In fall 1859, slaves burned all the wheat of neighbor Lamuel Fletcher's while he was away on business in Warrenton. In early November Tee responded with righteous indignation: "I would see the fire kindled and those who did it singed and burnt until the last drop of blood was dried within them and every bone smolder to ashes," she wrote. At least she wanted the "heartless, ungrateful wretches" and "the vilest ones" confined to protect her community.

Fletcher's misfortune, coupled with rumors of additional slave threats to the property and body of those in authority, fed whites' heightening worries about their safety. Tee and her sister feared for their lives. As night approached, Tee reported feeling "a dark foreboding" creep over her. She could not find peace, as doom "clung" to her "through the night over an anon." Despite all being quiet, she worried, "O! What is to come of us? Will the kind hand of Providence protect us?" There was a deep fear that despite Brown's failure at Harpers Ferry, he might have set into motion a chain reaction of slave protests. Female relatives flocked to Belle Grove to cluster together with the unmarried Edmonds women, and Tee's eldest brother dared not leave them. He stayed up two nights "watching with his arms" for any trouble. None came.

After a couple of days, Tee's spirit rebounded. She visited Paris, Virginia, and played a prank on her favorite first cousin, physician Tommy Settle. She took a pair of the young doctor's trousers, wrote upon them, sewed the pockets shut, and returned them with a bouquet of herbs, chrysanthemums, and turnips.

Tee Edmonds could act frolicsome once she was convinced that all would be quiet until Brown's execution. Her sister and a female friend whose slaves had burned her wheat crop were not as optimistic. Stress and "suspense concerning the darkeys" kept them sleepless, "looking dreadful," and in "very low" spirits, according to Tee. But Tee's confidence increased; she believed bold action must be taken against the enemies of Virginia. She cheered the news that Northerners had been expelled from Charles Town, and that, after weak-willed Paris residents had allowed an itinerant abolitionist preacher to stay for days preaching in their church, men chased the predicant out of their village.

On November 19, Tee Edmonds felt some apprehension over rumors of fighting at Charles Town and suspicious fires in the mountains, which might have indicated lurking enemies. The next day her fears were allayed. The rumors proved to be false. She was comforted by reports that searches throughout the mountains revealed no enemies, and by the sight of nearly 100 volunteers moving by her home with "their armed wagons and swords dangling on their sides" as they moved toward Charles Town. Tee Edmonds might not have been aware of all the profound changes that accompanied Brown's raid.[12]

"The crisis of Harpers Ferry," as C. Vann Woodward has so ably stated, "was a crisis of means, not of ends." The question of abolition, he wrote, did not originate with John Brown or Harpers Ferry, but had been debated "for a generation." The Republican press at first denounced Brown, but as the praise for Brown spread, these papers gradually drew distinctions between their repudiation of Brown's raid "and their high regard for the courageous and noble old man who led the raid." Many abolitionists now embraced violence as an acceptable way to end slavery. Extremist William Lloyd Garrison maintained that "every slaveholder" who hindered emancipation "had forfeited his right to live." A Boston minister,

Edwin M. Wheelock, praised "the sacred, and radiant treason" of John Brown. Transcendentalist Theodore Parker predicted the South would be the victim of "The Fire of Vengeance," which would spread "from man to man, from town to town." Parker asked himself, "What shall put it out?"—only "the White man's blood." A man of the cloth in New York bluntly suggested, "Rather than slavery continue it would be infinitely better that three hundred thousand slave holders were abolished, struck out of existence."[13]

It is little wonder that the abolitionists' call for shedding Southern blood had a profound impact on white Southern paranoia. In the white Southern mind the distinction was blurred between moderate Republicans, such as Lincoln, who were the most numerous faction of the party, and the radical wing of abolitionists. Lincoln was emerging on the national scene from debates with Stephen A. Douglas for the US Senate and was becoming a prospective presidential candidate. Lincoln repeatedly denounced Brown's raid as a "reckless exhibition of madness" and vehemently argued that no Republican took part, and the party's beliefs did not foster such acts. He said Brown's attack violated the law and was futile. The rangy attorney from Illinois argued Brown's raid was unique: "It was not a slave revolt. It was an attempt by white men to get up a revolt among slaves, in which the slaves refused to participate. In fact, it was so absurd that the slaves, with all their ignorance, saw plainly enough it could not succeed... We have a means provided for the expression of our belief in regard to Slavery—it is through the ballot box—the peaceful method provided by the Constitution." At Leavenworth, Kansas, on December 3, 1859, the day after the execution of Brown, Lincoln addressed threats to break up the Union: "If we constitutionally elect a President, it will be our duty to see that you submit. Old John Brown has just been executed for treason against a state. We cannot object, even though he agreed with us in thinking slavery was wrong. That cannot excuse violence, bloodshed, and treason."[14]

The Chicago *Tribune* defended the Republican Party, and attempted to lessen Southern fears claiming Southerners had nothing to fear from it or from the Wide Awakes, militaristic political clubs in the North. They were the most numerous of the paramilitary organizations created to attract young men to the Republican Party by enabling them to perform at rallies. They marched in uniforms with a robe or cape and a black hat, carrying a flaming six-foot torch and the image of a large eyeball as their banner. The editorial concluded, "The enemies of the South are 'of her own household,' and if she will take care of them she need fear nothing form our Wide-Awake boys at the North. There are no 'John Browns' among them. They are for the Union, the whole Union, 'now and forever, one and inseparable.'"[15]

Fear was not limited to the South. Southern rhetoric in support of economic independence from the North was disturbing, but the call for total separation alarmed

Northerners, regardless of party. To placate Southern fears Northerners expressed sympathy and support for the South in Union meetings. These celebratory mass gatherings took place in Philadelphia, Harrisburg, New York, Boston, and Jersey City, and included music, speeches, banners, flags, and pictures of famous national leaders in celebration of the Union. Thousands gathered to cheer and applaud. Speaker after speaker condemned John Brown and all fanaticism, reaffirmed allegiance to the Union and the US Constitution, expressed support for Southerners, and reassured the South that Northerners were not enemies but friends who would not interfere with Southern property rights or interfere in its domestic affairs—sentiments that were reaffirmed in resolutions. Letters were often read from prominent Americans such as former President Pierce and General Winfield Scott; these evoked great applause and cheers.

On December 7, 1859, a Union mass meeting in Jayne's Hall in Philadelphia overflowed into the street, where an additional impromptu meeting took place. New York newspapers ran the call for a Union meeting: "The undersigned, regarding with just abhorrence the crimes of John Brown and his confederates, desire to unite with our fellow citizens of New York and vicinity, in a public and formal denunciation of that and all similar outrages, and to declare our unalterable purpose to stand by the constitution in all its parts, as interpreted by the Supreme Court of the United States." An overflow crowd also converged on the spacious Academy of Music in New York on the evening of Monday, October 19. It filled adjoining streets and prompted three additional Union meetings, where thousands relished the military music played by a band on a balcony, with "the roar of artillery, brilliant fire works and blazing bonfires." Pictures of George Washington and banners with presidential quotations hung from buildings: "The Union must and shall be preserved.—Jackson"; and "I stand upon the constitution, I need no other platform.—Webster" Hanging over the speaker platform were smaller banners with the names of "Jackson, Webster, Benton, Clay, Monroe, and Madison." Behind the stage bold letters proclaimed, "Justice and Fraternity."

On Thursday, December 8, 1859 in Boston's Faneuil Hall a meeting addressed "recent events which have so disturbed the public mind." The meeting organizers professed support in resolutions and speech for the Union and Constitution, and made an "unqualified condemnation of every demonstration or sentiment, public or private" that in any way supported or approved "the conduct or character of the criminal actions in the late outrage in Virginia." In an attempt to reassure the public that abolitionists need not be feared, it was "Resolved, that the people of Massachusetts, however many of them have been misled into extremists' opinions and actions, are nevertheless disposed in general to obey the laws."

The headlining speakers were two famous native sons of Massachusetts, prominent politicos whose careers included terms in the House of Representatives and posts as foreign ministers. The first to speak was Edward Everett, who would be the main speaker before Lincoln made his historic remarks at the dedication ceremony of the Gettysburg Cemetery in November 1863. At the Boston meeting Everett eloquently pointed out "the enormity of John's Brown's Harper's Ferry raid and the terrible consequences that would have ensued had he been successful" by reading "a short account of the horrors attending the servile insurrection in St. Domingo" and concluding with his "emphatic denunciation of every tendency toward disunion." The response of the immense crowd was electric. Everett was given "nine vociferous cheers," according to the Baltimore *Sun*, followed by thunderous "clapping of hands, waving of hats and handkerchiefs and every demonstration that a sincere people could give of satisfaction and delight."

Deafening applause greeted the second speaker, Caleb Cushing, who was just a few years away from serving as attorney-general under Franklin Pierce. His dramatic and emotional speech rivaled, if not surpassed, Everett's, but he alienated some in the crowd, and there was some hissing among the applause. Cushing commenced with, "Who denies that John Brown was guilty? Who says he did not undertake invasion and perpetrate it? Who says that he did not meditate treason and endeavor to perpetrate it? Who says that he did not slay unarmed and inoffensive men in the streets of Harper's Ferry? No man denies it." Those were, said Cushing, "atrocious and ferocious felony." He continued, "I say... honor to the State of Virginia for apprehending [and executing]... this traitor and murderer." The crowd applauded and cheered Virginia. Cushing moved the audience, describing "husbands torn from the arms of their wives... ruthlessly slaughtered in cold blood" and the "merciless" murder of youthful sons at Pottawatomie Creek. He said the man responsible was John Brown—"his sword dripping with the gore, and that sword from the State of Massachusetts." Not all in the crowd approved, responding with hisses, someone yelling, "That's a lie"; others cried, "Put him out," as others applauded their approval of the speaker. Cushing continued, "I say that murderous acts of John Brown [in Kansas]... was the commencement of bloodshed in these United States, and it was with the same spirit... [that Brown] with an insane ferocity of cruelty, proposed to ravage the peaceful inhabitants of the State of Virginia, and millions upon millions of white women, too, to servile insurrection and civil war, and to outrages indescribable, impossible to imagine."

Cushing went on. "Gentlemen, shall I speak openly?" "Yes, Yes" was the response. "I say in this commonwealth of Massachusetts and in the adjoining state of New York, there is a handful of men, of intellectual men of highest culture, literary and scientific men... Wendell Phillips [applause and hisses], Lloyd Garrison [applause and hisses], Theodore Parker, Waldo Emerson [applause and hisses and cries of 'Go on' and 'name them'] and Gerrit Smith [cries of 'Good,' and 'Go on']." "[They would not] injure even a hair on my head—unless upon the question of slavery, and then such is the atrocious ferocity of mind into which they have been betrayed by this monomania... [they have] set up in this Commonwealth a religion of hate—aye, of hate, such as belongs only to the damned devils in hell." Concluding, Cushing said, "But I speak for no party—I speak for the Union."[16]

The most raucous meetings were on December 15 in Philadelphia and New York. Much excitement occurred in Philadelphia when an anti-slavery convention was held, and a Union meeting took place in front of the building with attendees praising the deeds of John Brown. Things grew more chaotic in New York, where a "John Brown Sympathy Meeting" was held in the Cooper Institution. A series of speakers, including Dr. Cheever and Wendell Phillips, compared Brown to the greatest men in history—even Jesus—arguing Brown had been given the right to end slavery by God, the Bible, and natural rights. They were repeatedly interrupted by hecklers, loud applause, even louder hisses, and cries of "No, No," "Yes, Yes," "Three cheers for Governor Wise," and "Three groans for John Brown." Speakers were frequently forced to stop talking. A reporter from the Baltimore *American* wrote, "Confusion was almost indescribable." Policemen struggled to remove the most disruptive, only to have them return and resume their disturbance. Even the addition of more lawmen failed to restore order. Often during the chaotic interruptions the band would play a familiar song. During one interlude the dissenters unanimously voted that Cheever should be tarred and feathered. In the midst of Phillips's talk a loud voice could be head stopping his speech: "I want to know who constituted John Brown the judge of the laws of the United States, whether they are constitutional or unconstitutional—whether he, by himself, with a few friends he had at Harper's Ferry, deluded like himself, whether he is constituted the judge of the laws of the United States as laid down." In reply, Phillips said, "I will give you an answer to that question," which was met with cries of "No, Yes," and "Answer!"

"God made him [Brown] a judge when he made him a man… Law is nothing but parchment, with the bayonets behind it." Phillips added, "I had rather be with John Brown in his grave, if I were worthy of it—" when an interrupting voice shouted, "I wish you were."[17]

Brown helped divide not only North from South but also factions of Northerners. Northern Union meetings—attended by large masses in support of the Union—did not resonate in the South. The only thing most residents below the Mason–Dixon Line found believable were the horrors of slave insurrections. These were vividly depicted by speakers such as Edward Everett and Caleb Cushing. Even Lincoln's and other moderate Republicans' messages repudiating Brown's actions fell on deaf ears; all Republicans were repugnant to the South. Indeed, no Yankee could be trusted. A Virginia lady in Fairfax County was distrustful of the more than 200 Northern families who moved into her county in the antebellum era (many of whom, she suspected, were abolitionists). She requested that Governor Wise send her a Sharps rifle. She claimed to have "plenty of nerve, and all she wanted was the means to exercise it." According to a letter printed in the New York *Herald,* the governor sent her a rifle, along with the request that she raise a "volunteer corps of women in her region."[18]

The fear of slave revolts and outside attacks served as a powerful stimulus for Southern mobilization. Soon after the Harpers Ferry raid, the governor of Maryland ordered the sheriff of Washington County to deputize men who lived near the Pennsylvania line. The sheriff summoned 500 men to arrest and detain "the assembly of unlawful characters or men whose character and purpose" were "not known." South of the Potomac, in Berkeley County, Virginia, border guards were formed for public protection. This move was duplicated by many other counties and towns.

Even the nation's capital, in many ways a Southern city, shared the fears of trouble from black people (the District had 1,800 slaves and 9,000 free blacks). Despite attempts in the mid-1840s to revive Washington's militia, in the fall of 1859 the District had only four small companies. The US military force in the capital city consisted of nearly 100 Marines, who had been sent hurriedly to Harpers Ferry to deal with Brown. Several months earlier the Secretary of War had received an anonymous letter warning of impending and simultaneous attacks to be made upon the armories at Harpers Ferry, Wheeling, and Washington. News of Brown's raid hit Washington on Monday, October 17. The prophecy of the anonymous letter seemed to be coming true.

Aware of Washington's defenselessness, the mayor rapidly obtained arms from the War Department. He sent men on horseback to guard all roads to the city, with instructions to the men to give a signal by a previously agreed-upon system if they saw anything suspicious. An anxious chief of police handed out 200 muskets to policemen and volunteers, loaded from a government supply of 5,000 rounds of buck and ball cartridges, and had bayonets fixed. Black people found on the street were arrested and searched for concealed weapons, and those possessing weapons were detained. Permits that had been issued to blacks granting them permission to hold parties and festivals were revoked. After hearing news of the Harpers Ferry events, municipal clerks, militiamen, and policemen were kept on alert throughout the night. Precautions were taken to secure the Capitol and grounds; the security force there was furnished with revolvers.[19]

Governor Wise and the Defense of Virginia

Like the citizens of the national capital, residents in the Old Dominion's capital were also greatly alarmed when told about Harpers Ferry. The excitement affected all of Richmond, including Governor Wise's young son, John. The lad ran breathlessly to tell his father the news about Harpers Ferry that he had read on a bulletin board of a Main Street newspaper office. He found his dad in the library, roused from his afternoon nap and reading telegrams about Harpers Ferry. Soon the governor pulled the Virginia Code from the shelf, studied it, and sent word to the commanders of the militia near the invasion. He had telegrams sent to President Buchanan and the governor of Maryland, asking for permission to pass through the District and

Maryland "with armed troops, that route being the quickest route" from Richmond to Harpers Ferry. Later that evening the governor waited for further news at the drab old depot in the center of town, which was usually dark and gloomy at night, but was now brightly lit. Outside on the dim streets, curious masses swarmed about to catch a glimpse of militiamen with three days' rations waiting near the railroad cars.

Amid such excitement, young John Wise donned a little blue jacket with brass buttons and a navy cap, grabbed a long-barreled squirrel-rifle (half again as tall as the boy), took a powder horn and bullets, and joined the few militiamen who were able to board the train on a few hours' notice. Young John's glory was short lived. Before the train left, the governor's slave butler, "Uncle Jim," pulled the mortified youngster from under a train seat and took him home while onlooking militiamen laughed heartily. As an adult John would write, "Jim may have been father's slave, but I was Jim's minion, and felt it. There was no potentate I held in greater reverence, no tyrant whose mandates I heard in greater fear."[20]

At 8:00 p.m. the train left and proceeded north to Aquia Landing, with the governor and 60 men of Company F of the First Regiment of the Virginia Volunteers. At Aquia Landing the small force boarded a steamer for Washington, where it was joined by the Alexandria Rifles, a force of 28 men from across the river. After a long delay in the District and at the Relay House, 10 miles south of Baltimore, they proceeded to Harpers Ferry, arriving at 1:00 Tuesday afternoon, October 18. They were too late to assist in capturing Brown. The majority of the Richmond militia never made it to Harpers Ferry, as it took until 7:00 on the morning of Brown's capture for 223 men of the First Regiment and the 41 members of the 179th Regiment to ready themselves for departure. At Fredericksburg they were reinforced by 16 militiamen and three musicians of the Washington Guard. This force of 283 followed the identical route taken earlier by Wise and Company F. After being fed dinner aboard ship at the cost of $0.75 per man, a price the commander, Colonel T. P. August, felt was excessive, they disembarked in Washington. There they were told the raid was over and received the governor's order to return.

It was imperative to Governor Wise and many others that Virginia should show it could handle any threat to security. After Brown's execution, Wise told the state legislature, "I did not remove the prisoners further into the interior, because I was determined to show no apprehension of a rescue; and if the jail of Jefferson had been on the line of the State they would have been kept there to show they could be kept anywhere chosen in our limits." Wise rejected offers by the governors and militia companies of North Carolina, South Carolina, and Georgia to send military aid to protect the Old Dominion. The following companies telegraphed Wise in late November volunteering their services to Virginia: the Oglethorpe Infantry of Augusta, Georgia; Washington Light Infantry of Wilmington, North Carolina; Hancock Vanguard of Milledgeville, Georgia; City Light Guard of Columbus, Georgia; and by letter, Independent Grays of Elizabeth City, North Carolina. Wise "respectfully and thankfully declined all offers." Maryland Governor Thomas H. Hicks ordered a special scouting and policing detachment for the counties that bordered the Old Dominion: Allegheny, Washington, and Frederick.

Wise's zealous pursuit of Harpers Ferry fugitives evoked a concerned reply from Samuel P. Chase, the Republican governor of Ohio: he said he could not consent to invasion of his territory by armed bodies from other states, even for the purpose of pursuing and arresting fugitives. This did not blunt Wise's efforts to ferret out plans proving Harpers Ferry was part of a Northern conspiracy. During Brown's trial he would send attorney Henry Hudnall to Charles Town to gain proof from the papers taken from the Kennedy house that Wise had excitedly perused at Harpers Ferry the night after Brown's capture. By November 17 Hudnall had completed instructions from the governor to transcribe papers that "either directly or collaterally connected with Brown's scheme for an armed invasion of the south, and more particularly with reference to his late attempt on Virginia soil." Hudnall had to wade through a mass of written materials, including letters, journals, memorandum books, the Provisional Constitution, newspaper clippings, materials relating to the Kansas wars, random thoughts on scraps of paper, maps, and notes about weapons suppliers. Surprisingly, most of the letters were not written to Brown, but to Tidd. The rough lumberman had the most correspondence, a half bushel of letters from all over the North, from loving family members as well as Quaker ladies who took an interest in Tidd. Leeman also received touching letters in the delicate hand of his sister, and Kagi had letters from his relatives, but none were more moving than those received by Dangerfield Newby from his wife, who was in bondage nearby.[21]

Three days after the raiders' capture, Wise returned to the governor's mansion in Richmond, fatigued and suffering from a bad cold. He was enthusiastically welcomed by a crowd and Company F, the militiamen who had originally accompanied him to Harpers Ferry.

Wise responded with a speech. He summarized the raid and said he had matters under control. He told his audience that on the morning of the pivotal capture, he had wired Colonel Robert E. Lee with instructions to make "no terms with the raiders" before Wise had arrived. Despite Wise's orders, Lee was not under his command. Lee commanded federal troops to regain federal property, but the "invasion was on Virginia's soil" and, Wise argued, should have been terminated by Virginians. That it had not been greatly annoyed him. "I would have given my right arm to its right shoulder," Wise declared, "for the feat to have been performed by the volunteers of Virginia on Monday before the marines arrived." But his audience cheered when informed that their governor had told "officers of the United States" that Virginia had first jurisdiction over the "impudent invaders," and that he, Wise, had remained after the raid to accompany the prisoners to Charles Town to protect them from "Lynch Law" and guard them "with the law, and the mercy and might" of Virginia's "sovereignty."

Furthermore, said Wise, if federal authorities would not protect their property at Harpers Ferry, authorities in Virginia would. "Virginia and... other slaveholding states must rely only on themselves," Wise insisted. Harpers Ferry "is a severe lesson and we must profit... by its teachings. It urges upon us... the necessity for the thorough organizing, arming and drilling of our militia. I shall implore [Virginians] to organize and take arms in their hands and to practice [using them]," Wise continued, "and I will cause depots to be established for fixed ammunition along our border at every assailable point."[22]

Despite the confident air of his Richmond speech, Wise and many Virginians were worried. They faced the challenges of defending the state and both protecting and guarding the prisoners. The governor ordered militiamen, especially from counties that surrounded the raid site, to be sent to Charles Town. Militiamen, dressed in a vast array of colors, came from many regions of the state to the county seat of Jefferson County, Virginia (now West Virginia), about six miles from the raid. From late October to early December, the eyes of the nation focused on Charles Town as Brown was speedily tried; found guilty of treason, conspiracy, and murder; and sentenced to be hung on December 2. Visitors and curious onlookers flooded the small town. Rumors dominated conversation. Any sudden death of livestock suggested the fiendish hand of abolitionists. The eerie night burnings of barns, outhouses, stables, wheat, and haystacks around Charles Town and neighboring counties were interpreted by local whites as clear signals for slaves to revolt. Other slave-revolt signs were reported by vedettes who confused chimney sparks for rockets on the neighboring mountains. Women in the area were fearful of being killed or raped and barricaded themselves indoors.[23]

Contrary to Lewis Washington's and others' claim that slaves' behavior returned to "normal" after the raid, things were not so tranquil. Incendiary vandalism and livestock poisoning seemed evidence of this discontent, forming the bulk of black people's major protests after the raid. The Richmond *Enquirer* noted about the nightly burning: "the heavens are illuminated by the lurid glare of burning property."

Five barns and outbuildings near Charles Town were burned within 24 hours. The unidentified arsonists were unquestioningly assumed to be black people or abolitionist friends of Brown. The property of three of Brown's convicting jurors—John Burns, Walter Shirley, and George H. Tate—was torched. The citizens of Jefferson County sent a petition to the Virginia state legislature on January 12, 1860, asking that the jury's foreman, Walter Shirley, be compensated for his losses, citing that three stock yards were burned by so-called Negroes who received their orders from Cook. Wheatland, the home of George Turner, a victim of the raid whose slaves disliked him, was set aflame. His brother William F. Turner's horses and sheep suddenly died from an assumed poisoning. Even Brown expressed concern in a letter to his wife that the incendiary acts would be unfairly blamed "on our friends." On November 12 he wrote her, "There is now here a source of much disquietude to me… the fires which are almost of daily and nightly occurrence in this immediate neighborhood."[24]

The situation was devoid of humor—except to many Northerners who felt the South was greatly overreacting to Brown's raid. James Moore, who had mistaken bird calls for the sound of neighbors being massacred, was used as an example of the slightest thing's tricking Southern imaginations into seeing a menacing abolitionist behind every bush and treason in every peddler. A New York editorial claimed that if a raid as meager as the size of Brown's had occurred in the North it would have simply been quelled by the town police and would not have required "the interposition of Governors, Presidents, marines, militias and mobs." To Southerners this missed the point. It was not the size of the raiding party but the likely chain reaction on the institution of slavery that concerned them. A newspaper clipping from Pittsburgh, sent to a Charles Town resident, ridiculed Virginia's anxiety. It was reprinted in the Virginia *Free Press* as an example of "dirty" Northern printing and poor taste. The article suggested that the Pittsburgh "Hannibal Guards, colored infantry [should offer]… their service to Gov. Wise to protect the terrified residents of Charlestown." The Hannibal Guards "would be able to restore" to "the lilly-livered Virginians" a sense of safety. It was further recommended that the "guards take a large supply of a celebrated 'Scalp Tonic'… to be used on the hair of these Virginians to prevent it from falling out or turning grey prematurely from fright."[25]

Both hostile and friendly letters were sent to Brown and Governor Wise, telling of impending rescue schemes. A few sent money to the jailed Brown. Occasionally others received caveats. An unsigned letter from Harrisburg, Pennsylvania, warned Charles Harding, the Commonwealth Attorney for Jefferson County, that a sizable force from the North planned, on the day prior to Brown's execution, "to fire Charlestown in several places and amid the confusion" to rescue the raider leader. One hostile letter writer attempted to intimidate and worry Wise by using reddish ink to simulate bloodstains.

Most of Brown's mail told of help that was forthcoming. A few letters were in code or script. "A friend" of Brown "and enemy of Wise" wrote, "I will… command 5000 men" armed with "Pike's rifles" and "four pieces of cannon" to free Brown. Another letter, written in script and code, to "Captain" Brown, stated, "Die like a man—Your death will increase our numbers tenfold. We hope before you Suffer Martyrdom—in this glorious cause—you will hear of a much more successful campaign" before "those Hell-Hounds bring Satan's Kingdom (we mean Slave holders) to bear upon us." The letter went on, "Should the Sentence be carried out in your case—rest assured that Vengeance and 'blood' Shall be visited on the heads of those—who… dared to murder innocent men. Let Gov. [Wise] remember that 'blood' will flow and that freely for all the wrongs perpetrated by them—in order to Sustain their hellish [slave] traffic." Less threatening but still unacceptable was a letter to Wise from an abolitionist minister in Cincinnati, who offered to be hung in place of Brown. The Virginia governor's answer, according to the press, was that Brown's life could not be spared, but if the minister was anxious to be hanged and would come to Virginia, he "would try to have him accommodated."

On November 4 the verbose governor gave his most measured response about Brown's sentence and a plea for leniency in a letter to the ex-mayor of New York, Fernando Wood:

> MY DEAR SIR: I have duly received and weighted every word of your letter. I give it all credit for good motive and good morals, and as suggesting what, perhaps, is good policy. Now listen to me, for my mind is inflexibly made up.
>
> Had I reached Harper's Ferry before these men were captured (and I would have reached there in time had I been forwarded as I ought to have been from Washington and the Relay House,) I would have proclaimed martial law, have stormed them in the quickest possible time, have given them no quarters, and if any had survived, I would have tried and executed them under the sentence of court-martial. But I was too late. The prisoners were captured, and I then determined to protect them to the uttermost of my power, and I did protect them with my own person. I escorted them to prison, and placed around them such a force as to overawe Lynch law. Every comfort was given them by my orders. And they have been scrupulously afforded a fair and speedy trial, with every opportunity of defense for crimes which were openly perpetrated before the eyes of hundreds, and openly confessed... And the crimes deliberately done by them are of the deepest and darkest kind which can be committed against our people. BROWN, the chief leader, has been legally and fairly tried and convicted, and admits the humanity of his treatment as a prisoner, the truth of the indictment, and the truthfulness of the witnesses against him. He has been allowed excess of counsel, and the freedom of speech beyond any prisoner known to me in our trials. It was impossible not to convict him. He is sentenced to be hung... and requires no duty from me except to see that it be executed. I have signed no death-warrant. If the Executive interposes at all, it is to pardon; and to pardon him I have received petitions, prayers, threats from almost every State in the Union. From honest patriotic men, like yourself, many of them, I am warned that hanging will make a martyr. Ah! Will it? Why? The obvious answer to that question shows me above anything the necessity for hanging him. You ask, "Have you nerve enough to send BROWN to the State Prison for life, instead of hanging him." Yes, if I didn't think he ought to be hung, and that I would be inexcusable for mitigating his punishment... But was it ever known before that it would be impolitic for a State to execute her laws against the highest of crimes, without bringing down upon herself the vengeance of a public sentiment outside of her limits, and hostile to her laws? Is it so that it is wisely said to her that she had better spare a murderer, a robber, a traitor, because public sentiment elsewhere will glorify an insurrectionist with martyrdom? If so, it is time to do execution upon him and all like him. And I say to you, firmly, that I have precisely the nerve enough to let him be executed with the certainty of his condemnation. He shall be executed as the law sentences him, and his body shall be delivered over to surgeons, and await the resurrection without a grave in our soil. I have shown him all the mercy which humanity can claim...[26]

Letters sent to Brown were screened before they were forwarded to him. Authorities at Charles Town made terse endorsements, ranging from "idle stuff," "doubtful," and "rather bold, concerned," to "villainous" and "contemptible nonsense." The letters ranged from condemning Brown to praising his actions that would obtain heavenly rewards; in the words of a friend, his death would make him one of history's greatest martyrs and, "the gallows as glorious as the Cross." Others told of impending rescue attempts. A few letters were deemed improper and were not forwarded to Brown, including a letter from a former "Pro-Slavery man in Kansas Territory" who wrote, "You are now about to embark in the unenviable occupation of hemp-pulling; but... when your mind reverts to the innocent blood shed at your hands in Kansas and Virginia, what can you say, but that you deserve death in its most horrid form." However, an emotional letter from an aggrieved widow and mother, whose husband and two sons were victims of Brown's Pottawatomie Creek massacre in 1856, was forwarded to Brown:

> Chattanooga, Tennessee
> November 20, 1859
>
> Sir:—Although vengeance is not mine, I confess that I do feel gratified to hear you were stopped in your fiendish career at Harpers Ferry, with the loss of your two sons. You can now appreciate my distress in Kansas when you then and there entered my house at midnight, and arrested my husband and two boys, and took them out of the yard, and in cold blood shot them dead in my hearing. You can't say you done it to free slaves—we had none, and never expected to own one—but has only made me a poor disconsolate widow, with helpless children. While I feel for your folly, I do hope and trust that you meet your just reward. Oh how it pained my heart to hear dying groans of my husband and children. If this scrawl gives you any consolation, you are welcome to it.
>
> Mahala Doyle

Left destitute after Brown had taken her husband and two sons' lives, Mahala Doyle moved to Chattanooga, Tennessee. There she remained in poverty, supported only by the meager wages of her 18-year-old son John, a dray driver for a commission house, whom she had begged Brown to spare. The editor of the Charleston *Daily Tribune* cited the sympathy expressed in the North through $100 and $50 checks sent to Brown's widow: "Will not the benevolent, the affluent and the chivalric of the South contribute to the necessities of this deserving woman? Are there no sympathizers in the South" for "the suffering widow and children of James Doyle?"[27]

Brown admitted participation in the Kansas massacre to Sheriff Campbell but offered what a reporter called excuses for his actions. Mrs. Doyle's letter had a forceful and dramatic effect. It challenged the persona he so actively worked to create during his incarceration: that of a moral crusader and courageous victim. A reporter for the *Evening Star* contended, "The feeling produced against him by Mrs. Doyle's letter, the charge of murdering her husband and two sons, not being denied by him, is most intense. He is no longer admired for his truthfulness and bravery, but is now regarded as a hardened and unprincipled hypocrite."[28]

Mahala Doyle's letter's appearance in newspapers had a far greater impact than further tainting the Old Man's reputation. It became just one of the many pieces of "evidence" reinforcing Southern fears of the "insane fanaticism" threatening them. A Southern lady in a free state who was caring for her elderly mother wrote on lace-bordered stationery, warning Governor Wise, "The n****** headed by the abolitionists intend rescuing Brown and accomplices," who "boast the Ohio river shall run with blood" if Brown and his men are executed. "Look well to Northern and Eastern, indeed you may include all... free States as a threat."

Indeed, plans were proposed to save Old Osawatomie. These ranged from the legal to the unlawful and spanned the period between the start of Brown's incarceration to the end of November. All would fail. Legal redress was first sought after Brown's conviction. His attorneys petitioned the state Supreme Court of Appeals to overturn the conviction on a writ of error. The appeal was denied, and Brown's conviction was upheld. The only other legal recourse was clemency from the governor. Any pardon would have to have the approval of the state legislature, but the governor could delay the execution and let the new soon-to-be governor handle the matter. But postponing the matter was not Wise's way.

Brown's attorney hoped to spark Wise's clemency on the grounds of Brown's insanity. George Hoyt, a young attorney who had recently joined Brown's defense team, traveled to Ohio, obtaining affidavits from 19 of Brown's acquaintances that stated insanity went throughout his family and included Brown himself. Much of it was hearsay or second- and third-hand information from those who hoped to save Brown's life. The pleas of insanity had not worked during the trial, and Brown adamantly repudiated them. After Wise first met Brown, the governor believed Brown was sane and praised him as a man of courage and "clear head." Nevertheless, Wise considered sending Brown to an insane asylum, saying that if the Old Man was insane he ought to be cured. On November 10 Wise ordered the superintendent of the Lunatic Asylum at Staunton, Dr. Francis T. Stribling, to Charles Town to examine Brown. Stribling never went, as Wise soon had a change of heart and countermanded the order.

The governor's position was hardened by threatening letters. He confided in Andrew Hunter that after receiving letters from the North he would not reprieve or pardon any of the prisoners. Later he had a partial change of heart. Shortly before Edwin Coppoc's execution, Wise appeared before the state Senate and House committees for Courts and Justice, saying he favored commuting Coppoc's sentence to life imprisonment. Despite receiving praise in the North and South, Wise failed to convince the members of the Senate committee, who were annoyed by a recently published letter from Coppoc to Mrs. Brown in which Coppoc referred to the people of Harpers Ferry as "the enemy." This, along with information the young Quaker had killed Mayor Beckham, doomed the legislature's approval of a commuted sentence.[29]

Rumors of illegal attempts, spawned in Massachusetts, Kansas, and Ohio, to rescue Brown and his men approached fantasy at times. Such was the early talk that two men could easily go up and down the enormous chimney in Brown's jail room and rescue him. Another story involved a Kansas lady, Miss Mary Partridge, who was selected and was eager to visit Brown to deliver a rescue plan. She was to embrace him most affectionately and deliver the written message into his mouth. Financial and physical difficulties, along with Brown's attitude, kept her in Kansas.

Brown felt his death would further his cause to end slavery far more than his escape, which would diminish martyrdom. He also felt an obligation to John Avis, his jailor, for his kindness and had promised not to try to escape. Even threats to Wise disturbed Brown, provoking him to say it was difficult to believe they were made by his supporters.[30]

The most ardent rescuers were John W. Le Barnes and the Reverend Thomas Wentworth Higginson, along with James Redpath and R. J. Hinton. Le Barnes sent youthful George H. Hoyt to Charles Town, ostensibly as counsel but primarily as a spy to see if Brown could be freed. Convinced by the formidable security around the prisoner and by Brown's emphatic rejection of being rescued, Hoyt wrote to supporters that rescuing the Old Man was hopeless. His second warning on October 30 was even more emphatic: "There is no chance of his [Brown's] ultimate escape; there is nothing but the most unmitigated failure, & the saddest consequences." He was heavily guarded, argued Hoyt. "If you hear anything about such an attempt, for Heaven's sake do not fail to restrain the enterprise."

Undaunted, the intrepid Reverend T. W. Higginson, who agreed with Brown that violence was justified in a righteous cause, persuaded Mrs. Brown to visit her jailed husband in hopes she could convince him to allow a rescue. Once Brown, who may not have known Higginson's real intent, found out his wife was coming, he had her contacted by telegraph in Baltimore and turned back.

George L. Stearns of Boston unsuccessfully tried to enlist the free-soil Kansas guerrillas called the Jayhawkers to help free Brown. Even German immigrants in New York claimed to be willing to march southward—for a fee and under the leadership of John Brown Jr.—to liberate the captured raiders. They, along with men from Ohio, were to rendezvous away from Charles Town on November 27; free the prisoners, either on November 30 or on the day of Brown's execution, December 2; take the horses of the cavalry companies; and escape. The demand of $100 per man, the cost of safe places for the families of German liberty fighters, and the lack of a force coming from Ohio doomed the plan's implementation.

The boldest plan of all was devised by Bostonian abolitionist Lysander Spooner. His plan proposed navigating a tugboat down to Virginia and up the James River to Richmond, kidnapping Governor Wise, and holding him (at sea or in the North) "as a hostage for the safety of Brown." Spooner hoped such a bold move would terrorize the South, but the financial cost of this and other schemes doomed their implementation.[31]

Another approach in the attempts to save the condemned man came in the form of individual requests to Virginia's governor. Often the less threatening of the nearly 500 letters sent to Wise about Brown were those that appealed to Wise to magnanimously spare the abolitionist's life; some quoted scripture and argued it was the Christian thing to do. Even Southerners cautioned Wise that execution would elevate Brown to martyrdom in many eyes. Some of Brown's supporters pleaded he should be pardoned, on grounds of insanity. One of the more interesting appeals set forth arguments for the need for political equality for women and for pardoning Brown on religious grounds (because the taking of human life violated God's law). Such was advocated by Julia Cowles of Oaksville, Connecticut, who wrote Wise, "Can you say that you are not a murder, if Bro. John Brown and his associates are killed on the gallows[?]... There must be a Revolution in the United States... so... women's knowledge" will "make Laws, as well as men... Woman was created to Save, what men condemns to be killed... Bro. Wise do be wise and learn [from] woman how to save the Lives of all God's Creatures."

As well as letters, other items were mailed to Richmond and Charles Town. These ranged from money to assist Brown in his defense to rope for terminating his life. According to newspaper accounts, Francis Keeyes of Alexandria, Virginia, sent "sixteen feet of cotton rope with a noose, carefully knit by himself" to the Jefferson County sheriff. A note accompanied the package stating the intended use.

Anxiety escalated as the execution date neared. On the last day of November the number of letters to Brown that claimed help was coming increased. One deciphered on the 21st said 20 men "left this morning and thirty-five started Thursday—They will bring you with them or die." On the 24th another offered encouragement: "I write you these few lines to inform you that there are large companies of men forming in all the Northern States which will in due time march to your rescue." A November 29 letter told Brown not to give up hope: "I have collected 2,500 men all in arms and they have been quietly entering the town for some time past and the 1st [December] at 12 o'clock at M we will make an attack and endeavor to release you." An anonymous letter written five days earlier to prosecutor C. B. Harding told of an unknown number of armed men with Colt revolvers "by the day of execution of Brown's [plan]... to fire Charlestown in several places and amid the confusion that ensues," to rescue Brown. In late November the sheriff also received a letter warning of a rescue attempt. Earlier, in late October, the clerk of the court received a warning: "You had better caution your authorities to be careful what you [do] with 'Ossawatimi Brown.' So sure as you hurt One hair of the head—mark my word the following day you will see every City—Town and Village South of Mason & Dixon's line in Flames."[32]

Authorities considered most threats to be idle ones, but the ominous messages nevertheless fed doubts and frayed nerves. Wise had determined to keep Brown in the Charles Town jail as a show of Virginian strength. Wise's actions prior to Brown's death, nevertheless, reveal trepidation. Pressure was intensely felt by the tobacco-chewing governor, who was described as usually dressing in a slovenly manner and possessing such "rapidity of penmanship"—paralleling the speed of shorthand—that he was able to respond personally to 25 or 30 letters in a day in addition to his other duties, including receiving visitors. Barton H. Wise, grandson and biographer of the governor, described his grandfather as "largely a creature of impulse," with an "exceptionally excitable" temper. As a reign of terror settled upon Charles Town, Harpers Ferry, and the vicinity in November, with each periodic threat of an impending force's descent, Wise sent militia units back and forth between the homes of the men and the Charles Town area.

The governor was not alone in his anxiety. Local authorities stationed sentries throughout the region. Upon the advice of special prosecutor Andrew Hunter, the "old Southern system of mounted patrols was established in every precinct" of Jefferson County. On November 2, Colonel J. Lucius Davis, then in command of the militia at Charles Town, informed Richmond he was ready: "If [an] attack be made, the prisoners will be shot by the inside guards." During Brown's trial surveillance of strangers was in full force. Any unknown person traveling about at night without a countersign was in danger of a visit to the guard house. By November 12, Mayor Thomas Green ordered all strangers be removed from Charles Town unless they could prove an acceptable reason for their presence. A week later Colonel Davis, whose confidence to meet threats had evaporated, frantically wired Wise, "Send me 500 men armed and equipped"…"[to stop] a large body," which he claimed was said to be approaching from Wheeling to rescue Brown.

By mid-November mysterious fires and rumors of invaders coming to liberate Brown shook Davis's confidence and erupted into the greatest panic since the raid. Rumors of men crossing the Ohio to liberate the prisoners troubled people not just near Charles Town but also in Washington, Baltimore, Alexandria, Richmond, and throughout the Old Dominion. The threats echoed with menace throughout the South. Bold headlines in the New York *Herald* warned, "VIRGINIA ARMING FOR WAR." News of Brown's jurors' property torching was deemed irrefutable proof of the treacherous work of Brown supporters. One correspondent wrote that the burning of a wheat shock on the night of November 17 by an unknown arsonist worried Davis and was perceived by Davis to be an abolitionist attack. Without sending a party to investigate, Davis immediately sent a dispatch to Governor Wise to send two companies of cavalry. Eighty-four men hurried from Alexandria, armed with rifles, sabers, and ammunition taken from the Washington arsenal. Some traveled over the B&O. The others, 60 men with four guns, went by special train from Manassas Junction to Strasburg, walking the 18 miles to Winchester, and from there they rode the rails to Charles Town.

Angst also intensified at the time of the torching, with the arrival of the excited Smith Crane; he hurried from his home near Wheeling to Charles Town to warn citizens of their ominous fate. Crane claimed to have overheard a "conservation between some men who had organized a band of five hundred" to march and release "Brown and the other prisoners at Charlestown." Upon hearing this, Colonel Davis panicked and wired Governor Wise for help against the impending assault from above and rumored fighting that had occurred between citizens and a party of strangers in nearby Clarke County. Wise immediately sent help to Charles Town as militiamen from Richmond, Alexandria and Petersburg accompanied with artillery arrived within the next several days, totalling about 550 men. Wise, it was reported, did not believe the rumor of an imminent attack by a large force, but thought there were individual troublemakers in the area. Accompanying 400 militiamen from the state capital, Wise immediately left Richmond by special train to calm the nerves of the counties in the north and to discourage rescue attempts. Men from Petersburg, including Private Roger A. Pryer, a newly elected member of the House of Representatives, secessionists, and future Confederate general and venerable reporter Hugh R. Pleasants would travel by boat to Washington, arriving at Charles Town the day after Wise and the men from Richmond.[33]

Rumors of Colonel Davis's pleas for help also sparked panic in Richmond, Washington, and Baltimore. As militiamen scurried about the streets of Richmond on the night of November 17 preparing to accompany their governor to Charles Town, rumors spread that 900 abolitionists were nearing Harpers Ferry and preparing to assault the Virginia troops. It was rumored that abolitionists had burned half of Charles Town, Brown had escaped, and Wise was going to capture him. On November 20 Wise and 400 of his men arrived at the Ferry, greeted by militiamen in their best uniforms. Half the new arrivals stayed at Harpers Ferry, and the rest were taken to Charles Town by the yard engine that had been fixed up because the other engines were too heavy to run on the tracks to Winchester. Once at Charles Town, they impressed locals with their maneuvers. Around 9:00 p.m. a nervous sentinel fired, sending the town into a panic. Infantrymen and cavalrymen scurried through the streets, trying to avoid mud in the dark. A person was arrested, but the reason for the panic-triggering shot remained unexplained. A Richmond *Dispatch* correspondent wrote that the concentration of militiamen as a show of force "may be regarded as unnecessary preparations; but when you consider that the object of assembling so many troops here to annihilate all hope of a successful rescue, and thus prevent attack, which in any case would be disastrous, you acknowledge that as precautions they are commendable."[34]

It was cold weather, and many of the men who responded to Davis's call for help had left without overcoats, causing Wise to order 150 heavy overcoats on November 22. The following day the impulsive governor returned to Richmond. Before leaving, he and other military visited the condemned leader and his men. They were received by the prisoners courteously, but Brown vigorously argued he was correct in doing what he had done. Brown grumbled about the large crowd of visitors to one of the interviewers: "He objected to being made a monkey of."

Cook was the most talkative and frank. He is said to have stated that he was prepared to die, and "would be perfectly willing to be shot, but has a horror of being hung." He only "intended to assist runaway slaves" and thought the punishment handed down by the jury was too severe for the crime. He received no sympathy from Wise, who reassured citizens he would not interfere with the decision of the court and said, "The only man who stood the least chance of mercy was Coppoc and he stood no chance at all." Once back in Richmond, Wise received a dispatch from Governor Parker of Pennsylvania offering the services of 10,000 men, and "offering to station a guard along the dividing line between Pennsylvania and Maryland." Wise thanked Parker but assured him "Virginia was able to protect her honor." The numerous offers of military help from all quarters of Georgia and North Carolina received the same response.[35]

Once those who went through the scare realized Colonel Davis had severely overreacted without properly investigating, his reputation declined. Virginians fumed and said he had made them "appear ridiculous before the country."

No doubt the excitement caused by the warnings and the uncertainty of a rescue attempt, no matter how remote, were factors in the constant movement of militiamen to the vicinity of Charles Town. Several days after Wise went to Charlestown, telegrams were sent to Richmond that asked for men and arms to be sent to Northampton and Accomac counties, on the eastern shore, to foil a "plot to run the areas' slaves off to Canada on November 25."

Fear prompted individuals to arm themselves as best they could. Within a month of the raid Baltimore arms dealers sold over 10,000 Colt revolvers to Virginians.[36] Anyone who provided security was deeply appreciated; on March 14, 1860, the Booker sisters returned $40 to the state for assessed damage to their property in the occupation of troops at Charles Town. Others who were reimbursed for damages, although appreciative of militia protection, did not feel compelled to return the money.

Imaginary threats of impending abolitionist incursions brought martial law to Charles Town, to Jefferson County, and to neighboring Clarke County, as well as some degree of mobilization in nearby counties. By late November the Clarke County seat of Berryville was billeting the Clarke Guards into a building hastily converted into barracks. Numbering 72 and varying in age from 16 to 70, this recently formed company donned uniforms as soon as local women could make them. They anxiously opened three packages containing 60 Minnie rifles and bayonets; they drilled and fired at targets on a daily basis; and they conducted day and night patrols, occasionally turning away what the locals called "dangerous Yankee pedlars." For this work, like most other militia companies the governor had called to defend the state, their privates were later paid $11 a month, or $0.36 for each day of service. Musicians earned $12; corporals, $13; sergeants, $15; and lieutenants and captains, from $50 to $70. For those dealing with the John Brown raid, the Virginia General Assembly appropriated $81,140.02 for the payment of 1,799 men, totaling 797 days of service. This included $169.92 for eight days' service by 12 band members in the 1st Regular Virginia Volunteers. Those on duty after this appropriation were later compensated. Payment was slow in coming, and militiamen returned to their

NAMES OF COMPANIES, &c.	No. of Officers and Men.	No. of days in Service.	Under Act of assembly, pay for actual Service.	Under Joint Resolution, extra pay.
Ashby's Mountain Rangers, - -	64	38	3,970 29	1,398 50
Carter's Loudoun Light-horse, - -	42	21	1,931 65	1,304 90
Do. forage omitted on pay roll,	-	-	493 50	
Rady's Young Guard, twice in service—average,	49	21	731 35	1,526 30
Duffey's Alexandria Artillery, - -	49	38	969 87	814 65
Smith's Mt. Vernon Guards, - -	52	19	761 92	1,448 99
Mayre's Alexandria Rifles, - -	58	21	693 74	1,401 93
Cary's company F, 1st reg. Va. vol., -	89	19	1,184 22	2,149 55
Bowen's Clarke Guards, - -	66	33	2,376 55	1,387 00
Butler's Hamtramck Guards,* - -	62	19	1,660 70	
Rowan's Jefferson Guards, still in service—average number, - -	73	60	3,833 69	
Capt. Sherrard, drill officer to 77th regiment, -	1	5	19 75	
J. D. Smith, acting quartermaster's sergeant,	1	15	18 00	58 25
Band of 1st reg. Va. vol., - -	12	8	169 92	
Comp. A, 1st reg. Va. vol. (Greys), -	95	20	1,365 60	2,211 76
Comp. C, " " (Montgomery G'rds),	74	23	806 16	1,802 03
Comp. E, " " (Blues),	86	24	1,258 11	2,078 41
Scott's company of Black-horse, - -	45	30	1,645 66	1,070 00
Mallory's Monticello Guard, - -	52	15	524 50	1,437 50
Alburtis' Wise Artillery, - -	72	28	2,079 52	1,603 55
Sibert's 10th Legion Artillery, -	63	17	721 37	1,424 36
Rocky Ridge Rifles, - -	29	4	60 87	313 14
Comp. K, 1st reg. Va. vol., - -	57	22	469 08	1,345 84
Randolph's Howitzers, - -	80	17	729 69	1,852 21
Senor's Washington Guard, - -	44	15	460 70	1,194 80
Lamb's Woodis Rifles, - -	70	23	1,966 92	1,639 63
Berkeley Border Guard, - -	95	30	2,897 96	2,059 38
Old Dominion Greys, - -	44	26	1,011 04	1,039 02
Gilkerson's Rifles, - -	38	30	885 92	815 74
" " detachment, -	20	6	115 80	183 20
Rhinehart company of Cavalry, -	75	20	2,512 18	1,494 84
" " forage for detachment,	-	-	673 57	
Baylor's West Augusta Guard, -	56	17	549 61	1,545 84
May's City Guard, - -	60	33	1,064 71	1,153 60
Hunter's Executive Guard, - -	26	80	2,591 13	79 86
	1,799	797	$43,215 25	$37,924 77

The Virginia General Assembly's Partial Payment for Militia Service Regarding John Brown's Raid

homes before being paid. Early in 1860, the citizens of Petersburg donated funds for their volunteers, amounting to $425.50 for each company.[37]

Other jurisdictions surrounding Jefferson County also responded to the anticipated threat. Captain Shreve's cavalry company was called into service to guard that portion of Loudoun County lying on the Potomac River, especially the fording areas. Fairfax County, east of Loudoun, formed patrol companies for each magisterial district. Virginia counties to the south and west of Charles Town followed suit. A new volunteer company was formed at the Culpeper Court House, drawing upon the inspiration of the American Revolution; it was called the Culpeper Minute Men. In Warren County the Front Royal Guards met to decide a course of action, and men in the Shenandoah Valley at Woodstock organized a voluntary company they called the 10th Legion Riflemen. Men in Berkeley County, near the southern banks of the Potomac, rushed to arms at Martinsburg, forming two companies of the Berkeley Border Guards and single companies at Mill Creek, Darksville, Hedgeville, and Falling Waters. Mobilization for defense also took place north of the Potomac River in Howard County, Maryland, with the formation of cavalry and infantry companies.[38]

In the third week in November, when rumors flourished about armed abolitionists gathering in the Blue Ridge, Wise rushed—as he was moving hundreds of militiamen to Charles Town—more than 40 men of the Alexandria Artillery and their two artillery pieces to Berryville. They traveled via the Manassas Gap Railroad to Strasburg and continued on foot through Winchester. In the meantime, according to the Clarke *Journal*, a dozen of Clarke County's "gallant citizens," on a moment's notice and at 2:00 a.m., rode 12 miles in "a pelting storm" to ferret out abolitionists at the Underwood farm near Berry's Ferry. The trip was in vain. Similar efforts by squads of the Clarke Guards, Alexandria Artillery, and private citizens, scouring the Blue Ridge from Smoketown to the Jefferson County line, found nothing.

Occasionally, in November and December, shots rang out in the night in Clarke and Jefferson counties when nervous sentries stumbled through the underbrush and fired at imaginary attackers. The same occurred east of the Blue Ridge in Loudoun County, where the Short Hills and the southern banks of the Potomac were guarded by men on horse and foot, protecting what a local newspaper editor called "our soil from the polluting tread of enemies of our institutions." Any sudden light in the sky was interpreted by someone as a rocket giving a sinister signal to Brown supporters. Men who were repeatedly sent to investigate any suspicious nightly occurrence exhausted themselves, marching toward the source of the noise. About suspected rockets, they heatedly debated whether they were actually comets. If the source was discovered at all, it turned out to be simple sparks from a fire.

One night several sentries fired at a riderless horse, mistaking the creature in the darkness for approaching abolitionist assailants. People were curious about military sights. Berryville residents were fascinated by two cannons temporarily abandoned in their town by the Alexandria Artillery. Mesmerized by these uncommon weapons, local citizens took them to the outskirts of Berryville, claiming to search for what the town's newspaper called "vagabond abolitionists." Finding none, according to the Clarke *Journal*, they "touched" off the pieces "a few times for the sake of variety."[39]

CHAPTER 6

The Rush to Judgment

The nation's attention shifted away from Harpers Ferry when Brown and his captured associates were taken a half dozen miles southwest to the Jefferson County seat, Charles Town. The town was named after its founder, Charles Washington, the younger brother of George Washington; in 1786 Charles gave 80 acres of land and laid out streets, naming many of them after his brothers and his wife. He specified the four corner lots at the intersection of George and Washington Streets for public buildings, contingent upon the town's becoming the county seat. On three of those lots were constructed buildings that would play a significant role in the trial of Brown and his men. The courthouse, where the judicial drama was played out, was a Romanesque building with four imposing Doric columns and a commanding bell tower, surrounded by an iron fence. It occupied the intersection's northwestern lot. Directly south across the street was a three-story structure that housed and fed many who swarmed to witness the proceedings, as well as militiamen who swelled the streets. Those at the center of the drama, the prisoners, were locked in the brick jail diagonally across the intersection from the courthouse.

The Trial of the Century

While measures were being taken to secure the prisoners, many issues found forum in the Charles Town courthouse, among citizens as well as in newspapers; topics for debate included jurisdiction, a speedy and fair trial, proper legal defense for the accused, Brown's sanity, and his possible execution. It would be a trial of many firsts. A special telegraph line was constructed from Charles Town to Harpers Ferry to the national network so reporters could send accounts through the Associated Press telegraph service to newspapers throughout the nation. This relatively recent innovation was revolutionary, and the national coverage led to claims that Brown's trial was the first modern trial, a memorable event in the development of modern journalism. Called the trial of the century, it was the first to be extensively reported nationwide by reporters who swarmed to Charles Town from all US regions. It also was the first trial in which the defendant cited a "higher law" to justify his violent

Charles Town courthouse (right), Gibson Hotel (center), front of jail (far left). (*Frank Leslie's Weekly*, Library of Congress)

Charles Town jail. (West Virginia Archives, Boyd B. Stutler Collection)

crimes, and it was the first time a defendant was executed for treason against a state.[1] The trial, watched by the nation, reflected the most divisive issue that was shaking the foundation of the Union.

Sheriff James Campbell on the left and Jailor John Avis on the right. (West Virginia Archives, Boyd B. Stutler Collection)

Brown's trial and execution gave him the opportunity to salvage his reputation and (more importantly, in his eyes) his crusade against slavery, which had failed miserably. Several hours after Brown was captured, on the afternoon of his failed raid, his presence and eloquent words during the lengthy interview became his most effective weapons—weapons he would maintain until he stood on the gallows waiting for the trap door to open. Ironically, the man who believed the only workable means of ridding the nation of the evils of slavery was through violence and terror was far more successful making his case with words and nonviolence than with bullets.

Two paramount legal issues at his trial had to be immediately resolved: jurisdiction and treason. Brown had attacked and seized federal property and captured its employees. President Buchanan had sent the Marines, who quelled the raid and captured many of the raiders. Buchanan was well within his rights to insist on federal jurisdiction, but he acquiesced to the wishes of the insistent Virginia governor, who wanted to prove to all that the Old Dominion could defend its soil. This made the trial even more divisive. Instead of being charged for federal crimes against the nation, Brown was charged with acts against slaveholding Virginia and, by inference, all Southern neighboring states who upheld human bondage. The mercurial Governor Wise, however, at first vacillated over the jurisdiction of Brown's followers. On November 7, 1859, he instructed Andrew Hunter, special prosecutor for the State of Virginia, "You had better try Cooke and turn Stephens [Stevens] over to the United States Court. Do that definitely." Wise hoped this would somehow increase the chances of getting "greater villains implicated who are still out of our reach." Wise was bombarded with warnings and threatening letters telling of Northern conspiracies and attempts to rescue Brown. When Wise learned that on December 15 Buchanan asked by telegram whether Stevens had been turned over, the governor adamantly reversed his position of six week earlier. He said, "I say definitively that Stephens ought not to be turned over the Federal authorities for trial… I am convinced that there is a political design in trying to have him tried before the Federal courts."[2]

The other vexing question was whether Brown had committed treason against Virginia. His defense attorneys argued he had not. Brown was not a citizen of Virginia, and therefore he did not owe allegiance to the state, and could not be charged with treason against her. Furthermore, Brown came from Maryland and traveled only briefly on Virginia soil before seizing and occupying federal facilities.[3] Prosecutors vigorously contended the raider leader's actions were treasonous against the state. They said Brown was a citizen of the United States upon entering Virginia and owed allegiance to the state despite not being a resident. The judge, Richard Parker, sided with the prosecution, but the legal issue remained troublesome.[4]

There was also a question of whether the trial should be delayed. Brown and four of his men were arraigned on October 25, one week after the raid. The following day they were indicted for treason against the Commonwealth of Virginia, for conspiring with slaves to rebel, and for murder. They all pleaded not guilty, and when given the choice of being tried together or separately, they selected the latter. Brown's trial started on October 27. Three and half days later he was found guilty and sentenced to hang.

The rush to judgment raised cries of protest in the North, where a majority condemned the mad actions of Brown's raid. It appeared Brown was not being given time for a proper defense. Pressure for a speedy trial by judge Richard Parker emanated from the circuit court, which opened its term in Jefferson County on October 20, 1859, and by law was obligated to move to Winchester in the nearby county of Frederick, Virginia, by November 20. Additional factors were the cost and security of the prisoners; fears of attempts to liberate them would grow with delay. This influenced local authorities, such as the special prosecutor, Andrew Hunter, who vowed to have Brown "arraigned, tried, found guilty, sentenced and hung, all within ten days."

Brown's fast trial and his fate depended on men who formed the jury. They owned slaves and were contemptuous of what he had done. Some jurors had fought to subdue him. To Northern newspaper readers it appeared unlikely the raiders would receive a fair trial. This concern was reinforced by newspaper accounts and sketches that evoked sympathy among some by showing the hapless, seriously wounded Stevens, heavily guarded and hobbling to court in pain. He was struggling to breathe and unable to stand without assistance. His less severely injured cellmate was his elderly leader, whose impaired movement required him, at times, to be carried to court on a cot. Once there he lay on a cot in the courthouse. The special prosecutor, Andrew Hunter, was appointed at Wise's insistence because of the drunken ineptness of commonwealth attorney Charles B. Harding, who was relegated to assisting in the trial. Hunter's son had committed a vigilante act during the raid, which in normal times would have led to his being charged with murder after he shot a hapless William Thompson to avenge the death of a relative, Fontaine Beckham. (Despite Hunter's heading the prosecution, press accounts had him assisting Harding, whom Hunter held in contempt.)[5]

All involved in the trial, including the stout and stern-looking state circuit court judge, Richard Parker, were adamantly convinced of the raiders' guilt. The judge, prosecuting attorneys, and Brown's first lawyers were renowned jurists in the region. Despite their intransigent and predetermined views, they labored to follow proper legal procedures and argued they were giving Brown a fair trial. This involved going through three stages: the examining court, grand jury, and jury trial.

All three stages of the trial would meet in the courthouse, primarily in the large courtroom on the first floor, with its seating capacity in excess of 500. At the far end of the courtroom were three windows, and in front of them was a platform the width of the hall, with a railing in front and six steps at each end. Behind the large table sat the judge and magistrates. Below the platform and behind a second railing were the desks for the clerk, tables and chairs for lawyers and clients, and two rows of chairs for the jury. Two large woodstoves, connected to chimneys by long pipes covered with soot, provided heat. At night the room was illuminated by gaslights that dangled from the ceiling by long tubes. Above the first floor where the judicial drama was played out was a large hall for meeting or special events.

Despite the gravity of the situation and the seriousness of the actors in the drama, the room would take on an air of informality not totally unlike that of a circus or sporting event. During Brown's trial, the judge propped up his feet, attorney Harding fell asleep from excessive imbibing, lawyers hung their legs over the arm of their chairs, a wad of tobacco accidentally fell from an attorney's mouth to the floor. Under the feet of the hoard of listening and tobacco-chewing spectators, that floor accumulated several inches of chestnut and peanut shells. When they moved about it created a cracking sound. Uncouth and unrestrained spectators shouted curses at the accused, as others smoked or laughed out loud. Overcrowding necessitated the construction of plank scaffolding to protect court officials so they could perform their duties, and the lack of seats forced witnesses to sit or lie on the floor.[6] Attempts to ban and stop smoking were successful only for moments. Much of the time Brown lay on the cot with eyes closed until he was moved by what was being said; at those times he promptly spoke up.

Outside the courthouse, militiamen guarded all the entrances to the town. Rifle-muskets and ammunition were stashed in the jail, an armed guard patrolled the jail's perimeter, and cannons were positioned in front of both courthouse and jail and periodically checked for readiness to fire in case of attack. While court was in session the building was surrounded by men with gleaming bayonets. When summoned by the loud clanging of the bell above the courthouse, 80 or so militiamen would, with a drumroll, escort the defendants from jail. The prisoners were a pitiful sight at the start. Stevens and Brown lay in their beds groaning from their wounds. Brown's face was bruised and swollen. Hunter was afraid Stevens would die before he could be convicted and hung. Their sad condition was apparent on their way to court.

Brown and Coppoc were shackled together as they shuffled along the short distance across the intersection from jail to courthouse.[7] Jailer John Avis wanted armed men inside the courtroom, but Judge Parker had a strong aversion to arms in his courtroom. Instead four stout men were selected to serve as the prisoners' bodyguard in the courtroom.

Brown was concerned about his safety. This was first displayed the morning of his capture. A correspondent for *Harper's Weekly* who visited Brown and the other prisoners in jail wrote: "The only thing Brown seems to fear is lynch law. He vows his dread of it, and has condescended to ask protection from it from those about him. To give him the assurance (rather than from any well-grounded fear of disturbance), an armed guard accompanies him in his daily rounds between the jail and the court-house."[8]

Eight prominent men, all slave-owners, served on the examining court, convening at 10:00 Tuesday morning (October 25) and concluding its work four hours later. The court opened with Judge Parker instructing the court of the necessity of providing the proper "strict and impartial justice," regardless of the "enormity" of the guilt of those who "invaded by force a peaceful and unsuspecting" community "to create insurrection" and "shoot down without mercy Virginia citizens defending Virginia soil from their invasion." The examining court's task was not to determine the guilt or innocence of the accused but to determine whether there was probable cause to hold them, sending to the matter to a grand jury.[9]

First there was the matter of legal counsel for the defendants. The entrance and departure of attorneys for Brown was a game of musical chairs, and during his trial six lawyers would serve as legal counsel. The first three, local Virginians appointed by the court, would leave and be replaced by three more sympathetic to abolitionists. A seventh attorney would join Brown's legal team soon after his conviction.

Soon after incarceration Brown sought legal help. Suffering from his wounds, he requested Sheriff Campbell write three identical letters to lawyers he believed to be sympathetic to his cause. They were informed he had assets for their fees, including $250 in gold that the sheriff was holding for him, plus weapons at the Kennedy farm (Brown was apparently unaware they had been seized by authorities and taken by neighbors). When the legal proceedings began, Brown had not heard back from the prominent Northern attorneys, Judge Thomas Russell of Boston; Rueben Chapman of Springfield, Massachusetts; and Judge Daniel R. Tilden of Cleveland, Ohio.

Once Sheriff Campbell had read the charges, Harding suggested the court appoint a defense attorney. The head magistrate, Braxton Davenport, asked Brown whether he had an attorney. The Old Man appeared to have forgotten that he had begged for mercy upon his capture, and he surprised his listeners with a defiant response: "Virginians—I did not ask for any quarter at the time I was taken. I did not ask to have my life spared." He said the governor promised "a fair trial, but under no circumstance whatever will I be able to have a fair trial. If you seek my blood, you can have it at any moment without this mockery of a trial. I have had no counsel; I have not been able to advise with anyone... I am ready for my fate." He said his memory was only returning after sustaining injuries, he did "not ask for a trial" and repeatedly requested and begged "no mockery of a trial—no insult... but if we are to be forced with mere form—a trial for execution—you might spare yourselves that trouble." Concluding, Brown said he had little to ask other than, "I may not be foolishly insulted only as cowardly barbarians insult those who fall into their power."

Wanting to avoid delay, Davenport appointed two attorneys who had helped subdue Brown during the raid, Lawson Botts and Charles J. Faulkner. Botts accepted, but Faulkner was appointed despite questioning the court's right to appoint him as a lawyer for a man he emphatically pronounced guilty, a defendant who considered the legal process a mockery. When asked whether he would accept the two attorneys, Brown verbally sparred with commonwealth attorney Harding and was evasive.

Brown said he had sent for his own attorneys and wished to have counsel if he was to receive a trial, "But if I am to have nothing but the mockery of a trial, as I said, I do not care anything about counsel—it is unnecessary to trouble any gentleman with that duty." Harding immediately shouted, "You will have a fair trial." Finally, in exasperation, Harding asked Brown whether he accepted the two men as his attorneys: "Please answer yes or no." Brown refused, stating, "I would prefer they should exercise their own pleasure," as it was of little importance to him. "If they had a design to assist me as counsel, I should have wanted an opportunity to consult them at my leisure." Taking this as a yes, Harding asked the same question of the other defendants, Stevens, Coppoc, Green, and Copeland, who agreed without debate.

Ten witnesses were called, starting with Lewis Washington, Archibald Kitzmiller, Armistead Bell, and John Allstadt. After the last witness the magistrates concluded their work at 2:00 p.m. They were unanimously of the opinion that the prisoners were guilty of the charges and they instructed the matter be sent to a grand jury. The grand jury was already impaneled in another room in the courthouse and was ready for the case. The jury worked and listened to witnesses until 5:00 p.m. before adjourning until the morning. When court was not in session, Judge Parker went outside, where he found prominent citizens who were frustrated with the slowness of the judicial process talking of storming the jail and taking the law into their hands. Some thanked the judge and rethought their position when he pointed out that such opinions would merit harsh punishment.

The grand jury reconvened Wednesday morning. Prosecuting attorney Hunter presented jurors with a long, flowery indictment of the raiders, in legalese, for "conspiring with negroes to produce insurrection, treason in the Commonwealth" and "murder" that they approved of. The charges were spelled out in four indictments. The first was treason. John Brown, Stevens, Coppoc, Green, Copeland, and unknown "evil minded and traitorous persons... not having the fear of God before their eyes, but being moved and seduced by false and malignant counsel of other evil and traitorous persons and the instigation of the devil... feloniously and traitorously made rebellion and levy war against the Commonwealth of Virginia." To "fulfill their... wicked and treasonable ends and purposes," which included overthrowing the constitution and government of the commonwealth and establishing a different government, a "band of organized soldiers" attacked, seized, and held Harpers Ferry, "made prisoners of loyal citizens," and made war upon and murdered "good and loyal citizens... defending the Constitution and laws of the Commonwealth."

The second count accused the prisoners of "maliciously, and feloniously" conspiring with others to induce "Jim, Sam, Mason and Catesbury... the slaves and property of Lewis W. Washington, and Henry, Levi, Benn, Jerry, Phil, George, and Bill, the slaves and property of John H. Allstadt, and other slaves" unknown to the jurors "to rebel and make insurrection against their masters and owners, and against the Government, the Constitution and the laws of the Commonwealth of Virginia."

The third and fourth counts of the indictment were murder. In the third indictment the prisoners "feloniously, willfully, and with malice aforethought... did make an assault... with deadly weapons... charged with leaden bullets," shot and killed Thomas Boerly, George W. Turner, Fontaine Beckham, Luke Quinn, and Hayward Shepherd. The fourth charge indicted John Copeland for "aiding, helping, abetting" the other prisoners "in the felony and murder" of Thomas Boerly, George Turner, and Fontaine Beckham. This indictment applied to all of Brown's captured men.[10]

Treason was not part of the original indictment, and it has not been explained why treason was added to the charges. The outstanding Brown collector and scholar Boyd B. Stutler has surmised that prosecutor Andrew Hunter included treason to prevent the mercurial Governor Wise from pardoning Brown, whom he had both praised and damned. The governor could have pardoned, commuted, or reprieved Brown and his men on all charges but treason—that would have required the approval of the state legislature.

With the grand jury dismissed, and the examining court and grand jury no longer in need of a meeting place, Judge Parker reopened the circuit court on Wednesday afternoon, October 26. Hunter immediately announced the judge had accepted Faulkner's request to step down from serving as Brown's attorney. At Botts's request another able local lawyer and the mayor of Charles Town, Thomas C. Green, replaced Faulkner. Before his attorneys could say anything on his behalf, Brown got up out of a chair and requested a "very short delay" to recover from wounds that enfeebled him and impaired his hearing so much that he was unaware of what was said in the courtroom. Consideration of his request was delayed until after arraignment. It took about 20 minutes for the clerk to read the charges, and all the defendants were required to stand. It was the most difficult for Stevens, who had to be supported. During the reading of the charges an annoyed Judge Parker, who forbade arms in his courtroom, banished an armed militiaman who wandered into the room. After the charges were read, the clerk asked each defendant for their plea, guilty or not guilty. First Brown argued there were things wrong in the indictment, and then he pleaded not guilty. More subdued and in awe of their situation than their leader, the others pleaded the same without additional comment. The clerk asked each prisoner whether they preferred to be tried separately, which they all confirmed. Hunter elected to try John Brown first.

Botts addressed the court, stating he was instructed by his client "to say he was mentally and physically unable to proceed with the trial at this time." He also needed additional time for the Northern attorneys he had written to, asking to defend him, to respond. Hunter cautioned against any delay. Judge Parker rejected waiting for a response from the Northern attorneys as a valid reason for delay, and then ruled a reasonable delay would be granted "if physical impairment was shown." To determine this, the judge sought the opinion of the physician treating Brown in jail. He was informed by Dr. Mason that Brown's wounds would not affect his comprehension or memory and he had not heard him complain about his hearing. One jailor's testimony seemed to support Dr. Mason's opinion, but it was challenged by the testimony of the head jailor, John Avis, who stated he frequently heard Brown complain to visitors that his mind was confused and his hearing impaired. Anxious to move the trial forward, Parker denied a three-day recess and ruled the trial would continue after a midday break.

At 2:00 p.m., when Avis responded to an order to bring Brown back to the courthouse, the prisoner claimed he was unable to get up. Avis had Brown placed on a cot and carried into the courtroom. He lay there for three hours while questions were asked of two dozen prospective jurymen about the raid. Questions ranged from where they were from to what they knew and whether they were opposed to execution. Anyone present during the raid was disqualified. Before adjourning for the day, 12 jurors who happened to live the farthest away from Harpers Ferry but still within Jefferson County were selected. Seven of them owned a total of 54 slaves. At 5:00 p.m. the judge adjourned court until 10:00 the next morning.[11]

News that Brown was carried to court on a cot and was lying there with his eyes closed was met throughout the South and by the prosecutors as Brown's faking to try for a delay. Suspicion was heightened by the fact he had walked that morning to the courthouse, sat in a chair, arisen and spoken to the court, and later walked back to jail.[12] Northerners, especially those sympathetic to Brown, saw denying him a delay and continuing the trial when he was so debilitated as unconscionable; their perception he would not get a fair trial was reinforced. Concerns were stirred among prominent attorneys in Massachusetts and Ohio, who tried to find legal help. Many urged Boston attorney John A. Andrew to go to Charles Town, but he countered he was not familiar with Virginia law and would be resented. They finally found a Virginian by birth who practiced in the nation's capital: Samuel Chilton agreed to go help Brown after he made proper arrangements for his caseload.

The first day of the trial was a busy one for all connected with it, and that night was made more stressful by a letter received that day by the superintendent of the

Brown walking to court following the bed he would lie on in the courtroom. (*Harper's Weekly*, Library of Congress)

The trial of John Brown. (*Harper's Weekly*, Library of Congress)

armory, Alfred M. Barbour. The letter claimed that abolitionists would attempt to free Brown and his men. As a precaution Secretary of War Floyd sent 40 Marines to Charles Town. Brown's raid also evoked cries in the press and elsewhere about why federal armories with millions of valuable weapons and equipment were left unprotected. In response to the outrage the Baltimore *Sun* reported on October 29, the day after Floyd left Harpers Ferry, 25 regular troops arrived to protect the armory until two companies of armory workers were properly trained to defend the property.

Brown had limited trust in his court-appointed attorneys and gave them written instructions on how his defense should be presented. In essence he repeated was what he had been saying since his capture. His actions were benevolent and designed only to free slaves, and he had no intent to kill anyone, firing only in self-defense when fired upon. He cited examples of his kindness and consideration for the hostages and the townsfolk. Brown began repeating this story as soon as he received visitors in jail (after his filthy bloodstained clothes were changed for washing).

During his incarceration Brown drew strength from reading his Bible and praying, and he busied himself reading mail, which was first read by prosecutor Hunter. Brown also wrote letters, responded to telegrams, studied newspaper articles about himself and the raid (making extensive notations in the margins), and chatted with visitors. Once in jail, one of his earliest opportunities to argue his case came when several reporters visited on October 21. Brown asked one of them to copy a letter he had written, and then he instructed them to tell all, both the favorable and unfavorable. He asked, "Have any of you here ever stated this fact, that we had no idea or thought of killing or wounding or injuring any person who did not interfere with us?" Brown added that his men behind bars would testify that he repeatedly ordered them not to fire even when fired upon, for fear of harming the innocent. When asked how he could explain the death of Beckham he became annoyed. He might well have been asked about the death of Hayward Shepherd and others killed as a result of his armed invasion and seizure of the town.

Brown instructed Botts and Green to stress his benevolent motives and defensive acts. He came to liberate slaves peaceably—but forcibly if necessary. If he had not been resisted, he said, there would have been no bloodshed; but the latter was caused by militiamen and townspeople's attacking him. To prove this Brown gave his counsel the names of witnesses who could testify the prisoners were treated "with the utmost kindness and humanity." He said many were given "perfect liberty" and allowed "to visit their families"; orders were frequently given that "no unarmed person should be injured" regardless of circumstances. Brown instructed his lawyers to get the names of the conductor and train passengers to testify he allowed the train to leave and personally escorted it across the bridge to ensure its safety. Witnesses could only be white because Virginia law prohibited a black or indigenous person from testifying against a white person.

Brown's trial continued on Thursday morning, October 27. Before the jury could be sworn in or the lengthy indictment read once more, Botts read aloud to the court a telegram he had received from C. J. Faulkner stating that insanity ran throughout Brown's family. This reinforced what many had expressed verbally and in the press: Brown's attack on Harpers Ferry was the act of a "mad man." If Brown were ruled insane, his life would be spared and he would be sent to an institution in Staunton, Virginia. Brown, however, would have none of this; he believed it was untrue and would totally discredit and diminish his raid to a mere irrational act by a madman who did not know what he was doing. Botts read the incriminating letter and stated that his client emphatically rejected insanity as a plea. Brown arose from the cot and addressed the court, reinforcing what he had earlier told Botts. His father's side of the family was free of the malady, but mental illness affected a number of relations on his mother's side. His first wife and two oldest sons showed signs of mental illness. He concluded by saying the insane "have little ability to judge… their own sanity; and if I am insane, of course I should think I know more than all the rest of the world. But I do not think so. I am perfectly unconscious of insanity, and I reject, so far as I am capable, any attempt to interfere on my behalf on that score."[13]

Judge Parker ruled out the issue of insanity on the grounds of lack of reliable evidence and rejected Green's request for a day's delay to allow defense attorney Daniel Tilden of Cleveland to arrive. While the jury was sworn in, and afterwards, Brown lay on his cot; he was given the option of not having to stand while the seven-page indictment was read. Harding opened the prosecution's argument, describing in detail the facts of the raid that proved treason, insurrection (conspiring with slaves to revolt), and murder. After reading the law on treason he urged the jury to put aside all their prejudices and hatred of abolitionists and give the prisoners a fair trial.

Green countered for the defense, reminding the jury that if they had "any doubts as to the law or fact of the guilt of this prisoner, they were to give the prisoner the benefit of the doubt." He explained the laws pertaining to the three charges, and he argued that treasonable intent to establish a new government must be proven by testimony in court, as the Virginia law invalidated confessions outside of court for conviction; conspiracy and murder must be proven to have taken place in the Old Dominion—not on federal property or in Maryland. Green said that although Brown "may be guilty of murder, it must be proven willful, deliberate and premeditated murder, to make it a capital offense. Otherwise, the killing was murder in the second degree and punishable by imprisonment." Green concluded, stating that regardless of "how much the jury may be convinced in their own minds of the guilt of the prisoner, it is essential that they must have proof positive of guilt in a case like this, involving both life and liberty." Botts reiterated what Green had said, and then, following Brown's instructions, Botts told the jury they must give due weight to the prisoner, who "believed himself to be actuated by the highest and noblest feeling that ever coursed through a human breast. His instructions to his associates were to destroy neither property nor life; and they would prove by those gentlemen who were prisoners that they were treated with respect, and that they were kept in positions of safety—that no violence was offered them."

Andrew Hunter concluded the opening remarks. He reaffirmed his commitment to fairness through an examination of the law and facts in the pursuit of justice, which would, he said, result in "either convicting or acquitting the prisoner." Hunter countered the arguments of the defense in this high-profile case of Commonwealth v. Brown. First, he argued, a case involving "high treason" against a state was unusual, and said his "friends on the other side were totally mistaken in their view that the laws of Virginia were like that of U.S. Constitution" on treason. "The U.S. Constitution requires proof of overt acts" for the conviction of treason; the Virginia Constitution does not. It is more extensive and includes establishing and supporting an illegal usurping government. Treason proven by two witnesses or confession in court "shall be punished by death." A dozen witnesses, Hunter said, would show that the prisoner "attempted to break down the existing government of the Commonwealth establishing on the ruins a new Government... He is doubly, triply and quadruply guilty of treason." As to Virginia's jurisdiction in the US Armory at Harpers Ferry, argued Hunter, there was legal precedent for Virginia's handling a murder case. He added Brown's own confession proved he was guilty of murder and conspiracy.[14]

After the midday recess the prosecution called Dr. Starry, Phelps, and Washington to the stand. Phelps's testimony was interrupted by Green asking the court to adjourn until the morning, because he had just received a telegram stating that counsel for the defense was coming from Cleveland. The judge had Phelps continue. After adjournment precautions were taken to prevent any outside influence upon the jury, the sheriff escorted members of the jury to Gibson Hotel, where they were fed and would spend their night sleeping two to a bed in a large room.[15]

Friday morning brought additional excitement. At 1:00 that morning Wise's agents arrived from Pennsylvania with Cook, who had had a $1,000 bounty issued for his capture. Locals rejoiced at the capture of the most hated of the raiders, who had lived among them, deceiving and betraying them. When court reconvened a fresh-faced, slight 21-year-old lawyer, George Hoyt, entered the courtroom. He would later say he was not ready to be involved in the defense. Botts informed the judge Hoyt was to assist them but felt unprepared to do so immediately. Doubts were expressed whether he was really an attorney and why he was there. Parker was finally convinced when letters were read that implied Hoyt was a member of the bar.

Any stranger or straggler was looked upon with suspicion as a potential troublemaker. According to the Baltimore *Sun* strangers "were required to give a good account of themselves" to those in charge of military security. Outsiders were subject to extensive questioning about their past, politics, and plans. Hotel registers were routinely scrolled for unfamiliar names, and these people were then sought.

On October 28 a photographer and his wagon and a soap and medicine peddler, according to the *Sun,* "were very properly ordered out of town."

Suspicions about Hoyt were justified. Brown's supporters in Massachusetts selected Hoyt for his youth and unimposing physical appearance, to reduce suspicion. Among the supporters, John W. Le Barnes gave Hoyt $75 in silver and sent him to keep them informed about Brown, his trial, disposition of troops, defenses of the jail, and any information that would be helpful in recusing the old abolitionist. Hoyt would advise them rescue attempts were futile.

Botts opened the Friday morning session by cross-examining Phelps and Washington. Hunter introduced Brown's printed copy of the Provisional Constitution into evidence and asked Sheriff Campbell to verify Brown's handwriting. Brown sat up on his cot and said the writing was his, but the prosecutor still wanted the sheriff's verification; then Hunter read from the document, which showed Brown and his men swore their allegiance to it, and it decreed that they were a military force. Hunter introduced a large bundle of more than 50 letters written to Brown from prominent Northern abolitionists, and some copies of Brown's responses. Many had been collected by the congressman-elect of the region, Alexander R. Boteler; he had recovered letters from people around the Kennedy farm who had pilfered the house before the Marines seized the remaining correspondence. The latter made their way to Hunter. He asked the sheriff in court to identify each letter, and then hand it to Brown, who glanced at each letter and loudly stated, "Yes, that is mine."

Hunter read the names listed as members and officers of Brown's constitutional convention and handed the list to Brown, who responded with a groan, "That's my signature." To prove the attack upon slavery was not limited to Brown and his men but was part of a larger Northern conspiracy to eliminate slavery, Hunter read letters to Brown from prominent outspoken Northern critics of slavery, including Joshua R. Giddings and Gerrit Smith. Botts insisted on the right to examine the letters before they were read.

To further strengthen his case against Brown, Hunter interviewed Armistead Ball, John Allstadt, Alexander Kelly, and Albert Grist, who primarily shared information that was already previously stated.[16] After the midday recess the prosecution called Henry Hunter, Thomas Gibson, and Benjamin T. Bell, recalled Dr. Starry and rested its case. Henry Hunter was the son of the prosecutor; the father did not question the son about his role in the vigilante death of raider William Thompson.

It was late Friday afternoon on the third full day of Brown's trial when the defense called their first witnesses, former hostages Joseph A. Brua and Archibald Kitzmiller, who testified about Brown's unsuccessful attempts to get townspeople to stop fighting and negotiate a truce. Describing the firing that erupted during negotiations, Kitzmiller testified, "Thompson, one of Brown's men, was a prisoner on the bridge." This prompted Brown to interrupt and ask for the circumstances of Thompson's death. An argument ensued when Green tried to prove how Thompson was killed. Andrew Hunter was angry and wanted to avoid embarrassment from his son's actions, and he claimed Thompson's death "had no more to do with this case than the dead languages." Judge Parker overruled his objection, and Green questioned young Hunter, who gave the gory details.

Next came two more defense witness, hostages William Williams and Reason Cross. Williams, the night watchman, said Brown told them he would not harm them but would torch the town if townspeople fired on the enginehouse. Williams said he heard two shots but did not see the shooting of Hayward Shepherd, and he was interrupted by Brown, who rose up on his cot to demand, "State what was said by myself." Williams replied, "I think you said that if he had taken care of himself, he would not have suffered." Cross was then called to testify about Brown's attempt to work out a truce to stop the firing and release the hostages while retaining control of the armory. Cross and Williams were sent to stop the firing, but Thompson was captured.

Cross was the last on Brown's list of witness to appear; there were others who did not appear. Brown assumed they had not been subpoenaed. Greatly agitated, Brown stood up from the cot to address Judge Parker: "May it please the court: I discover that, notwithstanding all the assurances I have received of a fair trial, nothing like a fair trial is to be given me, as it would seem." He had given instructions with witnesses' names and locations, he said, "but it appears that they have not been subpoenaed"; "if I am to have anything at all deserving the name and shadow of a fair trial, that this proceeding be deferred until tomorrow morning." The drama increased as the agitated old man declared, "I have no counsel, as I have stated before, in whom I feel that I can rely… I have nobody to do any errands, for my money was all taken when I was sacked and stabbed, and I have not a dime…" He requested a delay until the next morning to get other witnesses to court. He said, "If not, I am ready for anything that may come up." Brown's outburst apparently left him exhausted, and he returned to his cot, pulling the blanket over himself and closing his eyes as if he were asleep. Young Hoyt repeated the request in a strong appeal for the delay, adding he was inexperienced and counsel was on the way from Ohio.

Rebuffed in open court and feeling unappreciated by their client after they had labored diligently and skillfully, not surprisingly, Botts and Green withdrew as Brown's attorneys. To Brown they were unacceptable as legal counsel because they were members of a society that supported and embraced human bondage. To him they were the enemy.

Judge Parker rejected the idea of waiting for the arrival of defense counsel but wanted to know whether all Brown's witnesses had been subpoenaed. Botts proposed a solution. It was 6:00 p.m., and it would be only fair to adjourn court and give Hoyt all night to prepare. Botts said, "… in the meantime the sheriff can be directed to have other witnesses here tomorrow morning." Botts generously said he would give Hoyt all his notes and spend the night preparing him to take over the defense. Convinced, Parker adjourned until morning.[17]

When court reconvened at 10:00 Saturday morning Judge Parker announced two new attorneys who had just arrived to join Hoyt: Samuel Chilton, from Washington, and Hiram Griswold, from Cleveland. The judge granted the request they sent in a note for an hour's delay so they could talk to their client.[18]

At 11:00 Brown entered the courtroom and immediately lay on the cot, looking according to a reporter, "quite feeble and haggard," reflecting the stress of the previous day. His three attorneys accompanied him. After Chilton and Griswold were sworn in, Chilton requested an additional several hours' delay. He and Griswold were unprepared to conduct the defense; they had expected Botts and Green to be there. The judge ruled the case must proceed, as there were other cases to be tried, and the term of court would soon expire. Parker added that although their plight was not their making, it was exclusively brought about by their client's dismissal of his able attorneys.

Forced to do something, Hoyt questioned the purpose of papers introduced the previous day, claiming he objected to some of them. Hunter interrupted, stating, "Designate those you wish to object to." Hoyt responded, "I desire to know the object of counsel in introducing these papers." "The papers will speak for themselves," responded Hunter. "Designate those you wish to object to, we will go on at once." "I object," Hoyt said "to this autobiography of Capt. Brown, as having any bearing on the case." Hunter immediately replied, "I withdraw it." Hoyt then objected "to the letter of Gerrit Smith." "I withdraw that too," was the reply.

Forced to find another way to buy time, Hoyt read the list of names he had given the clerk the previous night to be summoned as witnesses: Samuel Striker, Henry Ault, Benjamin Mills, John E. P. Daingerfield, and Captain Simms. He added that he understood the captain had gone to Frederick and questioned whether he had been summoned. The sheriff explained Simms was in town the day before and had come to Harpers Ferry as a member of the Frederick militia to subdue Brown. Hunter, again annoyed by the delay, interrupted: "I hope we will proceed with some other witness." Daingerfield took the stand, followed by the other witnesses in attendance.

During their testimony Hunter protested they were repeating what had already been covered. Hoyt, like Botts and Green before him, was attempting to show that Brown fired solely as a defensive measure and displayed concern and consideration for the hostages while working for a compromise. Brown continued the unprecedented practice of a defendant's interrupting to question the witness and, in one reporter's words, interpose "verbal explanations relative to his conduct." During the testimony of the master armorer who had been a hostage, Brown carried on a running conversation with the witness, asking him questions that corroborated most but not all of the raider's own version of what had happened. Mills, who been a hostage, said he did not hear Brown say he had surrendered, but stated Brown allowed his "wife and daughter to visit him unmolested, and free communication was allowed with those outside. We were treated kindly, but we were compelled to stay where we did not want to be."

On Saturday afternoon the last witness, Captain Simms, arrived. He disapproved of what Brown had done but saw him as brave. "As a Southern man, I came to state the facts about the case, so that Northern men would have no opportunity of saying that Southern men were unwilling to appear as witnesses on behalf of one whose principles they abhor." His testimony closed the defense case. Hunter felt there was no need for cross-examination.

Despite Chilton's recent arrival and unfamiliarity with the case, he used his legal savvy to buy time. He rose from his chair and submitted a motion that the prosecution be compelled to select one of four charges and abandon the others, as it posed a hardship "upon the prisoner to meet various and distinct charges in the same trial." He also pointed out a problem with the second count that seemed nitpicky to some, arguing, "[This count] alleges a charge different from that which is endorsed on the back of the indictment." Chilton also maintained that the charge differed from the Commonwealth's statute. He said the law stated, "If a free person advise or conspire with a slave to rebel or make an insurrection, he shall be punished with death, whether such rebellion or insurrection be made or not." But, he argued, the second count stated that the prisoners "conspired together" and with others to induce certain slaves "to make rebellion and insurrection... There is a broad distinction between advising and conspiring with others to induce slaves to rebel." Chilton added that it was up to the court to decide whether the discrepancy between the law—which prescribed death to an individual who directly contacted slaves and incited them to rebel—and count two—which charged that the defendants conspired with each other and others to induce slaves to rebel—was reason to drop the second count from the indictment or "wait until the conclusion of the trial, and then move for an arrest of judgment."

Chilton supported his argument with quotes from Archibald Kitzmiller's testimony, maintaining the court had the discretion, when multiple charges were a hardship to the defendant, to require the prosecution to select one charge.

Harding first opposed the motion, arguing he did not see "the force of the objections made by the learned counsel... In regard to the separate offences being charged, these were but different parts of one transaction. Murder arose out of treason, and was the natural result of this bloody conspiracy." Hunter reiterated the same argument. Annoyed by Chilton's attack on the indictment, he said, "It is my work, and I proposed to defend it as right and proper." In support he read from two legal authorities, Chitty's *Criminal Law* and Robinson's *Practice,* showing a court does not exercise its discretion in reducing charges to one when "the prisoner is not embarrassed in making a defense." The present case, said Hunter, "would show the absurdity of the principle," if it were applied as broadly "as contended...

by my learned friend." Referring to Chilton's other point in his objection, Hunter said, "it was too refined and subtle for his poor mind." After Chilton made one last argument for his motion, Judge Parker ruled that although the difference between count two and the law may be grounds for asking for an arrest of judgment, that would have to wait until after the trial. He rejected the motion to reduce the charges. The jury was sworn to try the case on the indictment as it was drawn, he said: the trial must go on.[19]

By late afternoon all that remained were closing arguments. All the evidence had been presented. Griswold attempted once again to buy time through a delay until Monday by pointing out Brown's counsel had missed much of the trial, they had not reviewed the witnesses' testimony, and they were exhausted. Hoyt told Judge Parker that even if he had been prepared, he was physically incapable of speaking, having had only 10 hours' sleep in five nights. Chilton said his lack of preparedness made it impossible for him to make the closing argument.

Prosecutor Hunter strongly opposed any delay; he was for continuing until midnight to conclude the trial. After recognizing the position of the defense attorneys, he pointed out Brown was to blame for their plight, because he had dismissed his earlier attorneys. Brown had his rights, but the commonwealth and community had their rights as well, said Hunter. He told the court that jurors were anxious to return to their homes where wives and womenfolk feared for the safety. Hunter asked the jury their preferences and was told they wanted to go home as soon as possible. Hunter said he was treating this case like any other case; they should continue.

Confident about their position, Harding proposed they dispense with closing arguments and submit the case to the jury. Chilton protested, wondering aloud why he and Griswold had traveled great distances if they were not to make closing arguments. Judge Parker inquired how long their arguments would take and was told not more than two and a half hours. Once again Hunter protested any delay and was told by Parker he and Harding could start their closing arguments.

Harding spoke for 40 minutes, reviewing the testimony of witnesses and pointing out the absurdity for Brown, after a bloody attack upon Harpers Ferry, to expect to be treated "according to the rules of honorable warfare." Brown seemed to have forgotten, said Harding, that "he was in command of a band of murderers and thieves, and had forfeited all title to protection of any kind." The people, Harding said, demanded a verdict of guilty.

By 5:00 it was dark and all the key participants in the courtroom were tired. Parker adjourned the court until Monday morning. The remaining closing arguments would have to be heard at that time.[20]

On Sunday, Brown's three attorneys finally had an opportunity to confer with their client, and they spent three to four hours together in his jail cell.[21] When the court convened at 9:00 Monday morning, numerous onlookers crowded the courthouse and its entrances. Brown looked better than he had on Saturday but lay once more upon the cot, where he listened to the four and a half hours of closing arguments. The first three hours were consumed by his defenders—first Griswold and then Chilton—who did an able job of refuting the charges. Both attorneys said their client must be judged by the law, not by emotions, and should not be found guilty if the evidence did not prove without a doubt that he violated the law. Griswold argued Brown had not committed treason because he was not a citizen of Virginia, and the jury could not find him guilty unless they found him "guilty of associating with others to organize a government to subvert and overthrow the government of Virginia." His provisional constitution was not proof of this, Griswold said: "If it proves anything, it shows that the attempt was to organize a government in opposition to the government of United States, and not Virginia." Brown's constitution was nothing more than the rules and regulations of the "most harmless organizations of the country" or the regulations criminal impose upon their members, said Griswold. Chilton also argued Brown's provisional constitution showed itself not to be an instrument of subversion. It "expressly declares the foregoing articles shall not be construed so to encourage the overthrow of any State government or the general government, and looks to no dissolution of the union."

As for the murder charge, Griswold told the jury the shooting by the prisoners and ensuing deaths were not the result of a treasonous war against the Old Dominion or premeditated murder. They were simply self-defense by Brown and his men. Both defense attorneys phrased this argument in such a way as to make it seem Brown and his men had the right to return fire when fired upon. Griswold added there "was a great difference from levying war and resisting authority." Chilton later pointed out the lack of clarity in the circumstances of the killings, specifically referring to the death of Dangerfield Newby, who was shot in the dark perhaps by accident. Chilton further addressed the issue of murder: "By the indictment five prisoners are charged with the murder of four men. That they might have jointly done it he could understand. But they could not severally have done it". He declared it was almost impossible for the prisoner to make a defense against such a charge: it was too loose and vague. The only way his client could be convicted of first-degree murder under Virginia law was if it was premeditated, and, he said, "The evidence in this case does not sustain that charge." There was no malice, as Washington and Allstadt had testified. As a Virginian (although he was living in Washington), Chilton disapproved of what Brown had done and informed the jury of his opinion. He expressed this disapproval in his defense of Brown against the charge of murder; he seemed to question the sanity of Brown's acts: "However ridiculous his project, it would seem, could never have entered the mind of a sane man, he might still have believed he could carry out that project without bloodshed. At any rate, no sane man could be expected, with a mere handful of men, to accomplish the object by force, and it is but fair to take his declarations, especially when, coupled with his acts, that he did not intend to shed blood except in self-defense."

To refute the charge of conspiring with slaves to rebel, Griswold stressed that Brown's intent was only to run them away and not provoke insurrection; which is indicated by the fact local slaves did not rebel or participate in the raid. There was a great difference, he argued, "between an effort to run slaves, or steal slaves, and conspiring to induce them to rebel. Rebellion and insurrection was a rising up (against masters, whites and state) not to run away, although freedom may be the ultimate aim." Brown had openly admitted to wanting to run off the slaves, said Griswold, and accepted being tried under such a charge and nothing more. He attempted to explain away the seizure of Washington and Allstadt's slaves, contending they "were taken possession of for a temporary purpose and placed in the arsenal." The testimony of Colonel Washington proved "that not a slave took part in the matter except Phil, who at the suggestion of the prisoner, attempted to drill port-holes in the enginehouse. That was not done for the purpose of insurrection and rebellion, but to protect themselves."

Chilton concluded the defense's argument with a charge to the jury. He urged them to base their judgment upon the law "with an eye favorable to the prisoner, and when their verdict should be returned, no matter what it might be, he trusted every man in the community would acquiesce in it. Unless the majesty of the law was supported, a dissolution of the union must soon ensue, and all the evils which would necessarily follow in its train."[22]

Hunter rose to from his chair to make the prosecution's closing argument. His legal opponents had raised some valid legal questions. Making another stand for the fairness Brown was receiving, he pointed out that the governor could have declared martial law and administered "drum-head justice." He then addressed the issue of the court's jurisdiction and the defense's contention the crimes took place on federal property or Maryland, and not Virginia. Hunter claimed incorrectly the crimes were committed in Harpers Ferry, not on armory grounds. (Luke Quinn was killed on federal property, Beckham may have been, and Hayward Shepherd was killed on the Potomac bridge, within the jurisdiction of Maryland). Hunter countered the defense's stand that Brown had not committed treason because he was not a citizen of Virginia by pointing out Brown had planned to set up his provisional government in Virginia; therefore, when he came into the state he became one of its citizens. He augmented his claim by asserting the privileges and immunity clause of the US Constitution: "The citizens of each state shall be entitled to all privileges and immunities of citizens in the several states." This meant, said Hunter, that upon entering Virginia a person not only had the privileges and right of citizenship but also the responsibility of loyalty to Virginia and obedience to its laws. "By the Federal constitution, he was a citizen when he came here, and did that bond of Union—which may prove a bad bond to us in the South—allow him to come into the bosom of the Commonwealth, with the deadly purpose of applying the torch to our buildings and shedding the blood of our citizens." Hunter continued, "As to the conspiracy with slaves to rebel, the law says the prisoners are equally guilty, whether insurrection is made or not. Advice may be given by actions as well as words. When you put pikes in the hands of the slaves, and have their masters captive, that is advice to slaves to rebel, and punishable with death."

Hunter also refuted the contention that Brown's provisional constitution was harmless, as its intent was to take away the property of slaveholders throughout the South and shoot down any man who resisted. As mad as the attack upon Harpers Ferry may have seemed, he said, it was part of a larger sinister plan that claimed that thousands in the North would join them. Hunter rejected the idea Hayward Shepherd was mistakenly or accidentally killed as proof of lack of malice. "If Brown was only intending to steal negroes, and in doing so took life, it was murder with malice prepense." He said "[Brown] glories in coming here to violate our laws, and says, he had counted the cost, knew what he was about, and was ready to abide the consequences, that proves malice." The same was true regarding the claim that Brown's gunfire was purely defensive and only used against armed men. Beckham was unarmed. Hunter pointed out, "If the party perpetrating a felony takes a life it is conclusive proof of malice." Whether Brown's motive was just to run off slaves and whether he meant no harm, his actions resulted in deaths; that, Hunter proclaimed, was "murder with malice."

It was 1:30 in the afternoon when Hunter sat down. It was now up to the jury. During most of the arguments Brown lay on his back with his eyes closed. Parker refused Chilton's request to instruct the jury that if they believed Brown "was not a citizen, but of another state, they could not convict him of treason." The judge agreed to Chilton's request the jury be instructed that they "must be satisfied that the place where the offense was committed was within the boundaries of Jefferson County." The court recessed, and the jury went to decide Brown's fate.

It took the 12 men only three quarters of an hour to reach a decision. Tension heightened, according to one reporter, drawing curious onlookers into every available space in the courtroom "out through the wide hall and beyond the doors. There stood the anxious but perfectly silent and attentive populace, stretching head and neck to witness the closing scene of Old Brown's trial." Brown, who some claimed was the calmest person there, sat up on his cot to hear the verdict. After repeating the charges set forth in the indictment, the clerk of the court said, "Gentleman of the jury, what say you, is the prisoner at the bar, John Brown, guilty or not guilty?"

"Guilty," said the foreman. The clerk then asked him, "Guilty of treason, and attempting and advising with slaves and others to rebel and murder in the first degree?" "Yes," was the reply. Not the slightest sound was heard—no expression of jubilation uttered as the verdict was rendered. Brown said nothing, lying back down upon his cot and showing no emotion.

The jury's decision could not have come as a shock, even to Brown. Despite the judge's and prosecutor's rush to judgment, they and defense attorneys Botts and

Green knew the world was watching. They had worked diligently to adhere to state regulations and legal protocol to provide a fair trial. Although Griswold and Chilton ably contended conviction rested solely on proof of specific violations according to law, which was lacking, it was not enough. The defense could not overcome the nightmare of fear for life and property that engulfed the community, including the jurors. That fear was caused by the Old Man and his raiders.

Once Parker pronounced the sentence, Chilton moved for an arrest of judgment on the grounds of error in the indictment. He claimed the prisoner had been tried for an offense not on record of the grand jury, and there was error in the verdict: "The verdict was not on each count separately, but was a general verdict on the whole indictment." The judge was anxious to try the other prisoners, so a decision on the motion was deferred until the next day, and Brown was returned to his jail cell. Harding announced he was ready to proceed with the trial of Edwin Coppoc. The small prisoner entered the courtroom, where he sat between his attorneys, Griswold and Hoyt. Jury selection had to wait until the next day.

Brown had to wait two days to hear the sentence he must have expected. On Tuesday morning, November 1, Brown listened to Griswold's arguments supporting Chilton's motion for the arrest of judgment and Hunter's protest against it. Parker decided he had better get on with the trial of Coppoc and the other prisoners, postponing a decision until Wednesday. Coppoc's trial took up the rest of Tuesday and most of Wednesday. He was charged with the same crimes as Brown, with similar testimony by the same witnesses and similar arguments by his attorneys.

On Wednesday, while the jury was out considering Coppoc's fate, John Cook appeared for mere minutes in front of an examining court. Cook waived his preliminary examination, which rapidly moved his case to trial. His brother-in-law, Ashbel P. Willard, the governor of Indiana, had traveled to Charles Town with his state's attorney general, Joseph E. McDonald, and a brilliant young lawyer who would defend Cook, Daniel W. Voorhees. Willard advised Cook to confess his guilt and identify the innocent and guilty. Cook spilled all from his perspective, in his fluid prose, confessing he was recruited by the raider leader. His first confession implicated most of his companions whom Stevens had already identified, but it failed to implicate Brown's Northern supporters. At the insistence of prosecutor Andrew Hunter, who was under pressure from Governor Wise to get names of Brown's Northern conspirators, Cook added five more pages to the nearly two dozen of his earlier confession. In those extra pages he implicated Frederick Douglass, Gerrit Smith, Samuel Howe, Thaddeus Hyatt, and Franklin Sanborn. His confession incensed Brown, who detested the incrimination of others and felt Cook's actions were a betrayal. While Cook was being tried, an abbreviated version of his confessions was published to raise money for Samuel Young, a Harpers Ferry non-slave-owner who was seriously wounded by Brown's men. Despite Wise's opinion that Cook was the worst of the lot, attorney Voorhees hoped the confession would increase the likelihood a deal could be worked out with the Virginia governor after the trial, a deal that would spare the wayward Cook's life.[23]

Late Wednesday evening Brown was brought to a courtroom illuminated by gaslight that gave his face the look of death's pallor. As he entered, murmurs of denunciation could be heard. Parker rejected the defense's motion to arrest judgments.[24]

The clerk ordered Brown to stand and declare why he should not be sentenced. This came as a surprise to Brown. He had expected to be sentenced later, after all the raiders' trials. This would seem to be supported by a reporter who thought he spoke calmly but with timidity and hesitation; others said he spoke without any indication of nervousness. Despite having to speak off the cuff, he made a remarkable—if at times factually imperfect—speech. He praised the truthfulness and candor of most witnesses. Though he had earlier denounced his trial, he stated, "I feel entirely satisfied with the treatment I have received on my trial. Considering all the circumstances, it has been more generous than I expect; but I feel no guilt." He repeated his belief that his attack on slavery was divinely justified. At the start of his talk, and again near the end, he denied all the charges against him except what he had admitted to: "to free the slaves." He had intended to do what he had done the previous winter, he said: "[I] went into Missouri and there took slaves without snapping a gun on either side, moved them through the country, and finally left them in Canada. I designed to have done the same thing again on a larger scale. That was all I intended. I did not intend murder, or treason, or the destruction of property or to incite slaves to rebellion, or to make insurrection."

He argued that punishment for crimes he did not commit was unfair. Not only was it unjust to be punished for actions he had not committed, but, he said, "had I so interfered on behalf of the rich, the powerful, the intelligent... it would have been all right; every man in this court would have deemed it an act worthy of reward rather than punishment." Brown said once more he was justified in his actions by a higher law than those made by man; God's golden rule trumped the contradictory rules of man. "This court acknowledges, as I suppose, the validity of the law of God," he said. Referring to the Bible used for swearing in witnesses, he said:

> [The Bible] teaches me that all things whatsoever I would that men should do to me, I should do even so to them. It teaches me, further, to remember them that are in bonds as bound with them. I endeavored to act up to that instruction... I believe that to have interfered as I have done, as I have always freely admitted I have done, in behalf of His despised poor, is no wrong, but right. Now, if it is deemed necessary that I should forfeit my life for the furtherance of the ends of justice, and mingle my blood further with the blood of my children and with the blood of millions in the slave country, whose rights are disregarded by wicked, cruel and unjust enactment, I say let it be done.

He concluded by rejecting Cook's or anyone else's claim that they had been recruited: "Not one of them but joined me of his own accord"—and most "at their own expense." Brown said, "I fear it has been stated by some of them that I have induced them to join me, but the contrary is true. I do not say this to injure them, but as regretting their weakness." Brown's oration lasted less than five minutes.

As some have pointed out, Brown's actions in the Missouri raid and intentions at Harpers Ferry were not as benign as he depicted. In Missouri Aaron Stevens had killed a farmer, and property and livestock were confiscated. Prosecuting attorney Hunter had pointed out earlier that Brown's claim he simply came to Virginia to "stampede slaves" was contrary to statements he made when he first talked with Governor Wise, and Brown seemed embarrassed. After the trial Brown attempted to explain away the inconsistency by plausibly contending it resulted from his forgetting much of what he wanted to say because of the pressure of being hurried into making his statement to the court.[25]

His goal of terminating slavery had long been a constant, but the method of achieving it was fluid and may have contributed to the misstatement. He certainly had not made it clear to his men. In John Copeland's confession, he said, "I did not understand, at any time, until Monday morning of the fighting, that anything else than running off the slaves was intended." Copeland understood from Brown there were laboring men at Harpers Ferry who wished to get rid of slavery, and would aid in running them off. Others believed thousands would swarm to their aid. Osborne Anderson later stated that during the raid Captain Brown seemed to be puzzled. Charles Tidd would be more indicting. He felt at times that Brown had murdered his men by failing to heed his own sons' and others' opposition to the raid; attacking with an insufficient number of men; failing to burn the bridges as promised; and ignoring the repeated pleas of his men, Kagi, and Tidd himself to leave before they were trapped.[26]

Brown's "few words" range from his lying to save his life to pleading his case to an audience outside the court and indicting Virginia and the slaveholding South as the real criminals and violators of God's law. His final words in court were an earnest speech, not designed to deceive. His speech followed the goal of any good defense attorney to present their side in the most favorable light. He may have vocalized unrealistic intent and strategy, but it was what he believed. It is, however, difficult to see how he could have naively believed that he and some armed men could seize federal property, take hostages, and free slaves without causing bloodshed. Although he was well aware of public opinion, Brown was caught off guard when he had to talk and did not have time to calculate his speech to sway the public. He essentially repeated what he had been saying since his capture, which was no doubt crafted for public impact. In Brown's rationalized view, which justified his actions, he did not see slaves universally revolting. They would have to be freed by incessant small guerrilla raids. Somehow he seems to have naively believed that if all his demands at Harpers Ferry were complied with and his men not been endangered, loss of life could have been avoided. He also believed his men had the right to defend themselves. The attacks upon him, the shooting of his men under flags of truce and other atrocities upon them, his benevolent treatment of hostages, and the unreasonable rejection of exchanging hostages for his own and his men's freedom made him the victim. He saw himself as a victim persecuted for following God's law in attempting to justifiably launch a movement to end the cruel sin of human bondage.

To Southerners whose memories of Nat Turner were fresh and terrifying, anti-slave rhetoric since 1831 and bitter sectional conflicts that threatened their way of life meant they found Brown a heinous villain who had tried to bring upon the South the terror that had accompanied Turner's revolt. To Southerners the evidence was undeniable: Brown had stolen slaves and armed them, seized Harpers Ferry, and caused loss of life there. He possessed incriminating letters from Northern supporters, weapons stockpiles, and maps of Southern targets. His speech was viewed as blatant falsehood.

Millions of people north of the Mason–Dixon Line read Brown's speech. Unlike Southerners and a majority of Northerners, who viewed it as untruths and factual errors from a mad man, abolitionists accepted the speech. By now they were convinced that a great and noble man was sacrificing his life because he tried to right a terrible wrong. Brown's demeanor in captivity, along with his unflinching convictions, even gained him grudging respect from Southerners, such as Governor Wise and the extremist Edmund Ruffin, who nevertheless demanded the raider leader forfeit his life. On October 25, before Brown's conviction and speech, Ruffin recorded in his diary, "It is impossible for me not to respect his thorough devotion to his bad cause & the undaunted courage with which he has sustained it, through all losses and hazards."

Regardless of the intent of his speech and its immediate failure to sway the judge, Southerners, and a majority of Northerners, the ultimate result would be another step toward martyrdom, second only to his hanging.[27]

Brown concluded his talk with, "Now, I am done," and Judge Parker solemnly pronounced the sentence:

"Not a reasonable doubt can exist as to your guilt of each and every one of these offenses. Your own repeated admissions, and all the evidence in the case, fully sustain the verdict that has been rendered… The sentence of the law is that you John Brown, be hanged by the neck until dead [on Friday, December 2] between the hours of nine in the forenoon and four in the afternoon of the same day… And the court being of the opinion that for the sake of the example…" the execution would be done in public at a place selected by the sheriff. Much to the chagrin of prosecutor Hunter, Judge Parker postponed execution for 30 days, ignoring talk that such action would provoke violent citizen reaction, so Brown could "appeal to the Supreme appellate tribunal of the State for its decision upon the errors which are alleged by you and your counsel in the proceedings against you." This his counsel would do.[28]

Parker's sentence was received in silence except for someone clapping loudly, only to be quickly subdued and placed under arrest by the judge. Locals attempted to explain away the embarrassment by pointing out he was not one of them but a stranger from out of town. The condemned man returned to his cell free of taunts to await the fateful day, December 2.

The judge's decision set in motion the final act in bestowing martyrdom upon Brown. The ultimate act was his execution, but the 30-day delay for an appeal also contributed significantly. Brown used the time to fashion his image as a martyr, through his numerous visitors, the press, and exhaustive letter writing.

Not everyone found his trial thrilling, including a writer for *Harper's Weekly*: "The law, in its awful majesty—its mumbling of essential formulas, its wise delays, its careful sifting of evidence to prove what seems already patent, its hair-splitting principles, its squeamishness in terms, its quirks and quibbles—has few attractions... A criminal trial and a crowded room is a lingering bore to one who loves action and the out-of-doors."[29]

Fate of the Other Conspirators

After Brown was sentenced, the jurors in Coppoc's trial returned. They had deliberated for less than an hour and found Coppoc guilty on all counts.

The work of the court was unfinished. The judge and two prosecutors relentlessly pushed forward trials for the remaining defendants, beginning with Shields Green, whom *The Spirit of Jefferson* described as "a regular out-and-out tar-colored darkey," followed by a trial for John Copeland Jr., and then for John Cook. Copeland was the source of some angst back home in Oberlin, Ohio, in the last days of October, when his confession was published in the Cleveland *Herald* and Cleveland *Leader*. In the Charles Town jail he answered the questions of a visiting marshal of the Northern District in Ohio, and his answers implicated Oberlin attorneys Ralf and Samuel Plumb. Copeland stated he and Leary had met with the brothers in Samuel Plumb's law office, that the Plumbs had given Copeland money to join Brown's fight against slavery, and the brothers had wished good luck to both recruits. The damning stigma and threat of legal repercussions of being in any way associated with Brown's raid—even in Oberlin, a hotbed of anti-slavery feelings—made the Plumbs immediately write letters to the editor of the *Leader*. The lawyer brothers' denials of Copeland's allegations, which were probably true, reveal the degree of the overall Northern repudiation of Brown's actions.[30]

Attorney George Sennott of Boston arrived after Brown's trial and provided much of Green's and Copeland's legal defense. In many respects their trials were replicas of Brown's, with diminished drama. The witnesses, testimonies, and legal arguments were the same, but there were differences. Green, a runaway slave, and Copeland, described in the press as a "mulatto," would have the charge of treason dropped.

Sennott argued that because they were black the Dred Scott case denied them citizenship, so they could not be charged with treason. The judge agreed. Treason was dropped, and Green and Copeland were found guilty of murder, insurrection, and inciting slaves to insurrection.

Sennott became an irritant to the court and antagonized locals by proclaiming during the legal proceedings, "The system of slavery is illogical and absurd." His expressions of gratitude for the safety afforded him and the copious tears that ran down his rosy cheeks in court when he attempted to "give expression to his sympathetic tenderness for the defenseless and at present frightened condition of the women and children of this section of Virginia" were in vain. No amount of drama gained favor for him or his clients.[31]

Cook's trial was more complicated. He was the most hated of the raiders, having lived in Harpers Ferry and married a local woman, and he was believed by locals to have curried their favor while deceiving and bringing about a sinister plot to attack them. Wanting to see Cook get his due, a large crowd assembled early in the morning and discussed the merits of lynching. They waited for three hours for the courthouse door to be unlocked. Cook had prominent family connections, with a brother-in-law who served as governor of Indiana, and Wise changed his mind about turning him over to the federal government for trial. Instead Wise planned to submit Aaron Stevens for federal prosecution. Prosecutors Harding and Hunter, who were not fond of each other, engaged in a heated argument in open court when Stevens agreed to wait and be tried by a federal court. Harding was adamant he wanted to try Stevens; Hunter argued for the wishes of Governor Wise to place him in federal court in hopes that they might "strike at higher and wickeder game": those Northern Brown supporters. Wise unsuccessfully sent detectives to hunt down escaped members of Brown's force and to ferret out information about Northern rescue plans.[32]

Stevens and Albert Hazlett—who was captured in Pennsylvania and returned too late for Parker's court to try him—would not be tried that week, but Cook's trial proceeded. An indictment was handed down, and Hunter opened the prosecution's case. Hunter read Cook's confessions, which traced his association with Brown since Kansas and hinted vaguely that Gerrit Smith and other Northerners might have helped Brown. The least believable of Cook's contentions was that he knew nothing of Brown's Harpers Ferry raid until the morning it began. Brown's former attorneys Thomas Green and Lawson Botts had volunteered to join Cook's defense team. Green admitted in court that Cook had joined a conspiracy to induce slaves to rebel, something Brown had never admitted. Proving the charge of murder against Cook seemed to be problematic for Hunter, since Cook was not at the Ferry during the fighting and claimed to have killed no one. But the prosecutor found an out, using the part of Cook's confession in which he stated he fired shots from the other side of the canal to draw the shooting toward him. This, Hunter claimed—although no more than conjecture—killed George Turner, one of three local citizens killed during the fighting. The eloquent Voorhees, Cook's main attorney, then attempted to explain away Cook's actions. He praised the commonwealth's dignity and treatment of the raiders after its citizens had fallen victim to mad fanaticism. He pointed out that as a result of the raid, the institution of slavery was more justified than ever, and he passionately argued Cook was taken in by an evil man, a pirate and robber. Although it was wrong for his client to join Brown, said Voorhees, Cook had repented. As the lawyer begged for mercy for Cook, there were tears in the eyes of some in the audience, but the defense failed to sway the jurymen. They found Cook guilty of insurrection and murder, but surprisingly, not treason. Cook was a resident of Virginia, but was not found guilty of treason; while Brown, who was not a resident of the Old Dominion, was found guilty. For Cook not being convicted of treason opened up the remote possibility of receiving clemency from the governor without the state legislature's approval. It was a false hope, because Wise's disdain for Cook precluded any acts of mercy.

Sentencing took place on the morning of November 10. Neither Green nor Copeland addressed the court. Both Coppoc and Cook emphatically denied they knew about Brown's plan to seize the government facility until the morning of the raid. They expected to be punished but felt hanging was not justified. Parker was unmoved. After denouncing them for their crimes he sentenced all four to be executed on December 16. To conform to the whims of segregation the two black men would hang in the morning, and the two white men, in the afternoon.[33]

Life Behind Bars

Although most interest and attention centered on the raider leader, his imprisoned followers were also the object of curiosity for visitors and readers of newspaper columns. Townsfolk as well as relatives, friends, and concerned citizens such as Mrs. Rebecca Spring also visited them. The men behind bars wrote letters to family and friends, and Stevens wrote to his girlfriend, Jennie Dunbar. Books were sent to Stevens during his lengthy incarceration, so he spent much time reading while recovering from his severe wounds. His movements and his cellmates' were restricted not only by barred cells but by shackled ankles, which limited movement to shuffling half steps.

The prisoners developed a surprising and special relationship, one of respect and affection for their jailor, his helper, and some of the townspeople; this feeling emerged from the benevolent way they were treated. In a letter to his brother less than a week before execution, Copeland, who had favorably impressed the judge and prosecutor, wrote: "Believe me when I tell you, that though shut up in prison and under the sentence of death, I have spent more very happy hours here. You may think I have been treated very harshly since I have been here, but it is not so. I have been treated exceedingly well… My jailor [Captain John Avis] is a most kind hearted man, and has done all he could, consistent with duty, to make me and the rest of the prisoners comfortable… But since we have been in his power he has protected us from insults and abuse which cowards would have heaped upon us. Also one of his aides, Mr. John Sheats, has been very kind to us and done all he could to serve us. And now, Henry, if fortune should ever throw either of them in your way, and you can confer the least favor on them, do it for my sake."[34]

Albert Hazlett concurred. To Annie Brown on March 1, 1860, he said, "I do not think the citizens here thirst for my blood; they have treated me very kind and humane; the ladies come in to see us most every day, and gentlemen also."[35]

Brown's imprisoned followers spent their time in confinement in a similar way to their leader: waiting; thinking about what had happened to determine their fate; and coming to terms with the stark reality of their lives' abrupt ending, the end of cherished relationships with loved ones and friends, and not participating in any of the normal acts of the living. Regret, thoughts of what might have been, blame, and thoughts of what they faced in the future must have wandered through their minds. Thoughts of their bodies dangling at the end of a rope and being buried for eternity made them, like Brown, seek meaning in their deaths. They spouted rhetoric similar to Brown's: their lives would be sacrificed for a noble and righteous cause. Many turned to salvation as the town's ministers visited them during their incarceration and spent hours with them in prayer on the day before and the day of the executions. The condemned men's reflections, regrets, disillusionment, and feelings of being misled or betrayed are revealed in letters to loved ones and friends. Coppoc expressed the greatest regret and remorse. Even Stevens, one of Brown's stalwarts, wrote to his uncle, "I think now, from what I have seen, that the way we were trying to doo[sic] away with slavery, is not the best way, but I had to get this experience before I knew It." Despite an earlier letter that was extremely critical of white men who enslaved black men and were about to hang him, on his last day Copeland was more forgiving, writing his family, "And now, dear ones, attach no blame to anyone for my coming here for not any person but myself is to blame."

Despite any misgivings, they believed their deaths were noble and often professed to being cheerful about their fate, urging loved ones not to grieve for them and expressing the belief they would meet in heaven. Stevens wrote his uncle, "I suppose you hav[sic] seen by the papers about the Harper's Ferry affair, & that I and several more, are about as they say to dance on nothing. It is rather a queer way to leave this world, but if a person must di [sic], because he loves man & justice why, I think it becums [sic] on the best deaths… I shall meet it cheerfully, and it will not be many years, until I shall have the pleasure of seeing you all in the other world… I think the ruling power of the universe is working in all things, and we shall get our just reward."[36]

Hazlett wrote Annie, "I do not see that my death will do them any good," but two weeks later, on the day before his death, his attitude may have changed. He wrote in a letter thanking Mrs. Spring for seeing that he received a proper burial, "I am willing to die in the cause of liberty; if I had ten thousand lives, I would willingly lay them all down for same cause. My death will do more good than if I had lived."[37]

John A. Copeland stated a similar view. He wrote to his brother and protested the betrayal of black people:

> I am [not] terrified by the gallows, which I see staring me in the face, and upon which I am so soon to stand and suffer death for doing what George Washington, the so-called father of his great but slavery-cursed country, was made a hero for doing, while he lived, and when he died his name was immortalized... And now, brother, for having... engaged in a cause no less honorable and glorious, I am to suffer death. Washington entered the field to fight for the freedom of the American people—not just for the white man alone, but for both black and white... It is true that black men did an equal share of the fighting for American Independence, and they were assured by the whites that they should share equal benefits for so doing. But after having performed their part honorably, they were by the whites most treacherously deceived—they refusing to fulfill their part of the contract."

Evaluating his participation in Brown's raid to free the slaves, he wrote, "And how dear Brother, could I die in a more noble cause?

On Friday morning, December 16, 1859, just before leaving jail on the day Copeland was hung, he wrote an insightful final letter reflecting on his acceptance of death. It was addressed to his father, mother, brothers, and sisters and tried to reassure them he was and would be fine:

> The last Sabbath with me on earth had passed away. The last Monday, Tuesday, Wednesday and Thursday that I shall ever see on this earth have now passed by God's glorious sun... And now, dear ones, if it were not that I know your hearts will be filled with sorrow at my fate, I could pass from this earth without regret. Why should you sorrow? Why should your hearts be racked with grief? Have I not everything to gain and nothing to lose by the change... I am leaving a world filled with sorrow and woe to enter one in which there is but one lasting day of happiness and bliss....And now dear ones I must bid you that last, long, sad farewell. Good-day, Father, Mother, Henry, William, and Freddy, Sarah and Mary, serve your god and meet me in heaven. You Son and Brother to eternity, John A. Copeland."[38]

Two of the more revealing letters, aside from the many that flowed from Brown's pen, were by John Cook and Edwin Coppoc. But no one wrote a more detailed account in one lengthy letter expressing their feelings, their view of the raid, and their fate than Cook. His lyrical epistle to his wife and infant son on November 6, 1859, starts with paragraphs telling of his love for them:

> My Ever dear Wife and Son: a dungeon bare confines me, a prisoner's cell is mine. Yet there are no bars to confine the immortal mind, and no cell that can shut up the gushing fountain of undying love. Distance cannot part the twining tendrils of affection, nor can time sever the golden links of that eternal chain which binds my throbbing heart to my life's partner and my child.
>
> The love I cherished for you in my hours of freedom has grown deeper and stronger while gazing through my prison bars. Alone, within my cell, my heart as ever turning to the fond memories of its loved ones, swelling, the memories history of life all the dear words, the loving

acts, and kindly smiles of those whose deep affections here has strewn the buds of hope and promise along the pathway of my life.

Regretting any previous unkindness to his wife, Cook asks forgiveness:

> Words have no power to tell the strength and depth of that love I bear for my boy and thee.
> Nor have they power to tell my deep regret for every harsh and ungentle word I ever gave thee... The memory of every unkind Act, like Banquo's Ghost, is with me now to tell me of the wrong. But oh! For every unkind act and each ungentle word, I humbly ask forgiveness. And I feel and know the deep devotion and thy love will pardon all. Forgive me errors—all my faults forgive, and love me still, although I wear a prisoner's chains.

John explained to his wife why he participated in the raid, and his role. He praised his fallen comrades and expressed disillusionment, emphatically claiming he and others in the raid had been deceived:

> You know that in the scheme which has resulted in the death of most of my companions, and which has made me a prisoner, that I was actuated only by the tenderest feeling of sympathy and humanity. I had been led to believe, as had my comrades, that it was the daily prayers and the life-wish of the masses of slaves for freedom. That they were groaning beneath the yoke of oppression, with no hand to aid them, or point them to the light of freedom. I know how dear my freedom was to me; and every sympathy of my heart was aroused for them. It had been represented to me and my comrades that once the Banner of Freedom should be raised, they would flock to it by the thousands, and that their echoing shout of Freedom would be borne by breeze to our most Southern shores, to tell of freedom there. I gave heart and hand to a work which I deemed a noble and holy cause. The result we were deceived: that the masses of the slaves did not wish for freedom. There was no rallying beneath our banner. We were left to meet the conflict all alone to dare, and do, and die... We have been deceived, but found out... when too late... Those who died, died like brave men, though mistaken... Let not the world judge them too harshly, for whatever wrongs they have done, for they erred on the side of sympathy and love. It was an error of their judgment not of their heart.
>
> The wrong I have done has not been by intention. In this work no man's blood rest upon my hands. I had no part in the death of those who were killed at the Ferry. My orders were to retrieve the arms for Capt. Brown's house and to guard them there. I obeyed orders to the very letter... I was anxious to know what was the cause of the firing at the Ferry...found my brave comrades surrounded... I contrived to draw fire of a part of their opponents upon myself, and succeeded. I tried my best to save them, but could not. I left them with a heavy heart. It was the saddest day of my life. Those who fell there were more than comrades—they were brothers.
>
> Whatever may be my fate, I trust that you will bear it with fortitude and submission. We all must die, and a brave man dies but once. Should such be my fate, then you must be for my child its guard and guide. Teach him to love the memory of his father. Teach him to love and worship God.
>
> John E. Cook[39]

Cook, like Brown, may have been writing with a wider audience in mind, thinking of those who might read his published letter and hoping to change his public persona as a villain and traitor. Perhaps he also hoped his life would be saved.

None of the jailed men were as contrite as Edwin Coppoc. He and some of the other young idealistic men had been naïve. Youth, inexperience, idealism, and Brown's lofty rhetoric about a noble crusade against evil compounded, and he failed to see or accept the danger and tactical flaws of the raid pointed out by Brown's own sons. The raid and incarceration were disillusioning for Coppoc. After his conviction he wrote an apologetic letter to his mother, expressing his regret and offering feelings of being misled by men who should have known better as explanation for why he violated pacifism, a cornerstone of their Quaker faith. Like Cook, he curiously claimed to have killed no one. Either he refused to believe he had killed Mayor Beckham or he was hiding the truth from his mother. He also claimed other raiders felt they had been deceived or betrayed:

> It is with much sorrow that I now address you, and under very different circumstance than I ever expected to be placed; but I have seen my folly too late, and must now suffer the consequences, which I suppose will be death, but which I shall try and bear as every man should. It would be a source of much comfort to me to have died at home. It had always been my desire that when I came to die, my last breath should be amongst my friends; that in my last moments they could be near to me to console; but alas! Such is not my fate. I am condemned and die a dishonorable death among my enemies and hundreds of miles from home.
>
> I hope you will not reflect on one [sic] for what has been done, for I am not at fault; at least my conscience tells me so, and there are others who feel as I do. We were led into it by those who ought to have known better, but who did not anticipate any danger. After stopping at Harper's Ferry we were surrounded and compelled to fight to save our own lives for we saw friends falling on all sides, our leader would not surrender, and there seemed to be no other resort than to fight. I am happy to say that no one fell by my hand, and am sorry to say that I was induced to raise a gun. I was not looking for such a thing. Never did I suppose that my hand would be guilty of raising a weapon against my fellow-man. After capture, which was the morning of the 18th, we were kept there until morning of the 19th, when we were removed to this place, where we have been ever since. We are well cared for; the jailor seems to do all he can to make us comfortable.[40]

Brown remained even busier than his comrades. He saw more visitors, wrote more letters, read more newspapers and, especially, his Bible, and prayed more often, while unavoidably thinking about his execution. He was well cared for and furnished with changes of clothing and washing at no cost and was offered by Wise "the best aid of physician and surgeon" when during the governor's visit Brown complained of kidney disease. He declined the offer, saying he was accustomed to "an habitual treatment, which he had already provided for himself."

A bond of friendship developed between the prisoner and his guards, John Avis and Sheriff Campbell. Brown's conviction increased interest in him. People wanted to see the number-one newsmaker and came from all regions of the country. He greeted his visitors cordially. One reporter wrote that he was among what Brown, on November 3, called "A batch of persons admitted to-day to see the prisoners." The reporter noted when he entered the spacious room Brown "was sitting on a chair at Stevens' bedside." The latter was "still in great pain from his wounds." Brown, having heard Forbes had left the country, anxiously questioned the reporter about Forbes's whereabouts.

Brown's plight made him a martyr to some Northern women who were magnetically drawn to him. In the midst of his trial in Charles Town, Lydia Maria Child, a pacifist abolitionist from Massachusetts, wrote to Brown. Her adoration of a man she had never met approached obsession: "In brief, I love and bless you... I think of you night and day bleeding in prison surrounded by hostile faces." Although unsympathetic to Brown's use of violence, Child admired his courage and was extremely sympathetic to his crusade against slavery. She not only wanted to visit the raider leader, but wrote, "I long to nurse you, to speak to you sisterly words of sympathy and consolation." In a letter on October 26 to Brown, enclosed in one to Wise, she made this request of Wise, as a person "of chivalrous intent" for his allowing her letter to be sent to the prisoner, as well as allowing her to visit. She promised not to use her visit in any way to promote her views but would only care for him. Wise, not a man of few words, welcomed her in a lengthy reply, stating he "would permit no women to be insulted" by rejecting her mission of mercy, even though she came to minister to "one who whetted knives of butchery for our mothers, sisters, daughters and babes." The governor, however, informed her that since Brown was being tried, the ultimate approval of her visit must come from the court, not from him.

Brown and his lawyers were adamantly opposed to Child's visit. Hoyt appealed to John W. Le Barnes of Boston (the man who had sent Hoyt to Charles Town at his own expense hoping to rescue Brown) to quietly inform other supporters, such as John Andrews of Massachusetts, to stop the visit. "Do not allow Mrs. Child to visit," Hoyt wrote to Le Barnes. "He does not wish it because the infuriated populace will have new suspicions aroused & great excitement and injurious results are certain. He is comfortable," Hoyt wrote, and said Brown had no need to be nursed. "He don't want women there to unman his heroic determination to maintain a firm and consistent composure. KEEP MRS. CHILD away at all hazards. Brown and associates will certainly be lynched if she goes there."[41]

Two other women who were deeply moved by Brown's plight felt compelled to come. Mrs. Russell and her husband, Judge Thomas Russell of Boston, to whom Brown had written for legal help, arrived at the end of his trial. Upon seeing Mrs. Russell, Brown said, "Oh, my dear this is no place for you." Noticing his torn coat, she skillfully mended it while her husband, looking at the wide chimney that might be an avenue of escape, conversed with the prisoner. During the conversation Brown told Russell he was not personally involved with the Pottawatomie murders. The Russells heard Brown ask Avis's permission to write his wife to inform her he would be hanged December 2. A weeping Mrs. Russell kissed the doomed man, whose mouth trembled slightly, and Brown said, "Now, go." They returned to their hotel, marveling at Brown's calm acceptance of his fate. The judge believed Brown had nothing to do with the massacre at Pottawatomie Creek.

In New Jersey Rebecca Spring felt compelled to go help Brown. She told her husband they had talked about someone doing something about slavery, and now Brown had taken action. With the permission of Judge Parker she went to Brown's cell, telling him, "It is better to die for a great idea than of a fever." She ministered to him and his suffering cellmate Stevens.[42]

From Massachusetts came Edwin Brackett, a sculptor who planned to make a bust of Brown. Brackett arrived with letters of introduction, his trip funded by Brown backer George L. Stearns. The sculptor was welcomed but told he would not be allowed in Brown's jail cell. When jailor Avis was busy at court, the assistant jailor allowed one of Brown's attorneys, Hiram Griswold, into the cell. He took measurements of Brown as Brackett stayed outside the cell sketching Brown. Brackett returned to Massachusetts and sculpted an admired marble bust of Brown.[43]

People came from far and wide and were looked upon with suspicion. So numerous were the visitors to Charles Town that Mayor Thomas Green (formerly of Brown's defense team) on November 12, 1859, with the approval of the town council, issued a proclamation banning strangers from coming to their town and expelling those who were already there. They still came. Visitors included folks from all over the country, some already renowned, such as old Edmund Ruffin and the soon-to-be-infamous John Wilkes Booth. From Kansas came Samuel C. Pomeroy, a future senator, who asked if Brown wanted his Kansas friends to rescue him. Brown repeated, "I am worth now infinitely more to die than to live." Also from Kansas came an enemy, Henry Clay Pate, whom Brown had defeated at Black Jack; he came to gloat at his former conqueror's plight. Marshall J. D. Donaldson traveled from Kansas, and a Mr. Scott, from California. An additional unpleasant visit was that of a Methodist minister, Norval Wilson. When Brown asked the clergyman whether he supported slavery, he replied yes. Brown told him, "Then I do not want your prayers. I don't want the prayers of any man that believes in slavery."

Among Brown's visitors were local newspaper editors, whose questions he answered freely, as long as he did not implicate others. Militiamen who helped capture him and those who later came to provide security also came to gaze upon the prisoner as if he were a zoo animal. At the end of October Captain Sinn and his Frederick militiamen came away amazed at the prisoner's composure and apparent contentment.[44]

The visitors appear to have been a source of controversy, especially between Sheriff Campbell and the jailor, John Avis. According to Edwin H. House, correspondent for the New York *Tribune*, the sheriff wanted to deny access to Brown "to any applicants from abroad" and had Mrs. Julia Child turned away at the entrance to the jail. Avis took the opposite view from his boss, declaring that Brown could "see anyone he wants to." Despite having fought against Brown in the raid, Avis had a growing respect for his prisoner and was "deeply impressed with Brown's heroic fortitude in his captivity." Avis was reported as saying that "he expects and means to witness his speedy death on the scaffold, but he will be very sad when that time comes." His admiration for the Old Man created some controversy, but Avis said he would give up his position as jailor "if the old man is treated without dignity." Brown seemed to reciprocate the feeling, promising Avis he would not try to escape and informing those who broached the subject he would not walk out of his cell if the door were opened because of his promise to the jailor, who showed him great kindness.[45]

Outsiders marveled at Brown's calm demeanor, but it was not easily crafted. The condemned man had to fortify himself and work at it, especially through prayer and reading the scriptures, and he wrote to a friend, "I am wonderfully strengthened from on high." As the days until the gallows dwindled one would think it became more difficult. His struggle for serenity was the primary reason he aborted the first attempt by his wife to visit him. Concern for her welfare in a hostile environment and the emotional strain of seeing her would unnerve him. In his words, "[My wife's visiting] would only tend to distract her mind TEN FOLD; and can not possibly do me any good… It would also use up the scanty means she has to supply Bread & cheap but comfortable clothing, fuel, etc. food and clothing… for herself & children… Her presence here would deepen my affliction a thousand fold." Rebuffed in her attempt to see her husband, Mary retreated to Philadelphia, nursing her feelings. There she was persuaded to stay in the homes of family friends, such as Mrs. Spring, who had just recently visited her husband, and Lucretia Mott. Mary Brown hoped it would enhance her availability to see her husband. She would express her great disappointment in a letter to Brown written on November 13, pointing out she could not visit and care for her husband, yet two other women were granted the privilege she was denied. She added that she did not want to do anything that would upset his peace of mind, but how gladly she would care for him if she could.

While she waited, on November 21 Mary wrote a touching letter to Governor Wise, with the help of a sympathetic minister, begging that the "mortal remains of my husband and sons" be returned to her for "interment among their kindred." Moved by her request, Wise replied, saying he took no pleasure in the execution of her husband. He included a copy of his orders to General Taliaferro, in command at Charles Town, to turn Brown's over body to either Mrs. Brown or her agent at Harpers Ferry. Mary's angst would have intensified prior to the receipt of the governor's letter had she known Wise had been considering less-dignified possibilities for her husband's body. Requests for the remains, for dissection, were made by University of Virginia medical students, and a Mississippi physician, who planned to exhibit the skeleton as a warning to abolitionists. The most ghoulish was the request by an anatomy professor in Richmond. He wanted the heads of Brown and the other condemned men severed from their bodies and sent to him for display in the museum of the Medical College of Virginia.[46]

On November 2 Brown wrote, "My Dear Devoted Wife" and said it would be fine with him when Virginia was through with him if "the people here [in Virginia] will [allow you to come and you]... can afford to meet the expense & trouble of coming here to gather up the bones of our beloved sons, & of your husband." Two weeks later, after receiving her November 13 letter expressing her disappointment for not being allowed to visit, Brown addressed the issue: "I would be most glad to see you once more, but when I think of you being insulted on the road, and perhaps while here and of only seeing your wretchedness made complete, I shrink from it... If you do come, defer your journey until about the 27th or 28th of this month." Her treatment on the journey would be different than the friendly treatment she was receiving, he said, from "kind hearted friends... Do consider the matter well before you make the plunge."[47]

The failed raid and impending execution forced Brown to reassess God's mission for him. He believed what happens is determined by God, but he wrote he was to blame for the failure at Harpers Ferry. God had, he wrote, "put a sword into my hand, and there continued it, and then kindly took it from him." He marked and re-read biblical passages, the majority dealing with persecution. His weapons for righteousness had shifted from the gun and bullet to the word—both written and spoken.

The latter was the precursor of the most potent weapon of all, martyrdom: dying for trying to end human bondage. His daily letters to family and friends soon found their way into print, carrying his message to the public. Some started looking upon Brown's actions at Harpers Ferry as those not of a madman, but of a courageous, misguided soul. On November 1 he wrote, "I am now wielding the "Sword of the Spirit." After his capture he believed his God-given mission was to be a martyr. He drew an analogy with Christ: "Jesus... suffered a most excruciating death on the cross as a felon; under the most aggravating circumstances." Like the early Christian leaders, Jesus "went through greater tribulations than you & I," he wrote to his wife and children. To his wife he wrote, "The sacrifices you & I have been called to make on behalf of the cause we love the cause of God; & of humanity: do not seem to me as at all too great. I have been whipped as the saying is; but am sure I can recover all the lost capital occasioned by that disaster; by only hanging a few moments by the neck; & I feel quite determined to make the utmost out of a defeat." To a friend he wrote, "These light afflictions which endure for a moment, shall work out for me a far more exceeding and eternal weight of glory." Since his cause was just, he repeatedly stated he felt no guilt and his execution was a "public murder" and a "judicial murder."

At the end of November Brown wrote to his family, "I am waiting the hour of my public murder with great composure of mind, & cheerfulness; feeling the strongest assurance that in no other possible way could I be used to so much advance the cause of God; & humanity." He advised them, "Do not feel ashamed on my account; not for one moment despair of the cause." He had earlier proclaimed to a friend,

"I neither feel mortified, degraded, nor in the least ashamed of my imprisonment, my chain, or my near prospect of death by hanging."

One would think he was somewhat unnerved or despondent when, a few days before his execution, he was contacted by the undertaker, Sadler, who was concerned Brown's body would deteriorate before its burial in New York. Sadler recommended his remains be sent north in a metal coffin. Brown seems to have calmly responded he did not think that would be necessary, as the weather would be cool, and he would keep in a wooden casket for that length of time.[48]

In addition to using his pen to cast the image of his execution as a noble sacrifice, he also used it to advise his family on how to live after he was gone. This was one of the points of his last letter to them on November 30, 1859. They must not, he said, forget those in bondage or succumb to the temptation of seeking wealth. "I beseech you all to live in habitual contentment with very moderate circumstances." Concerned about his children's rejection of his strict Calvinist beliefs, he sent them letters advising them on the subject. "I beseech you every one to make the Bible your daily & nightly study; with a childlike honest, candid, teachable spirit." Regarding the education of their daughters, he wrote his wife that it should be practical: "You well know that I always claimed that the music of the broom, washtub, needle, spindle, loom, axe, scythe, hoe, flail, etc., should first be learned, at all events, and that of piano, etc., afterwards."[49]

Brown divided his valued personal possessions among his children. All cash payments to his children or creditors, along with purchases, were to come from Brown's father's estate. To John Brown Jr. he left his surveying equipment and the old granite family tombstone in North Elba, to remain there as long as he lived there.

CHAPTER 7

Hemp Justice

The month between Brown's November 2 sentencing and his execution, on December 2, was one of preparation, for both the condemned man and the commonwealth of Virginia. Rumors ran wild as people rushed to Charles Town from as far away as Wheeling, 251 miles distant, or even farther, to inform authorities they had overheard men plotting to raise a liberating force to save Old Brown. Hundreds of letters clogged the mailbags—most to Wise, some to authorities in Charles Town, and some to Brown. Many pleaded with the governor to pardon Brown, often quoting scripture and arguing that freeing Brown was the Christian thing to do. Some people warned of coming incursions, thinking they were being helpful, while others made threats, claiming there would be "hell to pay" for the Old Dominion if Brown was executed. Most rumors were dismissed as nonsense, but the nervous governor and Virginians felt they could not discount the arrival of troublemakers.

State militia were quickly mobilized to secure not only the prisoners at Charles Town but also the northern borders. This mobilization was much to the displeasure of locals in Charles Town, whose lives were dominated by the military. Martial law curtailed their movement and freedom and was part of the mobilization in what was believed to be a war with evil forces from the North. As young men scoured the mountains and stood guard at Charles Town, Brown continued to pray, read the scriptures, and put pen to paper, to propagate the story that he was forfeiting his life for a noble cause.

Rumors, Fear, Mobilization, and Preparations for Death

Virginians believed every precaution must be taken. A Mr. Hunter, in Charles Town, even advocated tearing up the railroad tracks. Despite having more than 1,000 Virginians in arms, on November 25 an insecure Governor Wise asked the US President to return Colonel Lee to Harpers Ferry to keep peace among the states, as he believed desperadoes were assembling in Maryland, Ohio, and Pennsylvania to carry out an unimpeded invasion of Virginia. President Buchanan

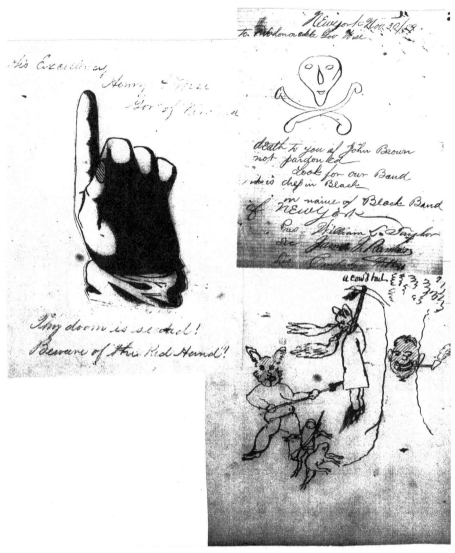

Drawings accompanying threatening letters to Governor Wise if he did not spare Brown. The sketch at the bottom shows a horned governor hanging by a cow's tail from a tree as birds pick at his mouth, a rabbit spearing the groin, frogs dancing, and a laughing face of an African American on the tree trunk. (Virginia State Archives, Executive Papers of Henry Wise)

sent Lee—who arrived on November 30 with 264 artillerymen from Fort Monroe to guard the bridges and to patrol federal property at Harpers Ferry until after Brown's execution—but Lee and the governors of Maryland, Ohio, and Pennsylvania (to whom Wise had sent copies of his letter to Buchanan) felt that Wise's imagination and unfounded fears had gained the upper hand. In the meantime, Wise planned to send more Virginia militiamen to Charles Town and ordered Major-General William B. Taliaferro, who had succeeded Colonel Davis as commander, to "keep full guard" with "mounted men on the line" of the "frontier from Martinsburg to Harpers Ferry" on the day of Brown's execution (December 2). Local people were to be instructed to arm themselves, protect their homes and patrol their communities, and to stay away from Charles Town. The militia were ordered to "prevent all strangers and especially all parties of strangers from proceeding to Charlestown on 2nd Dec."

In contrast to Wise's and Virginia's anxiety, John Brown was calm. Actively playing the martyr, he displayed what his defenders described as "heroic firmness and devoted self-sacrifice." Brown had obtained lasting fame after a life of obscurity and business failures. He emphatically rejected overtures for his rescue and claimed he was "fully persuaded that I am worth inconceivably more to hang than for any other purpose."[1]

Edmund Ruffin a Southern agricultural reformer who believed in secession of the South from the Union, was just one of many whose curiosity brought him to Charles Town. Among those attracted to the dominant news event in the US were three New York pickpockets. They planned to prey on the pockets of the gathering crowd. Instead they were found out, their heads were shaved, making them look like shorn sheep, and they were unceremoniously sent back to New York.

John Wilkes Booth, who was six years away from his infamous terrorist act, temporarily took leave from the theater in Richmond and, with a borrowed militia uniform, joined the militiamen of the Richmond Grays to see Brown hung. While helping to secure Brown's incarceration, Booth visited the prisoners. He also frequently entertained local residents in the evenings at the Episcopal Church by reading passages from Shakespeare.[2]

Jennings Wise, editor of the Richmond *Enquirer* and son of Governor Wise, who would fight eight duels in the two years before the Civil War, came to Charles Town as a private in Company F of the Richmond Grays. John H. Zittle, editor of the Shepherdstown *Register,* apologized to his readers for "all shortcomings" of the December 3 issue, explaining that "all hands have been 'playing soldier,' for some time past, night and day." A seven-year-old drummer boy accompanied his company from Harrisonburg, Virginia, to Charles Town. The youngster impressed others by being scarcely "knee high to a lame duck," yet he handled the sticks "with the dexterity of an old soldier."

Charles Town's inns, boardinghouses, and private homes were overflowing with visitors, who swelled the town, with its usual population of nearly 1,500. The town was also full of militiamen, who took over all churches and the courthouse, and boarded at the Carter House, paying a dollar a day in hopes of being reimbursed by the state. The Charles Town Guard had been on duty in the region since October 17. Other units arrived daily as Brown's execution date neared.

One group of visitors was a company of German boys from the Shenandoah Valley who talked to each other in what seemed to outsiders a strange "foreign" language. "Smooth-faced Cadets from the Virginia Military Institute," 85 in all, they were accompanied by adult commanders including Colonel Francis H. Smith (the Superintendent of the Virginia Military Institute, VMI, and overall commander of the cadets) and Major Thomas J. Jackson (who was in charge of the 21 cadets in the artillery unit and two brass howitzers, the future "Stonewall"). The cadets impressed all with their precision in drills, surpassing their closest rivals in this regard, the Richmond Grays. The young students arrived in town in late November via Richmond and Washington, D.C., and wore red flannel shirts "crossed by two white belts" and "long gray overcoats," presenting a splendid sight. From Winchester came the Continentals, wearing buckskins reminiscent of the Revolutionary War years. All units from Richmond and elsewhere wore gray, while still others, lacking training or uniforms, came in civilian clothing. They presented a kaleidoscope of colors. Cerulean blue was worn by the men from Alexandria, striking crimson decorated those from southwestern Virginia, and in some companies, no two men had a uniform of the same color, with head gear varying from sloughed hats, to caps, to the latest style: stovepipe beavers. The more affluent men wanted showy uniforms. The Home Guard of Richmond, with 90 members present, decided on expensive black frocks, pants, and vests that prevented men of lesser means from joining.[3]

An eyewitness wrote, "the uniforms and semi-uniforms" of the militiamen at Charles Town were as "numerous and varied as if the army consisted of 50,000 instead of 1,000 men." Some wore "a sort of jager uniform, dark coats and pants braided with green and slouched hats with dark plumes." Some wore "light blue uniforms, like the National Guard of New York." Others wore "antique dresses, with high, awkward hats, like those which Britishers might have appeared in eighty years ago." Still others did not "pretend to any uniform at all," but simply wore "a white waistbelt over their ordinary clothes, with a bayonet, sheathed or unleashed as the case may be, stuck inside, and [carrying] their muskets over their shoulders." Cavalrymen strutted about "with sabres by their sides, horse pistols stuck in their belts or bosoms, with the butts sticking out, and spurs clanking at their heel." A witness reported, "They all wear their ordinary garbs, with these appendages. Their horses are turned loose in the yard of the Carter House... Most of the men, when not on duty, are sauntering about, smoking their cigars or pipes." A dozen or so members of the Richmond Young Guard went from house to house serenading the inhabitants, hoping to provide enjoyment for all, and especially to impress the fair maidens.[4]

Facilities were strained in Charles Town, and incomers had to be housed in churches, courthouse, schools and wherever shelter could be found. Early December found 1,000 to 1,400 armed men in Jefferson County, concentrated mainly in the county seat. Some listed the number as 1,500. Visitor Edmund Ruffin estimated

1,300, and the Virginia *Free Press* lists the total as about 1,000 (with 650 in Charles Town), counting both organized units and armed residents in Jefferson County. This did not include late arrivals, such as the 85 cadets from VMI or the August Mountain Guard, Valley Guards, West Augusta Guards, and the Newton Cavalry; these significantly expanded the number.

Militiamen such as Parke Poindexter from Richmond had daily rations delivered that had been prepared by excellent cooks from the state capital, but the men often opted for the hospitality of local citizens; they arrived at meal times requesting five to 15 men to come to their homes. There the men feasted on beef, poultry, mutton, and what Poindexter called "delicate parts of the hog." Hospitality went beyond meals. Upon becoming ill from a high fever and delirium, Poindexter was taken to a private home, where for five days he received constant and kindly care from ladies. The hospitality of the women was not enough to feed the growing number of militiamen, and a commissary department was established.

The 500 additional men who arrived a few days before the execution created an even greater food and housing shortage. When General Taliaferro learned of the cost of $1 a day per man, he immediately ordered that the men be furnished with cooking utensils and rations to do their own cooking. This did not solve the issue. To feed the growing numbers an order was telegraphed to Winchester for more than 600 pounds of bread and thereafter a standing daily order of 500 pounds. The following day after the original order, the bread was sent on the daily train to Charles Town. Men who patrolled the mountains were less fortunate, and an officer of the company at Darksville complained they had to depend on the kindness of area residents for food and should be stationed at Martinsburg, where food was more accessible.[5]

To solve part of the housing problem, the quartermaster ordered 560 beds to be made. Women of the town again addressed the still-worsening issue. With nimble fingers they used their sewing needles, thread, scissors, and thimbles, working through most of the night and all the next day to fulfill the order. The bed ticking they fashioned would be filled with straw.

As December 2 neared, the only available structures were public buildings and churches. Worshippers were displeased and protested when their houses of worship were commandeered for arriving troops' quarters. Keys were turned over to the military with reluctance.

By the end of November rumors increased of imminent rescue attempts as the (Charles Town) Virginia *Free Press* and other papers carried stories such as the daily activities of a sentry who "[paced] up and down the porch of the courthouse, frequently asking people if they would like to see inside where four companies were housed." According to the *Free Press*, "Viewers of the courtroom where Brown and his associates were tried found it had been temporarily transformed into a barracks for a Richmond militia company and Alexandria Artillery. Bed ticks filled with straw were piled up on one side [of the room]," arms were stacked in another, and "belts and cloaks hung" wherever a hook or nail "could be found on the wall." Frequently a "young volunteer sat in the judge's armchair," smoking a pipe, according to the paper. This scene was created by Company F of Richmond, who occupied the judge's platform and the space outside the bar where lawyers normally sat. The area inside the bar was filled by the Alexandria artillery; the large hall over the courtroom was the resting place of the Alexandria Riflemen; and the "front of the upper portion of the courthouse" was held by the Executive Guards.

The scene at the courthouse, a visiting correspondent wrote, "was in no respect comparable" to that of the churches. This observation was incorrect in one respect. The town churches were also crowded, and militiamen swarmed through and around them. Such was the case of a red brick Episcopal Church that sat on a hill north of the courthouse, overlooking both the courthouse and the field where Brown would be executed. The daily routine of the Wheeling militiamen in the churchyard and among the marble monuments and humble graves of the Episcopal Church cemetery included chopping wood, lighting fires, cooking pancakes and Virginia ham, and playing cards. Inside, the Sunday school room and tower floors were littered with straw beds, and the sanctuary had pew cushions scattered over the floor where men had slept. A few days prior to Brown's execution, a young militiaman filled the baptismal font with writing paper and envelopes and sat down to write letters home about his odyssey. In the other churches the general appearance was about the same.

The recently arrived Richmond Howitzers turned the Presbyterian Church into their barracks. One Howitzer, an older man who worked for the *Richmond Daily Dispatch,* wrote about his experiences, signed with a P (for Parke Poindexter), and telegraphed his articles to the paper. He was particularly impressed by the number of beautiful young women in Charles Town (who made him wish he was younger), the assistance of all the females in providing for them, and the brilliant yellow of the local butter. He wrote, "I never saw butter as they have here... which is yellower than gold and prettier, too... It seems absolutely to reflect its luster upon the plate."

The Howitzers were housed in the lecture room in the church basement, sleeping upon piles of straw the first night, November 26, until the town ladies made ticking the next day. The reporter-militiaman wrote his first article as the rest slept. This was done in the midst of loud snoring "in every note which belongs to the chromatic scale... some of them manage their flats and sharps with extraordinary skill. One squeaks like a reed of a clarinet, another comes in deep bass of a bassoon; a third, more ambitious than his neighbors', runs over the entire scale. It is a pity that such skillful performances have but the audience of two—the sentinel namely, and your humble servant."[6]

One of the perks for militiamen was a visit to the jail to see the man and his followers who were responsible for their presence in Charles Town. This made the jail a center of activity and the prisoners feel at times as if they were animals in a zoo. The Howitzers went by squads to view the inmates; one asked Cook for his autograph, which he gladly provided, in beautiful penmanship. The *Dispatch* correspondent was impressed with a great many things in the town, but Brown was not one of them. "Old Brown I hold to be the most truculent, ill-looking ruffian I ever saw. It must require a very strong imagination to make anything poetical out of him. He has full light eyes, very prominent, and as cold and freezing as though they were balls of ice. I should judge him a man to whom the very name of mercy was unknown."

The Howitzers, among others, would perform guard duty and scour the countryside at night. They were artillery men hurriedly formed on November 9 in response to Brown's raid; they lacked artillery and had to be trained through military drills to be infantrymen. Their unit and others who were in need of improving their efficiency were directed by the man who led the capture of Brown, Lieutenant Israel Green. He had been granted a furlough from duty. Since the raid he split his time between Charles Town and nearby Clarke County, where he had taken a bride. The Alexandria artillerymen also benefitted from his tutelage. Their one artillery piece was stationed opposite the courthouse, and it was there, in the middle of the town, where they received their training. Full dress parades were frequently held to show off new skills and provide entertainment for gathering onlookers.[7] Militiamen entertained themselves and satisfied their curiosity when off duty by roaming around the town and also outside its boundaries.

Every 24 hours scouting parties sent reports to their company commander, who sent reports on to Taliaferro, who forwarded them to the governor. Despite the anticipation of a rescue attempt, every report stated, "All is quiet—no disturbance of any sort."

On November 29 the *New York Herald* correspondent reported, "The town looks today as if the town was revolutionary. War, not peace, appears to be the order of the day." Major-General William B. Taliaferro, the commander of the Virginia militia, directed the military activities. By late November Taliaferro divided his 150 cavalrymen into three mounted sentinels spread at intervals forming a five-mile radius around Charles Town. Inside the circle of horsemen were three lines of infantrymen, each demanding the countersign before entrance was allowed to the town. It was cold hard work, as troops were often in the saddle from sunset to sunrise, without top coats, scouring the countryside 20 or more miles away. They responded almost every night to reports of gunshot in the mountains, when folks falsely assumed invaders were upon them. "It was an arduous task," T. G. Pollack, a member of Ashby Turner's Black Horse cavalry, wrote to his mother on Friday, November 25. "This is the first night I will touch a pillow since Monday… We turn day into night now entirely and rise at half past six in the Evening. Soldiering is very poor fun I can assure you."

Those scouting the mountains from Winchester northward had a more arduous task. The area was believed to be a likely place of penetration in the event of a rescue attempt. Also closely watched were the Potomac River crossings, and the B&O Railroad that followed the river westward. Some served for weeks before receiving pay, and around December 2 a few companies were called into service without pay. Companies were stationed from Martinsburg and Darksville to the Piedmont, exhaustingly scouting miles around, from mountaintops and gaps to the land below. Some lacked weapons, some had weapons but no ammunition, and others lacked cartridge boxes or scabbards. Most men were without overcoats, and many had no blankets. They suffered greatly during the chilling nights spent prowling the rugged terrain. Responding to repeated requests by company commanders, overcoats were ordered. Many did not reach the men prior to Brown's execution, as they went to men Wise had called into service shortly before that event, and had to be reordered. Despite their strenuous efforts, the scouts found nothing; neither did Wise's detectives who were sent to Charles Town and as far away as Ohio. The daily reports by scouts to Taliaferro still contained no sightings.[8]

Wise's military actions resembled those of a state at war. Virginia was preparing to defend herself against possible invasion by nebulous liberation groups from the North. This was fueled by Brown's raid, the conviction there were sinister forces at work in the North and the innumerable letters, often anonymous, speaking of forces varying in size from 5,000 to individuals infiltrating the Charles Town region. Most warnings were regarded by Old Dominion authorities as bogus, mere unfounded rumors, but enough doubt remained in their minds that they could not take the chance of being unprepared.

The governor held no doubts about the threats. Military reports of the lack of activity were superseded in impact by the numerous letters telling of threats. The hundreds of pages of letters had the desired effect. They convinced Wise there was no doubt his state would be invaded by the sizeable forces he claimed were mobilizing across the Virginia border in Maryland, Pennsylvania, Ohio, and beyond. He sent copies of his letter to President Buchanan and to the governors of those states, telling of the impending invasion. He said that if needed he would call upon "the entire force of the State" to ensure Brown's execution. He wrote the president on November 25, 1859, "I have information from various quarters, upon which I can rely, that a conspiracy of formidable extent" existed in the states north of Virginia to rescue "John Brown and his associates… The information is specific enough to be reliable. It convinces me that an attempt will be made to rescue the prisoners, and if that fails then to seize citizens as hostages and victims… I apprise you of these facts in order that you may take steps to preserve the peace between the States. I protest that my purpose is peaceful," but "if another invasion assails the State or its citizens, from any quarter, I will purse the invaders, wherever they may go, into any territory, and punish them whenever arms can reach them." Buchanan was not convinced. He wrote back to say Wise had given no specifics of the evidence he referred to, and it was the duty of the governors to police any gathering of forces of ill intent in their states.[9]

A repercussion of Wise's fears was the martial life imposed upon Charles Town. Citizens were awakened by a loud reveille that ushered in each day. Occasionally the sounds of nocturnal activity by the militia awakened anxious residents. Inexperienced, eager militia arrived daily. When the Mountain Guards, who came to Charles Town in late November, were told there was nothing for them to do until the dress parade at 3:00 the next day, they encamped in anticipation of the coming event. Alarmed citizens were less enthusiastic; they ran from their beds to inquire why drums were beating at 3:00 in the morning, only to find that the officer in charge of the Mountain Guards mistakenly believed it was time for the dress parade.

As the execution date neared, citizens of Charles Town became weary of the restrictions placed upon them by the military. They were afraid to go out at night for fear of being shot by a trigger-happy youngster playing soldier. Locals were impeded from moving about their homes and places of business. Even a celebrity, Edmund Ruffin, known throughout the country as a defender of Southern states' rights, was arrested for traveling in the town and taken to headquarters. The brother of commanding officer Taliaferro, a militia officer, met the same fate when out of uniform. Most locals blamed Governor Wise for the hypervigilance. This was the view of Harding, the commonwealth attorney for Jefferson County. He angrily opined, "The military power had completely extinguished the civil power, and that martial law was established, though not proclaimed." He was turned out of the courthouse and turned back by sentries when he tried to enter headquarters or leave town, despite his being told by Hunter (the special council of state) that it "was always opened to him."

The New York *Tribune* reported in mid-November that a well-known local gentleman who had too much to drink wandered from his home beyond the militia line set up to protect the town. When stopped by a guard demanding the countersign, the intoxicated man was unable to give it, and the guard—also inebriated from whisky—fired. He missed narrowly and scared the citizen "nearly to death." An outcry from vocal protestors demanding the commander of the military forces "must not keep putting firearms in the hands of drunken boys." None protested more vociferously than Colonel Robert Baylor, who commanded the militia during Brown's raid. He was among those arrested on December 1 for venturing within a restricted area. Highly incensed by this indignity, which was compounded by the governor's ordering him out of the militia the previous day, Baylor denounced Wise. He not only blamed Wise for his arrest but asserted the governor planned to destroy the Union and become president of a Southern confederacy.[10]

So disgruntled were citizens that they posted a proclamation around Charles Town ridiculing the military:

> Citizens around Charles Town:
>
> Citizens of the state of Virginia and the southern States, and well dressed citizens of the northern States, are requested to visit our town as hereto fore as they will be protected by citizens form the insults of the mushroom, corn-stalk military now quartered among us.
>
> Citizens of the town will hereafter be allowed to pass to their homes and places of business without being arrested as insurgents or n*****-stealers.
>
> By order Gen. Tumblebug, Comd in-chief
>
> Hon Dunghill, Military Secretary
>
> Charlestown, Nov. 30, 1859
>
> P.S. Come one, come all. The military shan't monopolize the show![11]

As the execution date neared Taliaferro turned to military and local authorities to address the challenges. With the assistance of Colonel Smith, commandant of the cadets, Lieutenant Green of United States Marines, commonwealth attorney Hunter, and Sheriff Campbell, Taliaferro chose an execution site and "made all arrangements for such a disposition of troops, citizens and strangers as will make the execution a solemn spectacle without the least danger of even a chance at rescue." On November 28 Taliaferro ordered a cavalry force of 40 men to patrol in the night "the country around Charlestown at a distance of eight hundred yards beyond the outlying picket guard. This patrol will form a circle around the town… sending out vedettes from time to time." His orders for the militia on the day of the execution, formed with the help of the above gentlemen, were even more extensive and detailed.[12]

While the town prepared for Brown's execution, a visiting Edmund Ruffin did his best to spread the idea of secession. He wrote in large letters on a label: "Sample of the favors designed for us by our Northern Brethren." He attached the label to a handle of a pike captured from Brown's hideaway. This attracted much attention, but it failed to shake the local residents' devotion to the Union. Most opposed secession. But Ruffin, a recalcitrant old "fire-eater" now in his mid-sixties, who would later (at the end of the Civil War) take his own life rather than live under hated "yankee rule," wished someone would attempt a rescue of Brown. Ruffin was convinced a rescue mission, whether it failed or succeeded, would cause the "separation of the southern from the northern states." There were things happening at Charles Town that Edmund Ruffin approved of. He was caught up in the martial spirit of the time and found the military events engaging: dress parades, music playing, flag waving, drum beating, and being saluted by militiamen from Richmond. On one occasion he accompanied General Taliaferro and his staff in a middle-of-the-night security check. Seeing an old friend, 67-year-old Hugh Nelson, in uniform as one of the newly arrived volunteers from Petersburg whetted Ruffin's appetite "to assume a similar position."

So Ruffin obtained permission from Colonel Smith, the commander of the VMI cadets, and was assigned to supervise the hanging of Brown, and to march with their color guard to the execution site.

On December 1, the day before his execution, Brown wrote a will and saw his anxious wife one last time. The next day Brown selected his respected adversary in court, prosecutor Andrew Hunter, to draw up his will, with jailor John Avis serving as witness. The document distributed his remaining assets among his family. John Jr. was to receive his surveyor's instruments and the family tombstone that was to remain in North Elba as long a member of his family lived there, to have carved on both sides inscriptions he would later send. Jason was to receive a silver watch with his father's name inscribed on it; Owen, his opera glass and rifle (if found) and $50 cash "in consideration for his terrible suffering in Kansas; and crippled arm from his childhood." Salmon was also to receive $50 and daughter Ruth Thompson, his "large old Bible containing family records." His sons and other daughters were to receive a "good coppy [sic] of the Bible" purchased at "some bookstore in New York or Boston at a cost of five dollars each." Each grandchild was to get "as good a copy of the Bible as can be purchased… at a cost of $3." Any remaining balance from his father's estate was to be divided equally and given by his brother in Ohio, Jeremiah R. Brown, to "my Wife & each of my children; & Widows of Watson and Oliver." Brown's property and money in Virginia were meager; much of the property had been carried away or confiscated. His attorney Sennott—entrusted earlier with Brown's financial interest—attempted to collect Brown's property for the benefit of his family but recovered only 20 of the original 200 Sharps rifles. These were in possession of the jailor, who was anxious to have their value transferred to Brown. Edward H. House, a New York *Tribune* correspondent, assumed Brown's tents, axes, pikes, and other items would soon be sold. House was appalled the attorney Griswold had depleted Brown's cash by charging $250 to defend him.[13]

On November 30, Mary Brown traveled by rail with Philadelphia abolitionist friends J. Miller McKim and his wife, and Hector Tyndale, a promising young attorney. They arrived late at night in Harpers Ferry from Philadelphia. The next morning, seeking permission to go to Charles Town, she was introduced to Robert E. Lee, who referred her to General William Taliaferro. The general gave her permission to see her husband, but in accordance with the conditions specified by the governor, she had to go alone, could see no other prisoner, was subject to security procedures, and had to return that evening to Harpers Ferry to wait for the delivery of her husband's body. This was the last time she would see her husband alive, but she carried herself with dignity and composure. Early on the afternoon of December 1 she left by carriage, escorted by eight cavalrymen and a sergeant of the Fauquier Cavalry for the heavily guarded jail at Charles Town, leaving behind her two companions and the lawyer.

News of Mary Brown's arrival drew people away from the execution site to the jail. Outside the jail a large crowd gathered, in addition to the military force that performed military maneuvers found in Scott's Manual (the standard military manual of drills and tactics). An opening in the sea of humanity had to be made to allow the carriage to pull up to the front of the jail. The carriage moved through a pathway lined by bayonets. Gawking onlookers, hoping to get a good look at the doomed man's wife dressed in black, were disappointed: her face was hidden by a veil. Finally inside the jail, Mary Brown had to endure a quarter of an hour's worth of introductions before she was searched by Mrs. Avis, the jailor's wife, to make sure Mary did not slip a weapon or strychnine to her doomed husband. In the meantime, General Taliaferro informed Brown his wife had arrived and asked how long he wanted the interview to last. Three or four hours, Brown responded. The general apologetically replied, "I shall not be able to oblige you"; Mrs. Brown had to return to Harpers Ferry that night. Seemingly accepting the restriction, Brown responded he had no favors to ask of the Old Dominion.

Mary was escorted to her husband's cell by the jailer, John Avis, who was required to remain with them during her visit. They met in emotionally charged silence. They kissed but were speechless and stood embracing as Mrs. Brown sobbed for five minutes. They had not seen each other since June, about six months earlier, and had been separated for two years, except for a few days. Mary placed her head on John Brown's chest and her arms around her doomed husband's neck. Finally composing himself, he broke the silence by telling her, "Wife, I am glad to see you."

Freed of the manacles that rubbed his ankles raw, Brown accompanied his wife to the Avises' parlor, where they sat on the sofa to talk. They spoke of their children. Mary told her husband that in Harpers Ferry she had made some effort to recover the bodies of their two dead sons, and Colonel Barbour "kindly consented to give his assistance." Brown said he would also like the remains of the two Thompsons to be removed if they could be found. He suggested the most economical way of dealing with the remains of their dead sons, the Thompsons, and his own body was to "get a pile of logs and burn them together; that it would be much better and less expensive to thus gather up all their ashes together and take them to their final resting place." Mary found this repugnant and shifted the conversation to other topics. Much of their conversation was about what was to be done after his death, covering much of what he had spelled out in his will. He said each child would receive $50, but his property would go to Mary. He thought she should stay in North Elba and stressed the importance of educating the children.

During their conversation Mary asked whether he had heard Gerrit Smith had become insane and been placed in an asylum at Utica. Brown replied he had read about it in the papers and was sorry to hear of it, immediately changing the subject. Avis extended the invitation to dine with him and his wife in their living quarters in the jail. After dinner the Browns were told Mary must leave. This enraged Brown who lost his composure. He wanted her to remain, but they had been together for four hours, longer than initially approved. Orders said she had to return to Wagner House at Harpers Ferry that night. The couple did not embrace, but as they departed they shook hands as Brown said "Good bye; God Bless." She responded "Good bye, may heaven have mercy on you," keeping her composure until leaving the room. She cried for a few moments before leaving for the town where her family was decimated to face a restless night. On the way back Captain Moore, riding in the carriage with Mary, attempted to express sympathy for the doomed man's soon-to-be widow, but she "repelled all attempts," saying her husband had not done anything to deserve the stain of being branded a criminal, much less execution. She "regarded him a martyr in a righteous cause."[14]

Brown returned to his cell. Once again he turned to his pen, remembering he had forgotten to give Mary instructions for Oliver's, Watson's, and his own epitaphs, for inscription "on the old family Monument at North Elba." He introduced this request by bidding her "another Farewell: 'Be of good cheer' and God Almighty bless, save, comfort, guide, & keep; you, to 'the end.'" He wrote a last letter to his brother Jeremiah and read the comforting letter of a childhood friend, Lora Case, who wrote a blessing: may God give him strength and comfort him; she also asked for something in his handwriting to remember him. He went to bed at 9:00 p.m., sleeping well that last night.[15]

The last supper of John Brown and his wife in the parlor of John Avis, the jailer. (West Virginia Archives, Boyd B. Stutler collection)

While the Browns were having their farewell visit, the execution site was being prepared. The hanging was to take place east of town in a stubble field of corn and rye of about 40 acres. A company of soldiers, complying with part of General Taliaferro's extensive orders, fixed flags designating the area of each military unit that was to occupy the field. Most of the field had been planted in rye, though some reported it as half and half, and others said the field was only 10 to 20 acres. In the center of this farmland was a broom handle with a small piece of paper attached, which marked the spot where the gallows were to be assembled the next morning, the day of the execution. Until then the not-yet-assembled gallows lay in a pile in the field. The execution site was close to a new Baptist church that had been built by the carpenter in charge of constructing the gallows. The field attracted visitors throughout the day, including members of the Alexander artillery, who argued over the uses of the different parts of the gallows. Some men removed their pocketknives and cut away pieces of the gallows as mementos. A child's doll was found nearby and placed upon the scaffold, prompting coarse and crude jokes.

In a different part of town a carpenter's shop contained a black walnut coffin waiting for the doomed man. Brown was to be placed in the coffin in civilian clothes before his remains were delivered to his wife. Both the gallows and casket attracted curious onlookers, and the coffin was sketched by a German artist of *Leslie's Weekly.*

Leaving nothing to chance, those in charge of the hanging even tested rope prior to the execution. According to one reporter, "Some half dozen voluntary ropes for the execution" were sent to Sheriff Campbell. The first selected was tested the day before the execution and "broke when tried with the weight of fifty-sixes attached to it." This was a reference to the cotton rope made in South Carolina. The final selection was hemp rope from Kentucky. It was rigged, according to the *Tribune,* "to give the body a fall of only eighteen inches—scarcely enough it was thought by some, who expressed a desire that Brown might fall ten feet, so as to insure his death…"[16]

Death on the Gallows

A beautiful sky with an array of pinks greeted dawn on a balmy Friday, December 2, 1859. How much Brown noticed it is not known. When he awoke he returned to writing under the window, answering his childhood friend and adding a codicil to his will stating that it was his desire that Mary "have all my personal property not previously disposed of by me." This was his property that was scattered through Maryland and Virginia. He appointed Sheriff Campbell the executor and included, "I wish my friends James W. Campbell, Sheriff, and John Avis, Jailor, as a return of their kindness, each to have a Sharp-rifle of those belonging to me, or if none can be found a pistol." Brown wrote the codicil, reported the *Evening Star,* "with a steady hand, and apparently with a continuous flow of thought, unchecked by the slightest ripple of discomposure."

At sunrise newspaper representatives went to General Taliaferro to gain permission to visit the site where the gallows was being assembled. They received a lecture on failing to report at headquarters and were warned he wanted "no abolitionists or republican on the grounds." Taliaferro sent the reporters "off under military escort." When they arrived at the execution site they saw, according to an *Evening Star,* "a dozen men" placing together the yellow pine framework of the gallows. The uprights were of unequal lengths. Those over the trap measured 17 feet and the opposite ones were 14 feet long. The platform was 15 feet by 10 feet and was "reached by a rail flight" of a dozen steps.

Curiosity satisfied, the reporters went to the Carter House "for good corn bread and tough beef-steak." Much consternation was created by the announcement that all the bars and drinking houses were closed for 24 hours. This was to lessen the possibility of a disturbance. The proprietor of the Carter House lamented he "would lose 150 dollars prospective profits."

After breakfast the *Star* reporter went to the heavily guarded jail and found Brown examining papers. This time his hands were "somewhat tremulous" and he was looking rather "fagged out." Andrew Hunter, who was with Brown until the prisoner left for the gallows, would many years later contend the opposite, that there was "no sign of tremor or giving way in him."

Earlier that morning, about an hour and half before his execution, Brown had asked for Hunter to come see him. Despite feeling harried with the work of dealing with the execution, Hunter dropped what he was doing and went to Brown; despite having rewritten his will the day before, Brown wanted another rewrite. Hunter responded, "Captain you wield a ready pen, take it, and I will" guide you through the proper legal form. "It will be what is called a 'holographic will' being written and signed by yourself, it will need no witnesses." Brown was not satisfied and replied, "Yes, but I am so busy now answering my correspondence of yesterday, and this being the day of my execution, I haven't time and will be obliged if you will write it." Hunter wrote down what Brown told him, repeating what he had written the day before. After completing the document Brown made additional suggestions requiring a codicil to be added. While Hunter worked on Brown's will, the old insurrectionist busily wrote his last letters.

While the attorney finalized the will and the captain hurried to complete his last correspondence, Hazlett was one floor up, occupying the cell immediately above Brown. He was, according to a reporter, a "rough looking customer, with a crop of stiff hair bristling above his head." He had not yet been tried, and he acted as if he would not be identified as a member of Brown gang. He was passing time by spitting tobacco juice "with considerable accuracy of aim at the shed-roof below." In good spirits, he laughed with little provocation at "any odd or ludicrous incident" in the courtyard below. In the cell next to Hazlett, Cook was well aware of his plight and stayed away from the window.

The execution was to occur at 11:00 a.m. Around 10:30 Brown was told to prepare for his execution. As his hour of doom approached Brown asked to be taken into the cells of the men who followed him. He first saw Green and Copeland, instructing them to conduct themselves bravely and "not betray their friends, bidding them farewell and giving each a quarter, saying he had no further use for money." The two African Americans shook hands with Brown but said nothing. Next he visited the cell of Cook and Coppoc, who were handcuffed together. Seeing Cook evoked resentment in Brown, who believed he had been misled by Cook's scouting reports of support for the raid and betrayed by Cook's incriminating confession.

He immediately charged Cook, the man he had sent to Harpers Ferry to gather intelligence (after Cook had possibly lobbied to go there), with having lied in his "Confessions." Shocked and taken off guard, Cook asked what he meant. "You say I sent you to Harpers Ferry," was the reply. Attempting to show this was not the case, Cook asked whether Brown hadn't sent him to Harpers Ferry to find out what Forbes had revealed. Brown bluntly shot back, "You know I opposed it when first proposed." "Captain, your memory is very different from mine," replied Cook, and he dropped his head as Brown glared at him. Brown then turned to admonish Coppoc for making false statements but tempered his condemnation by saying he was glad Coppoc had corrected the error. He gave Coppoc a quarter and instructed him not to betray friends.

Brown's last visit was to his cellmate and trusted lieutenant, the hot-tempered Stevens. This was more amicable. As they shook hands with warmth, Stevens said, "Goodbye Captain, I know you are going to a better place." Brown replied, "I know I am," and then instructed Stevens to stand up like a man and not betray friends, giving Stevens a quarter and a note from Proverbs of the value of controlling one's temper. Brown refused to visit or address Hazlett, not wanting to implicate him as one of his men.[17]

Shortly before 11:00 a defenseless, old John Brown was taken from jail, escorted by the sheriff and jailor. Recounted one witness, "General Taliaferro and his entire staff" of 25, as well as "six companies of infantry and one of troop of horse," were waiting in front of the jail to greet the raiders' leader. Cavalry were at the rear and head of the column. A reporter contended Brown had earlier begged he be allowed to walk the approximate 400 yards to the gallows. There is little to substantiate this, and security would forbid it. As the old man left the jail, stated the New York *Daily Tribune* on December 6, 1859, and descended the steps, a mother held her black baby up to him, and he kissed the baby. The false story lingered in Brown lore for years before being discredited. So anxious were reporters for news that they were prone to embellishing, printing rumors they had heard as well as what they actually saw, making it more difficult for readers to tell fact from fiction. Another story that was printed and gained currency stated that as Brown was leaving the jail he supposedly looked upon his military escort and remarked, "I had no idea that

Gov. Wise considered my execution so important." Avis and the sheriff, who were with him as he left the jail and were the only two men on the gallows platform with Brown, would state years later in an affidavit that Brown had made no conversation or comments as he was leaving the jail. The sheriff did not initiate a conversation and then assess Brown's calmness on the way to the gallows.

Looking at the topography, Brown saw the Blue Ridge Mountains and the wispy clouds above to the east and the brown colors of late autumn contrasted with the vivid green of recently planted wheat fields on rolling farmland. He commented on the beauty of the area as he neared the place of his execution. It was unusually pleasant and warm for a December day. People threw open their windows, and reportedly birds were singing and bees were flying.[18]

Brown's execution suit was the clothes he had worn for the raid, which had been washed of dirt and blood. It was a well-worn suit of black cassimere.[19] He was dressed in what onlookers described as a "black frock coat, black pantaloons, black vest, black slouch hat, white socks, and slippers of predominating red" that were broken down in the back, a colored shirt, and gray wool undershirt; he wore no necktie or cloth collar. Witnesses said, "It was noticed that his neck and breast were as white as a woman's."

His arms tied behind his back with cord, Brown was placed in an open wagon of the undertaker and cabinet maker, and he sat upon a poplar box that contained his black walnut coffin.[20] The sheriff, jailor, and undertaker sat in the front seat; the latter's assistant sat on the coffin with Brown. The yellow wagon of the undertaker and furniture maker was drawn by two large white horses, slowly taking the condemned man to the slight rise east of Charles Town where the gallows rose up.[21]

The military and press had been waiting at the gallows for hours; the press since 9:00 a.m. and the military even longer, aligning themselves along the white flags denoting their assigned positions. According to the *Evening Star,* they formed "two octagons, one within the other with the gallows in the center." More simply put, there were two concentric lines of armed men forming a rough square, with the inner line 50 yards from the gallows. General Taliaferro took every precaution to counter rescue attempts and ensure control of the crowd. The night before the execution he had doubled the number of pickets and had the soldiers assigned to the execution site sleep with their weapons. Militiamen were stationed outside the jail on all sides; inside, daily visitors were supposed to be prohibited for several days before the execution. An artillery piece pointed menacingly at the jail, with another on execution day pointing at the gallows. Reportedly, outside the rail fence that contained the execution field "were long lines of cavalry, and the country in every direction as far as the eye could reach was dotted with squads of sentinel soldiers, their brilliant uniforms bringing their figures out in strong relief against the somber autumn brown." Among the multicolored militia east of the gallows were the cadets from Virginia Military Institute. An elderly Edmund Ruffin contrasted starkly

A contemporary sketch of the procession to the gallows along George Street in Charles Town. The courthouse appears in the upper right, and the back of the jail with its walled in exercise yard on the left. In front of the jail is part of the Gibson Hotel. (Virginia Archives, Boyd B. Stutler Collection)

John Brown riding on his coffin to the execution site. (*Frank Leslie's Illustrated Newspaper*, Library of Congress)

with the youthful cadets. He had not gone to bed the night before because he had accepted an offer to accompany the officer who was checking on troops from 2:00 to 4:00 a.m. The tired secessionist stood out, with long gray hair that touched his shoulders, a disabled left hand, a long gray overcoat, and a simple parade cap. He had marched more than a mile with the cadets of the Richmond Grays and Company F. All were well dressed, but the cadets stood out in their red shirts. Without their gray overcoats, the cadets presented a dashing "zouave look."[22]

Despite great numbers of people attempting to witness Brown's demise, civilians at the site were limited, perhaps to several hundred. They had been discouraged from attending. Controlling the crowd and security were the most vexing problems facing Taliaferro, who felt harassed by 500 requests from people wanting to witness the top news event of the time. An attempted solution was a proclamation warning people to stay away. It originated from orders by Governor Wise, who micromanaged troop movements and anything else that struck his restless mind. Following instructions, General Taliaferro, along with the mayor, sheriff, and commonwealth attorney, issued a proclamation that threatened with arrest any strangers found in Jefferson County (including Harpers Ferry and Charles Town). It said that strangers, especially groups who did not have "known and proper business" and who could not give "a satisfactory account of themselves, will be arrested." "That on, and for a proper period before" the execution all those who attempted to come "whether by railroad or otherwise, will be met by the Military and turned back or arrested without regard to the amount of force that may be required to affect this." Local residents were urged to stay home and protect their property. Women and children were barred from the execution site. Travelers on the Baltimore and Ohio line were "subjected to examination," and passengers were temporarily prohibited from riding on the Winchester Railroad. Militiamen patrolled the mountains and were ordered not to allow people to cross from Pennsylvania and Maryland into Virginia. Military forces were concentrated at Charles Town. John Garnett, head of the B&O Railroad, wrote a grateful Governor Wise that Colonel Lee had ordered transportation for "240 U. S. Troops to Harpers Ferry," who would arrive on November 30 by special train.[23]

Citizens were kept away the hanging site, wrote one reporter, by "bayonet—nearly a quarter of a mile from the scaffold." On the morning of the execution aspiring attendees outside the neighborhood were stopped from proceeding. Harpers Ferry was lined with many people who were angry that they were not permitted to attend the hanging. However, because of the dogged "persistence of Dr. Rawlings of Frank Leslie's paper, the order excluding the press was partially rescinded, reporters were assigned a position near" General Taliaferro's staff. This was a more favorable position than they had expected; they had thought Wise would have them placed away from hearing distance of Brown. Surprisingly, the governor was not in attendance; he stayed in Richmond to prepare for the coming meeting of the General Assembly.

All visitors had to pass through the main gate to the field at its southern boundary. Hunter's Guard secured that gate and separated those who were known—and sent to the right—from those not known—on the left. Captain Ashby's company of cavalry was assigned special guard duty patrolling the perimeter and preventing admission to the field through anywhere but the main gate.[24]

Some half dozen of the "privileged civilians" sat upon the gallows steps waiting for Brown. It was reported, "Not a female was to be seen by the naked eye in any direction, but by the aid of a glass some few were observed at the windows of distant dwellings. They along with children were banned from the execution site. A few colored people were seen along the road skirting the field… Almost every tree in the vicinity was loaded with boys." While spectators waited attention was drawn to a single carriage that entered the field carrying a disabled man. It proved to be Samuel C. Young of Harpers Ferry—one of the citizens wounded by Brown's men. His injuries entitled him to enter the line as a spectator.

As 11:00 neared, General Taliaferro and his sizable staff entered the field. They were followed by the prisoner and his military escort, who came up and "halted in front of the gallows." Brown ascended the steps to the platform in a sprightly fashion. According to some correspondents, he exchanged farewells and thanked Sheriff Campbell and jailor Avis for their kindness. He was described by witnesses as standing "erect and calm" as the sheriff and jailor "properly pinioned" him, tying his arms in front of him, binding his legs near the ankles, and placing a white linen hood over his face. They adjusted the noose, "attached to the hook above." When asked to move a few steps forward to the trap door Brown responded, "I can not find it blindfolded; guide me to it."[25] The breeze disrupted the position of the hood causing the sheriff to ask Avis for a pin. Brown raised his hand pointing to the collar of his coat where a couple of old pins had been quilted in. Campbell removed the pins attaching them to the hood making it more secure.

Facing southward, symbolically facing the land he was accused of wronging, Brown might have expected to instantly drop to his death, but he had to wait 10 to 15 minutes while the troops that formed his escort from the jail assumed their assigned places. This must have seemed like an eternity. The sheriff tried to explain the reason for the delay, but "I don't care," said Brown, "only don't keep me waiting unnecessarily." It was the last time the sharp nasal twang of his voice would be heard. Throughout it all, he seemed to remain extraordinarily calm, showing no sign of fear or trepidation. His calm demeanor impressed almost everyone. A militiaman near the gallows later wrote that "[Brown] mounted the scaffold as calmly and quietly as if he had been going to dinner" and did not "exhibit the slightest excitement or fear." Although Avis—who had become close to Brown during his incarceration, despite their dissimilarities in background and beliefs—found his role in the execution evoked sadness, he said "Respecting the statement that he 'walked cheerfully to the scaffold,' I will say that I did not think his bearing on the scaffold was conspicuous for its heroism, yet not cowardly." Another onlooker called the seemingly emotionless Brown's actions "wooden."[26]

Colonel Francis H. Smith, the commander on the field, finally announced, "We are all ready, Mr. Campbell." But the Jefferson County sheriff did not hear or comprehend. Again, but in a louder voice, the colonel repeated his statement. Eventually, the sheriff descended the steps from the platform of the gallows and, a witness wrote, "with a well-directed blow of a sharp hatchet, severed the rope that held up the trap door." As it opened the dead silence was broken as "its hinges gave a wailing sort of screech that could be heard on every part of the field." Down Brown "shot through the trap, then up, then down," wrote the *Evening Star* reporter. Brown fell a relatively short distance—eyewitnesses estimated it at one to three feet—and the "rope used to strangle Brown was only three feet long." Those around the gallows watched in "profound stillness" as the old man struggled, with "each abortive" effort to breathe growing "feebler and feebler." His knees were scarcely bent, his arms were drawn up to a right angle at the elbow, with clenched hands, but there was no writhing of his body, no violent heaving of his chest.

At each feebler effort at breathing, his arms sank lower, and his legs hung more relaxed, until, at last, straight and lank, he dangled and swayed "to and fro by the wind." His body slowly turned "round and round—this motion, with the fluttering of the coat-skirt in the breeze" gave it the appearance of a scarecrow in a corn field. It was a ghastly spectacle. The dangling body "did not fill out its clothes" despite

A sketch of John Brown ascending the scaffold for his execution on December 2, 1859. (*Frank Leslie's Weekly*, Library of Congress)

the weight Brown had gained in jail. As Governor Wise said, "he must have been a bundle of nerves and nothing else."

The corpse of Old Osawatomie hung from the gallows for 37 minutes. During that time, Major J. T. L. Preston, a Lexington attorney and early advocate of the establishment of VMI, broke the silence of those around him by uttering, "So perish all such enemies of Virginia! All such enemies of the Union! All such enemies of the human race!" Major Preston viewed Brown's face while the hood was moved aside, and he found the bearded long face, still dangling from the gallows, "awful,—to see the human form thus treated by men,—to see life suddenly stopped." Major Thomas Jackson witnessed the execution from the right of the scaffold and was also deeply moved by the solemn event. Before the trap door fell, Jackson "was much impressed" that before him "stood a man in the full vigor of health, who must in a few minutes enter eternity." The devout major and future Confederate hero silently prayed that Brown's soul be saved from eternal damnation and the "everlasting fire" of Hell.[27]

After perhaps 20 minutes a series of physicians ascended the scaffold to examine the body to determine whether Brown was dead. It was reported that first came "Drs. Storry [Starry], Cook and Straight," who wore blue ribbons, the badge of the Temperance Society, on their coat buttons. They "felt the hanged man's pulse, examined his neck: and placed their ears to his heart." They were followed by four regimental surgeons who did the same things. "Then they too retired (as the platform was not deemed strong enough to bear more than a half dozen persons at a time) and so on, (including slips of boy-surgeons) to the number of twenty." According to the *Evening Star* reporter, "'Porte Crayon,' Strother, the artist, a thin sickly looking young man, with others visited the platform for a moment." Strother had been standing almost under the gallows. He hurried up the steps to the platform, raised the hood from the face, and quickly sketched the hanging human form. He later said his drawing was for Maria Lydia Child, who said she wanted "to have a portrait or likeness of Brown in every condition to hang in her room."

It was reported that Brown's pulse did not stop for 35 minutes "and at the end of 36 minutes the body was cut down. The neck was not broken, and the medical examiners declined certifying death… until further examination to be held at the jail at 3 p.m." Dr. Mason believed "it was possible in such a case to restore life by galvanic action"—an electric shock by chemical reaction. It was estimated "that strangulation took place after less than four minutes suspension," as Brown did not drop far enough to break his neck.

It was reported the rope "left no mark of abrasion on the neck. The eyes of the corpse were open, but not startling so. The mouth was open and would not close. The face was not unnaturally distorted though the blood vessels were somewhat distended, as occurs in death by strangulation." The body was placed in the black walnut coffin, which was placed inside a poplar box. On its exterior the undertaker had penciled, "John Brown, Esq."

In a field northeast of Charles Town, Brown's body is surrounded by Virginia militiamen on foot and horse. Structures of the town are in the upper right. (*Frank Leslie's Weekly,* Library of Congress)

The body was taken to the jail and again examined by a group of physicians to make certain Brown's limp body was lifeless before turning it over to his grieving wife. At the Wagner House in Harpers Ferry she heard the news that had created consternation at Charles Town. It surfaced while her husband was being hung that the buildings on the farm of George W. Turner, who was shot at Harpers Ferry during the raid, were burned. Unaware of the falseness of the rumor, and distressed at her husband's fate, Mary Brown said she was pleased it was the work of black men, not whites.

Wise had given orders for her husband's and sons' bodies to be turned over to Mrs. Brown, but her husband's was the only one that would be taken to her. He instructed Taliaferro to hand the sheriff the note requesting the body be turned over to the general for protection from mutilation. In a later clarifying message the governor stressed he did not intend for the corpse of the conspirator to have a military escort or funeral honors, but rather be put in a simple box and "placed in safe hands to be delivered to Mrs. Brown & protected, if necessary by force from multination or injury." In compliance, the general had Andrew Kennedy recruit 14 other local citizen volunteers to escort the body safely from the jail. They left at 6:00 that evening via a special train to Harpers Ferry, where Kennedy turned over the remains to Mary Brown. She signed the requested receipt only after having the casket opened to make sure her husband's body was there.[28]

Mary Brown was anxious to retreat from the area of her horror, and she, her companion Mr. McKim, his wife, and the attorney who had accompanied her to the Ferry left at 3:00 in the morning with her husband's remains. She faced a difficult journey of approximately 600 miles by rail, road, and boat. Mary Brown was headed home to North Elba.

Burial of the Raider Leader

Despite Brown's praise-garnering demeanor, he was far from forgiven for his acts. Before the coffin left Charles Town, the New York *Herald* reporter claimed he heard a captain suggest, "A good dose of arsenic should be administered to the corpse" to ensure it was not revived. Others wished Brown's head was severed from the body and retained to prevent the body from being paraded through the North as if he were a martyr. "This amiable bloodthirstiness," the reporter continued, "is on par with that of the students of the Winchester Medical College which have skinned the body of one of Brown's sons, separated the nervous and muscular and venous systems, dried and varnished them, and have the whole hung up as a nice anatomical illustration."

After the execution people started taking mementos. The *Star* reporter wrote, "Almost immediately" after Brown was hung, "bits of the rope" with which he was hung "were flying about, also pieces of the gibbet and coffin [material] and one person exhibited a white lock of hair from Brown's head." Many at the scene left so rapidly that "almost before the corpse was cut down there was a stampede from Charlestown of visitors especially reporters," who had had great difficulty getting to Charles Town, now "with their pockets crammed with exciting newspaper material were… anxious to reach their respective establishments without delay." Fulton of the Associated Press reported "with ravenous news for all American newspaperdom to feed" he had a carriage standing by, paying quadruple the usual price to get him to the Ferry in 55 minutes so he could catch the train. "Horse flesh was at a premium throughout the afternoon." Virginians had unsuccessfully attempted to exclude reporters of the New York *Tribune*. At one time it had five reporters, and at the execution three, one of whom wore the uniform of the Richmond Grays, who guarded the scaffold.[29]

The military forces also rapidly quit the field. The brass artillery that had aimed at the gallows rumbled away, and carpenters started disassembling the gallows even before the wagon carrying the raider's remains had left the gate to the field.[30]

John Brown would have been pleased with both the Northern reaction and the decorum of his execution. His execution secured his martyrdom, which would grow and emerge as one aspect of his contradictory reputation as a villain-martyr. The speech making, bell pealing, and gun firing that proclaimed his martyrdom in the North on December 2 contrasted with the propriety and solemnity that marked the execution. There was no military music, no saluting. Even the setting was impressive. A witness reported that the gallows sat on "rising ground, and commanded the outstretching Valley" from the mountains to the east and west, while "white clouds" appeared, resting upon the mountains, reminding several militiamen of "the snow-peaks of the Alps." Moved by the emotional event and pageantry, one eyewitness hyperbolically referred to the "800 militiamen" at the execution as the "greatest array of disciplined forces ever seen in Virginia, infantry, cavalry, artillery combined, composed of the Commonwealth's noblest sons, and commanded by her best officers."

John Brown's name was now firmly etched in history, larger in death than in life. Brown's calm demeanor and a prophetic message he wrote were also pivotal in producing a cult of martyrdom. As he was leaving jail on the way to the gallows, he handed a guard this written message that is much quoted today but was unmentioned in almost all the newspapers at that time:

> I John Brown am now quite certain that the crimes of this guilty land: will never be purged away; but with Blood. I had as I now think: vainly flattered myself that without very much bloodshed: it might be done.[31]

Fortunately for Brown's reputation, he had survived Lieutenant Green's attack with a ceremonial sword on the morning of October 18. If Brown had died at the armory enginehouse, the martyr's mantle would have been denied him in the minds of many moderate Northerners. He would have failed again and been deemed a mere fanatic who had tried to liberate slaves by seizing federal property and invading a town of peacefully sleeping citizens. Dying at the end of the raid would not have denied him notoriety, anger, and the South's denouncement. It would, however, have eliminated the subsequent events of the next six weeks that bestowed martyrdom upon Brown: the trial, visits to the prison, rumors of a rescue, death by a hangman's noose, and countless columns in newspapers throughout the nation. Some of that press coverage extolled the virtues of an old man's giving his life for a cause he so devoutly believed in; all the media coverage kept the nation's attention fixed upon the 59-year-old abolitionist.

On the day of Brown's execution, public demonstrations and sympathy meetings by Northern abolitionists and sympathizers included prayer meetings, singing of hymns, eulogistic speeches (by both blacks and whites), resolutions, bell ringing, firing of guns, and individuals promenading the streets wearing crepe. Supporters formed committees and collected money for Brown's family. The impact of the execution was detailed in the New York *Herald* and other papers. In a New York church a speaker expressed sadness for Brown, "a Christian," having to "die for obeying Christ," but "prayed that the martyr might haunt his persecutors by day and by night, and never suffer them to rest."

According to the *Herald,* citizens of Syracuse, New York, packed city hall to listen to "over three hours of stirring speeches" and the "tolling of a city hall bell sixty-three times" in honor of Brown's age (though Brown was 59). An overflowing crowd assembled in the National Hall in Philadelphia to pray for Brown, reading aloud "a number of his letters," and listening to speakers who included Lucretia Mott, a Quaker leader, feminist, and abolitionist. A similar meeting occurred in Providence. In Albany a cannon was taken from the state arsenal, and 100 shots were fired in commemoration of Brown's execution. In Worcester, Plymouth, and New Bedford, Massachusetts, church bells tolled from 10:00 a.m. to noon, the time of Brown's execution. In Boston, it seemed as if all black people in the region turned out, along with many white ladies, to listen to the "who's who" of New England abolitionists, including William Lloyd Garrison. The *Herald* reported that the speakers' platform held "Virginia's coat of arms draped in black." The front of the rostrum "was decorated with a large black cross, underneath which was a photograph... of John Brown, which was draped in mourning." Brown was proclaimed a "Martyr to Freedom," and Governor Wise, "the modern Pontius Pilate." At a meeting one minister predicted, "The 2nd of December would hence forth be celebrated as the anniversary of martyrdom of one of the bravest and purest sons of freedom, and should be baptized 'Martyr's Day.'"

Prominent abolitionists continued the martyrdom theme. Ralph Waldo Emerson bestowed sainthood on Brown, proclaiming that his hanging would "make the gallows as glorious as the cross." On the day of execution writer Louisa May Alcott wrote: "Living [Brown] made life beautiful. Dying [he] made death divine." The American Anti-Slavery Society designated 1859 as "The John Brown Year." [32]

As Alcott wrote her eulogy, a Southern newspaper editor wrote that Northern demonstrations "[with] the tolling of bells, the firing of minute guns, the opening of churches, and the fanatical speeches... exhibit... a singular if not an alarming evidence of the unsoundness of the public mind in that section of the country." Even the *Philadelphia Journal* expressed a similar view: "How can we understand the speeches which were made, in which Brown was held up to the world as a hero and a saint... It is an alarming evidence of the unsoundness of the public mind that such sentiments should have been uttered, or received with approval, and we may well distrust the philanthropy which would thus confound all our notions of right and wrong, and would canonize the man of violence and blood as a Christian saint and martyr."

Even the legislature of Massachusetts, a state full of abolitionists, voted down a resolution to adjourn on execution day in honor of Brown. In Manchester, New Hampshire, Brown sympathizers gathered in the belfry of town hall to honor him. After several strikes of the bell, the mayor suddenly appeared, ordering them to desist. When one man refused, the mayor dropped him through the entrance to the belfry.

On the night of December 3, 1859, Princeton students expressed their disdain for Brown. "A large procession of students, headed by transparencies [transparent images], marched through the streets with banners inscribed 'John Brown, the horse thief, murderer, and martyr.'" Arriving in front of the college, the protesting students burned effigies of William Seward and Henry Ward Beecher, "amidst groanings and shouts," as the college faculty vainly attempted to suppress the proceedings, which included speeches and lofty cheers from the large student crowd. Brown was hung in effigy in Natick, Massachusetts, followed by pro-Brown supporters' hanging an image of Governor Wise. Brown was hung in effigy frequently in the South.[33]

Brown's hanging was a penetrating event. The Boston *Herald* tells of the near-fatal hanging of a youth named John Brown. On the day of Old Osawatomie's death, a group of young boys in Quincy, Massachusetts, held a mock trial and execution. The young John Brown was found guilty, placed on top of a barrel under a tree, with a "slip noose" placed around his body, and the rope was fastened to a tree limb. After the barrel was kicked out from under the youth, the rope slipped up and caught "the Young John Brown" around the throat. "His thoughtless companions, frightened by the blood that flew" from the nostrils of the dangling youth, ran from the scene. Fortunately, according to the Boston *Herald*, a quick-thinking woman in a nearby house ran out "with a big carving knife and cut the youth down saving his life."

Reactions differed in the South. In Southern eyes justice had been served by the executing a criminal; Virginia's authority was upheld. The editor of the Baltimore *American* accurately expressed the feelings of Virginia and its Southern sister states, that Brown's execution was just. His heinous acts had "disturbed the public mind," led to "the interruption of ordinary labors and pursuits of life," and brought about an enormous military expense:

> The State of Virginia, yesterday punished the leader in the attempt to stir up insurrection among her negro population, and who in that attempt made war upon her sovereignty and murdered her citizens. John Brown has justly expiated his crimes upon the gallows. Whether he was a fanatical and insane zealot, or a blood thirsty man willing to achieve his purposes through any amount of suffering and wrong inflicted upon others, does not in the least possible degree affect his guilt, nor ought it to have availed to alleviate his punishment—Fanaticism is no excuse for crime; nay, it is rather an added ingredient of criminality, inasmuch as it often being the pretense of a good purpose and of high enthusiasm in the achievement of deeds at which morality and humanity alike revolt. There was, therefore, nothing merciless in the justice which yesterday consigned John Brown to the scaffold and which holds the same fate in reserve for others of his convicted associates… John Brown having suffered the penalty of the law we hope Gov. Wise will cease his military display and allow the public mind to recover its tone.[34]

On the night after the execution rain and sleet washed away the balmy earlier temperatures. The next morning a large crowd gathered at the Charles Town depot and listened to Mayor Green heap praise upon the departing Richmond Grays, Company F, and the Alexandria Riflemen; a response by the captain of the Richmond soldiers evoked loud shouts. The same morning a newcomer to Charles Town named Otis was arrested near the courthouse after asking the guard for extensive information about the hanging of Old Brown. Vigilance in ferreting out troublemakers was still a priority. The most excitement that Saturday morning was created by an argument between a couple members of the Fauquier cavalry over the size of their companies. The dispute started in a hotel and was taken out into the street, where the men fought. Members of each company moved in to back their man, setting the scene for a large brawl. "Fortunately one of the commanding officers appeared," reported a Baltimore correspondent "and stopped the proceedings."[35]

Newspapers nationwide continued to chronicle the news of Brown's corpse's journey to its burial site. People gladly purchased papers such as the New York *Times* for two cents an issue. They read with interest accounts of the body's four-day trip, mostly by rail, but augmented by boat and road, to North Elba. With the news of the arrival of Brown's body at each stop, large numbers of black people gathered and dignitaries flocked. They were paying their respects to the widow, who was dressed in black mourning clothes. Interest did not wane after the burial; well into the night crowds questioned the funeral attendees, hoping for details.

Newspaper readers found amusement in a ruse devised by Mayor Henry of Philadelphia. He had Mary Brown's blessing to secretly move her husband's body from Philadelphia's Baltimore Station to the Walnut Street dock, and then on to New Jersey and New York. This altered the original intent to stop in Philadelphia on Sunday to give the exhausted widow a chance to rest while the body was taken to an undertaker. A huge crowd of mainly African Americans—and a few others who were less respectful of Brown, including medical students looking for a cadaver—mixed with the usual number of carriages and drays. An hour before the train's arrival at 12:40 Saturday afternoon the crowd blocked the depot's entrance. This alarmed the mayor, who feared for the security of the body and worried about a possible riot.

Black people were especially eager to witness the proceedings. Since Brown died attempting to help so-called "colored people," the correspondent for the Baltimore *American* reported, "The colored people appeared to imagine themselves entitled to an ovation over the remains." A committee appointed by the Shiloh African Church was among the earliest to arrive to pay respects, and they were permitted—much to the grudging eye of others—to enter beyond the fence that shielded the crowd from the depot. But they too were bitterly disappointed when they were forcibly told "to step outside." An old horse pulling a rickety furniture wagon driven by a "colored man" was pulled up at the depot. A large tool chest belonging to a carpenter at the depot loaded with tools and old iron was placed in the wagon, and a horse blanket placed over it, as policemen were stationed around it to enhance the deception. A row of boys on top of the enclosure broadcast what they could see to the crowd on the other side of the fence. They yelled to the crowd below, "There comes the coffin—thunder, what a big one." "Now they're getting it into the wagon!" "Hurry! There she comes." As the gate opened and the wagon emerged, "a shout went up from the mob, and a rush for the vehicle" was at once made by all the onlookers "that was like thunder in miniature." The old horse was lashed vigorously, trotting forward and pulling the rattling vehicle. A stream of panting pursuers followed. Those able to talk spoke to each other; the reporter wrote, "In dat coffin lays a bigger man the John Rogers." A black woman was reportedly overheard saying she was "going right to a spiritual medium, an ask Captain Brown if he was comfortable in the other world." Others not too winded to talk consistently indulged "in adulation for the unfortunate deceased." The running caravan, led by a panting gelding and a wagon jolting along Washington Street, passed factories, where the occupants came out to watch. Some workers took up the chase as others fell behind or dropped out of the pursuit. The poor heavily breathing horse gradually distanced himself from the multitude left behind, but it was not until "the rumbling vehicle nearly reached the dock at Walnut Street that all its followers were wearied out." There the few remaining discovered the fraud, to their dismay. Angered at being deceived, "One colored person, in a white necktie… indulged in profanity." Indignation spread to those who had not completed the chase when they realized they too had been intentionally duped.

While this was happening Brown's body was taken from the train at Baltimore Depot and carried by cart up 15th Street, free of any followers. It was safely delivered at 2:10 to the Walnut Street dock, taken by boat to New Jersey, and then by rail, to near New York City under the supervision of Philadelphia friend J. Miller McKim. Mrs. Brown stayed with friends in Philadelphia, going to New York the following day with Richard P. Hallowell of Boston and arriving in the afternoon.[36]

On Saturday evening Brown's body was taken from New Jersey to New York City, crossing the Hudson on the Amboy boat. The remains were quietly and secretly taken to McGraw and Taylors, undertakers in Brooklyn, around 11:00 that evening. The body remained there until about Sunday noon. The undertaker's assistant, Thomas Williamson, confided in a friend, who told others, and all the men who heard the news scurried to the site. The street in front of the undertakers' became crowded from 2:00 p.m. to midnight. The crowd clamored to see the body, often claiming they were there to purchase a coffin to increase the chance of entrance. The doorbell rang continuously, and six policemen had to guard the mortuary all night so the gate would not be broken down. So persistent was the crowd that at least 50 prominent men were allowed to enter the premises. For two hours they gazed upon the still remains.

Accompanying those at the viewing was the undertaker's assistant's wife, who was surprised at how well the corpse looked. A few days later she wrote to her brother, "I never saw a finer looking man of his age after such a death too. His countenance was as serene as if asleep just red enough to look life like. When he came in he was black in the face for they slung him in the coffin with his clothes on with his head under his shoulder and the rope he was hung was in the coffin, but the ice soon restored his looks."

The undertaker, J. M. Hopper, who charged $44.50 for services rendered, had performed his duties well. The clothing was removed, the remains washed and the body placed on ice. Hopper's itemized bill lists "Keeping the Corpse on ice" at $8.00, and "working and laying out Corpse" at a $3.00 charge. The body was dressed again in the washed clothing, including the worn cashmere coat Brown had worn to his execution. A cravat collar was added at a cost of $3.00. It covered any unsightly marks made by the noose and enhanced the remains' overall appearance. The refurbished corpse was then laid in a new "5 ft 10 walnut coffin" costing $16.00. McKim, no doubt with Mary's blessing, did not want Brown's body to spend eternity in a box made in the slave state that took his life. The original walnut coffin was discarded as eager viewers seeking souvenirs took "the screws out of the Coffin as relics." The rope was given away in inch-long pieces.

Eager viewers wanted the clothes, but McKim said no. Undertaker Hopper had his assistant's wife, Louisa Williamson, wash them. She found the "coat was pierced with bayonet stabs and through his vest too." In "his pantaloons pocket I found a rifle cap... which they tell me is the most valuable relic left." Louisa's evaluation of the deceased was that of many in the North: "We all esteem him here in reality a Good man but mistaken, or misguided, or he would never have done that last deed when he did, for he must have known if he were not monomania on the subject that he would be sure to fail."[37]

On Monday morning Wendell Phillips, a noted abolitionist orator who gave up the practice of law to fight slavery, joined Mrs. Brown and her party accompanying the body. They boarded the train on the Hudson River Railroad line; it took them north to Rutland, Vermont, where they spent the night. At 5:00 the next morning they proceeded north to Vergennes, where news of the arrival of Brown's body and widow spread rapidly. A large crowd assembled at the hotel, a temporary stopping point for the travelers before they moved westward for the last part of the trip. Leading citizens gathered to express their sympathy to Mrs. Brown. Just before the train left, a silent procession was formed in front of the carriages. Then, according to the *Tribune,* "All moved forward to the tolling of solemn bells." Arriving at the bridge over Otter Creek, a third of a mile away, "the gentleman who formed the procession halted," and they formed themselves "in a double line and uncovering their heads, allowed the body, with the stricken widow and her friends to pass through." The Vermonters' spontaneous tribute to Brown and his widow concluded.

The small caravan traveled about five miles to the shore of Lake Champlain. There a boat was waiting, changing its usual course to transport them to Westport, New York, on the other side of the lake. Once across, heavy rain and rapidly melting snow caused them to forgo sled runners in favor of a wheeled carriage and wagon, as they traveled to Elizabethtown, nearly 10 miles away. They reached a hotel owned by the county sheriff, E. A. Adams, as an inquisitive crowd followed Brown's coffin to the courthouse, which the sheriff offered as a safe place for the body to spend the night. Men crowded into the judicial center, wanting particulars of the execution and lamenting that they "could not understand how Wise could have executed such a man." The sheriff's son offered to ride through the night on a fast horse in the inclement weather to inform the family at New Elba of their approach. The kind gesture was appreciated but deemed an unnecessary and difficult task. As everyone else took to their beds, 12 young men, who included several attorneys, stood guard all night over the remains.

Before daylight the next day, Wednesday, the group set out to travel the last 25 miles of their journey—the most difficult leg of the trip. A reporter wrote, "The road lay over a mountain, and was well-nigh impregnable." Travel was reduced to a crawl over muddy, rutted, and slippery roads; the slowest stretch was at the gap in the Adirondack Mountains. "So short as was the distance, it would take the whole of Wednesday." They traveled into the night with only a brief stop at 10:00 a.m. for refreshments at the home of Mr. Phineas Norton, a neighbor and friend, who was surprised and saddened to find his good friend had been executed.

That night as the weary travelers approached Brown's home in North Elba they were mystified at seeing moving lights in the distance. Nearing the house, they realized the lights belonged to worried family members and neighbors who had taken lanterns outside and were anxiously awaiting the arrival of the tardy travelers.

The carriage stopped and all was silent. The weary, agitated widow had to be helped out, wrote a reporter for the *Tribune*. When she alighted, he wrote, "There was a sharp, low cry of 'Mother!' and in answer, uttered in the same tone of mingled agony and tenderness, 'O! Annie' and the mother and daughter were locked in a long, convulsed embrace." This scene of grief erupted into pitiful sobbing, flowing tears, and embraces and was repeated with the next daughter, Sarah, followed by the little girl of five. The daughters-in-law, Oliver and Watson's widows, came next, "And then there went up a wail, before which flint itself would have softened. It was a scene beyond description," wrote the reporter, who was moved.

Soon composure was restored, the guests were introduced, and the fatigued party partook of a meal that had been prepared earlier, though their appetites were dulled by exhaustion. Going into another room, Mrs. Brown asked Mr. McKim to explain what had occurred during her trip, and then everyone went to bed.

The Brown home was typical for the region. The four rooms downstairs and space above accommodated family and friends. The structure sat on what the *Tribune* reporter described as "the highest arable spot of land in the state, if indeed, soil so hard and sterile can be called arable." Visitors on this occasion asked why such an area had been chosen, a place "so difficult to cultivate, and yielding so poor," and requiring such hard labor. The land originally belonged to Garrett Smith, who had given it as a "free gift to certain colored people," and it was to aid these people that Brown "had originally come to a place so compromising for the agriculturist."

The lengthy funeral started at 1:00 the next afternoon. Neighbors from the sparsely settled region squeezed into the farmhouse, joining family and other guests.

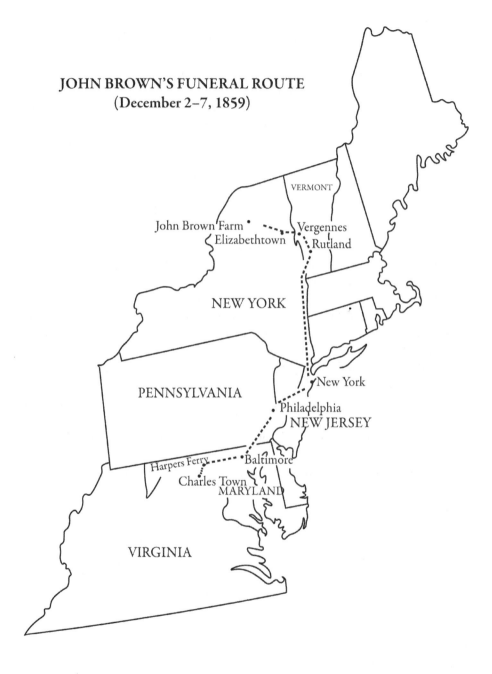

JOHN BROWN'S FUNERAL ROUTE
(December 2–7, 1859)

Services commenced with one of John Brown's favorite hymns, one he had sung to his children to lull them to sleep:

> Blow ye the trumpet, blow!
> The gladly solemn sound
> Let all the nation know,
> To earth's remotest bound
> The year of jubilee is come!

The Reverend Joshua Young of Burlington, Vermont, gave a moving prayer. He had traveled with a friend all night over the mountains through the storm to attend. Next J. Miller McKim spoke, expressing to the gathering that words were inadequate on such an occasion but words of comfort were due the weeping widow and the family. He read the letter written by Edwin Coppoc, delivered to Mary Brown at Harpers Ferry by the men who escorted her husband's body. Coppoc thanked her for the book to comfort him, *The Voices of the True Hearted,* which she had brought during her visit with her husband, although she was denied the possibility of giving it to Coppoc and visiting the other prisoners. (Jailor Avis saw that the book was delivered to Coppoc.) The latter part of the letter, describing how Coppoc attempted to comfort her suffering and dying son Watson, elicited much weeping from Mary. McKim, like the eulogy to follow, stressed Brown had struck a fatal blow against slavery and had achieved far more than he realized. He did "infinitely better than would appear his purpose of an armed exodus of former slaves."[38]

Wendell Phillips rose to speak. He delivered a flowery eulogy that perpetuated the image of John Brown as a noble and Christian soul, a great man who made a monumental contribution to humanity. To those who called Harpers Ferry a disaster, Phillips said in a sense it was, "But in no sense was it a failure." Brown's "words—they are stronger even than his rifles. These crushed a State. These changed the thoughts of millions and will yet crush slavery… Thus with the sword of the flesh and the sword of the spirit John Brown has performed a double mission, and the handwriting that dooms the system already flames out of control."

While another hymn was sung, the coffin was placed on a table by the door. Family friend Phineas Norton, whose home Mrs. Brown and her party had stopped at the morning before, invited guests to come forward to take one last look at their fallen hero. Gazing upon the dead man's face, the *Tribune* reporter was surprised. "It was almost as natural as life—far more than the ordinary corpse. There was a flush on the face, resulting from the peculiar mode of death, and nothing of the pallor that is normal when life is extinct." When the family came forward it was deeply moving, even to a stranger such as the reporter. "It was a touching sight as these widows, the eldest still in the prime of life and the younger ones in its opening buds, denied of their natural companions, leaning, as they stood around the coffin, on the arms of strangers. Such a sight I should not expect to see again if I should live a thousand years."

Despite their sorrow, the family took some small solace in the calm repose of their deceased loved one. Five months later Ruth Brown Thompson would write to a friend, "The calm peaceful face of our beloved Father as he lay in his coffin is ever before me, and I would have given anything if all our family could have seen it."[39]

When the viewing ended the mourners processed from the house to the gravesite Brown had selected. The site was about 50 feet from the house, next to a large rock, about eight feet high and 15 to 20 feet square. It was the most striking feature in the immediate area and immediately grabbed one's attention, said a reporter.

Mrs. Brown, supported by Wendell Phillips, led the procession; then came Oliver Brown's widow, leaning on the arm of Mr. McKim, who held hands with the small girl, Ellen. Next came Watson Brown's widow, on the arm of the Reverend Joshua Young; and the widow of William Thompson followed, on a family member's arm. The rest of the family followed, including the only son of John Brown in attendance, Salmon Brown, aged 23, who had auburn hair and a full beard. At the end of the procession walked friends and neighbors. As the body was lowered into the grave an outburst of crying came from the family. This gradually subsided when they heard the deep, mellow voice of the Reverend Young quote words of the apostle Paul when he appeared before Nero before his death. Among the soothing words were, "I have fought a good fight; I have finished my course; I have kept the faith; henceforth there is laid up for me a

Last viewing of John Brown in his home prior to internment. (West Virginia Archives, Boyd B. Stutler Collection)

The burial of John Brown at North Elba, December 8, 1859. Between his home and barn are parked carriages and oxen attached to a sled on the right. (West Virginia Archives, Boyd B. Stutler Collection)

John Brown's tombstone in front of a large boulder. (West Virginia Archives, Boyd B. Stutler Collection)

crown of righteousness which the Lord, that righteous judge, shall give me." This was followed by a benediction. The sobs were hushed as the family and friends returned to their house. The service and burial had taken two hours. It was now 3:00 p.m., and those who had traveled great distances were anxious to cross the mountain before dark; they said hurried goodbyes.[40]

Execution of the Remaining Prisoners

Brown's death did not release the South from the grip of paranoia or free all militiamen from duty. Even while Brown's body was being transported to Harpers Ferry, rumors raged through Charles Town that the property of several white farmers was in flames and their horses and sheep had been poisoned to death by sinister forces. Newspaper columns continued to swell with items pertaining to the remaining captured raiders and their subsequent executions on December 16, 1859, and March 16, 1860. At least for a while, life in Charles Town was similar to life before Brown's execution. Military parades and the shifting of militia units continued, and many militiamen who had been on duty for weeks were replaced by companies from other regions of the state. Several of the replacements were newly formed companies: the Wythe Grays, Fincastle Rifles, and Clarke Guards. The efforts of Wytheville were noteworthy. Within six days after notification by Governor Wise on December 2 that their militia was being called to duty, the people of Wytheville wired for and received from Richmond material for uniforms, made uniforms for 71 men, and sent their newly clothed warriors to Charles Town, a distance that was reported in the press as nearly 400 miles.

As residents in and around Charles Town waited for the next executions, according to the Shepherdstown *Register*, a "very cold spell of snow and sleet" gripped the region. "Chickens were frozen in their coops." Farmers took advantage of the cold to slaughter their swine for their yearly supply of pork. "Kill and eat" became the order of the day.

For two days before four of the raiders were executed, people again flocked to Charles Town. Despite the dark storm clouds and snow on December 13 that restricted movement and kept the ladies off the streets of Charles Town, they still came. Trains from Winchester, south of Charles Town, and from Harpers Ferry, from the north, were loaded with passengers attracted to the place that had been the center of excitement and drama in America for the last several months. They filled all the hotels, once more taxing the ability of the town to accommodate a crowd who wanted to make sure they were not turned back, the way people had been prior to Brown's execution. The Carter House filled its tables more than a half dozen times for meals to accommodate the swarm of newcomers. Local proprietors' profit margins swelled from the spending of visitors and militiamen, and farmers benefited from an expanded market for their hay and grain for military horses. It was a time of high entertainment as well as anticipation and excitement. The Woodstock Brass Band paraded through the streets during the day, visiting barracks and serenading the onlookers, concluding with visits to several private homes. The day's excitement peaked at noon with the news of the arrest of a stranger rumored to be "one of the venerable" followers of the late John Brown. Arrested under suspicious circumstances, the man "could give no satisfactory account of himself," repeatedly responding to his interrogators "I'm a Scotchman, have had my leg broken; and am twice fifteen." He was held in jail while they sought more information.[41]

Among the throng that arrived were Cook's two worried sisters who had helped raise him, and their husbands, one of whom was the governor of Indiana, Ashbel Willard. They came to see the condemned man one last time. Willard loved and was deeply concerned about his wife's brother. His earlier attempts to save Cook from the gallows by obtaining top legal counsel, urging Cook to write his confessions, and personal visit and appeals to Governor Wise had failed. Willard may have sought help from Cook's former employer, Peter Y. Culter, a law professor at the University of the City of New York, which proved to be as unsuccessful as his own attempt to move the governor. Cook had worked as a law clerk before going to Kansas, a move Cutler had strongly advised against. In a letter written to Wise asking for a pardon for Cook, Cutler said his contacts with his former law clerk after Kansas convinced him Cook "had become insane and I have no doubt that he was essentially deranged when recently at Harper's Ferry."[42]

Willard had done all he could, and he and three other members of Cook's family visited Cook for the last time on the afternoon of December 14. It was an emotional encounter. His sisters hugged their little brother and wept in anguish. When Willard and Cook embraced, the governor was "sobbing loud enough to be heard throughout" the two-story structure. They left at 6:00 p.m. vowing to return the next day. But upon returning to the Carter House, Willard said it was too difficult for them to see Cook again. The sisters penned notes to be given to their condemned sibling, and they and their husbands departed the next morning.

For arriving visitors and residents the day was more enjoyable, as they were treated in the afternoon to a grand dress parade by all the troops in Charles Town. A large crowd that included many ladies in fine carriages gathered on the field where Brown had been executed. The sun was reflected off gleaming bayonets as the brightly clad warriors, divided into four battalions, strutted impressively through their drills in the snow-covered field. They were reviewed by General Taliaferro, in full dress, sitting on his white mount. The second-most-noticed person was the adjutant Lieutenant Israel Green of the US Marines; not only was his uniform impressive but he was also the object of praise and appreciation for having trained the raw recruits from different parts of the state.

Amid the ceremony military orders for the next day of executions were read. Most found the arrival of a company of cavalry from nearby Middleburg, Virginia, the highlight of the grand dress parade. They dressed in black pants and red shirts, with drawn swords, and were mounted on fine horses.[43]

It was not as pleasant for the jailed raiders as the clock ticked off their last days and hours. Cook's spirits had been boosted by the news that his wife was coming to see him, but it turned out to be a false rumor. He had been ill for several days and looked unwell. No doubt his stressful situation was a major contributor to this condition. He was pleased to see his mother-in-law, Mary Ann Kennedy, who was devoted to him. She attended not only Cook's trial but the trials of the other conspirators in hopes of learning more about her son-in-law. During her visit she told him that if she had known what he was up to at the Ferry, "You would not be here." Cook agreed. Despite being despised by many, he attracted the curious, receiving a number of visitors during his incarceration, especially young women, many of whom asked for his autograph.[44]

His fellow shackled cellmate, Edwin Coppoc, also had visitors who had labored to save him from the hangman's noose. Coppoc was a physically unimposing, honest, and likeable young man from a pacifist Quaker family who evoked sympathy because of his character. He was also a model prisoner. His much-published letter to his mother in Iowa expressed remorse and claimed he had been led astray by men who should have known better. His father's death had led to Coppoc's leaving his mother in Iowa to go live with a Quaker farmer, John Butler, in Ohio, and Butler described Coppoc as a good but willful youth. Evidence of his willfulness included Coppoc's expulsion from the Society of Friends for dancing.

Butler and two other Ohio men of the Society of Friends came east in what proved to be a futile attempt to save his life. Their appearance in Richmond, and the extensive testimony of Governor Wise before the Virginia legislature that Coppoc's sentence should be commuted to life imprisonment, did not change a significant number of the hardened hearts. The governor could not commute the sentence; only the Virginia legislature could, because Coppoc had been convicted of treason.[45] Angry legislators, including the representative of the district that included Harpers Ferry, bellowed protests against commutation, saying Coppoc was unworthy of mercy. He had killed the popular mayor of Harpers Ferry and shown his disdain for Virginians in his condolence letter to Mrs. Brown, where he referred to the people of Harpers Ferry as "the enemy." The condemned man's claim he had not written the letter held no sway. It has been suggested that Cook, a gifted writer with dramatic phrasing, wrote the letter on behalf of Coppoc, who may have signed but not read it. Even if this is true, Coppoc referred to Virginians as the enemy in a November letter to his mother. This letter was published but received less attention because it appeared in the second week of December and was overshadowed by his more newsworthy condolence letter to Brown's widow.[46]

On the afternoon of the day before the execution, Wednesday, December 14, the prisoners were visited by local clergymen from the town. The jail was temporarily turned into a religious sanctuary for all the prisoners.[47] Solemn religious services were held. The tones of preachers' voices uttering prayers asking for divine forgiveness and salvation for the condemned men echoed through the cells. Cook and Coopoc were the loudest, wrote a witness, with "professions of a change of heart, and in hope of Divine forgiveness—They freely admitted their guilt." This proved to be a sham, wrote one reporter. Later that night they attempted to escape.

The clergymen left the jail feeling satisfied they were highly successful in gaining the repentance of the prisoners, especially Cook and Coppoc. Darkness soon fell upon the town. Barrooms became crowded with men drinking, discussing the executions and the resignation of the prisoners to their fate, and generally agreeing that military duty was a bore. Suddenly at 8:15 a shot was heard outside the jail, followed by several more. The previous quiet was abruptly interrupted by a commotion and fear, the greatest the town had known since news of the Harpers Ferry raid. The military immediately swarmed through the town. Rumors ran wild. One reporter wrote, "The true cause of the excitement, and rumors of the most extensive character floated into the bar-rooms, only to be contradicted by momentarily new arrivals of citizens driven from the streets."[48] Rumors ranged from an attack by an abolitionist liberation force to the prisoners' escape.

The hubbub had actually started with a man named Thomas Guard, a tailor in civilian life who was serving as a military sentry near the back of the jail when he saw a man standing on the wall. When the man, Cook, refused to answer the challenge, the sentry fired. Another head suddenly appeared—Coppoc's—but was soon pulled back. Cook was not intimidated and seemed ready to jump but when the sentinel threatened to impale him, Cook stayed put. Both prisoners retreated to the jailyard and surrendered to the sheriff and jailor. Cook later said, wrote a reporter, "if he could have gotten over the wall and throttled the guard he could have made his escape." Once again Cook was the victim of poor timing; when he was captured in Pennsylvania the plan to let him escape from jail there had been foiled by a warrant mistakenly issued in his name for Hazlett. Some later surmised that if Cook had waited until later at night his chances might have improved. He seems to have been unaware of the guard outside the jail wall, but regardless of the hour, making an escape attempt later would have provided less darkness under which to escape, and success would still have depended on the position and vigilance of the guard. Cook stated he had planned to escape the previous night, but postponed it, fearing the embarrassment it would be to his sisters and brother-in-law, Governor Willard, who had labored on his behalf. He also claimed he had encouraged Coppoc to escape without him, but Coppoc refused.[49]

Over 10 nights Cook and Coppoc had labored when they were alone at night, making an escape hole through the prison wall to the prison yard. Their tool was a Barlow knife—a large, strong pocketknife—a guard had loaned them to cut a lemon and had forgotten to retrieve. The knife was used to remove a screw from their bedstand, which they used as a chisel to pry mortar from the brick wall. From fellow prisoner Shields Green they acquired the blade of another knife and with it made some teeth in the Barlow knife, which allowed them to cut off their shackles. When they were ready to escape they pried off their irons, using bedclothes to muffle the sound of cutting off iron shackles. They removed bricks from the inner wall, concealing them in the stove drum, and hiding the dirt, plaster, and mortar between their bed sheets. Bricks in the outer wall, with the mortar chipped away, were left until the moment of escape. Their escape hole was underneath a barred window behind their bed, which hid their work. They squeezed through the opening in their cell wall on the second floor and slid down a drainpipe to the fenced-in jailyard, about 18 feet below. There they faced a 15-foot wall. Seeing the scaffolding of Brown's gallows stored there, they moved it. They were scaling the wall when they were thwarted by a sentinel on the outside the wall.[50]

The attempted escape accelerated rumors, including the story that Cook and Coppoc had received inside help. Taliaferro's fear that security was inadequate had been proven, and both the military and local authorities were embarrassed. General Taliaferro raced to the scene and telegraphed Governor Wise about the incident. The most embarrassed and humiliated staff were also under the greatest suspicion: jailor Avis and Sheriff Campbell. They had strongly resisted the military's attempt to increase its control over the jail and ignored both its warning of escape attempts and its suggestions for tightening security. Taliaferro had written Wise a week earlier, on December 7, asking the extent of his authority over the jail and expressing concern about security. He lamented that the sheriff and jailor had ignored his suggestions. Taliaferro was concerned there was no guard in the jail yard outside the window on the first floor and the suggestion of Colonel Smith of VMI that the doors should be opened at night and lights placed to shine on the prisoners so any movement by them could be detected were ignored. Five days after writing the governor the concerns of Taliaferro and one of his staff were heightened when they went to identify Hazlett. They found the front door to the jail open, along with the doors to corridor in front of Hazlett, Stevens, and their cell. They were not greeted by anyone for five to 10 minutes except for a 12-year-old girl with a child in her arms, who, upon seeing the military men, rapidly disappeared. Finally a man they did not know appeared. Upon entering the cell they found other strangers visiting Hazlett and Stevens. This experience was relayed to the governor, who left the sheriff and jailor in charge within the walls of the jail and Taliaferro in charge outside.[51]

After a tremulous night, it was execution day for Cook and three other conspirators. Security was heavy. In the morning three local minsters—the Presbyterian Reverend North, the Methodist Reverend Waugh, and the Reverend Leech, whose religious affiliation was not given—again visited the cells of the doomed. They arrived when the men were washing and putting on clean underclothing. Avis, the jailor, told the prisoners that if they had anything to say to do it now in front of the 15 to 20 people present. Cook responded, thanking the ministers, jailor, sheriff, and guards and naming citizens of Charles Town who had shown kindness and concern for their welfare. A reporter wrote, "At this point Coppoc looked up and said 'Them's my sentiments too gentleman.'"

On the execution field, the military had taken its early morning position. At 10:30 a.m. General Taliaferro and his staff of 25 were set up with the military units necessary to safely escort the two African Americans, John Copeland and Shields Green, to the gallows. Between the soldiers at the front door of the jail was an open wagon carrying their coffins. At 10:45 the sheriff and jailor helped Copeland and Green into the wagon, where they sat on their coffins without looking around. Soldiers sat beside them, and a large crowd, five times the number that attended Brown's hanging, waited with anticipation to see the executions. The procession entered the field at 10:53, and the two condemned men, according to one reporter, "cast a shuddering glance toward the gallows erected on the rising ground in its center." They were also accompanied by the three ministers; Copeland and Green gave them an affectionate farewell and said they hoped to see them in heaven.

Green and Copeland rapidly ascended the steps, along with the sheriff and the Reverend North, who made one last prayer. Copeland remained silent as ropes were adjusted around their necks and caps were pulled over their heads, but Green frantically prayed out loud until the trap door dropped. He died quickly, and his death was reported as "very easy, his neck broken by the fall and the motion of his body very slight." Copeland was not as fortunate and "seemed to suffer very much, and his body writhed in violent contortions for several minutes." Some surmised the rope had been too short, and the fall not far enough to break his neck. Their bodies remained hanging for a half hour until physicians examined them and their lifeless forms were cut down.[52]

Their bodies were placed in poplar coffins and taken back to the jail, arriving there at 11:45. Interment was planned for the next day at the gallows site, but the bodies remained there only briefly. Medical students from Winchester had other ideas and dug up the caskets; one student stood guard with a revolver. The bodies of Copeland and Green were taken to Winchester, joining the cadavers of Watson Brown and Jeremiah Anderson, which had been seized shortly after the end of the raid. Copeland's father's repeated pleas to Governor Wise for permission to get his son's body had failed. Four days prior to the execution Wise had responded to the senior Copeland that he could not travel to the state; only a white person could retrieve the body. He further instructed a physician that if "proper relatives" were not there at the time of the execution, the convicts' remains would be turned over to the medical college.

A few days after the execution the Oberlin, Ohio, mayor, A. N. Beecher, received a telegram from Governor Wise saying the bodies of Copeland and Green had been taken to the Medical College for dissection. The mayor, with whom Copeland's father had pleaded to help retrieve his son's body, sent an Oberlin professor, James Monroe, to the medical school. Professor Monroe was reluctant to go and received a chilly reception in Winchester on his way to the college. The medical faculty agreed to his request for Copeland's body, but adamant students, who were led by a lean, tall, redheaded Georgian, blocked the removal. They claimed they had gone to considerable trouble, that their leader and his "chums" had faced considerable danger digging up the corpses, and the students—not the faculty—owned the remains. Before leaving empty-handed, Professor Monroe was given a tour of the college. He left with the indelible memory of seeing the physically well-developed body of Shields Green in the dissection room lying on its back on a table, with glassy eyes staring skyward.[53]

Back on execution day, around the time when Copeland and Green's bodies arrived back at the jail, Cook and Coppoc were told they had one hour remaining. The preachers were in the cells with them finishing prayers. Outside military movements similar to those earlier in the day were taking place, and a wagon with two more caskets waited. Cook gave instructions for the disposition of sentimental items on his person. He requested the breast pin he wore not be broken during execution and afterwards be given to his wife or his baby boy, if the child lived. He also had a necklace holding a highly polished daguerreotype with a lock of his son's hair, and he wanted to wear it until after his death. It was to be given to his wife. Both men requested their wrists not be tied so tightly that it caused great discomfort.

Cook had been asked to explain all about his jailbreak attempt, and that morning he wrote a letter that exonerated the sheriff, jailor, and guard and included details about the escape attempt. He started the fluent letter with, "Having been called upon to make a fair statement of our means of breaking jail, I have agreed to do so from a sense of duty to the sheriff of this county, our jailor, and the jail guard. We do not wish any one should be unjustly censored on our account." It was signed by both Cook and Coppoc.[54]

Like Brown and other raiders, Cook and Coppoc saw themselves as martyrs. They wanted to believe their deaths would have a meaningful purpose, making it a little easier to face the hangman's noose. Cook told a gentleman that he believed slavery was a sin and would be abolished in Virginia in 10 years, by Virginians. He had nothing to regret and was "prepared to die for such a cause." Coppoc remarked that he feared the affair was not over and friends in the North would not rest until they had revenge.

Seeing Coppoc struggling to keep his composure, an elderly Quaker man remarked, "It is hard to die." Coppoc responded, "It is the parting from friends and not the dread of death that moves us." According to a reporter in the room, Coppoc gave away his old slouch hat to the Quaker from Ohio who raised him, "[saying] that the dark one should be put on him was a present from Governor Willard."

A blue cloth cape was thrown over Coppoc's shoulders, and a dark one placed on Cook's, and their arms were pinioned.

Coppoc and Cook walked downstairs and were allowed to proceed to Stevens and Hazlett's cell. They cordially shook hands and said goodbye. To Stevens, Cook said, "Good Bye!—My friend, good bye." Stevens replied, "Good bye!—Cheer up!—give my love to my friends in the other world." They shook Hazlett's hand but refused to call him by name for fear of identifying him. After saying goodbye to the guards, they left the jail and were helped into the open wagon. They sat on their walnut

Shields Green. (Library of Congress)

John A. Copeland. (Library of Congress)

John E. Cook. (Library of Congress)

Edwin Coppoc. (Library of Congress)

coffins. The Baltimore *American* reported, "The appearance was rather of hopeless despair than resignation, and they seemed to take but little notice of anything as the procession slowly moved on the field of death."

Cook, however, was not totally stoic. A reporter from a different paper contended that Cook was surprisingly cheerful. Recognizing several men as he left the jail, he bowed politely to them and told one gentleman to remember him to his Harpers Ferry friends. At 12:47 the men reached the scaffold, where Cook shook hands with a large number of people and bowed politely to Mayor Green. A reporter contends Coppoc had a look of despair, and tears streamed down Cook's face. As the crowd got a look at the physically unimposing Coppoc, they remarked about his "genteel appearance." Both men ascended the steps to the scaffold without hesitation. Stepping upon the trap door, Cook looked up at the hook from which the noose hung. Like Brown and Copeland, he would have spoken if he had been given a chance. Reverend North made a brief prayer, the nooses were placed around their necks, and the hoods were placed on their heads. Cook said, "Stop a minute, where is Edwin's hand? The sheriff placed their hands together for one last handshake. Cook then said, "God bless you."

The angst at that moment became so intense for Coppoc that he said in a loud tone, "Be quick as possible." To prevent a repetition of Copeland's death struggle, the sheriff carefully adjusted the nooses. In the words of one reporter, seven minutes after ascending the scaffold, "Both were launched into eternity."[55]

The bodies of Cook and Coppoc were taken to Harpers Ferry by a train waiting at the Charles Town depot. Coppoc's uncle Edwin had his nephew's body taken to Ohio for a burial that was attended by a large crowd. Cook's remains were shipped to Robert Crawley in New York. He was Cook's non-governor brother-in-law and friend.

There were difficulties moving Cook's body and locating a funeral site. Crawley did not have a permit, so it was with great difficulty that he was able to get the remains through a town and across a ferry in New York. Finally the bruised body with a broken neck, distorted face, and discoloration arrived at its destination. All were denied viewing because of its deteriorated condition, including the widow, Virginia (Jenny) Kennedy Cook. The undertaker had a formidable job, standing the corpse upright as it was embalmed to drain blood from the face.

Hundreds gathered at the mortuary, wanting to see the body, with many claiming to having been a friend of the deceased. Meanwhile, Crawley and the minister of his church were shocked when the ruling body denied them permission to use the church Crawley had attended for 15 years. The funeral was finally held in a private citizen's large home on December 20. The rosewood casket was open, and family members and Cook's teenage widow saw her husband (of only three quarters of a year) for the first and last time after the raid. The emotional service concluded with the minister's reading from Cook's last poem. Jenny Cook removed her husband's pin and pendant. He was buried first at Cypress Hill Cemetery and later moved to a Crawley family plot in Brooklyn's Greenwood Cemetery.

Jenny Cook lived for a brief time with her in-laws, but it didn't work out. Being from a modest background, she was ill at ease around members of high society, especially her strong-willed mother-in-law. She had told them she and Cook had married a year earlier than the actual date, hoping to hide the shame and condemnation of a pregnancy out of wedlock. Jenny had supported her husband and been faithful in keeping silent when Cook had told her before the raid that they were going to liberate the slaves. She would later find employment among Brown's friends in Boston and would marry a Union soldier.[56]

The Final Executions

After Coppoc and Cook's hanging three months lapsed until the last of Brown's men—Aaron Stevens and Albert Hazlett, who was calling himself William H. Harrison—would meet the same fate. First they had to be tried. The haggling between Virginia and the federal government over which entity should try Stevens delayed his execution, and the question of identifying Hazlett and proving he was at Harpers Ferry could not be resolved before the fall court session expired. Their trial would have to wait until spring session. Until then, maintaining security and executing Brown and his convicted followers were the first orders of business.

The trial of Stevens and Hazlett, identified in the indictment by the alias William Harrison, a name he and his jailed friends used to hide his identity, commenced on February 2, 1860. Boston attorney George Sennott defended them pro bono. He hammered hard at prosecutor Hunter, who had attempted to obtain a court order that would have allowed Stevens to decide whether he wished to be tried by the federal or state governments. It was all in vain; the convictions of Stevens and Hazlett were a foregone conclusion. They were found guilty on February 14 and sentenced to be hung a month later. Hearing his sentence, Hazlett told the court he had been kindly treated, but he was innocent of the charge of murder of which he had been convicted. "I deny ever having committed murder, or ever having contemplated murder, or even having associated with anyone contemplating murder… I repeat I am innocent of murder but I am prepared to meet my fate." Stevens denied he had ever proposed burning Harpers Ferry, which a witness swore he had done. He said, "When I think of my brothers slaughtered and my sisters outraged, my conscience does not reprove me for my actions."[57]

Attempts to save the two men included legal appeals and petitions; personal visits to Wise's successor, Governor Letcher; and illegal rescues. Time was running out, and in desperation Richard J. Hinton, Thomas Wentworth Higginson, and several other Brown supporters attempted to organize a raiding force to free the two men. They raised money, acquired weapons—including rockets—and recruited men.

Attempts were made to get a dozen or so German revolutionist refugees in New York who were supposedly interested, but they failed. Eight comrades of Stevens and Hazlett in the Kansas wars came east to Harrisburg, Pennsylvania, to join a liberation force of 20 men—one fewer than Brown's. The eight Kansas comrades were referred to in written correspondence as "machines" and were led by a seemingly mild-mannered man, James Montgomery, who was relentless in combat. The plan was to travel for five to 10 nights down South Mountain carrying weapons and provisions from Harrisburg to free the two men. First, three men in two separate scouting expeditions revealed there was little chance of success. It was decided that the tight security at Charles Town, and frequent heavy snows that hindered travel and would lead to easy detection, should abort all plans for a rescue.[58]

Petitions from Ohio and elsewhere to commute the death sentences of Stevens and Hazlett failed to sway Governor Letcher. Personal visits from Stevens's girlfriend, Jennie Dunbar, to Richmond two days before the hanging met a similar fate. Letcher greeted her cordially and then dashed all of her hopes of saving Stevens's life. The governor rejected commutation for Stevens, stating he was the worst of the insurrectionists, "reckless, hardened and dangerous to society," and it was the governor's duty to rid the world of him.

Stevens endured much suffering from being wounded six times, with severe injuries that were, for a time, considered terminal. He had mostly recovered by the end of his 169 days of incarceration, but facial paralysis restricted laughing and made singing, the joy of his life, difficult. Nevertheless, Stevens retained his sense of humor. The jailor, Avis, recounted that Stevens and Hazlett debated who should have the noose placed around their neck first. One day he found them "chucking" pennies. Avis witnessed: "Stevens tossed the coin again and called out: 'Head or tail?' 'Tail,' shouted Hazlett. 'It's head—I've won!' exclaimed Stevens, as he went over and picked up the coin. 'What have you won?' asked the jailor. 'The privilege of selecting you to put the hangman's noose around my neck!' was the cool reply." While walking up the steps of the gallows Stevens is said to have whispered to the jailor: "Captain, remember I won first choice."[59]

The day before their execution both Hazlett and Stevens had relatives visit one last time. Hazlett's brother of Armstrong County, Pennsylvania, visited him. Stevens's sister, Lydia Pierce, came from Connecticut, as well as the woman he loved, Jennie Dunbar of Ohio, with whom he shared a keen interest in music. Hazlett's brother counseled his brother to tell all—which he did not do—and to not expect commutation or amnesty.

Jennie Dunbar's presence was a delightful gift on the next to last day of Stevens's life, which was his 29th birthday. She had just returned from Richmond and told Stevens of her unsuccessful visit with the immovable Virginia governor to save his and "Harrison's" (Hazlett's) lives. Stevens said he was sorry she pleaded with the governor, whose response was what you would expect. After this Stevens was cheerful. They sang, laughed (although earlier Stevens had written to a friend he could do neither), and ate snacks Dunbar had brought. Stevens read aloud about Spiritualism, finding comfort in the belief they would reunite in the spirit world. The two women stayed well into the night, having supper in the jail.

The next morning they rejoined Stevens and shared breakfast together, eating oysters—which he had requested for his last meal—at a table that was set up in the jail hall for all the prisoners and guests. Stevens remained cheerful. His shackles had been removed, and his clothes had been washed. He asked for a brush to polish his shoes with, saying he wanted to look well when walking up the steps of the gallows. His distraught sister left, weeping, and tears welled in Jennie's eyes. She was the woman he desperately wanted to marry, but despite her fondness for Stevens, some contended she might not have loved him. Her efforts on Stevens's behalf, including waiting at Harpers Ferry with his sister until after the execution, and accompanying the corpse to its burial site, would tend to make one think otherwise. At the least, the two shared an extremely strong bond of friendship.

Shortly after breakfast, according to the Charlestown *Spirit of Jefferson,* "the friends of the criminals bade them a long farewell and took a carriage for Harper's Ferry, where they remained until the bodies of the executed reached that place."[60]

As the three visitors departed, throngs crowded the town to witness the last in the trilogy of executions. It was the greatest gathering of spectators of all of the executions, estimated at about 3,000. Many waited on the field where the scaffold had been reassembled, on the same spot as the previous hangings, but far more waited at the jail. There they accompanied the local militia escort, consisting of Hamtramck Guards, Jefferson Guards, and Bott's Greys from Charles Town. They were led to the gallows by Colonel John Gibson, General Taliaferro's replacement. The number of militiamen had expanded from 80 men to 11 small companies. Waiting around the gallows were the Berkeley Border Guards, Floyd Guards, Floyd Riflemen, Armory Guards, Letcher Cadets, Continental Morgan Guards, and Letcher Riflemen. There were other militia units nearby that could arrive at Charles Town within two to three hours if needed. Four hundred militiamen would remain at Charles Town for several weeks after this execution.

At 11:50 a.m. on Friday, March 16, Stevens and Hazlett arrived by wagon at the execution site, sitting on two plain boxes with their names boldly written on them. Inside the plain boxes lay two fine walnut coffins. Like Brown, the doomed men refused ministers who offered to pray for their souls in jail or on the gallows. Also like Brown, they walked up the gallows steps with resolve. Hazlett was the first to ascend the steps and did so, according to a reporter, "with an easy, unconcerned air, followed by Stevens. Both seen to survey with perfect indifference the large mass of persons in attendance and neither gave the least sign of fear." While the ropes were being adjusted around their necks they exchanged affectionate farewells

Shields Green, John Cope and and Albert Hazlett in the Charles Town jail. (*Frank Leslie's Illustrated Newspaper*, West Virginia Archives, Boyd B. Stutler Collection)

Albert Hazlett. (Library of Congress)   Aaron D. Stevens. (Library of Congress)

with the only other men on the scaffold, the sheriff, the jailor, and the jail guard. "Just before the caps were drawn over their heads, Stevens and Hazlett embraced and kissed."

When the trap doors were dropped Hazlett's neck was broken and he died quickly with little struggle, but the muscular Stevens—like Copeland—struggled for a considerable time. (Stevens had earlier described hanging as when one "danced on nothing.") The knot had slipped on Stevens's neck, causing him to "writhe in contortions for several minutes." The bodies were permitted to hang for approximately half an hour, and then they were examined and pronounced dead.[61]

Friday, March 16, 1860, saw the end of the lives of the last of John Brown's captured men. Mrs. Rebecca Spring had made arrangements for Stevens's and Hazlett's bodies to be shipped by the Adams Express Company to her home in Englewood, New Jersey for proper burial. She had them shipped to her husband, Marcus, who had sent $50 to cover the costs. When the bodies arrived, they had deteriorated almost to the point of being unrecognizable. An undertaker got to work, and after he had finished, a bell rang at 10:30 a.m. on March 18 to signal the start of the funeral. Mourners assembled in the parlor of the Springs' home, in a community for socialists led by Mrs. Spring's husband, Marcus. Among the mourners was Stevens's sweetheart, Jennie Dunbar, whom the New York *Herald* called his "betrothed bride." She had accompanied her boyfriend's body from Charles Town. Others were curious onlookers—socialists who did not attend the ceremony but stared from the balconies of a large nearby building.

A traditional religious service was conducted. The two men were eulogized; traditional hymns were sung, including "Nearer My God to Thee"; and Mrs. Spring read letters written by what the New York *Herald* called "The last of the Harper's Ferry Conspirators." At the end of the service Stevens's body was placed in the hearse, and Hazlett's, in a common farm wagon. They were taken to the nearby Socialist Cemetery half a mile away and buried in shallow graves three to four feet apart. Before leaving to go home, mourners threw evergreens on the caskets as a symbol of the immortality of the soul. Within an hour the decedents' last resting place was filled with dirt.[62]

With the exception of a few papers, including the Charles Town paper, the New York *Tribune,* and the New York *Times,* coverage of the execution was reduced to a brief synopsis hidden among other cursory news. News from fall to spring of the conspirators and the previous executions gave people pause about the execution of Brown's men. Somehow they now seemed less menacing, more human, although flawed. The thirst for their blood had waned. Shortly after the execution of Stevens and Hazlett the Charles Town *Spirit of Jefferson* expressed its disdain for further bloodshed: "Although it is known that at least four of the Brown party yet remain unwhipped of justice, still the desire is that no more blood be shed, and that the remaining wretches be permitted to wander through the world with the sting of a guilty conscience and scorned by all honest men, rather than our country shall be made the theatre of another season of excitement."

The most scathing indictment of the execution of Brown's men was published in the Cleveland *Daily Herald* the day after Stevens's and Hazlett's deaths. "Virginia has wreaked her judicial revenge upon two more of the misled victims of John Brown's madness, but the world in looking back upon the three day's execution of the seven men who have dangled from the Charlestown gallows, will point with a sneer at that cowardice of Virginia [which did not have one drop of mercy] to mix with her cup of vengeance ... The civilized world has seen no such barbarity as Virginia has displayed under the mockery of justice."[63]

CHAPTER 8

Rehearsal for War

John Brown's raid and the trauma at Harpers Ferry prompted a call to arms and revitalization of the militia system that springboarded mobilization for the Civil War. The November after the raid the New York *Herald* repeatedly ran the headline "VIRGINIA ARMING FOR CIVIL WAR," as well as similar headlines that said the South was doing the same.[1]

Historically, Americans have viewed the militia system, which originated in Colonial days, as the shield and protector of American freedom. After the American Revolution many believed the state militia was the keystone of individual freedom. In the early national period a number of Americans strongly disliked the idea of having a large national standing army, as it could be used by the central government to coerce states and suppress individual civil liberties. Taking into account this fear, plus the need to rally a sizable force to meet national emergencies, domestic insurrections, and foreign invasions, Congress passed the Uniform Militia Act of 1792.[2] President Washington had hoped this legislation would establish uniformity in the nation's militia, but it did not. About the only uniformity created by this law (which bestowed upon the militia what meager central direction it was to have for the next 111 years) was a form of universal military training for able-bodied males in the United States from the age of 18 to 45. "The Uniform Militia Act," wrote historian John K. Mahon, "had the weight not of law but of a recommendation to the several states" and did "amount to virtual abdication by the federal government of all authority over the state militias." In extreme national emergencies the militiamen served the nation, but for the most part, they served their respective states. Service varied from mere ceremony to keeping the peace, enforcing quarantines, and, in the South, slave patrols.

States implemented the Uniform Militia Act as they saw fit. All states enacted legislation that recognized the right of citizens to have and bear arms, made the governor the commander in chief of the militia, provided for exemptions from service including conscientious objectors (with some states requiring payment of commutation fees), and prescribed fines for nonexempt citizens who failed to discharge militia duties. Militia drafts were recognized, as it was the right of the draftee to procure a substitute. Captains of militia units were required to give advance notice of muster or training days, either by leaving summonses at homes or by printing notices in newspapers. Once notified, militiamen were expected to show up with weapons on time and in the right place. Most states provided for the election of company officers, but states varied in their methods of selecting upper-level leaders and in the frequency of muster or training days. Some met only once a year. After the war of 1812, the compulsory militia waned, and the volunteers, another type of service within the militia system that had existed since 1792, waxed.[3] A number of the militia regulations and customs of the early national and antebellum eras—such as the age limit for service eligibility, election of officers, draft, commutation fees, exemptions, and preferences for volunteers—were precursors of military procedures later followed by the belligerents of the Civil War.

Voluntary militia service lacked the repugnant mandatory element that plagued the line organizations and offended the American sense of individualism. Unlike the line, volunteers were almost autonomous military fraternities.[4] This explains in large part why, despite long-standing historical roots back into the colonial era, many Southern and Northern line, or compulsory militia, units in the 1850s were poorly trained and poorly equipped. Without the stimulus of an immediate danger, they received only lukewarm public support.

Muster days were frequently similar to festivals or carnivals. This was especially true for the infrequently held training days for regiments and battalions. People often traveled great distances to see the peddlers and vagabond entertainers who were attracted to militia muster sites. People also came to witness the ill-clad, all-too-often inebriated, and half-hearted warriors, armed with "deadly" corn stalks and brooms, imprecisely attempting to perform military drills and exercises.[5] Despite the military imperfection and the fact that frequently, little if anything was learned along the lines of militia drills, general muster days were the biggest events of the year—even bigger than circus days. Thomas Gold, in his history of Clarke County, Virginia, provides a vivid description of militia day: "It was a holiday for all. Bullies strutted arrogantly and were willing to whip anybody" who dared to test them. Little boys roamed about; each one could be the "proud possessor of a horse cake or a stick of peppermint candy." It was an occasion that brought the people together and helped gratify the ambitions of "those who wanted to be colonels or majors."[6]

During the antebellum era, the militia—especially voluntary units, which were better uniformed and better armed than those of the line—helped quench the public's thirst for excitement and pageantry that 20th-century sports would later also satisfy.[7] The playing of drums and fifes and the marching and maneuvering of the militiamen created an appealing spectacle. Militia were commanded by mounted officers wearing uniforms that rivaled the splendor of peacocks, complete with long plumes worn on hats that were turned up jauntily. Both boys and men had flights of fantasy, dreaming that, if they were needed to defend state and family, it would be an honor to participate in the glories and splendor of war.[8] In the early months of the Civil War, this illusion would be shattered by the realities of the boredom of camp life, the fatigue of protracted marches, and the suffering and hardships of combat.

Attempts to upgrade the militia system had only limited success. Despite remedial legislation enacted in Virginia throughout the 1850s, especially in 1853 and 1858, the militia in the Old Dominion had severe flaws—particularly the line.[9] Large numbers of public arms dispersed by the state to the militia had fallen into the hands of individuals who used them, illegally, for private purposes. So sloppy were the periodic militia parades, and so acrimonious were feuds among militia members, that the editor of the *Democratic Mirror* stated in 1859 that the militia system in Loudoun County, Virginia, was on the verge of self-destruction. Languid discipline and ineffective leadership resulted in the trial of a militiaman by his commanding officer, a colonel, in a court of inquiry in which the colonel was the presiding officer. For misconduct during a parade, the militiaman was charged with mutiny. The trial was marred by even less order than the parade; the proceedings consisted of shouting, yelling, throwing chairs, and the exploding of "torpedoes," as bedlam reigned. Finally the trial was terminated, as the accused was found guilty of disobedience and fined $5.[10]

Under more somber circumstances the inadequacies of militia units in Loudoun County were further revealed. Despite the nearness of Loudoun's boundary to Harpers Ferry, none of the county's line militia responded to the call to action. A few days after John Brown was captured, 50 volunteers from Hillsboro and the vicinity marched to the northwestern frontier of the county, just east of Harpers Ferry, believing they were protecting their community from abolitionists' incursions. Fifteen members of this force were so young their mothers begged them not to go, while others were ancients, including one venerable gentleman in his eighties. Armed ineptly with outdated and inferior weapons, such as flint pistols, bludgeons, and blunderbusses, this band of Loudouners made at best a feeble gesture to protect their homes from imagined imminent danger.[11]

The local press praised the volunteers' efforts but condemned the "contemptible militia system" that left Loudouners "perfectly defenseless." The *Democratic Mirror* demanded "arms" and urged "citizens to form volunteer companies and patrols throughout the state." The *Richmond Index* agreed. "The peculiar character of... Southern Institutions" and the threat to them by abolitionists "has made the volunteer system no longer a mere gaudy display of fine dress, but a real necessity."[12]

Fearful residents held community meetings and passed resolutions proclaiming that areas like Loudoun County were in imminent danger of having slave insurrections ignited by abolitionists and John Brown sympathizers; residents believed such characters might be traveling through the region masquerading as "pedlars" and "book agents." To meet this danger, volunteer companies such as the Hillsboro

Border Guard, Loudoun Artillery, Loudoun Guard, the Leesburg Civic Guard, and the North Fork Guard were formed. These groups attracted both the young and the old. Seventy-year-old Marshall W. Butts, a veteran of the war of 1812, was appointed first sergeant of the Hillsboro Border Guard. "Though tottering toward the tomb," according to some, Butts seized his musket and marched with his company, ordered into the service of the state, as the members of this unit scoured the Short Hills and Blue Ridge Mountains and patrolled the Virginia side of the Potomac River. Bridges and landings along the river were areas of great concern to the patrols.

To provide better security, arms and munitions were procured. Uniforms were ordered, but—to the dismay of the editor of the *Democratic Mirror*— not from a Southern company but from a firm in Philadelphia. To finance the uniforming of volunteers, a military fair was held in Leesburg, and numerous oyster suppers were organized in several larger hamlets in the region. Such fundraising was also an occasion for militant speeches. None reflected the combative spirit within the county better than the speech of Captain A. L. Rogers in early January of 1860. Rogers stated that three months previously, at the time of John Brown's raid, not an armed company and scarcely a musket were in Loudoun, but as of the first day of 1860, there were eight organized and equipped companies of volunteers. He concluded that the true feelings of most were "for the Union, Constitution, and peace," but in view of John Brown's raid, "[we] are armed to the teeth and ready for war! Being determined to defend our institutions from all assaults of abolitionists, if need be, at the point of bayonets and cannons' mouth."[13]

Neighboring counties to the west of Loudoun seem to have improved their line militia prior to Brown's raid, but their greatest interest seemed to be forming and supporting volunteer companies, such as the well-drilled Hamtramck Guards and Jefferson Guards of Jefferson County. In 1858 in Charles Town, a Mexican War veteran, Lawson Botts, organized the Jefferson Cadets for boys aged eight to 16. Volunteers, like the Jefferson and Hamtramck Guards, played a crucial role in the entrapment of John Brown and his men, and they provided security during the raiders' executions. Brown's raid led to the demand for additional volunteer companies. For example, in Jefferson County alone after Brown's raid, four recently formed companies joined the two older companies to form the Second Regiment of Virginia Volunteers. In nearby Frederick County, a local paper told of 70 men over age 45 who formed, in December 1860, the "Silver Grays" (also known as the Winchester Home Guards), in "preparation for an 'irrepressible conflict' that may be forced upon" them. Farther south residents of Lynchburg, Virginia felt especially vulnerable with the state of their militia—the "Barefoot militia," as it was called because of the various kinds of dress worn by the men, who drilled once a year with sticks and umbrellas. It was urgently reorganized as the One Hundred and Thirty-first Virginia militia. Other companies were formed, such as the Wise Volunteer Troop.

Meanwhile, according to a Lynchburg historian, town residents cried "To arms! To arms! The South will soon be invaded"![14]

During the waning days of Wise's governorship he called for reform of the militia system in two lengthy messages to the Virginia General Assembly. Addressing the legislature on December 5, 1859, he stressed the dangers to slave states revealed by what Southerners called "the outrage at Harpers Ferry." He demanded "each State in the Union state their position on the future of slavery and the provisions of the Constitution and laws of the United States." The agitated governor denounced President Buchanan's "refusal to help keep the peace" and warned of the dangers of civil war: "We must rely on ourselves, and fight for peace! I say then to your tents, organize and arm!" He advocated for reorganizing the militia system, having an "active militia of men 18–25 fully equipped and frequently drilled compelled to duty" that included "patrols and organized into regiments, battalions or companies as the density of the population will admit."[15]

Failure to comply would result in "heavy and summary fines and penalties." Officers were responsible for arms and fines for loss or abuse. This branch of the militia was exempt from working on roads or serving on juries. Men over 25 who were not volunteers would assemble but once a year and pay $1 tax per man for exemption from active duty, "unless actually called into service." The governor was to appoint all general officers with the approval of the senate, all field officers, and captains, who were to supervise the election of lieutenants on down. Major-generals through captains should have the authority to call out the militia in sudden emergencies. The Virginia Military Institute was to be part of the militia system, "subject to orders from the governor alone." Wise urged establishing "depots of arms and ammunition at numerous points," modifying old muskets, and procuring rifle-muskets.

To reduce the dangers of slave insurrections and escapes, Wise advocated greater vigilance and restriction. He called for legislation that would prohibit the distribution by mail, newspapers, or booksellers of incendiary materials. To prevent the escape of slaves, "vessels of all waters" would be inspected thoroughly and frequently. Intercommunication and "intercourse of slaves with free negroes to or from the north of Virginia" must be rigorously regulated, and all "secret and nightly associations of negroes, free or slaves should be banded." Uncomfortable with having free black people in his state, Wise proposed restrictions, some of which would form the heart of the Black Codes during Reconstruction: "Do not drive free negroes north, but force them to be constantly employed. Compel all idlers, vagabonds, persons of bad behavior to public works and labor under guard." Wise went even further: "Allow them to have no real estate." Many of the governor's proposals would see fruition, but not the bill to establish a Virginia Military Academy in the northwestern part of the state on equal footing with the Virginia Military Institute.[16]

In 1860 volunteer companies became not only more numerous in Virginia and the South but also better trained and equipped. The 1860 Virginia militia law required each volunteer company to muster at least six times yearly. The law also provided for election of officers (a common practice) and the adoption of bylaws, which gave volunteers a degree of local autonomy over their company, a feature they found most appealing.

The 1858 militia law in Virginia required the line to meet three times a year: a regimental muster in April or May and a company muster in the same two months. Volunteers were to meet in companies four times—in April, May, June, and October—in addition to a regimental or battalion muster. After Brown's raid, the 1860 militia act increased these requirements to at least six musters a year. Each muster of the line or volunteers was to last from two hours to one day long, with muster time set at 11:00 a.m. Commanding officers were required to notify militia members at least 10 days before the muster by running notices in local newspapers; in 1853 15 days' notice was required by law. Northern Virginia papers from 1858 to 1860 were cluttered with such notices. If a local newspaper did not exist, notices were to be placed in three "separate public places in the respective companies' district."

Commissioned officers, when on duty, were required to wear a uniform "prescribed by the regulations of the army of the United States, except the buttons shall have the Virginia coat of arms." Training militia officers in tactics was conducted annually by the brigade inspector, who was appointed by the brigadier-general. Instruction occurred at the county courthouse three days preceding the regimental muster. In addition to providing training, the commanders of each company were required by law to submit to the brigade inspector a report on the number of militiamen of each company and condition of each company's arms. To assist in the training program the inspector could employ, at $2 per day, a drummer and fifer, who also received $.04 a mile for travel expenses. Brigade inspectors were paid $5 per day and $.10 a mile for travel. Officers who failed to attend training were fined $5 for each day missed. The 1860 law increased training frequency to semiannual three-day sessions. A list of males required to serve in the line, men from 18 to 45, was prepared by the commissioner of revenue for the county, city, or town, as he had assessed and recorded taxable property in his jurisdiction. Commissioners were paid $.02 for each name they placed on the muster roll.

Men who failed to report for muster were fined $.75 by the court of inquiry, a key administrative arm of the militia system created primarily to deal with those who did not fulfill their militia duties. Courts of inquiry existed on the company, battalion, and regimental levels; regimental courts of inquiry also served as an appeals court for the battalion court of inquiry and met annually in October or November.

The clerical work of keeping the court records was carried out by the clerk of the court of inquiry. He was appointed by the commandant of each regiment's battalion or company. The clerk kept records of proceedings of the court of inquiry and issued tickets of all fines the court assessed. Tickets were given to the sheriff, who had to collect fines.

Expenditures of the militia for services of officers, clerks, and others were paid from the militia fine fund. After Harpers Ferry the 1860 militia law increased fines: adjutants failing to make the proper reports forfeited allowances and faced a fine from $10 to $20. Regimental staff officers failing to appear at rendezvous when lawfully ordered to do so could be fined $15 to $75. Failure to attend musters could mean $5 to $10 fines. Noncommissioned officers and privates failing to comply with duties faced fines smaller than those imposed upon personnel in command positions.[17]

Volunteers were not always content. Virginia Governor John Letcher's commutation of an elderly slave, Jerry, who had been sentenced to be hung for "seditious language" for talk of burning property after Brown's raid, angered white residents and the Clarke Guards. Guardsmen gathered in the streets of Berryville on March 6, 1860, reportedly "biling" with righteous indignation over Letcher's failure to allow the eternal silencing of Jerry's menacing tongue as a warning to others. They talked of demonstrating and hanging the governor in effigy and vowed, according to a reporter, "If Jerry was taken out" of the Berryville jail and moved to Richmond, "he would not get out of town alive!" Governor Letcher ordered the ringleader, First-Lieutenant Thomas G. Flagg, court-martialed in Berryville on May 1, 1860. Flagg was eventually reprimanded at the next regimental muster, and some Clarke Guards resigned in protest of the reprimand. So strong was the feeling on behalf of Flagg that a local newspaper editor expressed concern that the incident would lead to the disbanding of the Clarke Guards.[18]

There were many advocates of the intolerance and vigorous suppression of troublemakers that Flagg and his friends espoused. Shortly after Flagg's sentence was announced at the end of May, a citizen sent a letter to the Clarke County *Journal* denouncing the lack of forceful action against "dangerous" travelers throughout northern Virginia:

> When John Brown came to the Ferry, the people of Virginia were like a parcel of startled horses; some running to meet him; some running from him; and others too scared to run either way, but all vowing vengeance. Organ grinders, pedlars, clock menders, and such… could not show their faces for fear of being roughly handled, but now six months after our country is flooded again with such characters, and see by one of the last papers that the black-hearted wretches of the North, are again at work, and making threats against the South… Can you tell why it is that the people have quieted down so and will permit all these scamps to wander around from house to house, not for any good purpose, as the writer… is well aware of but for the black-hearted [villains] meddling with such things that do not concern them.[19]

Numerous Southerners had the same concerns as this letter writer. Dangerous revolutionaries were believed to be lurking throughout the South. Two such "suspicious characters," one fully conversant with the geography of Virginia, Maryland, and Pennsylvania and possessing "a bundle of charts of the Potomac River landing clearly marked," were arrested and detained in September 1860 in the town of Waterford, Virginia. Knowledge of geography and maps, coupled with rumors of recent attempts to burn property near this picturesque town, though not overwhelming evidence in a court of law, was definitive proof of guilt to area property owners.[20]

The psychological scars of Brown's raid that were seared upon the Southern consciousness made militia seem indispensable to Southerners' well-being and the security of the South. Concern for the security of Virginia's northern frontier, as well as anticipation of the return of militiamen whose homes were far from Charles Town and Harpers Ferry, caused Governor Wise to urge residents on the northern border from Point of Rocks to Wheeling to organize efficient militia companies to protect the "line of the Potomac." Wise pledged to arm them with the best weapons and proposed reorganizing the state's militia to make it combat-ready.[21]

Wise did not achieve a comprehensive militia reorganization in his waning days as governor.[22] Nevertheless, one of his first official acts after Brown's execution was an attempt to improve the training of the state's militiamen. He ordered the superintendent of VMI to have an officer write a manual on tactics for Virginia's militia. Within a year (1860), the *Manual of Introduction for the Volunteers and Militia*, by William Gilham, was published.[23] On January 21, 1860, the Virginia legislature appropriated $500,000 to buy arms and munitions—with some distributed to the "most exposed parts of the state"—and to purchase "patents rights of any newly invented arms, as may be necessary for the successful operation" of the Richmond armory. Following Virginia's example, Alabama allotted $200,000 for its defense, Mississippi, $150,000, and South Carolina, $100,000.[24] The fear of slave revolts and outside attacks in the aftermath of the Harpers Ferry raid served as a powerful stimulus for a Southern mobilization that proved to be a rehearsal and a spark for later mobilization—for the great American Civil War.[25]

It would be a gross oversimplification to say John Brown's raid was the sole cause of sectional conflict and the Civil War. Sectional issues, especially slavery, and vivid memories of the jarring trauma of Nat Turner's revolt had plagued America for decades, becoming even more divisive in the 1850s. The Fugitive Slave Act, Kansas-Nebraska Act, "Bleeding Kansas," the Dred Scott decision, and the Lincoln-Douglass debates preceded and helped to set the emotional and political stage so that Brown's feeble raid had a monumental impact. All these events enabled an unknown old man who had failed throughout life to become, in the fall of 1859, a household name, a symbol.

To Northern abolitionists and black people, Brown became the martyred paladin of downtrodden enslaved people. To Northern and some Southern moderates, he was a courageous, though misguided, man. But to most Southerners, Brown was the symbol of an insane Northern conspiracy to shed Southern blood.

The fear Brown inspired tainted all Republicans as dangerous enemies of the South, whether they were moderates or abolitionists. Lincoln's election was, therefore, the event that first fractured the Union, as seven lower Southern states responded by seceding. Secession set in motion the seizure of federal forts and firing on Fort

Sumter. In turn, Lincoln called for 75,000 volunteers to suppress the "insurrection," which caused the final waves of secession, including the Old Dominion and three other sister states. Americans were now at war with each other. Compromise—the answer to settling earlier sectional crises—would now fail despite many proposals by Congress, the Crittenden Compromise, and Virginia Peace Convention. The repercussions of Brown's raid played a major role in their failure. Although not the sole cause of disunion, John Brown's raid was unequivocally a pivotal factor in widening and deepening sectional bitterness, a bitterness that tore apart the Union in a bloodletting civil war.

John Brown's Elusive Place in History

Information about John Brown and the Harpers Ferry Raid is extensive, and it varies in accuracy and interpretations perhaps more than most historical events. This is due in part to the chimeric character of Brown himself. He directed vicious murders at Pottawatomie Creek and the seizure of a US defense plant all in the name of God and of freeing humans from bondage. His violence and terrorism, which many have found repugnant, contrast with his noble goal of ridding America of its greatest sin, making Brown the most controversial 19th-century American. He is viewed as both a madman and a saintly martyr.

Brown's world was one of absolutes, right and wrong. Compromise on the immoral issue of slavery was unacceptable. He therefore rejected and had no faith in what he saw as a corrupt political system: the Democratic and Republican parties, the federal government, and governments of slave states. He attempted to reorder society as spelled out in his own "Provisional Constitution" and "Declaration of Liberty" while asserting in the provisional constitution it was not meant to encourage the overthrow of state governments or disunion, "but simply to Amend and Repeal." This proved to be an unconvincing disclaimer, especially to Southerners after Harpers Ferry. Brown's two documents were patterned after the two most significant documents in the creation of the United States, the Declaration of Independence and the United States Constitution, to give a sense of order and legitimacy to his actions.

Fear was a paramount weapon and objective in his war on slavery. He hoped his attack and the liberation of slaves would terrorize slave-owners who, for their self-preservation, would give up those they held in bondage. Both modern terrorists and Brown justified their actions as carrying out the will of the divine against an immoral enemy. Unlike modern terrorists, who support indiscriminate killing of people they consider their enemy, Brown did not kill women and young children in his heinous Pottawatomie Creek Massacre. Before the Harpers Ferry raid he cautioned his men to use restraint and not fire unless fired upon. He felt the deaths of those who owned slaves, however, were justified. Despite the dissimilarities between terrorists of the 21st century and Brown, like them, he used terror—especially in

Portrait of John Brown during the last year of his life. Abolitionist proclaimed Brown a "martyr to freedom" while Southerners denounced him as a murderer and terrorist. A failure in more than a dozen business ventures and as a revolutionary, his raid upon Harpers Ferry greatly widened the sectional chasm and intensified bitterness as well as the start of Southern mobilization for war. (Harpers Ferry National Park)

the form of fear. Fear was his key weapon against slavery. He was willing to kill, if necessary, those who supported slavery or militarily fought against him. As with modern terrorists, working outside the law did not bother him. Both claim their violent actions are a moral crusade and are justified against evil for the betterment of mankind.

Historians wrestle with the issue of causation when attempting to explain events in history. This is certainly true in explaining Brown's role in history and the issue of his mental health. The question of Brown's sanity has never been answered conclusively. In the fall of 1859, between Brown's conviction and execution, it was reported in the New York *Times* many Virginians claimed the plea that the Old Man was insane was "started by his friends in the North for the purpose of gaining time to outfit an expedition for this rescue." Those who conclude Brown was insane cite 19th-century evidence that many of Brown's relatives had mental illnesses. However, the vague and all-encompassing meaning of insanity in the Brown era included diseases such as epilepsy and multiple sclerosis, and the 19th-century affidavits—made mainly by Brown's friends and relatives to save him from the gallows—cast doubt on the validity of those psychological observations. The many vague connotations of insanity are such that the term is not used diagnostically in modern medicine. Only in the modern legal world is an insane person defined, as a person not responsible for their behavior. Despite whatever character flaws Brown had, by today's legal standards he was sane.

Historians still debate the issues of Brown's sanity and his motives for his anti-slavery activities, including attempts to provide explanations for the killing and mutilation of the five pro-slave men in the Pottawatomie Creek massacre. Was it insanity, hatred of slavery based on moral convictions, spawned by his Calvinist religion or by psychological turmoil emanating from his childhood? Others have suggested that Owen Brown's harsh treatment of his son might have led John Brown to vent his repressed hostility for his father on the slave-owner who also subjugated other humans. If he was insane, was it inherited or the result of traumatic life experiences, not only in childhood, but in adulthood? Brown withstood demoralizing loss with the deaths of his first wife and children, the murder of a son in Kansas, and extensive bouts of illness, including malaria.

He was described by many in the 19th century as a monomaniac, a term frequently used in that era. In the 1950s Allan Nevins made a similar assertion. According to Nevins, Brown had "reasoning insanity. On all other subjects but one—slavery and the possibility of ending it by one swift stroke… he was sane." Among modern historians no one has addressed this issue more extensively, refuting a number of traditionally held views, than Robert McGone in his penetrating biography of Brown. More recently, David Reynolds articulates the prevalent view that Brown's actions at Pottawatomie Creek were not that of a deranged man but must be considered in the context of the violence in Kansas as an act responding to the barbarity of the pro-slave forces. In summing up the confusing issue of assessing Brown's sanity another of his biographers, Stephen B. Oates, concludes that when comparing Brown with others in the 1850s, including those for and against slavery and violence, it is difficult to tell "who's mad."

Newspapers, eyewitness accounts, and other sources on the raid buffet the reader with conflicting information. It can be difficult to know what to believe. The human proclivity for making black-and-white judgments of "good versus bad" and "right or wrong" has led defenders to see Brown's actions as entirely justifiable, viewing Brown as a freedom fighter for the enslaved. Brown saw himself as sanctioned not only by divinity but also by the principles laid out in the Declaration of Independence, as well as by the resulting liberation of two and a half million colonials in the Revolutionary War from the tyranny of Great Britain; he was freeing four million African Americans from the tyranny of human bondage. At the same time, Southerners who were paranoid about slave rebellions viewed Brown as an evil madman who was willing to take their property, and to do it in a way that would cost their lives. Moderate Northerners could understand Brown's opposition to slavery but not his methods. Many assumed he must be mad. Over the years the printed pages about Brown depict him as either a benevolent crusader or a malevolent blot on the nation's history.

Time has also influenced how Brown is viewed. Generations are removed from 1859 and from the immediacy of the consequences—real and imagined—of the Harpers Ferry raid. Lifestyles, values, and experiences are different, and there is a lack of understanding of mid-19th-century life that has shifted both the public and the historical view. Modern opinion has more in common with that of the minority view of abolitionist defenders of Brown than with the more prevalent condemnation of the insurrectionist that persisted in the 19th and most of the 20th centuries. The radical and violent abolitionist who was often called American's first terrorist has had a shift in image, from a fanatical murderer to a benevolent figure whose courageous acts and death inspire admiration and recognition. Brown is now seen as having profoundly influenced the course of our history by bringing on the splintering of the nation into bloody civil war, terminating slavery, and sparking civil rights; as well as, less desirably, having influence as a mentor of modern terrorists.

After death Brown has gained a reputation of far greater success than he enjoyed in life. He is more viewed as a revolutionary who correctly fought for freedom of the oppressed—a view that understandably resonates with African Americans who award him hero status. In an era of political correctness and demand for the removal of all public display of statues, names and symbols considered tainted by slavery or segregation, the view of Brown being on the correct side of history has been enhanced. Modern Americans agree with Brown that slavery is reprehensible and intolerable. Admiration of his futile attack on slavery to rid the nation of something so repugnant, his explanation of his motives, his demeanor after capture, and his execution suppress condemnation of his methods that cost innocent lives. If the

Harpers Ferry raid happened today it would be totally unacceptable, legally and in public opinion. Yet today the view of Brown has morphed to that of, at the very least, a "good terrorist."

John Brown is a constant reminder of our struggle with the use of violence to resolve the plight of mankind when such action goes against the accepted norms of civilized behavior. Judging the past by present values and seeing our motives and values in the past—sometimes referred to as "presentism"—can hinder understanding of previous eras, and also gives each generation different perspectives that trigger the inevitable, continual rewriting of history. Our views of Brown are determined by our emotions as well as our minds. A clear perspective of Brown's place in history is sometimes obscured by a veil covering the past, and it can be challenging to lift that veil to see history's true face. What really happened remains inconclusive.

Bibliographical Comment

Materials used in preparing this volume are cited in detail in the endnotes. Materials, primary and secondary, are extensive and scattered over depositories across the US from one coast to the other. The press extensively covered events of the raid, making the newspapers of that time important grounds for research. One of the most valuable sources is the Boyd B. Stutler Collection of John Brown in the West Virginia Archives, accessible at www.wvculture.org/history/. The titles mentioned below were selected because they are generally accessible for further reading.

Brown has made a lasting impact upon Americans. Counter to his condemnation, he has been immortalized in statues, plays, poems, literature, art, movies, and song, and by organizations such as John Brown Heritage Associations and the John Brown Society. Biographies of John Brown and other works related to specific aspects of his life, his family, and the men who followed him continue to flow from presses. Interest in John Brown seems to never wane as new books appear with the coming of each year. A fine starting point would be Oswald Garrison Villard's *John Brown* (1910), written half a century after the raider's demise. Despite the work's age, and despite newer research, the work's detail and inclusion of primary material continue to make it in some ways the most complete biography of Brown. Villard's work was the dominant study of the raider until the readable *To Purge This Land with Blood* (1970) by Steven B. Oates appeared. A number of recent biographies have competed for attention. Of these, *John Brown's War Against Slavery* by Robert E. McGlone (2009) stands out as a revisionist and psychological study. David S. Reynolds' *John Brown, Abolitionist: The Man Who Killed Slavery, Sparked the Civil War, and Seeded Civil Rights* (2005) proclaims the far-reaching influence of Brown and integrates his life with the lives of other significant figures of that era. Other more recent biographies include *Patriotic Treason: John Brown and the Soul of America* (2006) by Evan Carton; Louis A. Decaro Jr., *"Fire from the Midst of You": A Religious Life of John Brown* (2002), and Ted A. Smith, *Weird John Brown: Divine Violence and the Limits of Ethics* (2015).

The first books on Brown were by sympathetic contemporaries and supporters. Despite their pro-Brown bias, they are useful in the study of Brown. The first was *The Public Life of Captain John Brown* (1860), by James Redpath, followed by *The Life and Letters of John Brown* (1891), edited by Frank B. Sanborn, and Richard J. Hinton's *John Brown and His Men* (1894). Continuing a pro-Brown view is W. E. B. Dubois' *John Brown* (1908). Robert Penn Warren in *John Brown: The Making of a Martyr* (1929) is critical of the abolitionist. An early and useful collection of material on Brown's life is *A John Brown Reader*, edited by Louis Ruchames (1959); the more recent *John Brown* (1972), edited by Richard Warch and Jonathan Fanton, and *Meteor of War: The John Brown Story* (2004), edited by Zoe Trodd and John Stauffer, have a similar approach. The latter part of the 20th century saw a number of studies on Brown: Oates's biography and his *Our Fiery Trial: Abraham Lincoln, John Brown and the Civil War Era* (1979); *Man on Fire: John Brown and the Cause of Liberty* (1971) by Jules Abels; Richard O. Boyer's *The Legend of John Brown: A Biography and History* (1973); and the brief study by John Anthony Scott and Robert Alan Scott, *John Brown of Harper's Ferry* (1988). A unique and comprehensive pictorial history is *John Brown: "The Thundering Voice of Jehovah"* (1999), by Stan Cohen. Addressing the issue of Brown's sanity is "The Madness of John Brown" in

After the Fact: The Art of Historical Detection (1986), by James W. Davidson and Mark H. Lytle. For Brown's role in the strife in Kansas during the1850s, see Thomas Goodrich's *War to the Knife: Bleeding Kansas, 1854–1861* (1998), and *Bleeding Kansas* (2004), by Nicole Etcheson.

Dealing primarily with the raid on Harpers Ferry, at the top of the reading list should be Tony Horwitz's *Midnight Rising: John Brown and the Raid That Sparked the Civil War* (2011). A briefer account by National Park Service is *John Brown* (1980, 2009). Both editions are excellent overviews of the raid and aftermath. Other titles include Allan Keller's *Thunder at Harper's Ferry* (1969); *The Raid* (1953), by Laurence Greene; *Six Years of Hell* (1996), by Chester G. Hearn; and *John Brown's Raid on Harpers Ferry: A Brief History with Documents* (2008), by Jonathan Earle. "Recollections of John Brown's Raid" (1883, 1885), by Alexander R. Boteler is reprinted in *John Brown's Raid at Harpers Ferry* (n.d.). Other contemporaries' and press views about the raid are found in Bob O'Connor's *The Perfect Steel Trap: Harpers Ferry 1859* (2006). An individual Southern view of the raid is presented in *I Rode with Stonewall* (1961), by Henry Kyd Douglas. Important documents in attempting to figure out what happened during the raid are *The Select Committees of the Senate* (1860) reprinted in The Michigan Historical Reprint Series. Virginia Ott Stake authored a useful volume, *John Brown in Chambersburg* (1977).

For information on individuals pertinent to the Brown saga consult the autobiography of Frederick Douglass, *Life and Times of Frederick Douglass* (1892); Sarah Bradford's *Harriet Tubman: The Moses of Her People* (1886); Craig M. Simpson's *A Good Southerner: The Life of Henry A. Wise of Virginia* (1985); John A. Wise, *The End of an Era* (1899); Kate C. Larson, *Bound for the Promised Land: Harriet Tubman, Portrait of an American Hero* (2005); Jeffery Rossbach, *Ambivalent Conspirators: John Brown, The Secret Six and a Theory of Slave Violence* (1982); Edward J. Renehan Jr., *The Secret Six* (1995); and *Companions in Conspiracy: John Brown & Gerrit Smith* (1996) by Chester G. Hearn. An interesting study of Brown's most flamboyant raider is the well-researched *John Brown's Spy: The Adventurous life and Tragic Confession of John E. Cook* (2012) by a professor of law, Steven Lubet. He tells the story of the man some called the most impressive of Brown's men in *The "Colored Hero" of Harpers Ferry: John Anthony Copeland and the War Against Slavery* (2015). Stonewall Jackson's widow's massive *Memoirs of "Stonewall Jackson"* (1895) contain interesting material, as do Douglas Southall Freeman's *R. E. Lee* (vol 1, 1934) and *"Right or Wrong, God Judge Me"* (2001), edited by John Rhodehamel and Louise Taper. Bonnie L. Schultz's *The Tie That Bound US: The Women of John Brown's Family and The Legacy of Radical Abolitionism* (2013) represents—along with Lubet's book—the trend for more detailed research of those around the raider leader.

The role of African Americans in the raid is discussed by Jean Libby, in *Black Voices from Harpers Ferry* (1979) and *John Brown Mysteries* (1999); she refutes the prevailing view that "slaves refused to fight with Brown in support of their liberty." The issue is also addressed by academic Benjamin Quarles's *Allies for Freedom & Blacks on John Brown* (1974). Osborne P. Anderson, an African American member of Brown's raiding party, who escaped, wrote a not-altogether-accurate account entitled *A View from Harper's Ferry* (1861). It was reprinted in 2000 accompanied by essays by three African American civil rights crusaders. Pertinent information is also available in *Prophets of Protest* (2006) edited by Timothy P. McCarthy and John Stauffer; *Migrants Against Slavery* (2001) by Philip J. Schwarz; and a textbook classic by John Hope Franklin, *From Slavery to Freedom* (1947).

The trial and execution are covered in Robert De Witt's *The Life, Trial and Execution of Captain John Brown, Known as "Old Brown Of Ossawatomie," with a Full Account of the Attempted Insurrection at Harper's Ferry* (1859). Brown's trial is admirably covered in *John Brown's Trial* (2009) by Brian McGinty. An eyewitness account is *The Capture and Execution of John Brown* (1906), written by Elijah Avey. The trial and execution of two black raiders is traced in *The Capture, Trial and Execution of John A. Copeland Jr and Shields Green* (2003), by the Jefferson County Black History Preservation Society.

The legacy of Brown has received much attention, especially recently: see Merrill D. Peterson, *John Brown: the Legend Revisited* (2002); the wide-ranging collection of responses to Brown's raid found in *The Tribunal: Responses to John Brown and the Harpers Ferry Raid* (2012), edited by John Stauffer and Zoe Trodd; *John Brown Still Lives!: America's Long Reckoning with Violence, Equality, and Change* (2011), by R. Blakeslee Gilpin; and *His Soul Goes Marching On: Responses to John Brown and the Harpers Ferry Raid* (1995), edited by Paul Finkelman.

Information about the history of the area of the raid and trial can be found in Millard K. Bushong's *A History of Jefferson County West Virginia* (1941); Dolly Nasby's *Then & Now: Harpers Ferry* (2007); *Harpers Ferry Houses* (2008), by Stowell Architects; Mike High's *The C&O Canal Companion* (2000); and *A Walker's Guide to Harpers Ferry West Virginia* (1995), by David T. Gilbert. Merritt Roe Smith's *Harpers Ferry Armory and the New Technology: The Challenge of Change* (1977) is a superb and important work.

Books on terrorism are numerous. Two stand out as starting points: *The Terrorism Reader* (2007), edited by David J. Whittaker; and *Origins of Terrorism: Psychologies, Ideologies, Theologies, States of Mind* (1998), edited by Walter Reich.

Endnotes

Chapter One: The Making of a Terrorist

1 Joseph Barry, *The Strange Story of Harper's Ferry with Legends of the Surrounding Country* (Martinsburg, W. Va.: Thompson Brothers, 1903), 6–10 (hereafter cited as *Story of Harper's Ferry*). National Park Service, *John Brown Raid* (Washington, D.C., 1973), 15; Merritt R. Smith, *Harpers Ferry Armory and the New Technology: The Challenge of Change* (Ithaca, N.Y.: Cornell University, 1977), 146–50, 328–32. In 1858 the 400 workers at the Harpers Ferry armory produced 8,581 rifled muskets (M1855) and 1,719 percussion rifles (M1841 & M1855). Earlier resentment of the government insistence upon uniformity in work habits of armory workers led to the "Clock Strike" of 1842. Unlike those at Harpers Ferry, workers at the Springfield armory in Massachusetts embraced technological changes, in part to out-produce their Virginia rivals.

2 See Barry, *Story of Harper's Ferry*, 4–46; Laurence Greene, *The Raid: A Biography of Harper's Ferry* (New York: Holt, 1953), 1–78; and Smith's *Harpers Ferry Armory and the New Technology*, 24–50.

3 Thomas Jefferson, *Notes on the State of Virginia*, ed. by William Peden (Chapel Hill, N.C.: University of North Carolina, 1955), 325.

4 New York *Times*, October 20, 1859.

5 Baltimore *American and Commercial Advertiser*, October 21, 1859; Steven Lubet, *John Brown's Spy* (New Haven, Conn.: Yale University Press, 2012), 41–4; Richard Warch and Jonathan F. Fanton, eds., *John Brown* (Englewood Cliffs, N.J.: Prentice-Hall, 1973), 2–5; James Redpath, *The Public Life of Captain John Brown* (Boston: Thayer and Eldridge, 1860), 49; David S. Reynolds, *John Brown, Abolitionist: The Man Who Killed Slavery, Sparked the Civil War and Seeded Civil Rights* (N.Y.: Alfred A. Knopf, 2005), 74–7.

6 James W. Davidson, Mark H. Lytle, *After the Fact* (N.Y.: Alfred A. Knopf, 2d ed., 1986), 169–71.

7 Letter, Anne Brown Adams to Garibaldi Ross, December 15, 1887, The Gilder Lehrman Collection Online Exhibition.

8 *The Good News Bible* (N.Y.: Thomas Nelson Pub. 3rd. ed., 1976), 269–70 (Judges 7); Louis A. Decaro, Jr., *"Fire from the Midst of You": A Religious Life of John Brown* (N.Y.: New York University Press, 2002), 20–4, 30–6; Werner Keller, *The Bible as History* (N.Y.: William Morrow and Co., 1958), 163–4; Judges 7, King James Bible, (Philadelphia: The National Bible Press, n.d.); Stephen B. Oates, *John Brown* (N.Y.: Harper & Row, 1970), 197, 395; James Redpath, *The Public Life of Captain John Brown* (Boston: Thayer and Eldridge, 1860), 203. John Brown's favorite hymn, "Blow Ye the Trumpet Blow," was based on one of Gideon's tactics. The hymn was later played at Brown's funeral.

9 Erich Gruen, *The Last Generation of the Roman Republic* (Berkeley: University of California Press, 1974), 20–1; Richard J. Hinton, *John Brown and His Men* (N.Y.: Funk & Wagnalls Company, 1894), 24–25; Reynolds, *John Brown*, 52–6, 164–5. Other prominent slave revolts occurred in New York City in 1712; the Gabriel plot in Richmond, Virginia, in 1800; a slave revolt in New Orleans in 1811; and Denmark Vesey's revolt in Charleston, South Carolina in 1820.

Spartacus was born free, served in the Roman army, deserted, and was captured and sold into slavery. He was then trained as a gladiator. In 73 B.C.E. he and about 70 slaves took knives from the cook's shop and gladiator weapons from a wagon, and then escaped and hid on Mount Vesuvius. Spartacus hoped to lead the slaves who joined him over the Alps and out of Italy. They refused and insisted on plundering much of Italy. At the height of the revolt Spartacus led about 120,000 former slaves. After a number of impressive victories the revolt was crushed by combined Roman legions under Crassus in a battle in southern Italy. It is assumed Spartacus was killed in the battle. His body was never found among the thousands of mangled corpses.

10   Sarah E. Bradford, *Harriet Tubmam: Moses of Her People* (New York: George Lockwood, 1886), 14–15, 33, 35, 55, 54–91; Virginius Dabney, *Virginia: The New Dominion* (N. Y.: Doubleday, 1871), 225; Hinton, *John Brown and His Men*, 106–10; John B. Duff & Peter M. Mitchell, ed., *The Nat Turner Rebellion: The Historical Event and the Modern Controversy* (N.Y.: Harper & Row, 1971), 6–7, 19–29; Ulrich B. Phillips, *American Negro Slavery* (Baton Rouge: Louisiana State Press, 1966), 480–481; Washington *Post,* March 10, 2013. Harriet Tubman was born Araminta Harriet Ross in Dorchester County, Maryland, and died at Auburn, New York, on March 10, 1913, from pneumonia at the age of 93. Her early nickname was Minty. She later married a free black man, John Tubman, who refused to accompany her when she fled to Pennsylvania; he feared being sold. A recent biography by Kate Clifford Larson, *Bound for the Promised Land: Harriet Tubman, Portrait of an American Hero* (New York: Ballantine Books, 2003), revises the story of Tubman's life, contending that she made 13 trips, freeing 70 to 80 people, and the reward for her capture was only a fraction of the claimed $40,000. She was not struck in the head by a two-pound weight thrown by her owner—for at that time she was hired out to a farmer and worked in the flax field—but was hit by an overseer who was angered by her refusal to restrain a runaway in a dry-goods store (it is debated whether he meant to hit her). The injury she suffered as an adolescent would plague her for the rest of her life with debilitating seizures, headaches, narcoleptic attacks, and vivid dreams and visions she interpreted as divine revelations.

Nat Turner launched his revolt in Southhampton County, Virginia, during the night of August 21, 1831. Like Brown, Turner felt he was carrying out a divine mission. In addition to basing this on the Bible, he had visions. He claimed, "I saw white spirits and black spirits engaged in battle, and the sun was darkened—the thunder rolled in the Heavens and blood flowed in streams—and I heard a voice saying, such is your luck, such you are called to see, and let it come rough or smooth, you must surely face it." When questioned after his capture, he was asked if he was not mistaken in interpreting a vision, claiming "the Spirit" ordered him to take up the yoke of Christ, "for the time was fast approaching when the first should be last and the last first." Turner replied, "Was not Christ crucified?"

Before the rebellion was ended by local militia, the numbers of whites killed were 10 men, 14 women, and 31 children.

11   J. D. Randall and David Donald, *The Civil War and Reconstruction* (Boston: D. C. Heath, 2d ed., 1961), 23; Reynolds, *John Brown*, 63–64, 118–21; Oswald G. Villard, *John Brown, 1800–1859 A Biography Fifty Years Later* (Rev. ed., New York: A. A. Knopf, 1910), 42–3, 50, 659–61. Other Sambo errors included wasting his money on expensive clothing, accessories and expensive parties and joining "Free Masons Odd Fellow Sons of Temperance, & scores of other secret societies instead of seeking the company to intelligent wise & good men from whom I might have learned much that would have be interesting, instructive, & useful…"

12   Villard, *John Brown*, 45–6.

13   Frederick Douglass, *Life and Times of Frederick Douglass* (Hartford: Park Publishing Co, 1882), 71–5. Frederick Douglass noted the Brown home "reflects the character of its occupant… In it there were no disguises, no illusions, no make-believe. Everything implied stern truth, solid

purpose, and rigid economy." Brown was indeed the head of the family, Douglass writes. "His wife believed in him, and his children observed him with reverence. Whenever he spoke his words commanded attention."

14 Villard, *John Brown*, 53–5.

15 Jules Abels, *Man on Fire: John Brown and the Cause of Liberty* (New York: Macmillan, 1971), 1–12, 45–6,76–7, 116–17; Richard O. Boyer, *The Legend of John Brown: a Biography and a History* (New York: Knopf, 1973), 148–54, 558; Richard J. Hinton, *John Brown and His Men* (Rev. ed., New York: Funk & Wagnalls, 1894), 29–36, 421; Allan Nevins, *The Emergence of Lincoln* (New York: Scribner, 1950), vol. II, 9–10; Stephen B. Oates, *To Purge This Land with Blood: A Biography of John Brown* (New York: Harper & Row, 1970), 64; *Valley Spirit* (Chambersburg, PA), October 26, 1859; Villard, *John Brown*, 11; Warch and Fanton, eds., *John Brown*, 7. In his first meeting with Douglass, Brown informed Douglass he did not want to bring about a widespread slave insurrection, but said he was "not averse to the shedding of blood."

16 Abels, *Man on Fire*, 34–35; Hinton, *John Brown and His Men*, 26; Reynolds, *John Brown*, 121–4; Villard, *John Brown*, 50–1; Warch and Fanton, eds., *John Brown*, 7. The Fugitive Slave Act angered Northern white and black abolitionists; some called for violent resistance. Neither their talk nor the Gileadites' led to the means of their rhetoric.

17 Abels, *Man on Fire*, 64–65; Oates, *To Purge This Land with Blood*, 114, 126–39; Thomas Goodrich, *War to the Knife: Bleeding Kansas, 1854–1861* (Mechanicsburg, PA: Stackpole Books, 1998), 123–7; Robert E. McGlone, *John Brown's War Against Slavery* (New York: Cambridge University Press, 2009), 114–42; Reynolds, *John Brown*, 103–4, 150–3, 158–63, 176–7; Louis Ruchames, ed., *A John Brown Reader: The Making of a Revolutionary: the Story of John Brown in His Own Words and in the Words of Those Who Knew Him* (New York: Abelard-Schuman, 1959), 194, 201; Warch and Fenton, eds., *John Brown*, 9; Villard, *John Brown*, 149–52. The men who accompanied John Brown on the raid were Henry Thompson, Theodore Weiner, and Brown's sons Owen, Frederick, Salmon, and Oliver. Technically, Brown did not personally murder any of the men. Brown did, however, order or allow the acts that occurred on May 24, 1856. Brown later wrote that he and his men were justified in what they did. Over the years Brown gave varying accounts of his role at Pottawatomie, ranging from what he originally told Jason, to an account in which he believed he might have been guilty of murder, to his belief that God had "ordained" the murders. Brown and his sons were frenzied by the news of the events in Lawrence, and their emotions were heightened by the news of the Washington, D.C., caning of Charles Sumner, the abolitionist senator from Massachusetts. Salmon Brown, one of Brown's sons in Kansas, stated that the news about Sumner made them go "crazy-crazy." John Brown Jr. and Jason Brown were upset by what happened at Pottawatomie Creek. According to an eyewitness, James Townsley, John Jr. resigned as captain of his company and became deranged for a period of time.

18 Letter of Salmon Brown to William E. Connelly, December 2, 1913, Boyd B. Stutler Collection of John Brown, West Virginia Achieves; Douglass, *Life and Times of Frederick Douglass*, 272–3; Oates, *To Purge This Land with Blood*, 150–4, 170; Reynolds, *John Brown*, 178–82, 186, 195–6; Villard, *John Brown*, 57–8, 202–24, 246–8. Brown was winning the battle of Black Jack but was nevertheless aided by his son Frederick, who galloped across the battlefield, shouting, "Hurrah! Come on, Boys! We've got 'em surrounded: we've cut off their communication." The commander of the enemy force, Henry C. Pate, then ordered his men to surrender.

19 Oates, *To Purge This Land with Blood*, 65–7; Edward J. Renehan Jr., *The Secret Six* (N. Y.: Crown, 1995), 107–9; Reynolds, *John Brown*, 215; Ruchames, ed., *A John Brown Reader*, 110. All but Gerrit Smith of the Secret Six had ties to the transcendentalists. Smith was impulsive and, like Brown, was a Bible quoter. Smith purchased 120,000 acres in the Adirondacks in northwestern New York for black families to settle and farm. The harsh weather caused few to come. Upon learning of

Smith's offer, Brown asked for a farm so he could be a mentor to "my colored neighbors." Smith sold Brown 244 acres at $1 an acre. Although it took Brown a while to pay for his purchase, while he lived in the new community called North Elba he was happy and eagerly helped the black people who settled there.

20   Hannah Geffert, "Regional Black Involvement in John Brown's Raid on Harpers Ferry," in *Prophets of Protest*, ed. by Timothy P. McCarty & John Stauffer (New York: The New Press, 2006), p. 170; Oates, *To Purge This Land with Blood*, 200–1; Renehan Jr., *The Secret Six*, 123–124; Villard, *John Brown*, 286. Forbes was born in Scotland. Before fighting with Garibaldi he worked as a silk merchant in Vienna. He fought in the Italian Revolution and then moved to France and married. Leaving his wife and children in Paris, he moved to the United States in the mid-1850s. Once he agreed to work with Brown, money was always an issue, despite Brown's obtaining a $600 advance from the Secret Six.

21   Martin Delany's family had been forced to flee Charles Town in 1822 to Chambersburg, Pennsylvania, after his free mother, Pati, was accused of teaching her children to read. Martin's father remained a slave in Martinsburg until his family purchased his freedom.

22   Oates, *To Purge This Land with Blood*, 243–51; Hinton, *John Brown and His Men*, 619–37, 637–43; McGlone, *John Brown's War Against Slavery*, 239; Ruchames, ed., *A John Brown Reader*, 111–13. The Provisional Constitution had a preamble and 48 articles. Brown's term as commander in chief was also three years.

23   According to John Cook in his confessions, Richard Realf was born in poverty but taken in by the family of Lady Noel Bryon, who recognized his talents and saw he received an education. Realf split with the family and struck out on his own when Lady Bryon censured him—a man of lowly origin—for falling in love with one of her female relatives.

24   Hinton, *John Brown and His* Men, 224–5; Renehan, Jr. *The Secret Six,* 123–4,150–2; James Redpath, *The Public Life of Captain John Smith*, 239–40; Reynolds, *John Brown, Abolitionist*, 239, 278–9, 284–5; Ruchames, ed., *The John Brown Reader*, 114–15; Boyd B. Stutler, "Captain John Brown and Harpers Ferry" (manuscript, John Brown/ Boyd B. Stutler Collection, West Virginia Archives), 13A; Letter, Boyd Stutler to Julia Davis Healy, June 15, 1961, Stutler Collection. Brown seemed to delight in upsetting the pro-slavery forces and seemed somewhat amused by the territorial governor's call for an end to the "dreadful outrage" (Brown's raid) and the marshal of Kansas's collecting a posse to "enforce the law." Brown' s attack on a pursuing federal cavalry force as they were crossing a stream also enhanced Brown's legend as a warrior in what was called the Battle of the Spurs. Panicking Federals dug their spurs into their horses' flanks as those who been dismounted leaped behind other riders. One man attempted to escape by grabbing the tail of a horse and being dragged. Brown and his men, who were outnumbered about four to one, chased the fleeing opponents six miles, capturing five of them.

Chapter Two: Launching the War of Liberation

1   Hannah Geffert (with Jean Libby), "Regional Black Involvement in John Brown's Raid on Harpers Ferry," in McCarthy & Stauffer (eds.), *Prophets of Protest*, 160–71.

2   Hinton, *John Brown and His Men*, 239–345; Reynolds, *John Brown, Abolitionist*, 297; *Report of the Select Committee of the Senate Appointed to Inquiry Into the Late Invasion and Seizure of Public Property at Harpers Ferry*, Report no. 278, Senate, 36th Cong., 1st Sess., 1860, 2–5 (hereinafter called the Mason Report). After the raid a local said that Brown and his companions arrived at Sandy Hook from Hagerstown in a hack. According to Philip Keller, a good friend of Cook and a groomsman at Cook's wedding (to local Virginia "Jenny" Kennedy six months before the raid), Brown and others in his group spent the night of July 3, 1859, at Orman Butler's hotel

at Sandy Hook. The man Brown met the next day was John C. Unseld, who said, upon seeing them, "Well, gentlemen, I supposed you are hunting minerals, gold and silver perhaps." "No," replied Brown, "they were looking for land." During their conversation Smith [Brown] was asked where he was from and "What have you been following there?" He replied, "The northern part of New York… farming, but frost had been so heavy of late years it had cut off their crops… so he sold out and thought they would come farther South and try it awhile." Mr. Unseld then rode on. "After returning from checking out the area, several hours later, Brown again met Mr. Unseld and asked him if any farms were for sale. The Kennedy farm was for sale, Unseld told him. Brown wanted to know if it could be rented, and Unseld said he did not know.

3   *The Atlantic Monthly,* December 1875, 710–11; Thomas Featherstonhaugh, *John Brown's Men: The Lives of Those Killed at Harper's Ferry* (Harrisburg, PA: Harrisburg Pub. Co., 1899), 11–13; *Republican* (Springfield, Mass.), January 12, 1902. Annie Brown later said, of the manners and behavior of the men assembled, "Taking them all together, I think they would compare well with the same number of men in any station of life I have ever met."

4   Osborne P. Anderson, *A Voice from Harpers Ferry* (Boston: printed by the author, 1861), 12; Letter from Franklin Keagy of Chambersburg, PA, to F. B. Sanborn, March 24, 1891; Boyd B. Stutler Collection; Mason Report, pt. 2, 225–34; Andrew J. Torget and Edward L. Ayers, *Two Communities in the Civil War* (New York: W. W. Norton & Co, 2007), 3–4; Villard, *John Brown,* 340–3. Judge Elmore declared his inability to decide a case involving a free-state man robbed by a pro-slavery man. Kagi then wrote, "A person who could not decide a case, when the clearest evidence was given, whether a convicted robber should restore stolen goods or retain them, was hardly qualified for a seat on the Supreme Bench of a territory." Upon seeing Kagi on the courthouse steps at Tecumseh, Kansas, a livid Elmore asked, "Are you the man who writes under the Signature of K?" When Kagi replied affirmatively the judge struck him. During his prison stay in Kansas, Kagi continued communicating with those outside the jail by hollowing out a plug of tobacco, shoving his message inside, covering it with a tobacco leaf, and handing it to a visitor. This looked to the authorities like a mere exchange of tobacco.

5   Anderson, *A Voice From Harpers Ferry,* 12; *Boston Traveller,* October 21, 1859; A. K. McClure, "An Episode of John Brown Raid," *Lippincott's Magazine* (Philadelphia, PA, September 1883), 380; Lubet, *John Brown's Spy,* 41, 43. 45; Redpath, *The Public Life of John Brown,* 49; *Springfield Republican,* January 12 & December 2, 1902. Another version of this incident is of Aaron Stevens intervening "hotly and rashly" when Captain James Longstreet, future Confederate lieutenant-general, harshly—and in Stevens's view, unfairly—disciplined a comrade during a drill. A fight ensued, during which Stevens "struck Longstreet down with his saber" and was arrested, facing a death sentence.

6   *Calendar of Virginia State Papers,* 310; Harpers Ferry Historical Association, *John Brown's Raid* (Virginia Beach, V.A.: The Donning Company Publishers, 2009), 26–7; *Governor's Message and Reports of the Public Officers of the State* (Richmond: William F. Ritchie, 1859) Doc. No. 1, 116–17; Philip J. Schwarz, *Migrants Against Slavery: Virginia and the Nation* (University Press of Virginia, 2001), 149–66. Accounts differ as to the number of children Dangerfield and Harriet had. Harriet Newby later remarried and moved back to Virginia. Harriet wrote letters to her husband Dangerfield on April 11, April 22, and August 16, 1859.

7   Dunkards were members of the Church of the Brethren who practiced triple immersion; opposed slavery, oaths, and military service; and observed "severe simplicity in dress and speech." Dunkards around the Kennedy farm were also referred to as Winebrenarians.

8   Brown received Old Dolly the mule on July 17, 1859. Accounts differ about the livestock Brown had at the Kennedy farm. In *John Brown and His Men* Hinton claims Brown only had a dog and a mule. This seem to be disproved by others, including Osborne Anderson, in *A Voice from*

Harper's Ferry; In The Public Life of Captain John Brown James Redpath, a local resident, implies livestock had remained on the farm since Dr. Booth Kennedy's death in spring 1859; apparently neighbors were feeding the animals. Redpath contends Brown purchased the hogs and cow and cared for the other animals until they could be sold.

9   Featherstonhaugh, *John Brown's Men*, 4–7. About two hundred Sharps rifles and an equal number of revolvers, procured three years earlier for Kansas, were kept first in Tabor, Iowa; then moved to Ashtabula County, Ohio; Chambersburg, Pennsylvania; and finally to the Kennedy farm.

10 Osborne P. Anderson, *A Voice from Harpers Ferry*, 19, 25; Henry Kyd Douglas, *I Rode With Stonewall* (Greenwich, C.T.: Fawcett Publications, 1961), 14–15; Testimony of Charles Blair, *Senate Select Committee on the Harper's Ferry Invasion*, 121–9; Villard, *John Brown*, 407. Kyd Douglas, who lived near Shepherdstown, Maryland, was walking across the bridge over the Potomac when he found a man who said he was Isaac Smith carrying "mining tools" in a farm wagon stalled in the mud at the bottom of a steep hill. Young Douglas went to his nearby home and got a horse and driver, who pulled Smith more than a mile to where he could proceed on his own. Douglas was greatly impressed with the old man's expression of gratitude. Only after the attack on Harpers Ferry did Douglas realize the man he had befriended was John Brown.
Brown's instructions were to make the blades for the pikes two inches wide and at least six inches long. Charles Blair's friend, a man named Hart, manufactured the blades, and another man made handles for the pikes. Brown also inquired of Hart about having two to three heavy wagons constructed. Hart expressed Brown's interest to another friend who made wagons. Nothing materialized because the wagon maker could not make them in the short time frame Brown wanted.

11 Villard, *John Brown*, 411–12. For a long time it was assumed Edmond Bibb, editor of the Cincinnati *Gazette,* wrote the letter to Floyd.

12 Hinton, *John Brown and His Men*, 248–58; Villard, *John Brown*, 408–9, 416–21.

13 Frederick Douglass, *Life and Times of Frederick Douglass* (Hartford: Park Publishing Co., 1882), 126, 139, 143, 170–9, 319–20; Geffert, "Regional Black Involvement in John Brown's Raid on Harpers Ferry," 170. Frederick Douglass was born in 1817, the son of an enslaved mother and a white father. Originally named Frederick Augustus Washington Bailey, he changed his name to Douglass after escaping to freedom. He gained fame as an abolitionist, writer, and orator. To prevent re-enslavement he went to Great Britain and Ireland (1845–1847) and collected enough money to purchase his freedom upon returning to the United States.

14 Hinton, *John Brown and His Men*, 258–260; Allan Nevins, *The Emergence of Lincoln* (New York: Charles Scribner's Sons, 1950), vol. II, 74–5; New York *Daily Tribune,* October 20, 1859; Oates, *To Purge This Land with Blood*, 211–12, 225–6, 248–50; Mason Report, pt. 1, 2–3; Villard, *John Brown*, 285–6, 298–9, 338–9. Twenty-five years after the raid Owen Brown states that only nine of the 21 men originally supported Brown in attacking Harpers Ferry. He also contends he and his father often discussed attacking Harpers Ferry during their wagon trips, pointing out, "You know how it resulted with Napoleon when he rejected the advice in regards to marching with his army to Moscow."

15 Hinton, *John Brown and His Men*, 259–65; Villard, *John Brown*, 415–424. Several years before the raid Kagi told Redpath the attack on Harpers Ferry was to occur in the spring, when slaves were busy working in the field. Redpath later contends in his book, *The Public Life of Captain John Brown* (243), his black and white supporters in Canada, New England, and elsewhere did not participate in the raid because they had been told it would occur on October 24, 1859.

16 Hinton, *John Brown and His Men,* 266, 332, 707–8; *Valley Spirit,* October 26, 1859. Oliver had also escorted the two women to the Kennedy house. On the way back he went with them as far as Troy, going by wagon to Chambersburg to catch the train. On the way to Chambersburg they were stopped by a constable, who searched their wagon. Once the train reached Harrisburg, they met Brown and Kagi. Brown visited Kagi often at Mrs. Ritner's. On one occasion Mrs. Ritner's seven-year-old daughter brought home with her a black toddler she had found wandering about lost and unattended. She entered the dining room exclaiming, "Oh, Mother! See here what I found, poor thing, it is lost! Won't you keep it?" Seeing this, Brown touched the old warrior, who proclaimed it "the grandest act he ever beheld, and a Sight worthy of the angels."

17 Villard, *John Brown,* 422–3. John Brown and Kagi's letters to John Brown Jr. were written October 1 and 13, respectively. The fact that John Jr. on numerous occasions maintained that the attack of the Ferry took him "completely by surprise" gives some credence to the argument that his mental instability was one reason he was sent north on a recruiting trip. Kagi in his letter tells John Jr. that Cook's wife and child had been sent from Harpers Ferry to Chambersburg and would probably rent there "until the *end."* Her rent was paid until November 1, "... but after that we shall expect you or some one under your direction, have it paid *monthly* in advance, from $10 to $15 besides the necessary etceteras, clothing and Etc. –This must be our last [communication] for a time."

18 Hinton, *John Brown and His Men,* 637–43. Jefferson changed the word "property" among Locke's list of natural rights to "pursuit of happiness."

19 Ibid., 424, 619–34. The Provisional Constitution states that all confiscated property shall be "held as the property of the whole" and may be "used for the common benefit." The Articles of Agreement for Shubel Morgan's Company says, "All property captured in any manner shall be subject to an equal distribution among the members."

20 Mason Report, pt. 2, 59–60; Redpath, *The Public Life of Captain John Brown,* 220.

21 Hinton, *John Brown and His Men,* 279–82; Redpath, *The Public Life of Captain John Brown,* 206; Villard, *John Brown,* 678–9. Probable captains included Stevens, Cook, Brown's three sons (Oliver, Owen, and Watson), Tidd, William Thompson, J. C. Anderson, and probably Leeman (whose captain's commission was found on his body). There is contrary evidence as to whether Hazlett was a lieutenant or a captain. Confusion also exists over the number of lieutenants. Cook wrote only two lieutenants were commissioned (Edwin Coppoc and Dauphin Thompson), but Colonel Robert E. Lee in his report lists Hazlett, Edwin Coppoc, and Leeman as lieutenants. There were only three white privates: Taylor, Barclay Coppoc, and Meriam.

22 Lubet, *John Brown's Spy,* 44; Mason Report, pt. 2, 30–1, 64.

23 Anderson, *A Voice From Harper's Ferry,* 29–31, New York *Weekly Tribune,* October 22, 1859. While in Kansas Kagi explained in great detail Brown's "Great Plan" to James Redpath. The first strike would be at Harpers Ferry "on account of the Arsenal... The Arms in the Arsenal were to be taken to the mountains, with such slaves as joined." No intention existed to take large numbers of slaves to Canada; rather, the plan was to "make a fight in the mountains of Virginia, extending it to North Carolina and Tennessee, and also to the swamps of South Carolina."

24 Mason Report, pt. 15, 214; Redpath, *The Public Life of Captain John Brown,* 193, 206, 203–205.

25 Hinton, *John Brown and His Men,* 672–77; Nevins, *The Emergence of Lincoln,* vol. II, 74–7; Oates, *To Purge This Land with Blood,* 64, 244, 274–9; Redpath, *The Public Life of Captain John Brown,* 204–05; Reynolds, *John Brown,* 149; Villard, *John Brown,* 427–8.

26 Hinton, *John Brown and His Men,* 280–3, 706–9; Oates, *To Purge This Land with Blood,* 288–9; Redpath, *The Public Life of Captain John Brown,* 204–5.

Chapter Three: Igniting the Fuse: The Attack on Harpers Ferry

1   Alexander R. Boteler, "Recollections of the John Brown Raid," *Century Magazine* (July, 1883) 399–401; Ralph Keeler, "Owen Brown's Escape from Harpers Ferry," *Atlantic Monthly* (March, 1874), 342; Allan Keller, *Thunder at Harper's Ferry* (Englewood Cliffs, N.J.: Prentice-Hall, 1957), 37–9; Mason Report, pt. 2, 22; National Park Service, *John Brown's Raid*, 27–8.

2   Oates, *To Purge This Land with Blood*, 223, 242–3, 248–50, 284–5; Mason Report 53; Villard, *John Brown*, 228–31.

3   Mason Report, pt. 2, 21–2.

4   Anderson, *A Voice From Harper's Ferry*, 33; Mason Report, pt. 2, 21–2. Accounts differ about John Brown's going to the arsenal and the rifle works. Daniel Whelan, the watchman at the eastern end of the armory, testified to the Mason Committee three months after the raid that Brown had stayed in the armory grounds. One of the raiders, Osborne Anderson, wrote at least two years after the raid that Brown went to these sites.

5   Mason Report, pt. 2, 29–41; Anderson, *A Voice From Harper's Ferry*, 33–5. Anderson presents a totally different and unconvincing view of the capture of Washington and Allstadt, depicting both men losing composure and crying, and Washington saying, "Take my slaves but leave me," and attempting to buy his freedom with bribes of liquor.

6   Ella E. Clark and Thomas F. Hahn, eds., *Life on the Chesapeake and Ohio Canal 1859* (Shepherdstown, W.Va.: American Transportation Center, 1975), 34; McGlone, *John Brown's War Against Slavery*, 161–2. Another version had Watson Brown capturing Patrick Higgins and locking him in the guardhouse at the end of the bridge, but Higgins escaped through a window of the guard house and ran to Wagner House.

7   McGlone, *John Brown's War Against Slavery*, 264. A more imaginative and overblown account of this incident can be found in *John Brown and His Men*, published in 1894 (see p. xx) by Richard J. Hinton, a staunch supporter and defender of the Old Man. As Higgins was returning with water for his friend, William Thompson stopped him and asked for a drink. "The bucket was handed to him." Thompson asked Higgins to go to the bridge and give Oliver Brown and "a negro" water. As he did so, Oliver supposedly said, "You're the buck that hit me last night, eh?" After Higgins replied yes, Oliver said, "Well, you did an unwise thing; it was only this leg that saved you," revealing a "cut near his left knee" from being "knocked into the bridge." Higgins is said to have asked, "What's all this fuss about, anyhow?" Laughingly, Thompson replied, "Oh, it's a darkey affair… pointing to the smiling negro and adding, 'I am one, here's another.'" Higgins is said to have responded "I'm on a darkey affair, too and that's to get water for a negro whom you have shot." Oliver said, "All right, go along. He brought it on himself by refusing to obey orders." Phelps testified he had started for the doctor when he was interrupted by seeing raiders leave the bridge and then by gunfire. The New York *Herald* reports that Throckmorton helped Shepherd to the ticket office and then also went for the doctor, which is likely, considering his friendship with the injured man. This suggests that tickets were sold not in the depot but in the office near the Shenandoah River.

8   Barry, *The Strange Story of Harper's Ferry*, 85–6; Boyd Stutler, "John Brown's Fort Is Back in Service of the Governments," Charleston *Gazette*, March 3, 1955. After Nat Turner's Revolt in 1831, white adult males throughout the South formed night patrols to ensure no black people (slave or free) were out at night and causing trouble. Free blacks in the South were looked upon as potential leaders of revolts and were required to leave or have permission of the county court to stay. This usually required a white person to vouch for and be responsible for the free black person.

9   Mason Report, pt. 2, 22–3; *The Life, Trial and Execution of John Brown*, published by Robert M. DeWitt in 1859, Boyd B. Stutler Collection, p. 60. The October 24, 1859, issue of the New York

Herald gives a slightly different and perhaps more imaginative account of the events after the train arrived. Throckmorton (whose name is spelled Throgmorton in the record of Brown's trial) claims the raiders cursed, threatened, and shot at him before he fired. He claimed two men passed him and another man standing on the platform as they returned to the bridge. Upon reaching the bridge the men called out to something the clerk and his companion could not understand.

10   Some accounts claim Dangerfield Newby shot Boerly, but if Newby was helping guard the bridge over the Potomac this is unlikely.

11   Phelps mistakenly testified that Coppoc told him, "You could have gone by 8 o'clock." The train had left Harpers Ferry an hour and half earlier.

12   Edward Hungerford, *The Story of the Baltimore & Ohio Railroad* (New York: G. P. Putman's Sons, 1928), vol. I, 335–8; *The Life, Trial and Execution of John Brown*, 60–1; Villard, *John Brown*, 434.

13   Mason Report, pt. 2, 4, 54–9; New York *Herald*, October 24, 1859; New York *Times* 20, 1859. Most secondary accounts contend Brown released the feeble Wagner Hotel bartender, Walter Kemp, in exchange for 45 meals. The amount of money Brown had during the raid reported in newspapers varies from $180 to "around $300" and $350. John at his trial claimed he did not have "a dime." He said, "I had two hundred and fifty or sixty dollars in gold and silver taken from my pocket." The October 22, 1859, issue of the New York *Times* reports, "Brown the day prior to the raid purchased a large wagon and team to pull it." Somehow the reporter may have confused Washington's large wagon and team for the purchase. There is no mention of a new wagon and team by any of the raiders. Osborne Anderson writes that before they left the Kennedy farm Brown's horse and wagon "were brought out" and some "pikes, a sledge hammer and crowbar were placed in it." The Mason Report supports this.

14   Mason Report, pt. 2, 13–16. This is what Byrne testified he thought he said, and he ended his statements by qualifying them, saying he was not sure the wording was exact.

15   Ibid., 54–5.

16   Ibid., 13–18, 55.

17   *The Life, Trial and Execution of John Brown*, 14; Mason Report, pt. 2, 54–5; Alexandria *Gazette* (Alexandria, VA), October 19, 1859; Virginia *Free Press* (Charles Town, VA), November 3, 1859.

18   New York *Herald*, October 24, 1859; Shepherdstown (Virginia) *Register*, November 3, 1859; Winchester (Virginia) *Republican and General Advertiser*, October 21 & 27, 1859.

19   Alexandria *Gazette* (Alexandria, Virginia), October 19, 1859; Elijah Avey, *The Capture and Execution of John Brown: A Tale of Martyrdom* (New York: Afro-Am, 1971), 11–15; Alexander R. Boteler, "Recollections of the John Brown Raid," *John Brown's Raid at Harper's Ferry, West Virginia: 1859* (Edgemont, Colo., n.d.), 12; Tony Horwitz, *Midnight Rising: John Brown and the Raid That Sparked the Civil War* (New York: Henry Holt and Co., 2011), 237; Oates, *To Purge This Land with Blood*, 293; Virginia *Free Press*, November 3, 1859; Mason Report, pt. 2, 26–7; Villard, *John Brown*, 436–7.

20   Mike High, *The C&O Canal Companion* (Baltimore: John Hopkins University Press, 2000), 70; Rayburn S. Moore, ed., "John Brown's Raid at Harper's Ferry: An Eyewitness Account by Charles White," *The Virginia Magazine of History and Biography*, LXVII (October 1859), 389 (hereafter cited as White, "John Brown at Harper's Ferry"); New York *Herald*, October 19, 1859; Virginia *Free Press*, October 21, 26, 27 1859; November 3, 1859. Several secondary accounts have Colonel Gibson making the decision as to what would be the plan of attack (see Kellar, *Thunder at Harper's Ferry*, 80–3 and the National Park Service, *John Brown Raid*, 35–36. In the "Report of Colonel Gibson to Governor Wise," *Virginia State Papers, Document 1, October 18, 1859*. Colonel Gibson reported, "... reached Harper's Ferry about 11 a.m. and took our position at Camp Hill. We immediately dispatched the Jefferson Guards... to cross the Potomac... about

a mile west of Harper's Ferry. Baylor reported the crossing site was near the old furnace located nearly two miles from the town."

21 George W. Chambers, Letter (February 3, 1888), *Tyler's Quarterly Historical and Genealogical Magazine* (April 1930), 225; Jennie Chambers, "What a School Girl Saw of John Brown's Raid," *Harper's Monthly*, January, 1902, 313; New York *Weekly Tribune*, October 29 and November 5, 1859; Edward Stone, ed., *Incident at Harper's Ferry* (Englewood Cliffs, N.J.: Prentice-Hall, 1956), 79–80, 82; Virginia *Free Press*, October 21, November 3, 1859.

22 Other conflicting details of Turner's death have him coming to town once he heard his friend Washington was a hostage. Some say he arrived unarmed and was given a shotgun, while others say he came with a gun.

23 Boteler, "Recollections of the John Brown Raid," 406–7; John A. Copeland "Letter from Charles Town Jail," West Virginia Memory Project, John Brown/Boyd B. Stutler Collection Database (hereafter referred to as Stutler Collection); New York *Herald*, October 22, 1859; Frank Sanborn, Scrapbook, Stutler Collection; Shepherdstown (Virginia) *Register*, October 22, 1859 (hereafter cited as the *Register*); New York *Times*, October 29, 1859; Villard, *John Brown*, 445; White, "John Brown at Harper's Ferry," 389. Conflicting accounts exist about the fighting at the rifle works and other aspects of the raid. Dr. Storry testified that around 2:30 to 3:00 p.m. he sent the men to the rifle works, instructing them to attack upon arrival. The numbers attacking Kagi and his men have been exaggerated. Thomas Drew, in *The John Brown Invasion: An Authentic History of the Harper's Ferry Tragedy* (1860), said it was a black insurrection headed by 250 whites, and 200 to 300 men fired "not less than 400 shots" at Kagi and his men. Copeland's letter written shortly prior to his execution refutes much of the version given in most Brown biographies, based on the writing of A. R. Boteler, the congressman for the district that Harpers Ferry belonged to. Boteler wrote when townsman James H. Holt waded out to Leary, neither his nor Copeland's gun would fire because they were wet, so Holt was in the process of using his weapon as a club when Copeland surrendered.

24 Baltimore *Exchange*, Frank Sanborn's Scrapbook, Stutler Collection; Barry, *The Strange Story of Harper's Ferry*, 85; Mason Report, pt. 2, 7, 28–9, 44; New York *Herald*, October 19, 1859; Villard, *John Brown*, 441. In 1909 Thomas Allstadt wrote that he was near Coppoc when he fired. His account at that time was more detailed than his testimony before the US Senate in 1860. The number of shots fired by Coppoc differs among accounts: from about a half dozen in the Mason Report to two in Allstadt's 1909 account.

25 Boteler, "Reflections of the John Brown Raid," 14; Cecil D. Ely, ed., "The Last Hours of the John Brown Raid: The Narrative of David H. Strother," *Virginia Magazine of History and Biography* (April 1965), vol. LXXIV, 171–2 (hereafter cited as Ely, "Last Hours of the John Brown Raid"); Mason Report, pt. 2, 39–40; New York *Herald*, October 24, 1859; *Register*, October 29, 1859; Virginia *Free Press*, November 3, 1859. Captain Alburtis was quoted in newspaper accounts as saying that on the road to Harpers Ferry, his men met "a company from Shepherdstown who proceded" his party to the town. He also stated that the Shepherdstown troops were to enter the armory from the east, and the Martinsburg men entered the armory from the west. Baylor reported that he ordered the two companies from Shepherdstown—"the Hamtramck Guards and the Shepherdstown Troops (dismounted and armed with muskets)"—to go only to the arsenal, just south of the armory.

A correspondent for the Baltimore *Sun* wrote Beckham's body was not removed for several hours until it was "finally removed by a woman, the sister of Mr. Foulke, upon a wheelbarrow."

26 Anderson, *A Voice From Harper's Ferry*, 46–9, 50, 158–62. Owen Brown states there were biscuits in the schoolhouse and implies he took many of them.

27 Ralph Keeler, "Owen Brown's Escape from Harpers Ferry," *Atlantic Monthly* (March 1874), 342–8; "John E. Cook's Confession," *The Life, Trial and Execution of John Brown*, 12–13.

28 New York *Daily Tribune*, Oct 20, 1859; Parke Poindexter, "The Capture and Execution of John Brown," *Lippincott's Magazine* (January 1889), 123–4.

29 New York *Daily Tribune*, Oct 20, 1859.

30 Boteler, "Reflection of the John Brown Raid," 408–9; *The Life and Trial and Execution of John Brown*, 6; Villard, *John Brown*, 447.

31 Villard, *John Brown*, 447–8. The three companies of Frederick militia that went to Harpers Ferry were Independent Riflemen under Captain Ulysses Hobbs, the Junior Defenders commanded by Captain John Richie, and the United Guards under Captain Thomas Sinn. Sinn responded to the summons to testify on behalf of John Brown during the trial. He did it "so that Northern men would have no opportunity to say that Southern men were unwilling to appear as witnesses on behalf of one whose principles they abhorred."

32 Gregory A. Stiverson, ed., "*In Readiness to Do Every Duty Assigned* (Annapolis, MD: Maryland State Archives, 1991), 9–21, 28–9; New York *Herald*, October 23, 1859; New York *Times*, October 20, 1859. The original report of Colonel Edward Shriver to Brigadier-General James M. Coale on October 22, 1859, is in the Governor Miscellaneous Papers, 1859, MSA S1274-37-1, Maryland State Archives. Shriver seemed to confuse the random shots fired by drunken men wandering about the town with shots by the raiders at the enginehouse guards.

33 Villard, *John Brown*, 447–8.

34 New York *Times*, Oct. 20, 1859. Israel Green states Lee arrived Monday at 10:00 p.m., Jeb Stuart claims it was midnight, and Edward Shriver reported it was 2:00 a.m. Tuesday. Lee testified he arrived at Harpers Ferry sometime between 11:00 and 12:00 and recorded in his memorandum book, "Reached Harper's Ferry at 11 p.m." The Baltimore *Exchange* reports on Monday evening at 7:30 a special train left Camden Station in Baltimore to go to Washington, pick up Lee, and take him to Harpers Ferry. Lee's arrival was likely to have been around midnight or later.

35 The five companies from Baltimore, Independent Greys, Law Greys, Baltimore City Guard, Shield's Guards and Wells and McComas's Riflemen left the city at 5:00 p.m., Monday 17 for Harpers Ferry by the B&O Railroad.

36 Israel Green, "The Capture of John Brown," *John Brown Pamphlets*, vol. 3, 1–6, Stutler Collection; Report of Colonel Robert E. Lee to Colonel S. Cooper, Adjutant General US Army, Washington City, D. C., October 19, 1859, 1–3, Stutler Collection (Hereinafter referred to as "Robert E. Lee's Report"); New York *Times*, Oct 20, 1859; Stiverson, ed., "*In Readiness To Do Every Duty Assigned, I 21, 23, 25;* Emory M. Thomas (ed.), "The Greatest Service I Rendered the State": J.E.B. Stuart's Account of the Capture of John Brown, *The Virginia Magazine of History and Biography*, July 1986, 345–53.

37 E. P. Dangerfield, "John Brown at Harpers Ferry," *Century Magazine,* June 1885. 267; Featherstonhaugh, *John Brown's Men*, 10–13; Mason Report, pt. 5, 9, 12; Villard, *John Brown*, 448–9. Testimony on the time of death of Oliver Brown varies from 15 minutes after he was shot to hours later, during the night. Edwin Coppoc in a letter after the raid writes: "Oliver Brown fell by the engine house. He died in about 15 minutes after he was shot. He said nothing." Another version says that after he was shot he stated his life was over.

38 Barry, *The Strange Story of Harper's Ferry*, 81; Oates, *To Purge This Land with Blood*, 294; Villard, *John Brown*, 419, 439, 686–7; Virginia *Free Press* (Charles Town, VA), October 27, 1859. Local residents claiming to have killed Newby include Jacob Bogert and Richard B. Washington. According to Alexander R. Boteler, in his "Reflections of the John Brown Raid," Newby was killed by Bogert, who fired a spike from the upper window of Mrs. Stephenson's house on the corner of Shenandoah and High Streets. Oates writes that upon Newby's mutilated body a letter was found from his wife pleading for him to come; that was written on April 11, 1859. She wrote

him two more letters; the last, on August 16, 1859, making her frantic plea for her husband to save her. It seems more likely if he carried any letter from his wife it would have been this one. After the Civil War Harriet Newby remarried.

39 Boteler, "Recollections of the John Brown Raid," 13–14; White, "John Brown at Harper's Ferry," 389; Villard, *John Brown*, 439–42; *Register*, December 10, 1859.

40 Charleston *Daily Courier*, November 7, 1859; Baltimore *Sun*, October 19, 1859; Hinton, *John Brown and His Men*, 534–5, Samuel V. Leech, *The Raid of John Brown at Harper's Ferry As I Saw It* (Washington, D.C., 1909) 9; New York *Herald*, October 24, 1859; Redpath, *The Public Life of Captain John Brown*, 259. Villard, *John Brown*, 440. Some accounts maintain Leeman's body was washed away by the currents; others maintain when this happened someone waded out in the river and placed his mutilated remains back upon the rock as a target.

41 Baltimore *American*, December 6, 1859; Villard, *John Brown*, 445; White "John Brown at Harper's Ferry," 389.

42 H. W. Flourney, ed., *Calendar of State Papers* (New York, 1968, XI, 77; New York *Herald*, December 5, 1859; Villard, *John Brown*, 464–5; Virginia *Free Press*, October 31, November 3, 1859; June 21, 1860. The spark that ignited the confrontation between Wise and Baylor was the governor's sending Colonel J. Lucius Davis, a West Point graduate, and an accompanying cavalry officer to Charles Town after the raid to evaluate the situation. Davis soon told Baylor he was in violation of the state militia law by illegally assuming command on October 17, as the command belonged to Colonel Gibson. Infuriated, Baylor wrote a lengthy letter to General William Richardson, the adjutant general, asserting that he was in compliance with the law, and that most people considered under his command the militia had been "wisely, prudently and cautiously managed"—especially given that citizens were held as hostages. He charged Wise with inflicting "gross injustice [on] the militia units" by criticizing their handling of the raid, by sending Colonel Davis, and by appointing Henry Hunter as the captain of a patrol company to report only to the governor. "If Col. Davis had not been sent here no difficulty would have arisen. There was not the slightest necessity for his presence here… If he sends us arms they will be of greatly more service than men… as we have too many already," Baylor added. When Wise became aware of the contents of Baylor's letter, he angrily refuted the charges and ordered Baylor "off Duty." Several weeks later another indignity further incensed Baylor. While at Charles Town the day prior to Brown's execution, the colonel was arrested for "venturing within the lines" off limits to all but the military. Although soon released, Baylor bitterly denounced the militia's show of force as a "vile political scheme" by Henry Wise "to destroy the Union" and enhance his chances of becoming the "President of the Southern Confederacy."

Baylor's removal from duty did not end criticism of him by state authorities. The state auditing board (February 27, 1860), in reviewing Baylor's claim for payment of $193.98 for militia service, awarded him compensation for only four days of service and repeated charges he violated the law by calling out the Winchester militia and failing to send a report to the governor. After Wise's term as governor expired, in an attempt to redeem his reputation, Baylor called for a Court of Inquiry. Convening at Charles Town on June 4, 1860, the court spent six days addressing three issues charged by the auditing board: (1) Had Baylor acted without orders, (2) improperly interfered with command since the raid as charged by Wise, and (3) acted in violation of state law by acting without orders and failing to report to the governor. To buttress the case against the colonel Wise's son Jenning wrote the court, charging Baylor illegally assumed power, acted without orders, was "guilty of cowardice in not storming the engine house" on October 17, and had used "violent and ungentlemanly language about his commander in chief Governor Wise." The court ruled in favor of Baylor, stating (1) although Wise sent Baylor no written order, the governor had sent him a verbal one "to scour the mountain opposite Harper's Ferry which Col. Baylor executed"; (2) Baylor did not improperly interfere with "any command"; and (3) the charge that Baylor failed to file a report was false as he sent one to Wise on October 22, 1859.

43 Benjamin Quarles, *Allies for Freedom* (New York: Oxford University Press, 1974), 101; Douglas Southall Freeman, *R. E. Lee,* (New York: Charles Scribner's Sons, 1934), I, 396, 398–9; Villard; *John Brown,* 452; Stiverson, *"In Readiness to Do Every Duty Assigned,"* 23.

44 It is possible that one or both of the Marines' shots came from raiders other than Brown.

45 Douglas, *I Rode with Stonewall,* 15–16.

46 Baltimore *Sun,* Oct. 26 & 28, 1859; Israel Green, "The Capture of John Brown," *John Brown Pamphlets,* III, 4–5; *Harper's Weekly,* November 5, 1859; New York *Daily Tribune,* Oct. 20 & Nov. 5, 1859; New York *Journal of Commerce,* Oct. 20, 24, 29, 30, 1859; New York *Herald,* Oct. 19, 21, 22, 24, 1859; Mason Report, II, 16–17, 19; New York *Times,* October 20, 1859; Richmond *Enquirer,* October 25, 1859; Robert E. McGlone, "Forgotten Surrender: John Brown's Raid and the Cult of Martial Virtues," *Civil War History* 40 (September 1994) 185–201; McGlone, *John Brown's War Against Slavery,* 296–306; Stiverson, *"In Readiness to Do Duty Assigned,"* 25; Thomas, (ed.), "The Greatest Service I Rendered the State," 353–4. Green contends the stories given by others describing what went on inside the enginehouse during the Marine attack "have been free from a many misstatements," including the account describing him "jumping over the right-hand engine more like a wild beast than a soldier." Green claimed the hostages were without food for 60 hours, but it was closer to 40.

A granite monument weighting 3,500 pounds honoring Private Luke Quinn was placed at Harpers Ferry on May 24, 2011.

47 Jennie Chambers, "What a School Girl Saw of John Brown's Raid," *Harper's Magazine,* January, 1902, 14; White, "John Brown's Raid at Harper's Ferry, 390; Quarles, *Allies For Freedom,* 105–107. For additional information on black support for the raid see Jean Libby, *Black Voices From Harpers Ferry* and Hannah Geffert, "Regional Black Involvement in John Brown's Raid on Harpers Ferry" in *Prophets of Protest.* Not permitted to join white militia companies, black men formed their own in Massachusetts, Ohio, New York, and Pennsylvania. Several were named for Crispus Attucks, a black protestor killed during the Boston Massacre, which preceded the Revolutionary War. Brown probably hoped to gain the support of these black militia for his cause.

48 "The John Brown Letters Found in the Virginia State Library in 1901," *The Virginia Magazine of History and Biography* (April, 1902), 389–390; (July, 1902), 17–18. Somehow the legend of Frederick the Great's presenting George Washington with a sword with the inscription "From the oldest to the greatest general" was believed by his descendants. Washington did possess a sword from Germany, but it was not from Frederick the Great. It was an inexpensive blade sent by a manufacturer of weapons, named Alte. Inscribed in German was the sentiment "Condemner of despotism." This differs greatly than the sentiment on the alleged gift from the Prussian ruler. The Lafayette pistols are genuine. One is in the State Library of New York.

49 *The Confederation* (Montgomery, ALA), October 27, 1859; Stan Cohen, *John Brown: "The Thundering Voice of Jehovah"* (Missoula, MA: Pictorial Histories Publishing Co., 2001), 150–1; De Witt, *The Life, Trial and Execution of John Brown,* 4, 7; Letter, Boyd Stutler to Sadavice Giddinn, November 12, 1948, Stutler Collection; Albert Lindert "The Revolvers of John Brown Raid," (unpublished manuscript, 1959), 1–2; New York *Times,* October 22, 1859; John C. Unseld, Testimony, Mason Report, pt. 5, 6–11. Brown's delinquency in payment resulted in only 954 pikes out of 1,000 ordered being delivered. Soon after Brown's raid unscrupulous vendors at Harper Ferry's rail station would sell poor-quality reproduction pikes to passengers for $2–$3. This became so annoying that by the end of November 1859 railroad officials had the sales stopped and the vendors driven from the platform. When the Confederates occupied Harpers Ferry in

April 1861 they carried off what would be of use to Richmond, which included 483 pikes and possibly 175 more with broken shafts. It has been asserted some of the pikes may have been given to Confederate cavalrymen (Texas unit) for use as lances in 1862 due to a shortage of weaponry. After the surrender of this unit near or in Alabama at the end the war the pikes were stored in the arsenal at Mount Vernon, Alabama. In the 1870s the pikes were burned in an arsenal fire and later shipped to the Rock Island Arsenal where they were rusting scrap iron—until they were purchased from the government and sold as souvenirs. It is unclear whether the rifles and revolvers (costing $6.50 apiece) that were stored at the Harpers Ferry arsenal after Brown's raid were destroyed when the government buildings were torched in April 1861 when the Confederates seized the facility.

50 Letter, James Ewell Brown Stuart to Jos Mother, written from Fort Riley, Kansas Territory, January 31, 1860, in the Virginia Historical Society, Richmond, Virginia.

51 Baltimore *American*, December 13, 1859; New York *Tribune*, December 12, 1859. In his condolence letter to Mrs. Brown in December, Coppoc wrote that Watson "complained of the hardness of the bench on which he was lying. I begged hard for a bed for him, or even a blanket, but none was obtained. I took my coat and placed it under him, and held his head in my lap, in which position he died without a groan or struggle."

52 Boteler, "Recollections," 411; Cecil D. Ely, ed. "The Last Hours of the John Brown Raid: The Narrative of David H. Strother," *The Virginia Magazine of History and Biography*, April 1965, 171–5; Excerpt of letter by Colonel L. T. Moore, Abram's Delight Museum, Winchester, VA; Parke Poindexter, "The Capture and Execution of John Brown," *Lippincott's Magazine* January, 1889, 124.

53 Reporters incorrectly assumed it was Jeb Stuart to whom Brown was referring.

54 New York *Herald*, October 21, 1859; Ely, "The Last Hours of the John Brown Raid," 177; Israel Green, "The Capture of John Brown," 3; Hinton, *John Brown and His Men*, 316–317; "Robert E. Lee's Report," 1; Mason Report, VIII, 12–13, 15–16; New York *Daily Tribune*, Oct. 20, 1859; New York *Weekly Tribune*, October 29, 1859; Stiverson, "*In Readiness To Do Duty Assigned,*" 27; Villard, *John Brown*, 454–6; Robert De Witt, *The Life, Trial and Execution of John Brown*, 8–15.

55 Joseph G. Rosengarten, "John Brown's Raid," (1865–1866) *John Brown Pamphlets*, vol 3, 2–6.

56 Brandon H. Beck & Charles S. Grunder, *The First Battle of Winchester: May 25, 1862* (Lynchburg, VA: E. Howard, Inc., 1992), 72–3; Featherstonhaugh, *John Brown's Men*, 20; OR, ser. I, vol. 23, pt. 3, 334–5; Horatio Rust to Mary Ann Brown and Ruth Brown, January 27, 1863, Stutler Collection; Ruth Brown Thompson to Thomas Featherstonhaugh, October 19, 1899, Stutler Collection; Boyd Stutler to E. N. Cotter, January 14, 1966, Stutler Collection; Boyd Stutler to Francis Drake, October 15, 1959, Stutler Collection. Residents of Winchester, Virginia, during the Civil War, and the Richmond *Whig* (June 7, 1862), contend Banks burned the Winchester Medical College (located at what is now 302 West Boscawen St.) because John Brown's son was dissected there. Banks did not order it to be incinerated. Orders were apparently given to set fire to the quartermaster's storehouse, described as "nearly opposite" the college, to prevent seizure by Jackson's Confederates, who were occupying the town. The fire started in the storehouse about 8:00 a.m. on May 25 and soon endangered the hospital. Before the fire reached the medical center nearly 250 patients were evacuated and cared for in the yard. Dr. Johnson's earlier removal of Watson Brown's body prevented it from being consumed by the fire. Dr. Johnson and other Union physicians stayed in Winchester to care for Union wounded during Jackson's brief occupation from May 25–30, 1862, before moving south to keep from being trapped. The professor of the Winchester Medical College's appeal to Dr. Johnson seems to have been after the federal troops

reoccupied Winchester. The professor also claimed he had the body of Brown sent to the college from Harpers Ferry and after consultation with other professors "decided to prepare the body of young Brown that it might be preserved in the museum of the college as a specimen, and as an object of interest and note."

The fire destroyed much of the institution's records and history. The hospital started in 1826 as the Medical College of the Valley of Virginia but was only active for three years. It was reopened in 1847 as the Winchester Medical College. The advent of the Civil War saw many students leave to join the Confederate army.

57 Featherstonhaugh, *John Brown's Men*, 18–24; Featherstonhaugh, *The Washington Post*, November 13, 1898. Later Dr. Libby escorted the remains of bodies taken from the bank of the Shenandoah River by rail to New York, and then to North Elba. Brown's 244 acres farm had been purchased by actress, journalist, and Brown admirer Kate Fields, so it could in the actress's words "be held as sacred ground, as proof that even in the 19th century there is such a thing as patriotic justice." The funeral for the above raiders, along with the bodies of Aaron Stevens and Albert Hazlett taken from their graves in New Jersey, was on August 30, 1899, the 43rd anniversary of the battle of Osawatomie. Programs were printed, and President McKinley was invited but did not attend. A parade consisting of the 16th US Infantry and their band escorted the single casket holding the remains of bodies from Harpers Ferry in the two-mile march from Lake Placid to Brown's home. About 150 to 200 mourners came early by foot and by a variety of conveyances and waited in the heat for the start of the 2:00 p.m. ceremony. The theme of praise for the deceased promoted the view of Brown and his men as noble, righteous, and patriotic. Three songs were sung in between three speakers; the concluding one was "John Brown's Body." To Brown supporters his gravesite was now sacred ground.

58 "Robert E. Lee's Report," 3; Thomas (ed.), "The Greatest Service I Rendered the State," 355; Villard, *John Brown*, 470.

Chapter Four: Anguish and Travail

1 Hinton, *John Brown and His Men*, 332, 481–2; letter, Anne Brown Adams to Garibaldi Ross, December 15, 1887. Materials providing details of the impact of the deaths of nonraiders do not exist.

2 Anderson, *A Voice From Harper's Ferry*, 113–17; Andrew J. Torget and Edward L. Ayers, *Two Communities in the Civil War* (New York; W. W. Norton & Co., 2007), 3–5. Five hundred free blacks lived in shoddy dwellings in the poorest part of Chambersburg, working as laborers and in whatever other physical jobs they could find.

3 Libby, *Black Voices From Harpers Ferry*, 166–72.

4 Richmond *Daily Dispatch*, November 30, 1859; Virginia Ott Stake, *John Brown in Chambersburg* (Chambersburg, PA: Franklin County Heritage, 1977), 85–8.

5 Keeler, "Owen Brown's Escape from Harper's Ferry," 345–51.

6 Keeler, "Owen Brown's Escape from Harper's Ferry," 353–5.

7 New York *Journal of Commerce*, October 29, 1853; Stake, *John Brown in Chambersburg*, 91–100. A correspondent of the Baltimore *American* wrote incorrectly that Cook came off the mountain with two loaves of bread in a handkerchief. He also wrote he had "a powder flask on his shoulder" and the pistol hidden in his shirt. Cook is reported to have requested that if his carpetbag was found, the pistol taken from Washington should be returned. He called Washington "a perfect gentleman" with whom he "had been shooting together frequently at Harper's Ferry."

8 Keeler, "Owen Brown's Escape from Harper's Ferry," 356–65.

9 Libby, *Black Voices From Harpers Ferry,* 189–210. The proceeds of John Redpath's two biographies of John Brown, written in 1859 and 1860, went to the Brown family. Most of $6,400 raised by the John Brown Fund, Haitian, and Redpath Fund went to Brown family members. The money in the Brown Fund for Anderson was raised by Thaddeus Hyatt by selling pictures of John Brown.

10 Hinton, *John Brown and His Men,* 564–8, 576; Virginia *Free Press,* February 9, 1860; Villard, *John Brown,* 682–3. John Brown had often been in Ashtabula county during 1858–9. According to *The Jefferson Gazette* 13 of his men had worked in the vicinity the summer of 1859. A number of the local citizens corresponded with Brown and his men at the Kennedy farm and after their arrest. The night after Brown was hung both Owen Brown and Barclay Coppoc spoke from the courthouse steps in Ashtabula County to a large and excited crowd. Today a plaque on the courthouse states Owen Brown was protected by the Blackstrings. It also lists other Brown followers, Barclay Coppoc, Francis Meriam, Osborne Anderson, and James Redpath, who sought protection in Ashtabula County.

Chapter Five: An Agitated Nation

1 Alexandria (Virginia) *Gazette,* October 19 & 20, 1859; Margaret Leech, *Reveille in Washington* (New York: Harpers & Brothers, 1940), 18–19, 236; New York *Weekly Tribune,* October 29, 1859.

2 McGlone, *John Brown's War Against Slavery,* 222, 239, 242, 244; Sanborn, ed., *The Life and Letters of John Brown,* 439–40, 469, 492, 515–16, 525; Renehan, Jr., *The Secret Six,* 142, 146, 206–7, 249–50; Jeffery Rossbach, *Ambivalent Conspirators* (Philadelphia: University of Pennsylvania Press, 1982, 4, 8, 188); Villard, *John Brown,* 526–7, 536. Fearing their arrest, Franklin Sanborn and George Stearns consulted the able attorney John A. Andrew, an abolitionist and future governor of Massachusetts, who felt they had been foolish, but with whom they and other members of the Secret Six were safe from extradition. Their peace of mind was soon shattered when Andrews told them he had found an obscure law he had been unaware of, and they could be arrested as witnesses and taken from the state.

3 Baltimore *Sun,* October 19, November 1 & 8, 1859; Torget and Ayers, *Two Communities in the Civil War,* 50.

4 Mason Report, pt. 1, 1–25; pt 2, 172, 146; Villard, *John Brown,* 580–3.

5 Villard, *John Brown,* 581–582.

6 Baltimore *Sun,* December 9, 1859; *East Floridian,* January 19, 1860; New York *Herald,* November 21, 1859.

7 Baltimore *Sun,* December 9, 1859; New York *Herald,* December 3, 1859.

8 C. Van Woodward, *The Burden of Southern History* (Baton Rouge: Louisiana State University Press, 1960), 64–6.

9 Cincinnati *Gazette,* November 26, 1859; Baltimore *Sun,* February 10, 1860; *Chronicle & Sentinel,* January 4, 1859. The first offense of free blacks immigrating to Maryland was a $20 fine; the second offense resulted in arrest and a fine of $500, with half going to the informer and the other half to the state.

10 Clarke County, Court Order Book, 1858–62; *Conservator* (Berryville, VA), November 9, 23 & 30, December 14, 1859, February 4, 1860; Scrapbook of newspaper clippings (1859–60) collected by Miss Catherine M, Wagner, Charles Town Library, West Virginia (hereafter cited as "Wagner scrapbook). Jerry was owned by Colonel Francis McCormick. Jerry was annoyed by the patrols because he and other slaves were not allowed to move freely without a pass. He protested by

turning to arson. Later at Berryville, Virginia, a court of five magistrates sentenced Jerry to be executed on Friday, February 17, 1860.

11   Baltimore *Sun*, February 10, 1860.

12   Nancy Chappelear Baird, ed., *Journals of Amanda Virginia Edmonds: Lass of the Mosby Confederacy, 1859–1867* (Stephens City, VA: N. C. Baird, 1984), vii–xi, xxiii, 2, 5–7, 31–36.

13   Woodward, *The Burden of Southern History*, 49–52.

14   Roy P. Basler. ed., *The Collected Works of Abraham Lincoln* (New Brunswick, N. J.: Rutgers University Press, 1953) III, 496, 502, 541; V, 160.

15   Chicago *Tribune*, October 30, 1859.

16   Alexandria *Gazette*, November 26, 1859; Baltimore *Sun*, October 19 and 22, November 7, December 8, 9,10, 12, 21, 1859, January 23, 31, February 10, 14, 1860; Chicago *Tribune*, October 30, 1859; *Chronicle and Sentinel,* January 4, 1860; *East Floridian* [Ferandina], January 3, 19, 1860; *Evening Picayune*, January 4, February 28, 1860.

17   Baltimore *American,* December 16, 1859.

18   Baltimore *Sun*, November 30, 1859; *East Floridian*, January 19, 1860.

19   Margaret Leech, *Reveille in Washington* (New York: Harpers & Sons, 1941), 18–19.

20   John S. Wise, *The End of an Era* (New York: Houghton, Mifflin and Co., 1890), 118–24.

21   Executive papers of Henry Wise, Boxes 271 & 477, MSS, Virginia State Library, Archives Division; *Governor's Message and Reports of the Public Officers of the State*, document 1, 51–117; New York *Herald,* October 26, November 27, 1859; Quarles, *Allies for Freedom,* 107.

22   Barton H. Wise, *The Life of Henry A. Wise of Virginia, 1805–1876* (New York: Macmillan, 1899), 256–9.

23   Alexandria *Gazette*, November 26, 1859; Baltimore *Sun,* November 21, 1859; *Conservator*, November 9, 21, 22, 1859; New York *Herald*, November 19, 1859; *Register*, February 11, 1860. Jacob Howe Jr., a native of Baltimore, Maryland, sent Brown $2 accompanied with the statement, "You will be rescued if we die for it."

24   Bushong, *A History of Jefferson County, West Virginia*, 131; Geffert, "Regional Black Involvement in John Brown's Raid on Harpers Ferry," 175–6; Quarles, *Allies For Freedom,* 107–8; Redpath, *The Public Life of Captain John Brown*, 371; Richmond *Enquirer*, November 19, 1859; Mason Report, pt. 2, 35; Virginia *Free Press*, October 31, 1859. It has been argued an indication of slave support during the raid is that the slaves carried weapons and were owned by Dr. Fuller and hired out to Washington, who was away from his house. Washington testified that upon hearing something was wrong, the slave "got in the wagon at Allstadt's. I understand that was the point he overtook them."

25   Quarles, *Allies for Freedom*, 106.

26   Villard, *John Brown*, 502–4

27   Charlestown *Daily Tribune,* December 15, 1859.

28   (Washington) *Evening Star*, December 2, 1859.

29   Executive Papers of Henry Wise, Box 472 & 477; Flourney, ed. *Calendar of (Virginia) State Papers*, vol. XI, 82–3; New York *Herald*, October 26, 1859; Quarles, *Allies For Freedom,* 107; W.W. Scott, ed., "John Brown Letters," *Virginia Magazine of History and Biography*, 322.

30   Alexandria *Gazette,* November 26, 1859; Baltimore *Sun*, November 21, 1859; *Conservator*, November 9, 21 & 23, 1859; *Register,* February 11, 1860.

31   Villard, *John Brown*, 511–17. The cost of the expedition to kidnap Governor Wise, including the cost of a boat and crew, would have been $10,000 to $15,000.

32   "The John Brown Letters, *The Virginia Magazine of History and Biography*, vol. 10, no. 1, 30; vol. 10 no. 3, 273, 274; vol. 11, no. 2, 167, 168.

33   New York *Herald*, November 19, 20, 21, 1859.

34   Richmond *Dispatch*, November 30, 1859.

35   New York *Herald*, November 24, 1859; Richmond *Whig*, November 25, 1859. Hazlett made the least favorable impression on the visitors; as the New York *Herald* reported, "He was very rough in his looks and has a dare devil manner of deporting himself."

36   Richmond *Dispatch*, November 30, 1859.

37   *Conservator*, November 9, 16, 23 & December 2, 1859; Clarke *Journal*, November 25, 1859 & February 10, 1860; *Democratic Mirror*, December 7, 1859.

38   New York *Herald*, November 21, 1859.

39   Clarke *Journal*, November 25; *Democratic Mirror*, December 7, 1859.

Chapter Six: The Rush to Judgment

1   McGinty, *John Brown's Trial*, 2–15. There were previous cases where individuals were tried for treason against a state, but they were not executed. The modern spelling for Charles Town is two words, but in 1859 it was one word, Charlestown.

2   McGinty, *John Brown's Trial*, 71, 82; Villard, *John Brown*, 477–8. By the end of October Wise took the recalcitrant position the federal government had failed to protect Harpers Ferry from Northern invaders and it was up to Virginia to defend herself: "I would not have delivered up these prisoners to any claim of priority of jurisdiction if the President of the United States had so ordered." If Stevens had been tried by a federal court, it would have been the US District Court for the Western District of Virginia, which at that time was to convene in southwestern Virginia in Wytheville, 250 miles from Charles Town.

3   This ignores the fact that Brown sent men to private homes under Virginia's jurisdiction to seize citizens and enslaved people.

4   Daniel Drape, "Legal Phases of the Trial of John Brown," *West Virginia History*, January 1940, typewritten copy, Stutler Collection, 1–11; McGinty, *John Brown's Trial*, 13–14. The question was unresolved whether sovereignty in the matter resided in the federal or state government. If Brown's actions were acts of treason against the federal government and Virginia, could the state prosecute the offender and disregard the federal jurisdiction?

5   Horwitz, *Midnight Rising: John Brown and the Raid That Sparked the Civil War*, 200; McGinty, *John Brown's Trial*, 86, 101, 104; National Park Service, *John Brown*, 51. Judge Parker lived in Winchester, Virginia, and was a slave-owner of 10. As for Brown's first attorneys, Lawson Botts was slave-owner of four, and Charles J. Faulkner, of 13. Jailor John Avis was a slave trader. The eight members of the examining court owned 105 slaves, and seven of the 12 jurors who found Brown guilty of the charges had a total of 54 enslaved.

6   Lubet, *John Brown's Spy*, 131.

7   Dewitt, *The Life, Trial and Execution of John Brown*, 53.

8   *Harper's Weekly*, November 12, 1859.

9   Heading the examining court was Colonel Braxton Davenport. The others included Dr. William Alexander, John J. Lock, John F. Smith, Thomas H. Willis, George W. Eichelberger, Charles H. Lewis, and Moses W. Burr.

10   Dewitt, *The Life, Trial and Execution of John Brown*, 62–5.

11   Ibid., 55–74. Prospective jurors were examined until 24 were approved by the court and lawyers to be competent jurors. From 24 men the defense had to right to strike off eight. Twelve were "drawn by ballot" from the remaining 16. The men on the jury were Richard Timberlake, Joseph Myers, Thomas Watson Jr., Isaac Dust, John C. McClure, William Rightstine, Jacob J. Miller, Thomas Osbourn, George W. Boyer, John C. Wiltshire, George W. Tapp, and William A. Martin.

12 McGinty, *John Brown's Trial*, 115–30. There are conflicting accounts about whether Brown was carried back to jail on the cot or walked.

13 Charleston *Daily Courier*, October 31, 1859; McGinty, *John Brown's Trial*, 132–6; New York *Herald*, October 28, 1859. Under Virginia law an insane person may be an idiot, lunatic, non compos (not of sound mind), or deranged. If the court had reasonable grounds to suspect insanity the normal proceedings were suspended until the jury decided whether the accused was insane or sane. If they were found sane, the trial continued, but if found insane, it was terminated and the person was sent to an asylum.

14 Charleston *Daily Courier*, October 31, 1859.

15 McGinty, *John Brown's Trial*, 154–5.

16 Charleston *Daily Courier*, October 29 & 31, 1859.

17 Ibid., November 1, 1859.

18 Samuel Tilden, who was expected to come, could not due to legal commitments. He sent Griswold in his place. Hilton received the unusually large fee of $1,000, paid by Brown's Massachusetts supporters, headed by John Andrew. Griswold received $250.

19 Charleston, *Daily Courier*, November 2, 1859.

20 Ibid.

21 McGinty, *John Brown's Trial*, 206.

22 Charleston *Daily Courier*, November 4, 1859.

23 Charleston *Daily Courier*, November 4, 1859; Dewitt, *The Life, Trial and Execution of John Brown*, 35–6; Lubet, *John Brown's Spy*, 171–80; McGinty, *John Brown's Trial*, 211–16, 221–3.

24 Parker had planned to make the ruling that morning, but not wanting to complicate and raise legal questions by ruling during Coppoc's trial, he waited until the jury was deliberating.

25 Brown attempted to correct his contradictory statements. He told Wise, who visited him in jail, his real object was not to carry off slaves and free them. This was followed up on November 22 with a letter to Andrew Hunter that elaborated and clarified his position by pointing out, "I intended to convey [the] idea, that it was my object to place the slaves in a condition to defend their liberties, if they would, *without any bloodshed, but not* that I intended *to run them out of the slave States.*"

26 Charleston *Daily Courier*, November 7, 1859; Horwitz, *Midnight Rising*, 237.

27 Villard, *John Brown*, 498–9.

28 Typescript of Parker's remarks in sentencing John Brown, November 2, 1859, Stutler Collection.

29 *Harper's Weekly*, November 12, 1859.

30 Charleston *Daily Courier*, November 7, 1859.

31 "The John Brown Invasion," newspaper clipping, November 18, 1859, Stutler Collection.

32 On November 7, 1859, Wise telegraphed Andrew Hunter to try Cook and turn Stevens over to the federal court. Wise wanted Northern supporters like Joshua Giddings, Gerrit Smith, Frederick Douglass, Samuel Gridley, and Franklin Sanborn to be subpoenaed to testify at Charles Town, but the subpoena power of the state ended at Virginia's boundary. They could be subpoenaed to testify in federal court, which Wise hoped would be done to expose the Northern conspirators that he believed made the raid possible.

33 Oates, *To Purge This Land with Blood*, 328–9; McGinty, 235–41; Villard, *John Brown*, 477–8. Brothers Terrance and James Bryne were among those who testified at Cook's trial.

34 Hinton, *John Brown and His Men*, 509–10.

35 Ibid., 526–7.

36 A. D. Stevens to his uncle, "The John Brown Letters," *The Virginia Magazine of History and Biography*, (July, 1902), 164–5.

37 Hinton, *John Brown and His Men*, 526–7.

38 Hinton, *John Brown and His Men*, 508–11; "The Letters of John A. Copeland," www.oberlin. edu/external/EOG/Copeland/copeland_letters.htm.

39 Baltimore *American,* December 13, 1859.

40 Ibid.

41 Charleston *Daily Courier,* November 7, 1859; Villard, *John Brown,* 479–80.

42 Villard, *John Brown,* 545–6.

43 McGinty, *John Brown's Trial,* 251–2.

44 Villard, *John Brown,* 544–6.

45 New York *Tribune,* November 18, 1859. Brown was aware an attempt or actual escape would undermine his grand plan of a martyr's image of sacrificing his life to end slavery.

46 Horwitz, M*idnight Rising,* 242; McGinty, *John Brown's Trial,* 256.

47 Horwitz, *Midnight Rising,* 241–2; Villard, *John Brown,* 513, 540–2, 248–9.

48 Baltimore *American,* December 6, 1859.

49 Villard, *John Brown,* 237–45.

Chapter Seven: Hemp Justice

1 Villard, *John Brown,* 524.

2 John Shadrach Alfriend, *History of Zion Episcopal Church* (n.p., 1973), [3].

3 James B. Avirett, *The Memoirs of General Turner Ashby* (Baltimore: Selby & Dulany, 1867), 62.

4 Parke Poindexter, "The capture and Execution of John Brown, 125; Letter and Order Book, William Booth Taliaferro Papers, Special Collection Research Center, Swem Library, College of William and Mary, pts. 1 & 4. Hereafter referred to as Taliaferro, Letter and Order Book.

5 The proprietor at Winchester told the commissary office he could provide up to 1,000 loaves of b On November 25 Wise ordered into service the following: from the 160th Regulars of Augusta County, one company of light infantry and one of riflemen; from the 145th Rockingham, one company of light infantry; from the 3rd Regular Volunteers of Norfolk, one company of light infantry; and from Wheeling, Ohio County, two companies "numbering together not less them 100 men" of light infantry riflemen. The companies called up "averaged at 50 men each rank and file."

6 Richmond *Daily Dispatch,* November 30, 1859.

7 Ibid.

8 T. G. Pollack, letter to mother, *The Fireside Sentinel,* January 1989, p. 4; Taliaferro Order Book, pts. 1–5. Taliaferro graduated from William and Mary, studied law at Harvard, fought as a captain in the Mexican War, and in 1850–3 represented Gloucester County, his place of birth, in the Virginia House of Delegates.

9 New York *Semi-Weekly Tribune,* December 13, 1859.

10 New York *Herald,* 1859; New York *Tribune,* November 18, 1859.

11 *Evening Star,* December 2, 1859.

12 Taliaferro, Letter and Order Book, pts. 1 & 3.

13 New York *Tribune,* November 18, 1859; Villard, *John Brown,* 668–9.

14 Baltimore *American,* December 3, 1859; Evan Carter, *Patriotic Treason* (New York Free Press, 2006), 330–1.

15 *Evening Star,* December 2, 1859; Horwitz, *Midnight Rising,* 245–7; New York *Herald,* December 3, 1859; Villard, *John Brown,* 249–53. Accounts differ on the wording in the departing of Brown's wife. Some have Brown saying, "God Bless you and the Children," and Mary saying, "God have mercy on you." Another account has her saying, "Good bye, may God have mercy on your soul." Among the gifts Brown gave to those who treated him well during his imprisonment was his prison Bible. This went to John Blessing, a local baker who gave Brown cakes and oysters.

16 *Evening Star,* December 2, 1859; New York *Tribune,* December 6, 1859; New York *Herald,* December 3, 1859. Ropes were sent by people from other states, including one from Alabama. The New York *Tribune* incorrectly reported one was from Missouri, made by the slaves of Mahala Doyle, who did not own slaves.

17 *Evening Star,* December 2, 1859; Hinton, *John Brown and His Men,* 389–91;Horwitz, *Midnight Rising,* 248; Redpath, *The Public Life of Captain John Brown,* 396; Charlestown *Free Press,* December 8, 1859. The exact wording of Brown's conversation with his men and others differs, especially in newspaper accounts. The Virginia *Free Press* states Cook replied to Brown's accusations, "Your memory is very different from mine." Brown answered, insisting, "I am right, sir." The *Evening Star* reports Cook said, "Captain Brown, we remember differently." Brown did not reply, "but sternly looked Cook down, whose eyes fell as the interview ended."

18 Horwitz, *Midnight Rising,* 249; New York *Tribune,* December 6, 1859; Oates, *To Purge This Land with Blood,* 351; Villard, *John Brown,* 670–1. The military companies that escorted Brown from jail to the gallows were led by General Taliaferro, and his staff included captain Scott's cavalry, Major Loring's Defensibles, Montpelier Guard, Petersburg Greys, Virginia Volunteers, and the Young Guard. All were under the command of Colonel T. P. August.

19 Brown's clothes, like those of the other prisoners, were washed as needed at no cost to them.

20 Some contend the outer box was pine. Cabinetmakers in that era were often also undertakers because they had the woodworking skills to make coffins.

21 Some accounts have Brown saying farewell to the sheriff and jailor in the jail prior to leaving; others have them shaking hands and saying goodbye on the gallows. The exact wording of Brown's last words varies with each correspondent.

22 Ruffin had anxiously pursued being one of the militia at the execution site.

23 Taliaferro, Letter and Order Book, pts. 1 & 4. The proclamation was signed by General Taliaferro; S. Bassett, military secretary; Thomas Green, mayor; Andrew Hunter, assistant provost attorney (also commonwealth attorney); and James W. Campbell, sheriff.

24 Avery O. Craven, *Edmund Ruffin, Southerner: A Study in Secession* (Baton Rouge, LA: Louisiana State University, 1966), 175; *Evening Star,* December 2, 1859; New York *Herald,* December 3, 1959 Scarborough, *The Diary of Edmund Ruffin,* vol. 1, 317–70; *Register,* December 3, 1859; Jennings C. Wise, *The Military History of the Virginia Military Institute from 1859 to 1865* (Lynchburg, VA: J. P. Bell, 1915), 106–7; Virginia *Free Press,* December 1 & 15, 1859. The Virginia *Free Press* in its December 1, 1859, issue lists the total force as about 1,000, with 650 in Charles Town. The paper counted both organized units and armed residents in Jefferson County and lists the following numbers of men, names of units and commanding officers of each company, all under the command of General Taliaferro: 84 Richmond Grays (Lt. L. J. Bossieux), 74 Company F (Capt. R. M. Cary), 44 Young Guard (Capt. John S. Ready), 43 Virginia Riflemen (Capt. F. C. Miller), 38 Mount Vernon Guards (Capt. William Smith), 40 Alexander Riflemen (Capt. Mayre), 38 Morgan Continentals (Major B. B. Washington), 60 Jefferson Guards (Capt. J.W. Rowan), 25 Executive Guards (Capt. H. C. Hunter), 45 Upper Fauquier Cavalry (Capt. John Scott), 45 Lower Fauquier Cavalry (Capt. Turner Ashby), 36 Petersburg Artillery (Capt. James Nichols), and 45 Alexandria Artillery (Major Duffey). This list numbers over 600 men at Charles Town, but it is an incomplete listing; it does not include late arrivals such as the VMI Cadets.

25 What was said and Brown's exact wording varies with each correspondent. Strother standing near the gallows said as Brown stepped from the wagon he had a "grim and greisly smirk." As "he passed our group" he stopped and "raised his pinioned arms and bid good morning" in a manner that seemed like "a trace of Bravado." Brown then sprightly ascended the steps to the rickety platform where he immediately took off this hat "offering his neck" for the placement of the noose.

26 Poindexter, "The Capture and Execution of John Brown," 125; Villard, *John Brown,* 671.

27   Mary Ann Jackson, *Memoirs of Stonewall Jackson* (Louisville, KY: The Prentice Press, 1895), 130–1.

28   Taliaferro, Letter and Order Book, pts. 1, 4, 5. Hinton, *John Brown and His Men,* 389–95. Andrew Hunter's description of the execution in the New Orleans *Times-Democrat* (September 5, 1887) contends that Dr. Mason, the jail doctor, was the first physician upon the scaffold and first to pronounce Brown dead. Later Governor Wise said the sheriff may decline his request to turn the body over to Taliaferro, "but I trust he will comply with it." Taliaferro also sent, along with the 15-man escort of Brown's body, a prisoner, W. G. Harvey, to be released at Harpers Ferry.

29   *Evening Star*, December 2, 1859; *The Indiana State Sentinel,* July 14, 1874.

30   *Evening Star*, December 2, 1859; New York *Herald*, December 6, 1859.

31   Villard, *John Brown,* 554.

32   Joseph Warren Keifer, *Slavery and Four Years of War* (New York: G. P. Putnam's Sons, 1900), vol. 1, 115; McGlone, *John Brown's War Against Slavery*, 517; George Brown Tindall & David Emory Shi, *America: A Narrative History* (New York: Norton & Company, 2013), vol. 1, 637.

33   New York *Herald*, December 3, 1859.

34   Baltimore *American*, December 3, 1859.

35   Ibid.

36   Baltimore *American*, December 6, 1859; New York *Daily Tribune*, December 13, 1859; New York *Weekly Tribune*, December 10, 1859.

37   Letter, Louis Williamson to Jedidiah Williamson, December 8. 1859, Stutler Collection; New York *Weekly Tribune*, December 10, 1859. One newspaper wrote when the body was "sufficiently frozen," it was dressed in "a neat shroud, with pleated trimmings and white cravat" and placed in a "solid rosewood coffin." The cuts in Brown's clothes were made by Israel Green's light dress sword when capturing Brown.

38   McKim also discussed Brown's will, his instructions for burial and inscriptions upon the tombstone, read Brown's last letter to his wife, and in an attempt to console the mourning family stated "in their sacrifice they had made a large contribution to the cause of Freedom and Humanity."

39   Letter, Ruth Brown Thompson to Mary E. Stearns, April 22, 1860, Stutler Collection.

40   New York *Daily Tribune*, December 10, 12, 1859; New York *Semi-Weekly Tribune*, December 13, 1859.

41   Baltimore *American*, December 16, 1859. The stranger was recognized by a militia captain from New Market as being arrested there a few weeks ago, but was released for lack of evidence. Serbert, the captain from New Market, claimed the man at Harpers Ferry fit the description of Barton Hassett who had a "heavy reward for the murder of a man named Evers, in Allegany County, Virginia several months ago."

42   Letter from P. Y. Cutler to Henry A. Wise, November 25, 1859. Wise Papers.

43   Baltimore *American,* December 17, 1859.

44   Baltimore *American*, December 16, 1859; Lubet, *John Brown's Spy*, 234–5.

45   In his appeal to legislature Wise claimed there was no proof Coppoc killed anyone. He said if given permission he would commute Coppoc's sentence.

46   Baltimore *American*, December 15 & 16, 1859; New York *Daily Tribune*, December 12, 1859; Villard, *John Brown*, 570–1. John Brown's daughter Annie Brown later contends Coppoc dictated the letter to Cook.

47   Baltimore *American,* December 17, 1859. The Revs. North and Dutton of the Presbyterian Church and the Rev. Beverly Waught of the Methodist Church were among those conducting the services. The Rev. North visited Cook frequently during his incarceration.

48   Ibid.

49   Horwitz, *Midnight Rising*, 264; Baltimore *American*, December 17, 1859.

50   Horwitz, *Midnight Rising*, 264; Baltimore *American*, December 17, 1859.

51 Letter and Order Book of General Taliaferro, pt. 2.

52 Baltimore *American*, December 17, 1859. The Shepherdstown *Register* reported on December 24, 1859, Copeland spoke out forcefully on the gallows: "If I am dying for freedom, I could not die in a better cause—I rather die than be a slave."

53 Baltimore *American*, December 17, 1859; Horwitz, *Midnight Rising*, 265–6. Jefferson County Black History Preservation Society, *The Capture, Trial and Execution of John A. Copeland Jr. and Shields Green* (n.p., 2003), 34–6.; *Valley News Echo* (Hagerstown, MD: December, 1859). Wise telegraphed the mayor of Oberlin, A. D. Beecher, on December 17, 1859, that the bodies were taken to Winchester for dissection, so James Monroe went there. After the faculty agreed to given him Copeland's body a delegation of upset students, led by a Georgian, went to explain to Monroe the situation, as he did not understand. Monroe claimed he was told by the Georgian: "This n***** you are trying to get don't belong to the faculty." It was not theirs to give, as the students had "risked their lives" getting his remains which made the thought of the faculty turning him over more than they could bear. Monroe returned to Oberlin on Christmas Eve. The next day, Christmas, a memorial service was held at Oberlin's First Church for Copeland, Green, and Leary. There he recounted the story of his failure to retrieve Copeland's body. His explanation was later read on a public radio station in Cleveland in 2001.

There were other attempts by groups and individuals, black and white, to retrieve the bodies of Copeland and Green. Governor Wise received a letter from abolitionists in New Jersey five days after the execution of Copeland and Green. He made no reply. Also unsuccessful in attempting to claim the remains were groups from Pennsylvania, Massachusetts, Ohio, and Baltimore.

54 Baltimore *American*, December 17, 1859; Lubet, *John Brown's Spy*, 245. Before leaving the jail, Cook gave a final letter to the jailor to mail to his wife. He also left several pages on a table about his escape attempt. Among the sheets of paper on the table was a memo written by jailor Avis: "Give me an accurate description, as possible as you can of the *age* and *personal appearance* of Owen Brown, Barclay Coppic, and J. T. Meriam." At the bottom of this Cook wrote he revealed this only to a woman sworn to secrecy.

55 Baltimore *American*, December 17, 1859; Horwitz, *Midnight Rising*, 266–7; New York *Herald*, December 17, 1859; Shepherdstown *Register*, December 24, 1859; Virginia *Free Press*, December 22, 1859. One reporter claims that while on the scaffold Cook waved a hand to the crowd, saying, "Good-bye, all!"

56 Lubet, *John Brown's Spy*, 246–50, 259–62.

57 Hinton, *John Brown and His Men*, 506, 519.

58 Hinton, *John Brown and His Men*, 520–6; Villard, *John Brown*, 573–80. Villard details the rescue attempt. "Eight machines," men from Kansas, arrived at a small town outside of Harrisburg on February 17, 1860, posing as cattle buyers and drovers. One of them, Montgomery, insisted on making a preliminary scouting trip to Charles Town. He, with John W. LaBarnes, who was among the first to plan a rescue of John Brown and retained G. H. Holt as an attorney for Brown, went openly to Charles Town. LaBarnes is said to have been arrested for drunkenness and thrown in jail. There he is said to have talked with the two condemned men, who were adamantly opposed to any rescue attempt, as it would cost the lives of their friends as well that of their benevolent jailor. Upon his release LaBarnes returned to Harrisburg to inform the intended rescuers. In the meantime another of the Kansas men, Joseph Garner, scouted the Underground Railroad route of the Quakers who ran slaves to the north. He apparently was too vocal in revealing his plans and had to return, having been found out and the Virginia governor having been alerted. Finally the conspirators agreed with clergymen Higginson "that fifteen or twenty lives ought not to be sacrificed in a hopeless attempt to save one or two." Traveling over snowy mountainous terrain

would have made rescue difficult. The cost of the aborted rescue was $1,721—funds given by sympathizers like Higginson, who also got permission from Brown's widow to use part of the funds he had collected for the welfare of Brown's family.

59 Hinton, *John Brown and His Men*, 500–1.

60 Charlestown *Spirit of Jefferson*, June 20, 1860; *Free Press*, March 17, 1860; Hinton, *John Brown and His Men*, 502–4; Horwitz, *Midnight Rising*, 168–71.

61 *Free Press* of Charlestown published in the *Commercial*, March 17, 1860; Letter, Francis Yates to Alexander R. Boteler, New York *Times*, March 20, 1860; New York *Tribune*, March 21, 1869; *Spirit of Jefferson* published in the *Commercial*, March 20, 1860. Lee ordered the 11 dead raiders to be interred, but left how this was to be done to others. James Mansfield was paid $5.00, some say $10.00, apparently hired by Charles Johnson who carried out Lee's order. His compensation was delayed by the drama and aftermath of the raid. Johnson finally submitted a bill to the Overseers of the Poor of Jefferson County for $55.00 that was not cordially received. One of the overseers, Francis Yates, in late March of 1860 wrote his congressional representative, Alexander R. Boteler, to assist in procuring federal money. Yates argued the taxpayers of Jefferson County should not have to pay for the burial ordered by a federal officer of ruthless non-citizens who were killed on federal not state land. It is unknown when or if Johnson received payment.

62 New York *Herald*, March 19, 1860.

63 Cleveland *Daily Herald*, March 17, 1860.

Chapter Eight: Rehearsal for War

1 New York *Herald*, November 21, 1859.

2 John K. Mahon, *History of the Militia and the National Guard* (New York, 1983), 46–53.

3 Ibid., 53–9, 61, 83.

4 For the organization of volunteer-militia companies, see Dennis E. Frye, "White Plums and Cornstalks: Jefferson County's Pre-war Militia (1858–61)," *The Magazine of the Jefferson County Historical Society*, vol. I (December 1984), 32–3.

5 Mahon, *History of the Militia and the National Guard*, 57, 81–3.

6 Thomas D. Gold, *History of Clarke County, Virginia, and Its Connections with the War Between the States* (Berryville, VA.: C.R. Hughes, 1914), 103–4.

7 Mahon, *History of the Militia and the National Guard*, 83.

8 Gold, *History of Clarke County, Virginia*, 103–4.

9 *Acts of the General Assembly of the State of Virginia* (Richmond, 1853) 34–9; Lee A. Wallace Jr., *A Guide to Virginia Military Organizations* (Richmond, VA.: Virginia Civil War Commission, 1964), 261.

10 *Democratic Mirror*, November 24, 1858.

11 *Democratic Mirror*, March 23 & 30, 1859; April 28, 1859; October 25, 1859; Charles P. Poland Jr., *From Frontier to Suburbia* (Marceline, MO: Walsworth, 1976), 171–2.

12 *Democratic Mirror*, October 25, 1859.

13 Ibid., November 2, 16, 23, 30, 1859; December 7, 21, 28, 1859; January 11, 1860; February 15, 1860; March 28, 1860.

14 W. Asbury Christian, *Lynchburg and Its People* (Lynchburg: J. P. Bell Co., 1900); *Conservator*, December 21, 1860; Frye, "White Plums and Cornstalks," 27–38; *Register*, December 17, 1859.

15 Wise pointed out the need to replace men guarding Virginia's northern boundaries from Point of Rocks to Wheeling.

16 *Journal of the Senate of the Commonwealth of Virginia*, (Richmond: James E. Good, Senate Printer, 1859), 1–43, 63, 154–5.

17 *Acts of the General Assembly of the State of Virginia,* (1852–3), 34–9; 33–7; (1860), 86–102.

18 Clarke *Journal,* May 4 and June 1, 1860; *Democratic Mirror,* February 15, 1860.

19 Clarke *Journal,* June 15, 1860.

20 *Democratic Mirror,* September 12, 1860.

21 *Register,* December 10, 1859. Wise wanted to arm Virginia's northern border; he sent pistols and Sharps rifles to the Shepherdstown troops in early December 1859. He placed great faith in the people of the Wheeling area to protect Virginia and the Ohio border: "The city [Wheeling] has shown her truth to Virginia, and I was proud of the corps she was prompt to send to prove it. I rely upon the Northwest which has nobly tendered service from every point."

22 Ibid. Wise wanted to reorganize the militia into two branches. One would be an active body composed of men "from 18 to 25 years of age, and of volunteers of any age; to be fully armed and equipped and frequently drilled, and compelled to do duty under heavy and summary fines and penalties." Those serving in an active branch would be "exempt from jury duty and working on the roads." Men of service age not in the active branch would form a reserve militia assembling yearly.

23 Wise, *The Military History of the Virginia Military Institute,* 114–15. *Gilham's Manual* was adopted by the US War Department to succeed *Hardee's Tactics,* but when the war started, it was supplanted by *Casey's Tactics.* In the Confederacy, *Gilham's Manual* "formed the basis of instruction for all arms throughout the war."

24 *Acts of the General Assembly* (1860), 127–31; Nevins, *The Emergence of Lincoln,* vol. II, 112. In addition to the $500,000 appropriated by the Virginia legislature on January 21, 1860, two days later the same body agreed to pay up to $150,000 for the costs of "defending the Commonwealth" in the Harpers Ferry raid. Costs included assembling, arming, equipping, and transporting troops, purchasing arms and munitions, and trying, guarding, and executing the captured raiders. The legislature appointed a commission on January 23, 1860, to accept and evaluate all claims presented (during the next six months) for services rendered in the "Harper's Ferry War." Supplementary acts enacted on March 6 and 28 appropriated additional sums of $75,000 and $31,000 to defray expenses that had been incurred by the state in the Brown affair. The March 6 law also rejected the commission's earlier acceptance of claims for allowances for horses and servants owned by officers but not in the service of their owner while he was in the service of his state. Such claims were to be re-audited and payment excluded.

25 "Muster-Roll of Winchester and Frederick County in the War in Defense of Virginia, 1861–5," 2.

Index